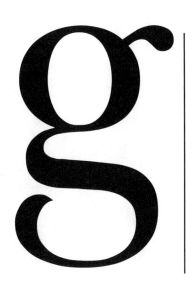

THE OFFICIAL
GUIDE COMPANION

12th Edition Official Guide for GMAT® Review
Quantitative Problem Explanations

This book provides detailed, step-by-step approaches to
every Problem Solving and Data Sufficiency question in
The Official Guide for GMAT Review, 12th Edition.

The Official Guide Companion

10-digit International Standard Book Number: 0-9841780-1-5
13-digit International Standard Book Number: 978-0-9841780-1-8

Note: *GMAT, Graduate Management Admission Test, Graduate Management
Admission Council,* and *GMAC* are all registered trademarks of the Graduate
Management Admission Council which neither sponsors nor is affiliated in any way
with this product.

The Official Guide Companion is a supplement to our

8 GUIDE INSTRUCTIONAL SERIES

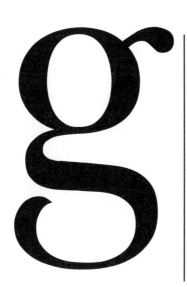

Math GMAT Strategy Guides

Number Properties (ISBN: 978-0-9824238-4-4)

Fractions, Decimals, & Percents (ISBN: 978-0-9824238-2-0)

Equations, Inequalities, & VICs (ISBN: 978-0-9824238-1-3)

Word Translations (ISBN: 978-0-9824238-7-5)

Geometry (ISBN: 978-0-9824238-3-7)

Verbal GMAT Strategy Guides

Critical Reasoning (ISBN: 978-0-9824238-0-6)

Reading Comprehension (ISBN: 978-0-9824238-5-1)

Sentence Correction (ISBN: 978-0-9824238-6-8)

ManhattanGMAT
the new standard

April 1st, 2010

Dear Student,

Thank you for picking up the Manhattan GMAT Official Guide Companion ("OGC" for short). This book is designed to accompany the *Official Guide for GMAT Review 12th Edition,* which we feel should be the primary resource for those studying for the GMAT. However, if there is one issue that our students cite about the Official Guide, it is that the explanations are not always as helpful as they could be. We hope that this book addresses that need by providing clear, step-by-step breakdowns of every math problem in the Official Guide.

There were many people involved in getting this book into your hands. We are indebted to our Instructors Josh Braslow, Faruk Bursal, Jen Dziura, Steven Jupiter, Stacey Koprince, Ben Ku, Ron Purewal, Jon Schneider, Emily Sledge, and Hemanth Venkataraman for their hard work drafting and editing the explanations. Our office hours ace Horacio Quiroga let us know which problems students routinely struggle with, giving rise to the Hot List. Graham Riske and Carrie Shuchart each took a turn reviewing before handing it over to David Mahler for his fine editorial eye. Last, Dan McNaney arranged and formatted the book in its current form.

We would also be remiss if we didn't acknowledge Zeke Vanderhoek, the founder of ManhattanGMAT. Zeke was a lone tutor in New York when he started the Company in 2000. Now, ten years later, MGMAT has Instructors and offices nationwide, and the Company contributes to the studies and successes of thousands of students each year.

At Manhattan GMAT, we continually aspire to provide the best Instructors and resources possible. We hope that you'll find our dedication manifest in this book. If you have any comments or questions, please e-mail me at andrew.yang@manhattangmat.com. I'll be sure that your comments reach Dave, Chris, and the rest of the team—and I'll read them too.

Best of luck in preparing for the GMAT!

Sincerely,

Andrew Yang
President
Manhattan GMAT

HOW TO ACCESS YOUR ONLINE RESOURCES

If you...

⊗ **are a registered Manhattan GMAT student**

and have received this book as part of your course materials, you have AUTOMATIC access to ALL of our online resources. This includes all practice exams, question banks, and online updates to this book. To access these resources, follow the instructions in the Welcome Guide provided to you at the start of your program. Do NOT follow the instructions below.

⊗ **purchased this book from the Manhattan GMAT Online store or at one of our Centers**

1. Go to: http://www.manhattangmat.com/practicecenter.cfm

2. Log in using the username and password used when your account was set up.

⊗ **purchased this book at a retail location**

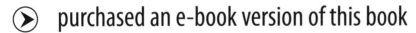

1. Go to: http://www.manhattangmat.com/access.cfm

2. Log in or create an account.

3. Follow the instructions on the screen.

Your one year of online access begins on the day that you register your book at the above URL.

You only need to register your product ONCE at the above URL. To use your online resources any time AFTER you have completed the registration process, login to the following URL: http://www.manhattangmat.com/practicecenter.cfm

Please note that online access is non-transferable. This means that only NEW and UNREGISTERED copies of the book will grant you online access. Previously used books will not provide any online resources.

⊗ **purchased an e-book version of this book**

Email a copy of your purchase receipt to books@manhattangmat.com to activate your resources.

For any technical issues, email books@manhattangmat.com or call 800-576-4628.

Please refer to the following page for a description of the online resources that come with this book.

YOUR ONLINE RESOURCES

Your purchase includes ONLINE ACCESS to the following:

⊙ 6 Computer Adaptive Online Practice Exams

The 6 full-length computer adaptive practice exams included with the purchase of this book are delivered online using Manhattan GMAT's proprietary computer-adaptive test engine. The exams adapt to your ability level by drawing from a bank of more than 1,200 unique questions of varying difficulty levels written by Manhattan GMAT's expert instructors, all of whom have scored in the 99th percentile on the Official GMAT. At the end of each exam you will receive a score, an analysis of your results, and the opportunity to review detailed explanations for each question. You may choose to take the exams timed or untimed.

The content presented in this book is updated periodically to ensure that it reflects the GMAT's most current trends and is as accurate as possible. You may view any known errors or minor changes upon registering for online access.

Important Note: The 6 computer adaptive online exams included with the purchase of this book are the SAME exams that you receive upon purchasing ANY book in Manhattan GMAT's 8 Book Strategy Series.

⊙ Official Guide Tracker

The Manhattan GMAT Official Guide Tracker tracks your accuracy and speed on problems from the Official Guide. It breaks down analyses by format, topic and subtopic. You can sort and filter by any field. This version has been updated as of September 1, 2009, and includes references to the 12th edition of the main OG and the 2nd Edition OG Quantitative and Verbal Reviews.

Manhattan GMAT* Prep
the new standard

TABLE OF CONTENTS

g

Part I
of
THE OFFICIAL GUIDE COMPANION

INTRODUCTION

Why This Book

Have you ever *wanted more from the explanations* in the Official Guide?

So have we.

Don't get us wrong—we love the Official Guide! As one of the few legit sources of retired GMAT problems, the "OG" should play a central role in your preparation for the exam. It forms a pillar of our curriculum as well.

The problems in the OG are fantastic, by and large. The *explanations,* on the other hand… well, some are just fine. But others can be inadequate, according to both our students and our instructors.

That's why we wrote this book.

Inside, you'll find *over 450 detailed explanations*—one for every quant problem in the 12th Edition of the Official Guide.

How To Use This Book

1) Do some OG problems.

Here is where to find all the quant problems in *The Official Guide for GMAT Review, 12th Edition*:

Section	Format	Numbers	# of Problems	Pages
Diagnostic Test	Problem Solving	D 1 – D 24	24	20–23
Diagnostic Test	Data Sufficiency	D 25 – D 48	24	25–26
Sample Questions	Problem Solving	PS 1 – PS 230	230	152–185
Sample Questions	Data Sufficiency	DS 1 – DS 174	174	273–288

Notation: a number with just a "D" in front of it, such as D 24, refers to problem 24 in the Diagnostic Test. Among the Sample Questions, "PS" refers to Problem Solving, and "DS" refers to Data Sufficiency.

When you do a set of OG problems, *should they all be the same topic?* At first, yes. This is a great way to learn a topic and build skills in a particular area. Later, you should start to mix topics, just as the GMAT itself does.

How many at once? Early on in your preparation, do just a few at once. Later, as the GMAT gets closer, you can lengthen out the sets.

Should you time yourself or not? At first, probably not. Give yourself space to struggle and learn. However, you also need to train yourself to "take a shot" under time pressure. To strike a balance, what some instructors recommend for your first time is that you write down an answer at the 2-minute mark, but keep going until you finish the problem. Record your total time, and if you took over 2 minutes & 30 seconds, put the problem on a list to redo for speed.

Later, as you do longer mixed sets, you should put yourself under exam-like time pressure. Do those sets as if they were "mini-GMAT's," averaging no more than 2 minutes per problem.

2) Go through our explanations.

Each problem is *Categorized* with a broad topic and a narrower subtopic.

There are five broad topics, corresponding to our five quantitative Strategy Guides (published separately):

1) **Number Properties** include subtopics such as Divisibility & Primes and Odds & Evens.
2) **FDPs** stand for Fractions, Decimals, & Percents.
3) **EIVs** stand for Equations, Inequalities, & "VICs"—in other words, Algebra.
4) **Word Translations** include various kinds of word problems, such as Rates & Work and Probability.
5) **Geometry** includes subtopics such as Triangles and Circles.

There are numerous subtopics, most of which are self-explanatory. **VICs** stands for "Variables In Choices," which are problems that include variables in the answer choices.

OG Page: We cannot legally reprint the full questions and answer choices, so you should turn to the OG Page in the 12th Edition to see the question itself as you review our explanation.

Within the text of each explanation, you'll find ***Bolded Tools*** or concepts in bold italics. These highlighted terms will help you keep track of major techniques, topics, and themes. For students using this book in conjunction with our Strategy Guides, these tools and concepts are explained in more detail in the Guides.

For some problems, we've included an ***Alternative Approach*** or a second explanation. We have been selective about these inclusions. Theoretically, many problems can be tackled in a variety of ways, but one of those ways is often better than the others. We like to emphasize the *best* way to solve a problem—and it's not always the classic textbook approach, either. We prefer methods grounded in solid conceptual foundations, but we also know that the best solution can be quick and dirty.

As a result, your toolkit will contain many different tools. So that you don't get confused on game day, you need to ***know what your first-choice tool will be for any problem***. That's why we've often included just one thorough explanation and process per question.

However, many problems lend themselves to more than one approach. Also, having more than one way to look at certain problems can deepen your understanding of a whole topic. When we've included a second or even third approach, we've done so for a good reason. ***Be sure to study Alternative Approaches thoroughly.***

Difficulty level: The problems in the Official Guide (outside of the Diagnostic Test) are numbered in order of difficulty, according to the GMAT folks.

How does the GMAT measure difficulty? By the percent of people who get the problem wrong during its experimental stage. The more people get it wrong, the harder the problem must be, right?

Sure… most of the time. But what if the problem is utterly confusing, but there's some backdoor way to guess the answer without understanding what's going on? What if the wrong answer choices aren't as well-designed as they could be?

When this happens, a truly hard problem might measure too easy on the GMAT's yardstick. Or an easy problem might measure too hard, in fact.

We think that in the OG, ***the vast majority of problems are positioned pretty well*** by order of inherent difficulty. But from mounds of student feedback, we know that some low-numbered problems are conceptually tricky, and some high-numbered problems are easier than their neighbors.

That's why ***our instructors have given each problem a difficulty range:*** 300–500, 500–600, 600–700, or 700–800. Use these grades, together with the OG numbering, to judge how hard a problem really is.

Finally, when you're reviewing, don't forget to **check the explanation in the *Official Guide!*** Sometimes these explanations can shed real additional light on problems. But if you find yourself getting confused, abandon ship. A few explanations in the Official Guide can actually make matters worse.

3) Redo the problem right away—or very soon.

Don't stop after you've read the explanation. To cement your learning, **put pen to paper one more time**. Force yourself to solve the problem all over again—maybe even right away. Or put it on a list for the weekend. But try to get two "touches on the ball" before you forget.

The goal is not exposure, but mastery. You're far better off doing fewer OG problems overall, if you can truly *own* those problems by doing them more than once. Here's the test: are you absolutely *certain* that you could do that problem again quickly, easily, and accurately, if you were to see it on the GMAT in a month? If not, you haven't mastered it. Put it on a list to redo.

4) Track your progress.

Keep track of your progress with our OG Tracker, an Excel spreadsheet that you can download from our website. ***Simply enter your answers and your times,*** and the OG Tracker will automatically crunch the numbers. You can easily analyze your accuracy and speed by topic and subtopic.

Horacio's Hot List

Students in our courses have access to weekly online Office Hours. Horacio Quiroga, one of our favorite instructors, has done thousands of Office Hour sessions with our students, who often bring OG problems for review. Over time, Horacio has seen many of the same problems come up again and again, so he's built a "Hot List" of ***33 extra-tricky problems that deserve your attention***.

Hot List Problem	*Beginning of Stem*	*Page in OG*	*Page in This Book*	
D 11 (Diagnostic Test)	Of the three-digit integers…	22	24	
D 13	If *s* and *t* are positive integers…	22	25	
D 15	The product of all the…	22	26	
D 16	If $\sqrt{3-2x}$ …	22	26	
D 24	Aaron will jog home…	23	29	
PS 11	Which of the following…	153	50	
PS 32	$\sqrt{(16)(20)}$…	156	59	
PS 50	If *y* is an integer…	159	66	
PS 82	If *n* is an integer…	163	79	
PS 87	A necklace is made…	164	81	
PS 89	If *s* is the product…	164	82	
PS 98	On a scale that measures…	166	86	
PS 130	Which of the following inequalities…	170	101	
PS 148	If *x*, *y*, and *k* are positive numbers…	173	109	
PS 149	During a trip, Francine traveled…	173	111	
PS 157	For any positive integer *n*…	174	115	
PS 163	This year Henry will save…	175	117	
PS 191	Pat will walk from Intersection X…	179	131	
PS 192	The ratio, by volume, of soap…	179	131	
PS 202	If *m* > 0…	181	137	
PS 204	John and Mary were each paid…	181	138	
DS 45	If *r* is a constant…	276	173	
DS 69	Of the four numbers…	278	185	
DS 73	If *m* is an integer…	279	187	
DS 87	Is the number of seconds…	280	194	
DS 89	Is the number of members…	280	195	*continued on next page…*

Hot List Problem	Beginning of Stem	Page in OG	Page in This Book
DS 90	If *k, m,* and *t* are positive integers...	280	196
DS 102	While on a straight road...	281	202
DS 115	For any integers *x* and *y*...	283	208
DS 128	A school administrator will assign...	284	216
DS 154	If *n* is a positive integer...	287	230
DS 156	Is 5^k less...	287	231
DS 171	What is the tens digit...	288	238

In the explanations that follow, we've marked these 33 problems with a ***Hot Tamale*** (🌶) and given additional care to our explanations on those problems.

We've also included a special appendix to identify recurring themes within the Hot List and provide further comments about each problem:

- How students typically go wrong
- What you should focus on in the problem
- What we think of the explanation printed in the OG (which occasionally creates more confusion than it clears up)

Look at the Hot List appendix (Part V) only after you've tried the problems.

Official Guide Problem Lists By Category

The last part of this book (Part VI) lists all the OG math problems by topical category. If you want a list of all the problems about Triangles, for instance, you can find it there. We have classified problems only by their major topic. For problems that involve more than one topic, this classification is a judgment call. For the sake of simplicity, each problem only appears once in these lists.

As we mentioned earlier, you should do topic-focused sets of problems while you are still learning the basic concepts and skills related to each topic. Over time, you should start to mix up the sets, so that you get used to seeing problems out of context. After all, the GMAT itself is a big mixed set.

Practice Tests

As a bonus for buying this book, you get free access to our 6 Computer Adaptive Tests, which contain over 1200 GMAT-like problems written by our instructors. Be sure to ***log onto our website*** and take advantage of these exams as part of your overall GMAT preparation. See pages 7–8 for details.

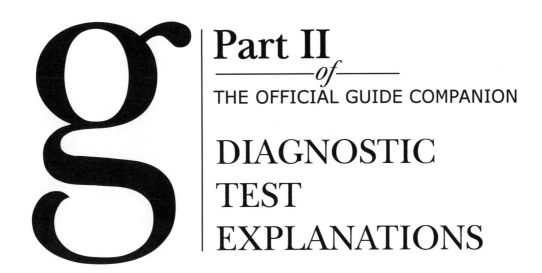

Part II

of

THE OFFICIAL GUIDE COMPANION

DIAGNOSTIC
TEST
EXPLANATIONS

D 1. <u>FDPs</u>: Digits & Decimals
Difficulty: 500–600   **OG Page:** 20

This ***Decimals*** problem requires us to translate the relationship described in the question into a mathematical expression. Then we must determine which of the given choices is equivalent to that expression.

First, we are told that the customer purchased a total of 6 compact discs, the first for $15.95 and the remaining 5 for $3.99 each. The total cost, then, can be expressed as follows:

5(3.99) + 15.95

Since this does not match any of the choices, we must figure out which choice is equivalent to the above expression. The easiest way to begin is to compare the 15.95 portion of the above expression to the choices.

(A) 5(4.00) + 15.90. Here, 15.90 is 0.05 less than 15.95. In order for this choice to be equivalent, the 0.05 needs to be made up for in the other part of the expression. Since 4.00 is 0.01 greater than 3.99, if we multiply 4.00 by 5, we will make up the 0.05 difference exactly. We can also express 4.00 as (3.99 + 0.01), which turns the expression into 5(3.99 + 0.01) + 15.90 or 5(3.99) + 0.05 + 15.90, which is the same as 5(3.99) + 15.95. **CORRECT**

(B) Since 15.95 is the same here, we can see that 5(4.00) is too large (by 0.05).

(C) Here, both 5(4.00) and 16.00 are too large (each by 0.05).

(D) 5(4.00 − 0.01) is the equivalent of 5(3.99). Thus, we would need to add 15.95. However, we are given only 15.90, which is too small (by 0.05).

(E) 5(4.00 − 0.05) is the equivalent of 5(3.95). Since 15.95 is the same here, we can see that this choice will be too small (by 0.20).

Notice that it would be slow and difficult to compute the actual total cost, as well as the values of the expressions in each of the answer choices.

The correct answer is (A).

D 2. <u>Number Properties</u>: Consecutive Integers
Difficulty: 300–500   **OG Page:** 20

This problem asks us to determine the difference between the ***Averages*** (arithmetic means) of two different sequences of ***Consecutive Integers***: 200 through 400, and 50 through 100. The ***Average Formula*** tells us that in general, the average of a set of numbers is found by dividing the sum of the numbers by the number of terms:

$$A = \frac{S}{n}$$

However, when the number of terms is large, finding the sum through simple addition would take far too long. Instead, we may use a shortcut: the average of an evenly spaced set of numbers is simply the middle term. Any set of consecutive integers is evenly spaced, so this shortcut is legal in this situation.

If the middle term is not particularly easy to find, we can use an alternative method for computing the average of an evenly spaced set: find the average of the first and the last term.

For the two given sequences, the means of each sequence can be found as follows:

$$A_1 = (200 + 400)/2 = 300$$

and

$$A_2 = (50 + 100)/2 = 75$$

The desired difference is therefore:

$$A_1 - A_2 = 300 - 75 = 225$$

The correct answer is (D).

D 3. <u>EIVs</u>: Formulas & Functions
Difficulty: 500–600   **OG Page:** 20

The problem gives us this ***Sequence*** for all $n \geq 3$:

$$A_n = \frac{A_{n-1} + A_{n-2}}{2}$$

This recursive formula for the sequence can be translated into words this way: Any term beyond the first two is equal to half the sum of the previous two terms.

We are given the third and fifth terms. Arrange them in a *Sequence Diagram*, leaving blanks for unknown terms (the question asks for the sixth term, so a circle is placed around the sixth slot):

We can use the values of the third and fifth terms to find the fourth term. If $n = 5$:

$$A_5 = \frac{A_4 + A_3}{2}$$
$$20 = \frac{A_4 + 4}{2}$$
$$40 = A_4 + 4$$
$$36 = A_4$$

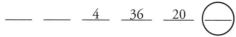

Now that we know the fourth and fifth terms, we can use them to get the sixth term:

$$A_6 = \frac{A_5 + A_4}{2}$$
$$A_6 = \frac{20 + 36}{2}$$
$$A_6 = 28$$

The correct answer is (E).

D 4. Word Translations: Overlapping Sets
Difficulty: 600–700 　　　 **OG Page:** 20

In this *Overlapping Sets* problem, people in the group invest or do not invest in municipal bonds. They also invest or do not invest in oil stocks. Some people invest in both bonds and stocks, and some in neither.

To avoid unnecessary computation, we can fill in a *Double-Set Matrix* with the given percents.

		Municipal Bonds?		
		Yes	No	Total
Oil Stocks?	Yes			
	No			
	Total			

Because we are using percents, the total population will be 100(%). 35 percent of the people invest in mutual bonds, so 35 goes in the bottom left box. 18 percent invest in oil stocks, so we put an 18 in the top right box. 7 percent invest in oil stocks AND municipal bonds, so we put a 7 in the top left box. Finally, the question asks for the probability that someone invests in municipal bonds but NOT in oil stocks, so we shade the middle left box, because that is the value that we want.

		Municipal Bonds?		
		Yes	No	Total
Oil Stocks?	Yes	7		18
	No	?		
	Total	35		100

In a Double-Set Matrix, the first two entries in any row or column will add up to the third entry. In the left column, 7 plus the value of the shaded box will equal 35. Therefore, 28 percent of the people invest in municipal bonds, but NOT in oil stocks. Thus, the *Probability*, which equals

$\dfrac{desired\ outcomes}{total\ outcomes}$, is $\dfrac{28}{100} = \dfrac{7}{25}$. This is the **answer**.

It turns out that the given total number of people (2,500) is irrelevant. However, we could use this piece of information to calculate the actual number of people in each category and fill in the matrix with the results:

(0.35)(2,500) = 875 people invested in municipal bonds,
(0.18)(2,500) = 450 people invested in oil stocks,
(0.07)(2,500) = 175 people invested in both.

		Municipal Bonds?		
		Yes	No	Total
Oil Stocks?	Yes	175		450
	No	?		
	Total	875		2,500

Of the 875 people who invested in municipal bonds, 175 of them also invested in oil stocks, so 875 − 175 = 700 people invested in municipal bonds but NOT in oil stocks.

The probability $\dfrac{\textit{Investors of muncipal bonds but NOT oil stocks}}{\textit{Total people in the group}}$

$= \dfrac{700}{2,500} = \dfrac{7}{25}.$

The correct answer is (B).

D 5. <u>Geometry</u>: Circles & Cylinders
Difficulty: 300–500   **OG Page:** 20

This ***Cylinders*** problem specifies that a closed cylindrical tank contains 36π cubic feet of water, which represents half of the tank's total capacity. We also know that, when the cylinder is upright, the height of the water is 4 feet. A diagram is not given, so our first task is to ***Draw a Picture***. Be sure to label the cylinder:

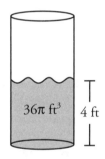

The problem asks us to turn the tank on its side and calculate the new height of the water above the ground.

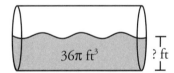

The water still represents half of the total volume of the cylinder regardless of whether the cylinder is upright or on its side. The new height, therefore, reaches halfway up the circular face of the cylinder. This height is equivalent to the circle's radius. If we find the radius, we will also have found the new height. We can calculate the radius using the formula for the ***Volume of a Cylinder***. When the cylinder is upright, the water has a volume of 36π cubic feet and a height of 4 feet.

$Volume = \pi r^2 h$

$36\pi = \pi r^2 (4)$

$36 = 4r^2$

$9 = r^2$

$3 = r$

The radius is 3 feet. Therefore, the new height of the water is also 3 feet.

The correct answer is (B).

D 6. <u>Word Translations</u>: Overlapping Sets
Difficulty: 500–600   **OG Page:** 21

In this ***Overlapping Sets*** problem, households can be classified in two ways: whether they use Brand A soap and whether they use Brand B soap. Some households use both brands, and some use neither.

This information can be best represented using a ***Double-Set Matrix*** to show which brands of soap are used. Begin by filling in the numbers given in the question.

	A	*Not A*	*Total*
B	?		
Not B	60	80	
Total			200

Summing the row that contains the "Not B" information, we can find that the total number of households not using Brand B is 140, and thus the total number of households using Brand B is 60. We are told that, for every household that used both brands of soap, 3 used only Brand B soap, which means that 3 times as many people used only Brand B as used both A and B. We can place an x in the box for "Both A and B," and a $3x$ in the box for "B but Not A."

	A	*Not A*	*Total*
B	**x**	**3x**	**60**
Not B	60	80	**140**
Total			200

We can now make an equation using the top row of our matrix:

$x + 3x = 60$

$4x = 60$

$x = 15$ 15 is the **answer**.

Notice that if we solved for $3x$, we would get 45, which is one of the wrong answers. Be sure to answer the question that is asked.

The correct answer is (A).

D 7. <u>Word Translations</u>: Probability
Difficulty: 600–700   **OG Page:** 21

If we select according to the order given in the problem statement (president, then secretary, then treasurer), then this *Probability* problem can be solved using the *Domino Effect* (multiplying consecutive probabilities). Remember that "AND" implies multiplication and that "OR" implies addition.

The probability that Harry is chosen as secretary incorporates two consecutive events: someone *other* than Harry must be chosen as president, AND then Harry must be chosen from the *remaining* candidates as secretary. These probabilities are 9/10 and 1/9, respectively, so the probability that Harry is chosen as secretary is $\left(\dfrac{9}{10}\right)\left(\dfrac{1}{9}\right)=\dfrac{1}{10}$.

For Harry to be chosen as treasurer, other candidates must first be chosen as president and secretary, with probabilities 9/10 and 8/9. Harry's subsequent probability of being chosen as treasurer is 1/8. As before, all three events must happen: someone else must be chosen as president, AND someone else must be chosen as secretary, AND finally Harry must be chosen as treasurer. The overall probability of Harry's being chosen as treasurer, then, is $\left(\dfrac{9}{10}\right)\left(\dfrac{8}{9}\right)\left(\dfrac{1}{8}\right)=\dfrac{1}{10}$.

Since Harry cannot be both secretary and treasurer, these outcomes are completely separate. So the probability that Harry is chosen as secretary OR treasurer is $\dfrac{1}{10}+\dfrac{1}{10}=\dfrac{2}{10}$ or $\dfrac{1}{5}$. This is the **answer**.

We can solve this problem more efficiently using *Symmetry*. There is nothing special about Harry or about any of the other members. Everyone has exactly the same likelihood of being chosen for any of the three positions. It does not matter that we are choosing these positions sequentially. Therefore, Harry has a 1/10 chance of being chosen as

secretary, and he also a 1/10 chance of being chosen as treasurer. He cannot be chosen as both. Thus, the chance that he is chosen as secretary OR as treasurer is $\dfrac{1}{10}+\dfrac{1}{10}=\dfrac{2}{10}$, or $\dfrac{1}{5}$.

The correct answer is (E).

D 8. <u>FDPs</u>: Fractions
Difficulty: 500–600   **OG Page:** 21

A toy store's revenue in January was a *Fraction* of its revenue in November, which was a fraction of its revenue in December. Since no specific amounts are given in the problem, we should pick *Smart Numbers* to solve this problem. The revenues in November and January are based directly or indirectly on the revenue in December, so we should pick a Smart Number for the December revenue and then calculate the November and January revenue.

In questions involving fractions, we can choose a Smart Number by multiplying all the denominators given in the question. If we use this number to perform calculations, it is likely that we will be dealing with integers all the way through the problem. In this case, we should choose $(5)(4)=20$ as the revenue in December.

The revenue in November is 2/5 the revenue in December, so:

$$\dfrac{2}{5}(20)=8$$

The revenue in January was 1/4 the revenue in November, which was 8, so:

$$\dfrac{1}{4}(8)=2$$

The average (arithmetic mean) of the store's revenues in November and January is $\dfrac{8+2}{2}=5$. Since 20 is 4 times 5, the store's revenue in December is 4 times the average of its revenues in November and January. This is the **answer**.

This problem can be solved algebraically (that is, by representing the quantities with letters and the relationships with equations). However, doing so would be more cumbersome.

The correct answer is E.

D 9. Word Translations: Statistics
Difficulty: 500–600   **OG Page:** 21

This ***Statistics*** problem refers to a set of performance scores with a specific ***Mean, Median,*** and ***Standard Deviation*** (the specific values are not given) and asks which of those will be affected by adding 5 to each of the scores.

Mean (average) is calculated by dividing the sum of the scores by the number of scores. If each score is increased by 5, the sum of the terms will increase by 5 × *(the number of terms)*, and thus the mean will increase by 5 as well.

The median is the middle score in the set if there is an odd number of scores or the average of the two middle scores if there is an even number of scores. If each score is increased by 5, the median will also increase by 5.

Standard deviation is a measure of how far away the scores are from the mean. If each of the scores increases by 5 and the mean also increases by 5, the spread of scores (i.e. their distances from the mean) will remain unchanged. Thus, the standard deviation will remain unchanged.

Putting it all together, we can see that only the mean and the median would change. This is the **answer.**

In theory, we could choose sample numbers to derive or verify these results. However, the transformation we are asked to consider (adding 5 to each term) is not very complex. Thus, we should try to reason out this problem using the properties of mean, median, and standard deviation.

The correct answer is (D).

D 10. Geometry: Lines & Angles
Difficulty: 600–700   **OG Page:** 21

We can simplify this problem by relating the labeled angles to something with which we are more familiar: the pentagon at the center of the star.

Label these five interior angles *a, b, c, d,* and *e.*

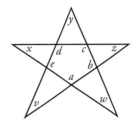

Use the formula for the ***Sum of Interior Angles of a Polygon:***

$$a + b + c + d + e = 180\,(n - 2) = 180\,(5 - 2) = 540$$

Now that we know what the 5 interior angles add up to, we can save ourselves a lot of time and energy by replacing *a, b, c, d* and *e* with numbers. As long as the numbers we choose add up to 540, we will arrive at the correct answer. The easiest numbers to choose will make every angle the same. We are taking advantage of ***Symmetry*** to make the problem simpler. The right answer must be the same for all cases, including the symmetrical one, so we know that we can find the answer this way—with less work.

540/5 = 108, so we can make *a, b, c, d* and *e* each equal to 108.

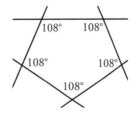

Now that we have values for the internal angles of the pentagon, we can also find values for their supplements. Each interior angle is supplementary to two angles in the small triangles surrounding the pentagon. Because we made every interior angle the same, every supplementary angle will be the same. Every angle will be 180 – 108 = 72.

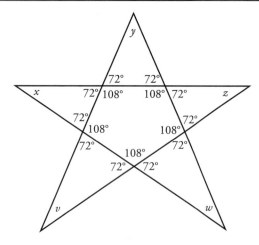

Now that we have the values of all the supplementary angles, we can find the values of v, w, x, y and z. Let's find the value of v. We know that $72 + 72 + v = 180$. That means that $v = 36$. But all five angles will be the same, because they are all the third angle in a triangle with two angles of 72. All five angles have a degree measure of 36. The sum is therefore $5 \times 36 = 180$. This is the **answer**.

If we get stuck, we can also **Estimate** the answer, as long as we draw a careful picture that is essentially symmetrical. With such a picture, we might estimate v to be somewhere between 30 and 40, which would put our answer between 150 and 225. Only one answer (180) fits that range. It turns out that estimation works rather well for this problem. However, we should still be sure to understand the first approach, which is based on useful geometrical principles.

The correct answer is (C).

D 11. FDPs: Digits & Decimals
Difficulty: 700–800   **OG Page:** 22

This problem requires us to tally a relatively large number of numbers that fit certain **Digits** criteria. The easiest way to do so is to find a pattern that will allow us to avoid counting out each specific number.

In this situation, we have two options. We can either find how many numbers meet the criteria, OR we can find how many numbers do NOT meet the criteria and subtract from the total. This is the **1 − x Principle**. For this problem, the latter option is preferable.

The range of **Consecutive Integers** from 701 through 999 contains $999 - 701 + 1 = 299$ numbers. From these 299 numbers we need to subtract all the numbers that have 0 digits in common and that have all 3 digits in common.

There are only 3 numbers that have all 3 digits in common: 777, 888 and 999. Subtracting 3 from the total gives us $299 - 3 = 296$ remaining numbers.

We can use the **Fundamental Counting Principle** from **Combinatorics** to figure out how many numbers have 0 digits in common. There are 3 possibilities for the hundreds digit (7, 8 or 9). That leaves 9 possibilities for the tens digit (the ten digits 0 to 9 minus the digit we picked for the hundreds digit) and 8 possibilities for the units digit (the ten digits 0 to 9 minus the two digits we picked for the hundreds and tens digits). The total is $\underline{3} \times \underline{9} \times \underline{8} = 216$ numbers that have 0 digits in common. $296 - 216 = 80$ numbers that have exactly 2 digits in common.

The correct answer is (C).

D 12. FDPs: Successive Percents & Percent Change
Difficulty: 500–600   **OG Page:** 22

We can solve this **Successive Percents** problem by **Algebraically Translating** the given statements into equations. Noting that "percent" is equivalent to division by 100 and that the word "of" implies multiplication, we get:

$$y = \left(\tfrac{50}{100}\right)\left(\tfrac{50}{100}\right)x = \left(\tfrac{2{,}500}{10{,}000}\right)x = 0.25x$$

and

$$\left(\tfrac{y}{100}\right)x = 100$$

Substituting for $0.25x$ from y the first equation into the second equation yields:

$$\left(\tfrac{0.25x}{100}\right)x = 100$$
$$\left(\tfrac{0.25x^2}{100}\right) = 100$$
$$0.25x^2 = 10{,}000$$
$$x^2 = 40{,}000$$

Because we are told that x is a positive integer, the only solution is:

$$x = 200 \qquad \text{This is the **answer**.}$$

Alternatively, we can *Test the Answer Choices*. We can plug in values for *x*, solve for *y* using the first relationship, and then test the second relationship. However, this approach is time-consuming. If we learn to write "*y* percent" as $\frac{y}{100}$, then the algebraic approach is faster and easier.

The correct answer is (C).

D 13. <u>Number Properties</u>: Divisibility & Primes
Difficulty: 700–800   **OG Page:** 22

The problem states that when *s* is divided by *t*, the quotient is 64.12. We are asked which of the answer choices could be the *Remainder*.

Let's use a simple example to make sure we understand the relationship between integer remainders and decimals in a quotient. If, for instance, 7 is divided by 5, the quotient is 1 (since 5 goes into 7 one complete time), and the remainder is 2.

However, when we do long division to find 7 divided by 5, we get 1.4. The 0.4 left over is *0.4 of 5—which equals 2, the remainder.* That is, the decimal part of the quotient (0.4) can be multiplied by the divisor (5) to get the integer remainder (2).

Thus, for the OG problem, the remainder is actually 0.12 *of the divisor t.* That is, 0.12*t* equals the remainder.

Now we are ready to *Test the Answer Choices.* Since a remainder must be an integer, see whether it is possible for 0.12 times an integer to equal each answer choice. Don't waste time actually doing the math if it is obvious that we are not going to get an integer.

A. If $0.12t = 2$, then *t* will not be an integer
B. If $0.12t = 4$, then *t* will not be an integer
C. If $0.12t = 8$, then *t* will not be an integer
D. If $0.12t = 20$, then *t* will not be an integer
E. If $0.12t = 45$, then $t = 375$ **CORRECT**

Alternatively, we can use *Divisibility Theory* to predict which answer choice will produce an integer. Again, split the original equation into a sum:

$$s = (64.12)t = 64t + 0.12t$$

64*t* is the multiple of *t* and 0.12*t*, as we've seen, is the remainder. This remainder must be an integer.

$$\frac{12}{100}t = \text{integer}$$
$$\frac{3}{25}t = \text{integer}$$
$$3t = 25 \times \text{integer}$$

Since 25 has no 3's in it, the integer on the right must contain a 3. (The *Prime Factors* on each side must match, because each variable is an integer.) So the remainder, which is that integer, must be a multiple of 3. Of the answer choices, only 45 is a multiple of 3.

The correct answer is (E).

D 14. <u>Word Translations</u>: Overlapping Sets
Difficulty: 600–700   **OG Page:** 22

In this *Overlapping Sets* problem, parents either volunteered to supervise children or did not volunteer. They also either volunteered to bring refreshments or did not volunteer. Some did both; some did neither.

First, we can *Name Variables* and let *x* equal the number of parents who neither volunteered to supervise children nor volunteered to bring refreshments. Therefore, 1.5*x* equals the number of parents who volunteered to bring refreshments.

Now set up a *Double-Set Matrix*, using the numbers given in the question. Notice that we are looking to find a value for 1.5*x*.

		Bring Refreshments?		
		Yes	*No*	*Total*
Supervise?	*Yes*	11		35
	No		*x*	
	Total	1.5*x*		84

Given that 11 of the 35 parents who volunteered to supervise the children also volunteered to bring refreshments, $35 - 11 = 24$ of the parents who volunteered to supervise the children did NOT volunteer to bring refreshments.

We can continue to fill in our Double-Set Matrix, noting that the number of parents who did NOT volunteer to bring refreshments is $24 + x$.

		Bring Refreshments?		
		Yes	No	Total
Supervise?	Yes	11	24	35
	No		x	
	Total	$1.5x$	$24 + x$	84

We can now set up an algebraic equation for the bottom row of the matrix. We are adding together the "refreshment" parents and the "non-refreshment" parents to get the total:

$(1.5x) + (24 + x) = 84$

$1.5x + 24 + x = 84$

$2.5x = 60$

$x = 24$

We are looking for the number of parents who volunteered to bring refreshments.

$1.5x = (1.5)(24) = 36.$

The correct answer is (B).

D 15. Number Properties: Divisibility & Primes
Difficulty: 700–800   **OG Page:** 22

The problem first requires us to identify all of the **Prime Numbers** less than 20. They are 2, 3, 5, 7, 11, 13, 17, and 19.

The problem next asks us to find the answer choice "closest to" the product of these prime numbers. As a result, we know that we can use **Estimation** on this problem. Our decision to estimate is further reinforced by the fact that the answer choices are very far apart. (If you have difficulty visualizing this, try writing out the numbers with all of the zeroes. For instance, $10^5 = 100,000$ and $10^6 = 1,000,000$.)

Since the answer choices are in **Powers of Ten**, the key is to *group the numbers* so that the products are close to powers, or multiples, of ten.

Given 2, 3, 5, 7, 11, 13, 17, and 19:

$2 \times 5 = 10$

$3 \times 7 = 21 \approx 20$

$11 \times 19 \approx 10 \times 20 \approx 200$

$13 \times 17 \approx 10 \times 20 \approx 200$

Notice that we have rounded in both directions to get more accurate estimates. For instance, we have

rounded 11 down and 19 up. The true product of 11 and 19 is 209, which is very close to $(10)(20) = 200$. There is less than a 5% difference.

Multiply the rounded numbers together:

$10 \times 20 \times 200 \times 200 = 8 \times 10^6$

Round this result once again:

$8 \times 10^6 \approx 10 \times 10^6 \approx 1 \times 10^7$ This is the **answer**.

Notice that we have to round 8 *up* to 10. The 8 came from the three 2's, which we should *not* have simply dropped or rounded down to 1.

Depending upon how we chose to group the numbers, we may have arrived at this answer differently. However, grouping and rounding is a far more efficient approach than multiplying all of the individual numbers.

The correct answer is (C).

D 16. EIVs: Quadratic Equations
Difficulty: 700–800   **OG Page:** 22

This **Quadratic Equations** problem asks us to solve for the value of $4x^2$. Therefore, instead of attempting to solve the equation for x, we can manipulate the equation until the term $4x^2$ appears in the equation. Since there are square roots on both sides of the equation, we must first **Square Both Sides** of the equation:

$$(\sqrt{3 - 2x})^2 = (\sqrt{2x} + 1)^2$$

Squaring the left side is straightforward. Taking the square of a square root cancels out the square root, leaving behind what was inside. In this case, that leaves $3 - 2x$ on the left side of the equation.

To compute $(\sqrt{2x} + 1)^2$, remember the **Special Product Quadratic:** $(x + y)^2 = x^2 + 2xy + y^2$

$$(\sqrt{2x} + 1)^2 = (\sqrt{2x})^2 + 2(\sqrt{2x})(1) + (1)^2$$
$$= 2x + 2\sqrt{2x} + 1$$

After squaring both sides, the equation becomes:

$3 - 2x = 2x + 2\sqrt{2x} + 1$

Since we do not yet know the value of $4x^2$, we must continue manipulating. None of the answer choices has a square root in it, so we should isolate $\sqrt{2x}$ and square both sides once more:

Combine terms: $2 - 4x = 2\sqrt{2x}$

Divide both sides by 2: $1 - 2x = \sqrt{2x}$

Square both sides: $(1 - 2x)^2 = (\sqrt{2x})^2$

Use Special Products: $1 - 4x + 4x^2 = 2x$

Finally, we isolate the $4x^2$ term:

$4x^2 = 6x - 1$ This is the **answer**.

Common errors are represented among the wrong answer choices. For instance, if we misread the right side of the original equation as $\sqrt{2x + 1}$ and then solve correctly for x, we will mistakenly choose (A).

The correct answer is (E).

D 17. <u>**Number Properties:**</u> Roots
Difficulty: 300–500   **OG Page:** 22

The best way to begin solving this ***Roots*** problem is to simplify the expression.

Roots can be distributed over division. That is, the square root of a fraction is the square root of the numerator over the square root of the denominator. Therefore, $\sqrt{\dfrac{16}{81}} = \dfrac{\sqrt{16}}{\sqrt{81}}$, or $\dfrac{4}{9}$, so n is equal to $\dfrac{4}{9}$.

Be careful, though! The problem asks not for the value of n, but for the value of $\sqrt{n}$. Therefore, we must take the square root of this expression *again*. As before, we can distribute the root: $\sqrt{\dfrac{4}{9}} = \dfrac{\sqrt{4}}{\sqrt{9}}$, or $\dfrac{2}{3}$.

This is the **answer**.

Notice that one of the wrong choices is indeed $\dfrac{4}{9}$. Always be sure to answer the actual question.

The correct answer is (D).

D 18. <u>**Number Properties:**</u> Divisibility & Primes
Difficulty: 300–500   **OG Page:** 22

$n = (1)(2)(3)(4)(5)(6)(7)(8)$. Thus, n has the following ***Prime Factors***: 2, 3, 5, and 7. But are there any other prime numbers that are factors of n?

For the non-prime factors of n (4, 6, and 8), we can take a prime factorization:

Thus 4, 6, and 8 are constructed of 2's and 3's only, which are already on our list.

Additionally, any products of the various factors of n are also factors of n. For example, the primes 2 and 5 combine to create a factor of $(2)(5) = 10$. However, all such products of prime numbers are non-prime. Indeed, they are all composed of the same prime factors we have already listed.

The prime factors of n are therefore 2, 3, 5, and 7. There are exactly four different prime factors of n. This is the **answer**.

A common misconception is that 1 is a prime number. This is not the case. By definition, primes have exactly two distinct factors: 1 and the prime itself. Since the integer 1 has exactly one factor, it is considered non-prime. By asking about "different prime factors greater than 1," the GMAT writers gave us free help by eliminating 1 from consideration.

The correct answer is (A).

D 19. <u>**Geometry:**</u> Triangles & Diagonals
Difficulty: 600–700   **OG Page:** 22

We are given that two of the three sides of the triangle have lengths of 2 and 7. We are also told that the third side k is greater than 2 and less than 7. By the ***Triangle Inequality*** law, the length of the third side of a triangle must lie between the difference and the sum of the two given sides, so $(7 - 2) < k < (7 + 2)$ or $5 < k < 9$.

To gain concrete understanding of this rule, ***Draw a Picture*** or two. Try drawing a triangle with side lengths 2, 3, and 7, or a triangle with side lengths 3, 7, and 10. In both cases, even if we put the two smaller sides end to end, we cannot span the largest side and form a triangle.

Now we can ***Test Possible Cases***. There are only 3 integer values of *k* that fulfill the criterion that 5 < *k* < 9. These values are 6, 7, and 8. However, only 6 is between 2 and 7 (the condition we are given). Thus, there is only one possible value for *k*. This is the **answer**.

Note that there is logic (even if it's incorrect logic) behind the wrong answers. For instance, "five" (E) is the difference between 7 and 2. Understanding the Triangle Inequality law is critical to solving this problem correctly.

The correct answer is (A).

D 20. Geometry: Circles & Cylinders
Difficulty: 300–500   **OG Page:** 23

Although this ***Circles*** problem might seem complex at the outset, it is straightforward if we follow a standard process. First, we should ***Draw a Picture***. Because the cone is inscribed in a hemisphere, draw the hemisphere first.

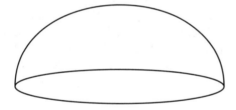

Next, draw the cone so that the base of the cone is the same as the base of the hemisphere.

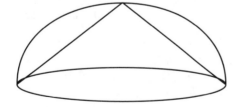

Finally, place a dot at the center of the circular base, and extend a line up to the top of the cone, representing the height.

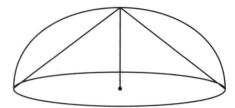

At this point, we can note that the height of the cone is the same as the radius of the hemisphere. After all, the height extends from the center of the sphere to the surface, just like any other radius. Thus, the ratio of the height to the radius is 1 : 1. This is the **answer**.

Because of perspective, a 3-dimensional diagram could appear distorted, as ours is. Don't try to get exact numbers out of a 3-D drawing. Instead, use it to visualize the situation conceptually.

The correct answer is (B).

D 21. FDPs: Percents
Difficulty: 500–600   **OG Page:** 23

When an annual ***Interest Rate*** is compounded quarterly, one-fourth of the annual rate (as a percent) is applied to the account every three months. The interest accrued every quarter then gets added to the principal. For instance, in the second quarter, John earns interest on both the original principal and the interest earned in the first quarter. This concept is critical in ***Compound Interest Rate*** problems. We should be sure to ***Follow the Money*** step by step.

If John deposited $10,000 at 4% annual interest, compounded quarterly, his account will be paid 1% of its balance every three months (1% is one-fourth of 4%). In the first three-month period, John will receive 10,000 × (0.01) or $100 in interest. That means that after three months, there will be $10,100 in the account. In the second three-month period, John will receive 10,100 × (0.01) or $101 in interest. Altogether, there will be $10,201 in John's account at the end of 6 months.

Note that adding 1% interest to the principal makes the new amount 101% of the principal. Another way to do the calculations in this problem is to multiply $10,000 by 1.01, which will give us the amount in the account after three months, and to multiply that value by 1.01 to give us the amount in the account after six months. Either method will give us the same answer.

$10,000 × 1.01 = $10,100
$10,100 × 1.01 = $10,201

The correct answer is (D).

D 22. <u>Geometry</u>: Circles & Cylinders
Difficulty: 600–700   **OG Page:** 23

In this *Cylinders* problem, we are told that a right circular cylinder of height 9 inches contains 36 cubic inches of water when it is half full. To begin the solution, we note that the cylinder would contain 72 cubic inches of water if it were completely full. In other words, the volume of the cylinder is 72 cubic inches.

The formula for the *Volume of a Cylinder* with base radius r and height h is:

$V = \pi r^2 h$

Of course, we should *Draw a Picture*.

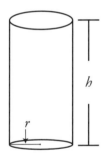

If the radius and height are given in inches, this formula yields a volume in cubic inches. Substituting for $V = 72$, $h = 9$ and leaving out the units, we obtain:

$$72 = \pi r^2 \times 9$$
$$8 = \pi r^2$$
$$\frac{8}{\pi} = r^2$$
$$\sqrt{\frac{8}{\pi}} = r$$

The *Square Root* of 8 can be simplified by factoring out a 4, which is a perfect square:

$$\sqrt{\frac{8}{\pi}} = \sqrt{\frac{4 \times 2}{\pi}} = \sqrt{4} \times \sqrt{\frac{2}{\pi}} = 2\sqrt{\frac{2}{\pi}}$$

Therefore, the base diameter, which is twice the base radius, is given by:

$$d = 2r = 4\sqrt{\frac{2}{\pi}}$$

The correct answer is (E).

D 23. <u>Number Properties</u>: Divisibility & Primes
Difficulty: 300–500   **OG Page:** 23

We can use our knowledge of *Factors and Multiples* to solve this problem.

If x is a multiple of 4 and y is a multiple of 6, then xy must be a multiple of 24. Any multiple of 24 is also a multiple of all of the factors of 24 (1, 2, 3, 4, 6, 8, 12, 24). Test each option individually:

I. 8 is a factor of 24. If xy is a multiple of 24, it is also a multiple of 8.

II. 12 is a factor of 24. If xy is a multiple of 24, it is also a multiple of 12.

III. 18 is not a factor of 24. If xy is a multiple of 24, it COULD also be a multiple of 18, but it certainly need not be.

Only I and II *must* be true.

The correct answer is (B).

D 24. <u>EIVs</u>: VICs
Difficulty: 700–800   **OG Page:** 23

We can approach this *Variables In Choices* problem by using the *Direct Algebra* method.

First, we rearrange the *Rate–Time–Distance Formula* ($RT = D$) to get $\text{Time} = \dfrac{\text{Distance}}{\text{Rate}}$.

Next, we should *Name a Variable* to represent distance. Letting d = the one-way distance from home, we can find the times for each part of Aaron's trip:

$$\text{Hours to jog from home} = \frac{d \text{ miles}}{x \text{ miles per hour}}$$

$$\text{Hours to walk back home} = \frac{d \text{ miles}}{y \text{ miles per hour}}$$

The total time Aaron spends jogging and walking is t hours, so we can add the two one-way times and solve for d, the value the question is asking for:

$$\frac{d}{x} + \frac{d}{y} = t$$

$$\frac{dy}{xy} + \frac{dx}{xy} = t$$

$$\frac{dy + dx}{xy} = t$$

$$dy + dx = xyt$$

$$d(y + x) = xyt$$

$$d = \frac{xyt}{x + y}$$

The problem asks for the one-way distance, which is d. Thus, we have the **answer**.

Alternatively, we could **Pick Numbers and Calculate a Target**. Because we have two different rates, we need to start backward and determine the total distance first. Suppose Aaron travels 12 miles away from home.

If he jogs $x = 4$ miles per hour, then he will jog for

$$\frac{12 \text{ miles}}{4 \text{ miles per hour}} = 3 \text{ hours. If he walks at } y = 2$$

miles per hour, then he will walk for

$$\frac{12 \text{ miles}}{2 \text{ miles per hour}} = 6 \text{ hours. His total traveling}$$

time is $t = 3 + 6 = 9$ hours. We can plug in these values into the answer choices to see which one results in 12 miles, our **Target Value**.

(A) $\dfrac{xt}{y} = \dfrac{(4)(9)}{(2)} = 18$ INCORRECT

(B) $\dfrac{x + t}{xy} = \dfrac{(4) + (9)}{(4)(2)} = 1\dfrac{5}{8}$ INCORRECT

(C) $\dfrac{xyt}{x + y} = \dfrac{(4)(2)(9)}{(4) + (2)} = 12$ **CORRECT**

(D) $\dfrac{x + y + t}{xy} = \dfrac{(4) + (2) + (9)}{(4)(2)} = 1\dfrac{7}{8}$

INCORRECT

(E) $\dfrac{y + t}{x} - \dfrac{t}{y} = \dfrac{(2) + (9)}{(4)} - \dfrac{(9)}{(2)} = \dfrac{11}{4} - \dfrac{18}{4} = -1\dfrac{3}{4}$

INCORRECT

The correct answer is (C).

D 25. <u>**FDPs:**</u> Digits & Decimals
Difficulty: 500–600   **OG Page:** 25

The problem asks us to determine the value of the **Units Digit** of some integer n. Since we are told that this units digit is greater than 2, it must be 3, 4, 5, 6, 7, 8, or 9. Now we must **Test Possible Cases** in each statement.

(1): INSUFFICIENT. If the units digit of n is the same as the units digit of n^2, we can narrow the possible values of the units digit by testing potential values for n. Use a **Table** to stay organized.

Possible n	n^2	Same units digit?
3	9	No, so n can't be 3
4	16	No, so n can't be 4
5	25	**Yes**, so n can be 5
6	36	**Yes**, so n can be 6 (stop)

As soon as we determine that there are at least two possible values for the units digit of n (5 or 6), we know that the statement is insufficient to determine n.

(2): INSUFFICIENT. If the units digit of n is the same as the units digit of n^3, we can narrow the possible values of the units digit by testing potential values for n. Remember to test each possible units digit in a table.

Possible n	n^3	Same units digit?
3	27	No, so n can't be 3
4	64	No, so n can't be 4
5	125	**Yes**, so n can be 5
6	216	**Yes**, so n can be 3 (stop)

As soon as we determine that there are at least two possible values for the units digit of n (5 and 6), we know that the statement is insufficient to determine n.

By the way, to avoid computing the cubes fully, we can take a little shortcut. If x and y are integers, we can find the units digit of xy by multiplying the units digit of x by the units digit of y.

In this case, after we know that $6 \times 6 = 36$, we can find the units digit of 6^3 by multiplying the units digit of 36 by 6. In other words, we don't need to multiply 36 by 6 all the way. The units digit of 36 is 6, so we can find the units digit of 6^3 by multiplying 6 by 6.

Without knowing the full value of 6^3, we know it ends in a 6. In this case, we don't save tons of time, but the shortcut is still worth knowing.

(1) AND (2) INSUFFICIENT. Statements 1 and 2 each permit the units digit to be either 5 or 6. Thus, when we combine the statements, both 5 and 6 are still possible units digits for n. As a result, we do not know the actual value of the units digit of n.

The correct answer is (E): Statements (1) and (2) TOGETHER are not sufficient.

D 26. <u>Number Properties</u>: Divisibility & Primes
Difficulty: 300–500   **OG Page:** 25

The problem asks for the value of p, an unknown integer. There is no need to rephrase the question.

(1): INSUFFICIENT. Given that the prime numbers 2, 3, and 5 are *Factors* of p, we can create the following *Prime Box* for p:

$$p$$
| 2, 3, 5, ... ? |

We do not know anything else about the possible prime factors in p, so we cannot determine a value for p.

(2): INSUFFICIENT. Similarly, we can create a prime box containing the integers 2, 5, and 7, but we have no information about other possible prime factors of p. Therefore, we cannot determine a value for p.

(1) and (2): INSUFFICIENT. Combining the statements, we know more about the prime factors of p, but we have no way of knowing whether we have been given *all* the prime factors of p. If we

were sure that we had the complete set of prime factors of p, we could determine the value of p by multiplying these prime factors together, but we cannot do so without that assurance.

Incidentally, the prime box we get by combining the two statements does not double-count prime factors mentioned in both statements:

$$p$$
| 2, 3, 5, 7, ... ? |

We can be certain that p contains the prime factors 2, 3, 5, and 7, but again, we have no information about other possible prime factors of p. Thus, we cannot determine a single value for p.

The correct answer is (E): Statements (1) and (2) TOGETHER are not sufficient.

D 27. <u>Word Translations</u>: Algebraic Translations
Difficulty: 500–600   **OG Page:** 25

This *Algebraic Translations* problem involves a typical situation: a telephone pricing plan.

In order to know how many minutes Wanda was charged for, we would have to know details about the pricing scheme. We would also need to know the total cost (or simply the number of minutes she talked).

(1): INSUFFICIENT. This statement gives only the cost of the call. To find the length of the call, we need information about the company's pricing structure.

(2): INSUFFICIENT. This statement gives some information about the phone company's pricing structure, but no information about the amount Wanda was actually charged. Therefore, it is impossible to determine the cost or length of the call.

(1) and (2): INSUFFICIENT. Even together, we do not have information regarding pricing and length of call. Thus, an answer cannot be reached. We can prove this through either of the following methods.

Algebraic Method: First, we should *Name Variables*. Let n stand for the length of the call, in minutes, and c the cost, in cents, of each minute *after* the first. In this case, Wanda was billed for 1 minute at $(c + 50)$ cents and for $(n - 1)$ minutes at c cents per minute. Thus, the total amount charged for the call was $(1)(c + 50) + (n - 1)(c)$, or $50 + nc$. Since the total charge was $6.50, which equals 650 cents, $50 + nc = 650$, or $nc = 600$. Many pairs of positive integers n and c satisfy this condition (for instance, 2 and 300, or 3 and 200). Thus, the two statements together are still insufficient to determine the value of n.

Pick Numbers: As is usual with Data Sufficiency number picking, the goal is to *try* to prove "insufficiency"—i.e., to look for two different values that fit the conditions but give different answers to the question.

First, **Simplify the Problem** by realizing that the extra $0.50 added to the first minute may be regarded as an extra charge. If this charge is considered separate, then the whole call is charged at the same rate per minute. Therefore, we can solve the problem as if the call were charged at a constant rate per minute, and as if the call cost $6.50 − $0.50 = $6.00 in total.

Let's test possible cases.

Try $n = 2$ minutes; the charge is $3.00 per minute. Try $n = 3$ minutes; the charge is $2.00 per minute.

With two plausible values for n, this information is insufficient.

The correct answer is (E): Statements (1) and (2) TOGETHER are not sufficient.

D 28. <u>Geometry:</u> Triangles & Diagonals
Difficulty: 500–600 **OG Page:** 25

By definition, an **Isosceles Triangle** is one in which two sides are equal. Even though we know that triangle *MNP* is isosceles, we do not know which two sides are equal. We need to **Test Possible Cases**, and for this problem, the best way to do so is by **Drawing Pictures**. We should draw 3 isosceles triangles with exaggerated sides, so that we can easily see which sides are equal and which are not.

In all of the triangles above, we have labeled $MN = x$. The perimeter of the triangle is either $2x + y$ or $2y + x$. To answer the question, we need not only x and y, but also the scenario (i.e. are the equal sides x or y?).

(1): INSUFFICIENT. $MN = x = 16$, so let's label the pictures accordingly.

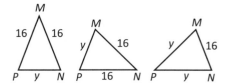

The perimeter is either $(32 + y)$ or $(2y + 16)$. We have uncertainty not only about the value of y, but also about which expression applies.

(2): INSUFFICIENT. $NP = 20$, so let's label the pictures accordingly.

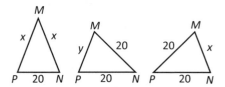

The perimeter is $(20 + 2x)$ or $(40 + y)$ or $(40 + x)$. We have uncertainty not only about the values of x and y, but also about which expression applies.

(1) and (2): INSUFFICIENT. If $MN = 16$ and $NP = 20$, we can again label all three sides in each picture:

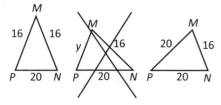

One scenario can be eliminated, as $MN \neq NP$. Although we know both x and y, we still do not know which two sides of the triangle are equal (i.e. are the equal sides 20 or 16?)

The perimeter could be either 16 + 16 + 20 = 52 or 20 + 20 + 16 = 56.

Whether we draw all these triangles or not, we must consider multiple scenarios. If we draw only one picture and assume that *MN* is one of the equal sides, then we would conclude, incorrectly, that the statements together are sufficient.

The correct answer is (E): Statements (1) and (2) TOGETHER are not sufficient.

D 29. <u>Word Translations</u>**:** Overlapping Sets
Difficulty: 600–700   **OG Page:** 25

This **Overlapping Sets** problem describes retailers surveyed who either owned their own stores or did not and who either purchased computers for business purposes or did not. The question asks whether we can determine what percent of retailers had purchased computers for business purposes. Using a **Double-Set Matrix**, we can identify what cell we are trying to fill. Since this is also a percent question with an unspecified amount, we can pick a **Smart Number** of 100 for the total number of retailers.

Purchased for Business?

		Yes	No	Total
Own Store?	Yes			
	No			
	Total	?		100

(1): INSUFFICIENT. Let's **Name a Variable**. If *x* is the number of retailers who owned their own store, 85% of those retailers (or $0.85x$) owned their own stores *and* purchased computers for business purposes. This also implies that $0.15x$ owned their own stores but did *not* purchase computers for business purposes. However, we cannot calculate what percent of retailers surveyed had purchased computers for business purposes.

Purchased for Business?

		Yes	No	Total
Own Store?	Yes	$0.85x$	$0.15x$	x
	No			
	Total	?		100

(2): INSUFFICIENT. Knowing that 40% of the retailers surveyed owned their own store tells us that 40 of the 100 owned their own store and 60 did not. Again, however, we cannot calculate what

percent of retailers purchased computers for business purposes.

Purchased for Business?

		Yes	No	Total
Own Store?	Yes			40
	No			60
	Total	?		100

(1) and (2): INSUFFICIENT. With these combined pieces of information, we know that 85% of 40 (or 34) retailers owned their own store and purchased computers for business purposes. This also tells us that 6 retailers owned their own store but did *not* purchase computers for business purposes. (Note that these numbers actually refer to percents of the total number of retailers surveyed, since we used 100 as a Smart Number.) However, we have no information about the percent of retailers who did *not* own their own store but *did* purchase computers for business purposes. Thus we are unable to calculate the total percent of retailers who purchased computers for business purposes.

Purchased for Business?

		Yes	No	Total
Own Store?	Yes	34	6	40
	No			60
	Total	?		100

The correct answer is (E): Statements (1) and (2) TOGETHER are not sufficient.

D 30. <u>EIVs</u>**:** Inequalities
Difficulty: 600–700   **OG Page:** 25

This **Inequalities** problem also involves **Algebraic Translation** from words to math.

Let's begin by **Naming Variables** for the two unknowns. Let *h* represent the number of hundred-dollar certificates sold, and let *t* represent the number of ten-dollar certificates sold. (Notice that there is a **Hidden Constraint** here: *h* and *t* must be integers, since we use them to count physical objects.) We can create two equations:

$h + t = 20$ (The store sold 20 certificates.)

$100h + 10t =$ Total Value

Notice that for the second equation, we have multiplied the monetary value of each type of certificate by the number of such certificates sold. (Some people confuse this step by thinking of the variables as *equal* to 100 and 10. This is incorrect, since our variables represent the *number* of such certificates, not their monetary value.)

The question asks us for the value of t.

(1): SUFFICIENT. This statement seems insufficient at first glance. After all, it does not give us an exact amount for the Total Value but only a range: the Total Value is between 1,650 and 1,800. Thus:

$$1,650 \le 100h + 10t \le 1,800$$

For this information to be sufficient, we must be left with only one solution for t. So let's **Test Possible Values** to see whether we can find two or more solutions. Given the lower boundary, we can start by testing $h = 16$ and $t = 4$. (We have to try values that sum to 20.) This set of test numbers yields $(100)(16) + 10(4) = 1,640$, which is too low.

Next, try $h = 17$ and $t = 3$. This yields $(100)(17) + 10(3) = 1,730$, which works. But is 1,730 the only value that works?

Let's also try $h = 18$ and $t = 2$. This yields $(100)(18) + 10(2) = 1,820$, which is too high.

Thus, 1,730 is the only possible Total Value between 1,650 and 1,800. As a result, we can say with certainty that $t = 3$ and that this information is sufficient. Notice that the integer constraint on h and t is crucial. Otherwise, there would be more than one possible Total Value in the given range.

(2): INSUFFICIENT. This statement tells us that $h > 15$.

This leaves multiple possible values for h (16, 17, 18, 19, or 20), and thus multiple corresponding values for t (4, 3, 2, 1, or 0).

The correct answer is (A): Statement (1) ALONE is sufficient, but statement (2) alone is not sufficient.

D 31. Word Translations: Statistics
Difficulty: 600–700   **OG Page:** 25

Standard Deviation measures the tendency of the terms in a set to cluster around the mean (average) of the set. To calculate standard deviation, we need to find the distance of every term from the average,

square these differences, take the average of these squares (this is called the **Variance**) and then take the square root of the variance. While this sounds like a rather complicated formula, do not be scared off by it. Our job is to know whether we can arrive at an answer—not to perform calculations.

We are asked whether a certain standard deviation is less than 3. This question cannot easily be rephrased.

(1) SUFFICIENT: If we know the variance of the set, we know the standard deviation, since the standard deviation is simply the square root of the variance. So if the variance is 4, the standard deviation is 2. Thus, we know whether the standard deviation is less than 3.

(2) SUFFICIENT: If we know that the difference between each term of the set and the average of the set is 2, we can calculate the standard deviation of the set.

First, square all the differences. This yields 4 for each term. Average the squares:

$$\frac{(4 \times 20)}{20} = \frac{80}{20} = 4$$

Take the square root of the average:

$$\sqrt{4} = 2$$

Thus, the standard deviation of the set is 2, and we know whether the standard deviation is less than 3.

Bear in mind, however, that we did not need to actually calculate the standard deviation in either statement. We needed only to determine whether it was less than 3. If we recognize that knowing the variance or the difference of each term from the average allows us to find the standard deviation, we don't need to do any calculations.

The correct answer is (D): EACH statement ALONE is sufficient.

D 32. Word Translations: Statistics
Difficulty: 700–800   **OG Page:** 25

This **Statistics** problem concerns the **Range** of a set, which is the difference between the largest and smallest numbers of the set. We cannot know the range of the set of numbers in this problem without knowing something about the two missing integers, x and y. Therefore, a natural rephrasing might be to ask what x and y are. However, notice that this question is a Yes/No question. Most such questions can actually be answered without precise knowledge of every quantity involved.

Therefore, in this case it is best to move on to the numbered statements without rephrasing the question, knowing that we are trying to figure out whether the difference between the largest and smallest numbers is more than 9. We will **Test Possible Cases** as we go.

(1): INSUFFICIENT. To begin, consider a simple concrete case. If $x = 0$, then y must be greater than $3 \times 0 = 0$. Now let's try **Extreme Values** of y, to see whether we can find cases yielding different results. Suppose that y is the smallest it can be: $y = 1$. In that case, 6 remains the largest number in the set, and the range is $6 - 0 = 0$, which is less than 9. Thus, if $x = 0$ and $y = 1$, the answer to the given question is *No*.

Now try a large value of y, with x still equal to zero. If $y = 10$, then the range is $10 - 0 = 10$, which is greater than 9. Thus, we can also answer the given question *Yes* while satisfying this statement. As a result, we cannot determine the answer to the question.

(2): INSUFFICIENT. We can proceed in a similar manner by testing numbers. This statement is satisfied as long as x is greater than 3 and y is greater than x. Again, start with the smallest possible case. If $x = 4$ and $y = 5$, the range is $6 - 3 = 3$, which is less than 9. Thus, the answer to the given question would be *No* in this case.

Now try a large value of y. If $x = 4$ and $y = 14$, then the range is $14 - 4 = 10$ which is greater than 9. Thus, we can also answer the given question *Yes* while satisfying this statement, and again, we cannot determine the answer to the question.

(1) & (2): SUFFICIENT. Combining the two statements, we know that x is an integer greater than 3, and y is an integer greater than $3x$. We start with the smallest possible case. The smallest that x can be is 4. Since y is greater than $3x$, we

know that y has to be at least 13. Thus, the range in this case is at least $13 - 3 = 10$.

If x is 5, then y has to be greater than 15. That is, y is at least 16, yielding a range of at least $16 - 3 = 13$. As x increases, y increases even faster, so the range widens further. As a result, the range will always be greater than 9, and we can answer the given question with a definitive *Yes*.

The correct answer is (C): BOTH statements TOGETHER are sufficient, but NEITHER statement ALONE is sufficient.

D 33. EIVs: Inequalities
Difficulty: 500–600   **OG Page:** 25

Before looking at the statements, we should see whether we can **Rephrase** the question. Notice that we will need to make use of both **Inequalities** and **Exponents** knowledge.

Is $\dfrac{5^{x+2}}{25} < 1$?

Note that 25 is simply 5^2. Therefore:

$$\frac{5^{x+2}}{5^2} < 1?$$

Since the numerator and denominator each have a base of 5, we can divide and subtract the exponents:

$$5^{x+2-2} < 1?$$
$$5^x < 1?$$

The rephrased question is simply "Is $5^x < 1$?"

(1): SUFFICIENT. $5^x < 1$. This answers our rephrased question directly.

(2): SUFFICIENT. x is negative. Therefore, 5^x is a fraction less than 1. We can **Test Numbers** to verify our understanding. For instance, if $x = -1$, $5^x = 5^{-1} = 1/5$. If $x = -3$, $5^x = 5^{-3} = 1/(5^3) = 1/125$. The more negative x becomes, the smaller the fraction will become.

The correct answer is (D): EACH statement ALONE is sufficient.

D 34. <u>Word Translations</u>: Overlapping Sets
Difficulty: 600–700   **OG Page:** 25

This ***Overlapping Sets*** problem does not specify the number of companies surveyed, so we can use 100 companies as a ***Smart Number*** to simplify the percentages given.

The companies surveyed either required or did not require computer skills. They also either required or did not require writing skills. The question asks for the companies that required *neither computer nor writing skills*. This quantity is shaded in our ***Double-Set Matrix***:

		Computer?		
Writing?		*Yes*	*No*	*Total*
	Yes	20		
	No		?	
	Total			100

(1): INSUFFICIENT. Note that half of the companies *that required computer skills* (not all companies surveyed) required writing skills too. Because 20 companies required both computer and writing skills, 20 companies required computer skills but not writing skills. This means that 40 companies required computer skills. However, the only other piece of information we can infer is that 60% of companies do not require computer skills. This is not enough information to answer the question.

		Computer?		
Writing?		*Yes*	*No*	*Total*
	Yes	20		
	No	20	?	
	Total	40	60	100

(2): INSUFFICIENT. We now know 65 companies required writing skills and 35 companies did not. We can input this information into the table, but we do not have enough information to answer the question.

		Computer?		
Writing?		*Yes*	*No*	*Total*
	Yes	20	45	65
	No		?	35
	Total			100

(1) and (2): SUFFICIENT. With both statements, we know that 15 companies required neither skill,

which means that 15% of all companies require neither computer skills nor writing skills.

		Computer?		
Writing?		*Yes*	*No*	*Total*
	Yes	20	45	65
	No	20	?	35
	Total	40		100

The correct answer is (C): BOTH statements TOGETHER are sufficient, but NEITHER statement ALONE is sufficient.

D 35. <u>EIVs</u>: Basic Equations
Difficulty: 500–600   **OG Page:** 25

The problem asks for the value of a ***Combined Expression,*** or Combo. The Combo is $w + q$. Note that we do not need the values of w and of q individually (although knowing those values would be sufficient).

(1): SUFFICIENT. The equation can be manipulated with ***Direct Algebra*** to determine the value of the Combo $w + q$:

$$3w = 3 - 3q$$
$$3w + 3q = 3$$
$$w + q = 1$$

Note that we cannot determine the values of w and of q individually, but we know the sum, and thus we can answer the question.

(2): SUFFICIENT. The equation can be manipulated to determine the value of the combined expression $w + q$:

$$5w + 5q = 5$$
$$w + q = 1$$

As above, we do not know the values of the variables separately. Nevertheless, we can answer the question.

The correct answer is (D): EACH statement ALONE is sufficient.

D 36. <u>Geometry</u>: Circles & Cylinders
Difficulty: 500–600   **OG Page:** 25

In this ***Circles*** problem, we must think about properties of the radius of a circle.

In order for point *Y* to lie inside circle *C*, the distance from the center of the circle to *Y* must be less than the radius of the circle. Since we are told that the radius is 2, we can **Rephrase** the question as "Is the length of line segment *OY* less than 2?"

(1): INSUFFICIENT. Given that point *X* lies inside the circle and that the length of line segment *XY* is 3, it is possible for point *Y* to lie inside or outside of the circle. To verify, we should **Test Possible Cases.** For instance, *X* and *Y* may be two points on the diameter of the circle, located 3 units apart.

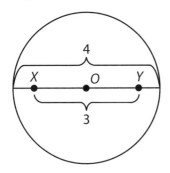

However, *Y* may be located outside the circle as well.

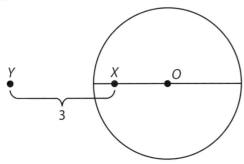

(2): SUFFICIENT. This statement directly answers our rephrased question. If the length of line segment *OY* is 1.5, *Y* must be inside the circle. The only possible locations for *Y* are shown on the dotted circle below.

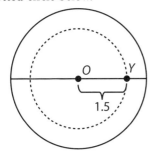

The correct answer is (B): Statement (2) ALONE is sufficient, but statement (1) alone is not sufficient.

D 37. <u>EIVs</u>: Basic Equations
Difficulty: 300–500   **OG Page:** 25

This **Basic Equations** question asks whether *x* is greater than *y*. The question involves **Inequalities**.

(1): SUFFICIENT. This statement tells us that *x* is equal to *y* + 2. We can conclude that *x* is greater than *y* (by 2 units, in fact) directly or by either of the following methods.

Substitution: Substitute the expression *y* + 2 into *x* in the prompt question, yielding "Is *y* + 2 > *y*?" Now we can subtract *y* from both sides, yielding "Is 2 > 0?" Since the answer to this question is unequivocally "yes," the statement is sufficient.

Number Line: Adding 2 to a number on a number line is equivalent to moving 2 units to the right. Since *x* = *y* + 2, we know that *x* is 2 units to the right of *y*. Finally, any number to the right of *y* on a number line is greater than *y*.

(2): INSUFFICIENT. We can see that *x* could be greater than *y* or less than *y* by either of the following methods.

Substitution: Multiply both sides of this equation by 2 to yield *x* = 2*y* − 2. We can now substitute into the prompt question, giving "Is 2*y* − 2 > *y*?" Simplify this inequality by subtracting *y* and adding 2 to both sides, yielding "Is *y* > 2?" However, we do not know whether *y* is greater than 2 or not.

Pick Numbers: Multiply both sides of this equation by 2 to yield *x* = 2*y* − 2. Since *x* is stated in terms of *y*, pick a value for *y* and calculate the corresponding *x* value. Try **Extreme Values** for *y*. If *y* = 100, then *x* = 200 − 2 = 198, so *x* > *y*.

However, if *y* = 0, then *x* = 0 − 2 = −2, so *x* is not greater than *y*. Since these two answers are contradictory, it is unnecessary to attempt further plug-ins.

The correct answer is (A): Statement (1) ALONE is sufficient, but statement (2) alone is not sufficient.

D 38. <u>EIVs</u>: Inequalities
Difficulty: 600–700   **OG Page:** 26

This *Inequalities* problem also involves *Rates*.

We are given Paula's average speed and asked about her time. Since the statements both provide information on the distance Paula drove, we should *Rephrase* the original question about time into an equivalent question about distance. We can use the *Rate-Time-Distance Formula: RT = D*, which can be rearranged into $T = \dfrac{D}{R}$.

Is $T < 3$ hours?

Is $\dfrac{D}{R} < 3$ hours?

Now, we do not have an exact rate, but we know that Paula's speed was "greater than 70 kilometers per hour." We can actually insert this fact into the inequality:

Is $\dfrac{D}{\text{a number over 70 km / hour}} < 3$ hours?

Now we can cross-multiply and simplify:

Is $D < (3 \text{ hours})(\text{a number over 70 km/hour})$?
Is $D < \text{a number over } 210 \text{ km}$?

Finally, asking whether D is less than a number over 210 km is equivalent to asking whether D is less than or equal to 210 km.

Is $D \leq 210$ km?

This question should make sense: if Paula drove home faster than 70 km per hour (but possibly only a little faster), then we can only guarantee she made the trip in less than 3 hours if her home is less than 210 km away.

(1): INSUFFICIENT. If $D > 200$ km, D might be either greater than or less than 210 km.

(2): SUFFICIENT. If $D < 205$ km, D is definitely less than 210 km.

The correct answer is (B): Statement (2) ALONE is sufficient, but statement (1) alone is not sufficient.

D 39. <u>Geometry</u>: Coordinate Plane
Difficulty: 700–800   **OG Page:** 26

In this *Coordinate Plane* problem, we know that line k passes through the point $(-5, r)$ and has a negative *Slope* (indicating that the line goes down to the right). Since we do not know the sign of r, the point $(-5, r)$ can be in quadrant II or III as pictured below. This yields many possible lines for k, three of which are shown below: k_1, k_2 and k_3. The question asks us whether the x-intercept of line k is positive. Note that k_1 has a positive x-intercept, whereas k_2 and k_3 both have a negative x-intercept. We will need to *Test Possible Cases* by drawing several lines, whether we have specific numbers or not.

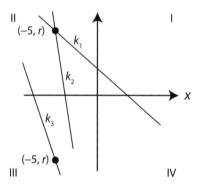

(1): INSUFFICIENT. A slope of -5 means that line k falls 5 units for every 1 unit of movement to the right. That means that if r were 25, the line would pass through the origin.

If $r < 25$, line k will have a negative x-intercept. Similarly, if $r > 25$, line k will have a positive x-intercept.

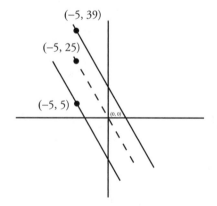

We don't know whether r is greater than or less than 25. Thus, we can't determine whether the x-intercept is positive.

(2): INSUFFICIENT. Just knowing that $r > 0$ is not enough to tell us whether the x-intercept of line k is positive. For both lines discussed in statement (1), $r > 0$, but one has a positive x-intercept, and one has a negative x-intercept.

(1) & (2): INSUFFICIENT. Knowing that the slope is -5 and that $r > 0$ is not enough. As discussed in statement (1), it matters whether $r > 25$, not whether $r > 0$. Line k could still have a negative x-intercept or a positive x-intercept.

The correct answer is (E): Statements (1) and (2) TOGETHER are not sufficient.

D 40. FDPs: Percents
Difficulty: 300–500   **OG Page:** 26

Given the information in the question stem, we can set up a **Simple Interest Formula** to show the knowns and unknowns involved in this **Percents** problem:

(Principal) × (Interest rate) × (Time) = Yield ($)

With this formula and the information given about the first investment, we can find p. Since the interest rate is given as *p percent*, we should write that rate as $p/100$. (The word "percent" means "per hundred," or "divided by 100.")

$$(\$5{,}000) \times (p/100) \times (1) = 500$$
$$p = 10$$

The second situation described in the problem is an investment at k percent simple interest. We know the time (1 year), and we want the yield to be the same as above ($500). We are left with two unknowns:

$$(\text{Principal})(k/100)(1) = \$500$$

To find the principal, we must know k. Thus, we can **Rephrase** the question as "What is k?"

(1): SUFFICIENT. Here we are given the relationship between k and p: $k = 0.8p$

As we already know the value of p, this relationship allows us to solve for k, which equals 8.

(2): SUFFICIENT. This statement gives us the value of k directly.

The correct answer is (D): EACH statement ALONE is sufficient.

D 41. Number Properties: Positives & Negatives
Difficulty: 600–700   **OG Page:** 26

This **Positives & Negatives** problem requires us to handle **Inequalities** carefully. It is tempting to cross-multiply here and assume we will get $x + y > 0$, but since we don't know whether z is positive or negative, we don't know in which direction the inequality will point (remember that we have to flip an inequality if we multiply or divide it by a negative). We do know, however, that if $\frac{x+y}{z} > 0$, then $x + y$ and z are either both positive or both negative. That is, $x + y$ and z have the **Same Sign**.

(1) INSUFFICIENT: Knowing that x is less than y does not tell us whether x is positive or negative.

(2) INSUFFICIENT: Knowing that z is negative tells us that $x + y$ is negative, but we don't know whether x itself is positive or negative. We could have a positive x and a negative y and still get a negative sum ($x = 1$ and $y = -3$, for example, sum to -2).

(1) & (2) SUFFICIENT: We know from statement (2) that $x + y$ is negative. We and from statement (1) that x is less than y, then x must be negative. In order to get a negative sum, at least one of the variables x and y must be negative. If x were positive, y would have to be a larger positive, and their sum would therefore be positive ($x = 3$ and $y = 5$, for example). Therefore, x must be negative.

The correct answer is (C): BOTH statements TOGETHER are sufficient, but NEITHER statement ALONE is sufficient.

D 42. Number Properties: Divisibility & Primes
Difficulty: 600–700   **OG Page:** 26

This **Divisibility** question asks us to determine whether integer k has at least three different positive **Prime Factors**.

Although it is not strictly necessary to do so, we can certainly answer the question if we can determine what the prime factors of k are, or at least a subset of three different prime factors.

(1): INSUFFICIENT. If $k/15$ is an integer, then k must be divisible by 15. Put differently, k must have the prime factors of 15 in its **Prime Box**, and therefore, k has 3 and 5 as prime factors.

However, we cannot tell whether k has at least three positive prime factors, since k may or may not have other prime factors besides 3 and 5.

(2): INSUFFICIENT. If $k/10$ is an integer, then k must be divisible by 10. Put differently, k must have the prime factors of 10 in its prime box, and therefore, k has 2 and 5 as prime factors.

Again, however, we cannot tell whether k has at least three positive prime factors, since k may or may not have other prime factors besides 2 and 5.

(1) and (2): SUFFICIENT. With these combined pieces of information, we know that k has 2, 3 and 5 as prime factors. Whether or not it has more prime factors, we are sure that k has a minimum of three different positive prime factors.

The correct answer is (C): BOTH statements TOGETHER are sufficient, but NEITHER statement ALONE is sufficient.

D 43. Word Translations: Statistics
Difficulty: 300–500   **OG Page:** 26

Was the **Average** (arithmetic mean) of a list of numbers greater than the **Median**? To answer, we need information about the average and the median. If we know the sum and the number of items in the list, we can calculate the average.

(1): INSUFFICIENT. We are given the sum and the number of elements in the list. This is enough to determine the average, but we still have no information regarding the median.

(2): SUFFICIENT. 60% of the elements in the list are less than the average. Imagine arranging the items in the list in order from least to greatest. We do not know anything about the last 40%, but we do know that each of the first 60% of entries is less than the average. When a list is arranged in order from least to greatest (or greatest to least), the medi-

an is either the middle number or the average of the two middle numbers. Thus, the median must be contained within the 60% of entries that are less than the average. The median is therefore less than the average.

The correct answer is (B): Statement (2) ALONE is sufficient, but statement (1) alone is not sufficient.

D 44. Number Properties: Exponents & Roots
Difficulty: 700–800   **OG Page:** 26

This tricky problem involves both **Fractional Exponents** and **Square Roots**. We also need to apply our knowledge of **Integers**. Before looking at the statements, we should figure out what conditions would make $(\sqrt{m})^n$ an integer. First of all, remember that if x and y are positive integers, then x^y is always an integer.

We know that m and n are both positive integers, so if $\sqrt{m}$ is an integer, then $(\sqrt{m})^n$ will also be an integer. That is, if m is a perfect square, then $(\sqrt{m})^n$ will be an integer, no matter what n is.

We can also express $(\sqrt{m})^n$ as a fractional exponent. $(\sqrt{m})^n = (m^{1/2})^n = m^{n/2}$. So we can see that if $\frac{n}{2}$ is an integer (that is, if n is even), then $(\sqrt{m})^n$ will be an integer, no matter what m is.

Thus, we can **Rephrase** the question to handle these two cases. Instead of asking "Is $(\sqrt{m})^n$ an integer?" we should ask "Is it true either that $\sqrt{m}$ is an integer or that n is even?" This question seems more complex, but it actually lays out the cases clearly.

Another option is to **Test Possible Values** to find patterns. Use a **Table** to stay organized.

m	$\sqrt{m}$	n	$(\sqrt{m})^n$	Yes/No
1	1	1	1	Yes
2	$\sqrt{2}$	1	$\sqrt{2}$	No
3	$\sqrt{3}$	1	$\sqrt{3}$	No
4	2	1	2	Yes

(*Notice that we get Yes when* m *is a perfect square.*)

m	$\sqrt{m}$	n	$(\sqrt{m})^n$	Yes/No
2	$\sqrt{2}$	2	$(\sqrt{2})^2 = 2$	Yes
2	$\sqrt{2}$	3	$(\sqrt{2})^3$	No
2	$\sqrt{2}$	4	$(\sqrt{2})^4 = 4$	Yes
2	$\sqrt{2}$	5	$(\sqrt{2})^5$	No

(*Notice that we get Yes when* n *is even.*)

(1): SUFFICIENT. This statement answers our rephrased question. We know that $\sqrt{m}$ is an integer, so we are done.

(2): INSUFFICIENT. Knowing that $\sqrt{n}$ is an integer does not tell us whether n is even. For example, if $\sqrt{n} = 2$, then $n = 4$, and the answer to our rephrased question is *yes*. However, if $\sqrt{n} = 3$, then $n = 9$, and the answer to our rephrased question is *no*. Because our answer is *yes* for some values and *no* for other values, this statement is insufficient.

The correct answer is (A): Statement (1) ALONE is sufficient, but statement (2) alone is not sufficient.

D 45. Word Translations: Minor Question Types
Difficulty: 600–700   **OG Page:** 26

This *Grouping* problem specifies that there are 66 people in an auditorium and that no more than 6 people have birthdays during the same month. The yes/no question asks whether at least one person has a birthday in January. The distinction, then, is whether we can tell that *nobody* has a birthday in January or that *one or more* people have a birthday in January. Because "one or more" opens up many possibilities, we should begin by determining what conditions would be necessary for *nobody* to have a birthday in January.

In order for nobody to have a January birthday, the 66 people need to be split among the other 11 months. As a result, the maximum allowed per month, 6 people, would have to be assigned to each of the other 11 months:

0 6 6 6 6 6 6 6 6 6 6 6
J F M A M J J A S O N D

If any month falls below the maximum (that is, has fewer than 6 people), we know that at least one person must have a birthday in January, because the extra birthday(s) cannot push any of the other monthly totals above 6 birthdays. Thus, we can **Rephrase** the question as follows: "Does any month besides January contain fewer than 6 birthdays?"

(1): SUFFICIENT. If there are more February birthdays than March birthdays, then March cannot have the maximum allowed (6). At most, March can have 5 birthdays. Thus, we know that at least one month besides January has fewer than 6 birthdays, forcing at least one person to have a birthday in January.

(2): SUFFICIENT. If March has 5 birthdays, then we can answer the rephrased question directly. Note that even if each of the other 10 months from February through December has 6 birthdays, we have only accounted for $5 + 6 \times 10 = 65$ birthdays. There is still one more birthday, which must happen during the one leftover month: January.

The correct answer is (D): EACH statement ALONE is sufficient.

D 46. Word Translations: Statistics
Difficulty: 600–700   **OG Page:** 26

Using a rearrangement of the **Average Formula**, (Average) × (# of terms) = (Sum), we can determine that the sum of the salaries of the employees last year was $42,800 \times 10 = \$428,000$. Since the number of employees has not changed, in order to calculate this year's average we need only know how this sum has changed.

We should **Rephrase** the question as "What was the sum of the salaries for the 10 employees this year?" Indeed, we did not need to calculate the sum of last year's salaries, since we are concerned only with finding this year's sum.

(1): INSUFFICIENT. For 8 of the 10 employees, this year's salary went up by 15%. We know nothing about the other 2 employees, so it is impossible to know the sum of all 10 salaries this year.

(2): INSUFFICIENT. We know that the salaries of two of the employees stayed the same, but we know nothing about the other employees', so we cannot determine the sum of this year's salaries.

(1) and (2): INSUFFICIENT. Even knowing that 2 salaries remained the same and 8 salaries increased by 15%, we cannot calculate a numerical value for the sum of the salaries this year. The result depends on the size of the 8 changing salaries. For example, imagine that last year 8 employees earned $10,000 each and 2 employees earned $174,000 each (producing a total of $428,000). Increasing those $10,000 salaries by 15% produces new salaries of $11,500. The total sum of all the salaries would be:

$2 \times \$174{,}000 + 8 \times \$11{,}500 = \$440{,}000$

If, however, the 8 employees earned $50,000 each last year, the 2 other employees earned $14,000 each, and we increase the $50,000 salaries by 15%, the new sum of all the salaries would be:

$2 \times \$14{,}000 + 8 \times \$57{,}500 = \$488{,}000$

If, in Statement (1), we were told that the salary of *each* employee was 15% greater this year than last year, even without knowing individual salaries we could compute this year's sum by multiplying $428,000 by 1.15. However, that is not the information we have been given.

The correct answer is (E): Statements (1) and (2) TOGETHER are not sufficient.

D 47. Word Translations: Overlapping Sets
Difficulty: 500–600   **OG Page:** 26

In this **Overlapping Sets** problem, books can be classified in two different ways: (1) fiction and nonfiction, and (2) Spanish and not Spanish. We construct a **Double-Set Matrix** according to these criteria, inserting the information from the prompt and circling the desired quantity. Be sure to fill in

as much of the table as you can. For instance, if we know that 24 of the 80 books are fiction, then we know that 56 are non-fiction.

	Spanish	*Not Spanish*	*Total*
Fiction	?		24
Non-Fiction			56
Total	23	57	80

(1): SUFFICIENT. Use *Algebraic Translation* for the specified relationship. Let's first *Name a Variable*. If we write the smaller number of books (those written in Spanish) as x, then the larger number (those not written in Spanish) is $x + 6$. Fill the numbers into the chart:

	Spanish	*Not Spanish*	*Total*
Fiction	x	$x + 6$	24
Non-Fiction			56
Total	23	57	80

Since all the rows in the matrix add up, we can write the equation $x + (x + 6) = 24$. This is a *Linear Equation* that can be solved for a single value of x. Thus, we can answer the question. (Incidentally, the value of x is 9, but you should try to avoid unnecessary algebra on Data Sufficiency questions.)

(2): SUFFICIENT. Again, translate the specified relationship. If we write the smaller number of books (the fiction books) as x, then the larger number (the nonfiction books) is $x + 5$. Fill the numbers into the chart:

	Spanish	*Not Spanish*	*Total*
Fiction	x		24
Non-Fiction	$x + 5$		56
Total	23	57	80

Since all the columns in the matrix add up, we can write the equation $x + (x + 5) = 23$. This is another linear equation that can be solved for a single value of x. Again, we can answer the question.

The correct answer is (D): EACH statement ALONE is sufficient.

D 48. Geometry: Polygons
Difficulty: 700–800   **OG Page:** 26

To attack this **Polygons** problem, we should first *Draw a Picture* of rectangle Q. We should also

Name Variables and label the sides, since the side lengths are used to determine the perimeter.

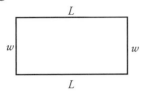

The perimeter is $2w + 2L = 2(w + L)$. Thus, we can **Rephrase** the question as "What is the value of $w + L$?"

(1): INSUFFICIENT. The diagonal of rectangle Q is given, so let's label the picture accordingly.

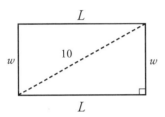

Cutting a rectangle in half diagonally creates two right triangles, so we can set up an equation for the diagonal using the **Pythagorean Theorem**.

$$w^2 + L^2 = 10^2$$
$$w^2 + L^2 = 100$$

From this equation, we cannot determine the value of $(w + L)$, nor can we determine the values of w and L individually.

(2): INSUFFICIENT. The area of a rectangle is wL, so $wL = 48$. From this equation, we cannot determine the value of $(w + L)$, nor can we determine the values of w and L individually.

(1) and (2): SUFFICIENT. We have two equations and two unknowns. At this point, we might think that because we have two equations and two unknowns, *of course* we can solve for the variables. However, this thinking is dangerous. Since neither equation is linear, we have no way of knowing whether the two equations are sufficient to solve for the variables or for an expression such as the one we are looking for (that is, $w + L$). As it turns out, we do not have enough information to find the variables themselves, but we can get a unique value for $w + L$.

There are several approaches at this point. The standard method is *Algebraic Substitution*: solve

one equation for one variable and substitute into the other equation.

From (2), we have

$$wL = 48$$
$$w = \frac{48}{L}$$

Substituting into the equation from (1), we get

$$w^2 + L^2 = 100$$
$$\left(\frac{48}{L}\right)^2 + L^2 = 100$$
$$\frac{48^2}{L^2} + L^2 = 100$$
$$48^2 + L^4 = 100L^2$$
$$L^4 - 100L^2 + 48^2 = 0$$
$$(L^2 - 36)(L^2 - 64) = 0$$
$$L^2 = 36 \ or \ 64$$
$$L = 6 \ or \ 8$$

When $L = 6$, $w = 8$, so $(w + L) = 8 + 6 = 14$.

When $L = 8$, $w = 6$, so $(w + L) = 6 + 8 = 14$.

As it turns out, we have enough information to get a unique value for $w + L$.

As we can see, the direct algebraic method is not only messy, but also time-consuming, since factoring the quadratic is difficult.

A better approach is to **Make an Educated Guess** about the values of w and L, then check whether the values satisfy both constraints.

One very common triangle on the GMAT is the *3–4–5* right triangle and its multiples, such as 6–8–10. Since the diagonal of rectangle Q is 10, side lengths of 6 and 8 would satisfy the constraint from statement (1). Do these values satisfy the constraint from statement (2)?

$$\text{area} = wL = (6)(8) = 48 \ \checkmark$$

Thus, $w + L = 6 + 8 = 14$.

Finally, if we recognize that we are given the components of a common quadratic form, we can use *Special Products*:

$$(w + L)^2 = w^2 + 2wL + L^2 = (w^2 + L^2) + 2(wL).$$

If $w^2 + L^2 = 100$ and $wL = 48$, then $(w + L)^2 = (w^2 + L^2) + 2(wL) = 100 + 2(48) = 196$.

Therefore, $(w + L) = \sqrt{196} = 14$. Notice that with this method, we do not try to solve or substitute for the individual variables w or L. Rather, we substitute for entire expressions, such as $w^2 + L^2$ and wL.

The correct answer is (C): BOTH statements TOGETHER are sufficient, but NEITHER statement ALONE is sufficient.

Part III
of
THE OFFICIAL GUIDE COMPANION

PROBLEM
SOLVING
EXPLANATIONS

PS 1. <u>Word Translations</u>: Minor Question Types
Difficulty: 300–500   **OG Page:** 152

To solve this **_Direct Computation_** problem, we should stay organized and go step by step.

If the budget is $12,600, spread out over 12 equal installments, then each installment should be $12\overline{)12,600} = \$1,050$.

After 4 months, $4 \times 1,050 = \$4,200$ should have been spent.

If $4,580 was spent instead, then the project went over budget by $4,580 - \$4,200 = \$380$.

The correct answer is (A).

PS 2. <u>EIVs</u>: Basic Equations
Difficulty: 300–500   **OG Page:** 152

This **_Basic Equations_** problem asks us to determine the value of x, given that the sum of 5, 8, 12 and 15 is equal to the sum of 3, 4, x, and $x + 3$. The word "sum" means addition, so in equation form, we must have the following:

$$5 + 8 + 12 + 15 = 3 + 4 + x + x + 3$$

We want to manipulate this equation, putting the unknown x on one side and everything else on the other side. To simplify our task, remember that we are free to add numbers in any order we want. Thus, we might combine the given numbers in ways that make the additions simpler. If we notice these sorts of combinations, we can both save time and avoid errors. Specifically:

$5 + 15 = 20$
$8 + 12 = 20$
$3 + 4 + 3 = 10$

We can now do **_Direct Algebra_** as follows:

$20 + 20 = 10 + x + x$
$40 = 10 + 2x$
$30 = 2x$
$15 = x$

The correct answer is (B).

PS 3. <u>Number Properties</u>: Divisibility & Primes
Difficulty: 300–500   **OG Page:** 152

To determine which of the answer choices yields a non-integer value for the given expression, simply plug each answer choice into the expression. Using **_Divisibility Rules_** will speed up the process.

(A) $= \dfrac{100+1}{1}$ Any integer divided by 1 is an integer.

(B) $= \dfrac{100+2}{2}$ Any even integer divided by 2 is an integer. 100 + 2 is 102, an even integer.

(C) $= \dfrac{100+3}{3}$ NOT AN INTEGER. A quick way to determine that 103 is not divisible by 3 is to add the digits of 103 (1 + 0 + 3 = 4). If the sum is a multiple of 3, the number is a multiple of 3 (and if the sum is not a multiple of 3, neither is the number). **CORRECT**

(D) $= \dfrac{100+4}{4}$ 104 divided by 4 is an integer. Since 100 is divisible by 4, we only have to consider the last two digits of any number over 100 to determine whether the number is a multiple of 4. Note that it is not necessary to calculate 104/4 = 26.

(E) $= \dfrac{100+5}{5}$ Any integer that ends in 5 is a multiple of 5, so 105 divided by 5 is an integer. Note that it is not necessary to calculate 105/5 = 21.

The correct answer is (C).

PS 4. <u>Geometry</u>: Polygons
Difficulty: 300–500   **OG Page:** 152

In a geometry problem, such as this **_Polygons_** question, it is often helpful to **_Draw a Picture_**. This way, we can visualize the information given in the problem.

Floor X has dimensions 12 feet by 18 feet. Floor Y is 9 feet wide, but we don't know how long it is. We can **_Name a Variable_** and let x represent the length of floor Y in feet.

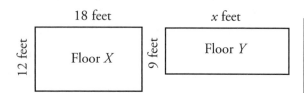

The formula for the **Area of a Rectangle** is

Area = Length × Width

Because Floor *Y* has the same area as Floor *X*, we can set the expression for their areas equal to each other.

Area of Floor *X* = Area of Floor *Y*

$$(12 \text{ feet})(18 \text{ feet}) = (9 \text{ feet})(x \text{ feet})$$

$$x = \frac{(12)(18)}{(9)} = \frac{12 \times \overset{2}{18}}{\underset{1}{9}} = 24 \text{ feet}$$

The correct answer is (E).

PS 5. Word Translations: Statistics
Difficulty: 500–600   **OG Page:** 152

This problem specifies four different salary levels ($20,000, $22,000, $25,000, and $30,000), as well as a different number of employees earning at each level. We need to find the average (arithmetic mean) salary for the 20 employees. Thus, we need to use the *Average Formula:*

$$\text{Average} = \frac{\text{Sum}}{\text{Number of Data Points}}$$

Thus, to find the average salary, we add up all the salaries and then divide by the number of employees (20).

Note that we should use multiplication to simplify the addition. For instance, we have 5 employees with $20,000 salaries each. The sum of five $20,000 salaries is simply 5 × $20,000 = $100,000. Thus, we should multiply each salary by the relevant number of employees, then add up the products. We can also save time by ignoring the "thousands" (the 3 extra zeros) until the end of the problem, because all the salaries are whole numbers of thousands.

5 × $20 = $100
4 × $22 = $88
8 × $25 = $200
3 × $30 = $90

The total amount of money earned is 100 + 88 + 200 + 90 = 478 thousand dollars. Now, we divide 478 by the total number of employees (20). We can use long division to perform this calculation:

$$
\begin{array}{r}
23.9 \\
20\overline{)478.0} \\
\underline{40} \\
78 \\
\underline{-60} \\
180 \\
\underline{-180} \\
\end{array}
$$

Alternatively, to divide 478 by 20, we can divide first by 2 and then by 10 (because 2 × 10 = 20).

478 ÷ 2 = 239
239 ÷ 10 = 23.9

Finally, write the answer using zeroes: 23.9 thousand dollars = 23.9 × 1,000 = $23,900.

The correct answer is (C).

PS 6. EIVs: VICs
Difficulty: 300–500   **OG Page:** 153

This *Variables In Choices* problem can be solved in several ways. The most straightforward method is **Direct Algebra.** Write each sentence or clause as an equation, replacing "contains" with "equals" (=).

First sentence: 1 case = *c* cartons
Second sentence: 1 carton = *b* boxes

Multiply both sides of the second equation by *c*:
       c cartons = *bc* boxes

Thus, we know   1 case = *bc* boxes

We can also think of this process as substituting "*b* boxes" in for the "carton" unit in the first equation:
       1 case = *c* (*b* boxes) = *bc* boxes

Now, translate the rest of the second sentence:
       1 box = 100 paper clips

Substituting in for the "box" unit in the previous equation, we get

$$1 \text{ case} = bc \ (100 \text{ paper clips})$$
$$= 100bc \text{ paper clips}$$

Therefore, 2 cases contain double this number, or $200bc$ paper clips. This is the **answer**.

Alternatively, we could *Pick Numbers and Calculate a Target*. Let $c = 3$ and $b = 2$. Thus each case contains 3 cartons and each carton contains 2 boxes.

Each case must contain $3 \times 2 = 6$ boxes. Since each box contains 100 paper clips, each case must contain $6 \times 100 = 600$ paper clips. We are asked for the number of paper clips in 2 cases, so doubling the number for one case, we get a *Target Value* of 1,200 paper clips. We can now plug $c = 3$ and $b = 2$ in to each answer choice to see which yields a value of 1,200:

(A) $100bc = 100(2)(3) = 600$ INCORRECT

(B) $\dfrac{100b}{c} = \dfrac{100(2)}{3} = \dfrac{200}{3}$ INCORRECT

(C) $200bc = 200(2)(3) = 1{,}200$ **CORRECT**

(D) $\dfrac{200b}{c} = \dfrac{200(2)}{3} = \dfrac{400}{3}$ INCORRECT

(E) $\dfrac{200}{bc} = \dfrac{200}{(2)(3)} = \dfrac{200}{6}$ INCORRECT

Only answer choice (C) yields the target value of 1,200.

The correct answer is (C).

PS 7. <u>Number Properties</u>: Divisibility & Primes
Difficulty: 300–500   **OG Page:** 153

This problem has no shortcuts, unfortunately. We can only solve it by directly listing all the *Prime Numbers* greater than 60 and less than 70.

To determine whether a number is prime, try to find *Prime Factors* of the number (similar to the technique used in assembling a number's *Prime Box*).

Try dividing by 2. The numbers 62, 64, 66, and 68 are divisible by 2, so none of them is prime. No even number larger than 2 is prime.

Next, try dividing by 3. Of the remaining numbers, 63 and 69 are divisible by 3, so neither is prime.

Next, try dividing by 5. Of the remaining numbers, 65 is divisible by 5, so it is not prime.

The remaining numbers, 61 and 67, are not divisible by any primes smaller than themselves, so they are prime. We only need to check up to the square root of the number in question. $\sqrt{61}$ and $\sqrt{67}$ are around 8, so we only have to check that 7 does not go into either 61 or 67; it does not.

Since the only primes between 60 and 70 are 61 and 67, the desired sum is $61 + 67 = 128$.

The correct answer is (B).

PS 8. <u>FDPs</u>: Percents
Difficulty: 300–500   **OG Page:** 153

For word problems that represent real situations, whether involving *Percents* or not, it is often helpful to *Draw a Picture* before diving into the math.

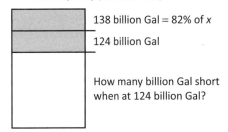

x = total capacity (in billion Gal)

138 billion Gal = 82% of x

124 billion Gal

How many billion Gal short when at 124 billion Gal?

The reservoir was short by $x - 124$ billion gallons prior to the storm, so we need to determine x.

138 billion gallons is 82% of x, so $138 = (0.82)(x)$, which implies that $x = \dfrac{138}{0.82}$. We should not bother to compute the exact value of x, as the question specifically asks "approximately how many...". Instead, we use *Estimation*. Note that we can reduce approximation error by rounding both numerator and denominator the same direction. As the numerator decreases, the fraction decreases. As the denominator decreases, the fraction increases. Therefore, by decreasing both the numerator and the denominator, we can offset the changes to the fraction.

$$x = \frac{138}{0.82} \approx \frac{136}{0.8} = \frac{136}{\frac{4}{5}} = \frac{136}{4} \times 5 = 34 \times 5 = 170$$

The reason to round to 136 is that we want a number divisible by 4, since we have 4/5 in the denominator of the fraction. This makes it easier to **Cancel Factors**.

The answer is approximately 170 − 124 = 46. The closest answer choice is 44.

The correct answer is (E).

PS 9. Geometry: Coordinate Plane
Difficulty: 300–500   **OG Page:** 153

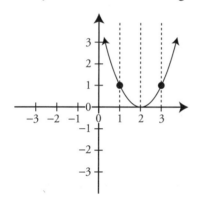

We know from the stem of this **Coordinate Plane** question that the graph (of what appears to be a parabola) is symmetric with respect to the vertical line at $x = 2$. This means that any two points on the graph with x-coordinates that are equally distant from $x = 2$ (i.e., one a certain distance *to the right* of 2, the other the same distance *to the left* of 2) will have the same y-coordinate. In other words, the left half of the graph is a mirror image of the right half of the graph, and we can apply **Symmetry** arguments.

The question asks us for the y-coordinate of the point at $x = 3$. This point has an x-coordinate that is 1 unit to the right of 2, so we must look at a point on the graph with an x-coordinate that is 1 unit to the left of 2 to get our answer (i.e., $x = 1$). The question tells us that when $x = 1$, $y = 1$. Therefore when $x = 3$, y must also equal 1. This is the **answer**.

Although the graph is not necessarily drawn precisely to scale, we should also be able to read off the graph that when $x = 3$, y is approximately 1.

We might not be sure about 1/2 as a possibility, but we can certainly rule out 0, −1/2, and −1, since the graph is clearly above the x-axis at $x = 3$.

The correct answer is (E).

PS 10. FDPs: FDP Connections
Difficulty: 300–500   **OG Page:** 153

For this problem, which draws **Connections Between Fractions, Decimals, and Percents**, we need to translate each of the pieces carefully. First, we must find 1/10 *percent* of 5,000. Note that "percent" literally means "per one hundred," signaling us to divide by 100:

$$\frac{1/10}{100}(5,000)$$

Next, simplify this term:

$$\frac{1/10}{100}(5,000) = \frac{1}{1,000}(5,000) = 5$$

Thus, 1/10 percent of 5,000 equals 5.

Next, we must simplify the second term:

$$\frac{1}{10}(5,000) = 500$$

At this point, we can deal with the surrounding language, which instructs us to subtract the first term from the second. Thus, we can solve:

500 − 5 = 495   This is the **answer**.

Alternately, we could have set up the entire equation before simplifying any of the terms:

$$[\frac{1}{10}(5,000)] - [\frac{1/10}{100}(5,000)] = 500 - 5 = 495$$

In either case, be careful with the phrasing of the problem. Note that the passive voice phrasing "is subtracted from" requires us to place the term that is first described at the end of the equation.

The correct answer is (D).

PS 11. Number Properties: Roots
Difficulty: 600–700   **OG Page:** 153

To solve this **Roots** problem, we can first find the cube root of 0.000064 and then find the square root of that value.

Step 1: The cube root of 0.000064 is 0.04. To find this value, we can start by realizing that 64 is the cube of 4. In other words, $4^3 = 64$. Therefore, 4 is the cube root of 64. Next, we deal with the *Decimal Places*. Since 0.000064 has six decimal places, its cube root will have one-third as many, or two decimal places:

$$\sqrt[3]{0.000064} = 0.04$$

We can also check this result by cubing 0.04 to get the original number: $(0.04)^3 = 0.000064$

Step 2: The square root of 0.04 is 0.2. Again, we can start with the fact that the square root of 4 is 2. Since 0.04 has two decimal places, the square root of 0.04 will have half as many, or one decimal place:

$$\sqrt{0.04} = 0.2$$

If necessary, perform a check: $(0.2)^2 = 0.04$

Thus, 0.2 is the **answer**.

Alternatively, we can look at the problem in terms of *Powers of Ten*. 0.000064 is equivalent to 64×10^{-6}. Therefore we can rewrite the problem and apply rules of exponents and roots:

$$\sqrt{\sqrt[3]{64 \times 10^{-6}}}$$
$$= \sqrt{(\sqrt[3]{64})(\sqrt[3]{10^{-6}})}$$
$$= \sqrt{(4)(10^{-2})}$$
$$= (\sqrt{4})(\sqrt{10^{-2}})$$
$$= 2 \times 10^{-1}$$
$$= 2 \times 0.1$$
$$= 0.2$$

The correct answer is (E).

PS 12. Word Translations: Probability
Difficulty: 500–600   **OG Page:** 154

In this *Probability* problem, we have a pool of tickets numbered 101 through 350, inclusive. We want to find the probability of selecting out of that pool a ticket that displays a hundreds digit of 2.

We need to apply the *Basic Probability Formula*. The general method for calculating the probability of success is to divide the number of successful outcomes by the total number of possible outcomes. Thus, we need to count the tickets whose hundreds digit equals 2, and we also need to count all the tickets.

In this case, the total number of tickets is given by $350 - 101 + 1 = 250$. Note that we must add 1 to the difference of the largest and smallest terms in order to include the endpoints of this *Consecutive Integer* set.

Next, we need to count the tickets with 2 as the hundreds digit. This group of tickets includes numbers 200 through 299. Therefore, the total number of desired outcomes is $299 - 200 + 1 = 100$.

Finally, the probability of success is given by the following ratio:

$$P = \frac{100}{250}, \text{ which reduces to } \frac{2}{5}.$$

The correct answer is (A).

PS 13. FDPs: Percents
Difficulty: 300–500   **OG Page:** 154

In this *Percents* problem, we first need to *Name a Variable*. Let's label the total value of the item t. Then we can express the portion of the total value that is in excess of $1,000 as $(t - 1,000)$. Finally, a 7% tax on this excess portion of the total value can be *Algebraically Translated* as

$$0.07 \times (t - 1,000), \text{ or simply } 0.07 \, (t - 1,000)$$

Since the tax paid is $87.50, set up an equation as follows:

$0.07 \, (t - 1,000) = 87.5$
$0.07t - 70 = 87.5$ Distribute the 0.07
$0.07t = 157.5$ Add 70 to both sides

Let's multiply both sides of the equation by 100 to eliminate the *Decimals:*

$7t = 15,750$

Finally, perform long division:

$$7\overline{)15{,}750} \quad \frac{2{,}250}{}$$

$t = 2{,}250$

The correct answer is (C).

PS 14. <u>Word Translations</u>: Statistics
Difficulty: 500–600   **OG Page:** 154

In this **Weighted Average** problem, we need to find the average weight of all the packages mailed on the two days. We can express the **Average Formula** in either of these ways:

$$\left(\begin{array}{c}\text{Average}\\\text{weight}\end{array}\right) = \frac{\text{Sum of weights of the packages}}{\text{Number of packages}}$$

or

(Sum of weights) =
(Average weight) × (Number of packages)

We'll need both of these versions as we go.

On Monday, 8 packages weighing an average of $12\frac{3}{8}$ pounds were mailed. Although we do not have the exact weight of each package, we can find the sum of the weights using the second formula above:

$$\left(\begin{array}{c}\text{Sum of}\\\text{weights}\end{array}\right) = \left(12\frac{3}{8}\right)(8) = \left(\frac{99}{8}\right)(8) = 99 \text{ pounds}$$

On Tuesday, 4 packages weighing an average of $15\frac{1}{4}$ pounds were mailed. We can find the sum of the weights of these in the same way:

$$\left(\begin{array}{c}\text{Sum of}\\\text{weights}\end{array}\right) = \left(15\frac{1}{4}\right)(4) = \left(\frac{61}{4}\right)(4) = 61 \text{ pounds}$$

Over the two days, the person mailed a total of 12 packages that weighed $99 + 61 = 160$ pounds. We can use the first formula above to find the average weight for all the packages over the two days:

$$\left(\begin{array}{c}\text{Average}\\\text{weight}\end{array}\right) = \frac{160 \text{ pounds}}{12 \text{ packages}} = \frac{40 \text{ pounds}}{3 \text{ packages}}$$

$$\left(\begin{array}{c}\text{Average}\\\text{weight}\end{array}\right) = 13\frac{1}{3} \text{ pounds per package}$$

This is the **answer**.

In this problem, we can quickly **Eliminate** unrealistic answer choices. We know the average of all the packages over the two days will fall between each day's average weights. If we examine the answer choices to see which ones fall between $12\frac{3}{8}$ and $15\frac{1}{4}$, we can immediately eliminate answer choices (C), (D), and (E).

The correct answer is (A).

PS 15. <u>FDPs</u>: Digits & Decimals
Difficulty: 500–600   **OG Page:** 154

This **Decimals** problem asks us to add three quantities. In order to perform the calculation correctly, we need to follow the **Order of Operations**, which we can remember using the acronym **PEMDAS**. In the context of this problem, PEMDAS means that we have to apply the **Exponents** first and then perform the Addition.

Begin with the second term: $(0.1)^2 = (0.1) \times (0.1)$

When multiplying decimals, first ignore the decimals and multiply the numbers: $1 \times 1 = 1$. Then count the number of ignored decimal places to the right of the decimal point. In this case, we ignored two decimal places to the right of the decimal. Insert the missing decimals back into the solution:

   1. → 0.01   Therefore, $(0.1)^2 = 0.01$

Then, compute the third term using the same method:

   $(0.1)^3 = (0.1) \times (0.1) \times (0.1)$.

Ignoring the decimals, we have $1 \times 1 \times 1 = 1$. We ignored three decimal places, so add those back in:

   1. → 0.001   Therefore, $(0.1)^3 = 0.001$

Finally, sum the three terms. Line up the decimal points, so that you don't accidentally add the digits incorrectly.

$$\begin{array}{r}0.1\\+0.01\\+0.001\\\hline 0.111\end{array}$$

The correct answer is (B).

PS 16. <u>Geometry</u>: Polygons
Difficulty: 300–500   **OG Page:** 154

This *3-Dimensional Geometry* problem requires us to understand how the capacity, or *Volume*, of a rectangular solid changes if we double its length, width, and height. Note that "capacity" is a code word for volume. Another clue is the unit "cubic feet": all units of volume are cubic lengths, such as cubic feet or cubic centimeters. The applicable geometric formula is

Volume = length × width × height, or
$V = lwh$.

In order to see what happens to the volume after doubling each dimension, we can substitute $2l$, $2w$, and $2h$ into the formula:

New $V = (2l) \times (2w) \times (2h)$

Rearranging the factors, we see that *New* $V = 2 \times 2 \times 2 \times lwh = 8 \times lwh$. The original volume was equal to lwh, so we can see that the new volume is equal to 8 times the original volume. This will always be true for a rectangular solid—if the length, width, and height are doubled, the volume will increase by a factor of 8.

In this problem, the original capacity is 10 cubic feet. Therefore, after doubling the length, width, and height of the sandbox, the new capacity will be 8 × 10 = 80 cubic feet. This is the **answer**.

Alternatively, we could *Pick Numbers* for the length, width, and height of the original sandbox. Let $l = 5$ feet, $w = 2$ feet, and $h = 1$ foot. (Choose any numbers that multiply together to 10 cubic feet and that are easy to deal with.) Then the new sandbox will have a length of 10 feet, a width of 4 feet, and a height of 2 feet. This new sandbox will have a volume of 10 × 4 × 2 = 80 cubic feet.

The correct answer is (D).

PS 17. <u>FDPs</u>: Successive Percents & Percent Change
Difficulty: 300–500   **OG Page:** 154

This *Percent Change* problem calls for *Direct Computation* according to the figures given. Note that there is no reason to convert from dozens to individual rolls, as both the given information and the requested answer are in units of dozens.

The bakery opened with 40 dozen rolls. Half of these, or 20 dozen, were sold by noon, leaving 40 − 20 = 20 dozen rolls. Of these 20 dozen *remaining* rolls, 80 percent, or (0.80)(20) = 16 dozen, were sold by closing time. Therefore, 20 − 16 = 4 dozen rolls remained.

The correct answer is (D).

PS 18. <u>Geometry</u>: Polygons
Difficulty: 300–500   **OG Page:** 154

For a *Square* with side length s, the area is s^2. Likewise, for a *Rectangle* with width w and length L, the area is wL.

Draw a Picture of each of these polygons and label the sides by *Naming Variables*. At the very least, name the unknown length of the rectangle.

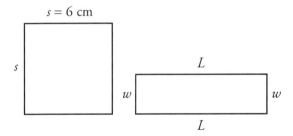

The area of a square with sides of length 6 cm is 36 cm². Since the rectangle with width 2.5 cm has the same area as the square, we can set the areas equal to each other and solve for L with *Direct Algebra*. We can drop the units during the calculation, since all the lengths are in centimeters.

$$\text{Area of rectangle} = \text{Area of square}$$
$$wL = 36$$
$$(2.5)L = 36$$
$$L = \frac{36}{2.5}$$
$$L = \frac{36}{2.5}$$
$$L = \frac{72}{5} = 14.4 \text{ cm}$$

The correct answer is (E).

PS 19. <u>FDPs</u>: Percents
Difficulty: 300–500   **OG Page:** 155

We can do a literal ***Algebraic Translation*** to obtain an equation for this ***Percents*** problem. First, we should ***Name a Variable*** to represent the question word "what." Let's use x. Represent "percent" by putting x over 100. Finally, represent "of" with multiplication, and solve for x using ***Direct Algebra***.

150 is what percent of 30?

$$150 = x\% \text{ of } 30$$

$$150 = \left(\frac{x}{100}\right)30$$

$$150 = \frac{30x}{100}$$

$$150 = \frac{3}{10}x$$

$$\frac{10}{3}(150) = x$$

$$x = 500$$

Thus, $x\%$ is 500%. This is the **answer**.

We can also solve this question by setting up a ***Percent Table***:

Part	150	x
Whole	30	100

From this, we can form the following proportion:

$$\frac{150}{30} = \frac{x}{100}$$
$$x = 500$$

Again, $x\%$ is 500%. Notice that the *part* here happens to be bigger than the *whole*. The whole is always identified as the word immediately following the expression "percent of," since a percent is always *of the whole*. Whenever the part is bigger than the whole, the part will be more than 100% of the whole.

The correct answer is (E).

PS 20. <u>Word Translations</u>: Ratios
Difficulty: 300–500   **OG Page:** 155

Begin by writing down the given ***Ratio***:

$$2 : \frac{1}{3}$$

Next, quickly scan the answer choices. Notice that all of the answer choices express the ratio in integers. Thus, we need to eliminate the ***Fraction*** from the right-hand side of our ratio without changing the ratio itself.

To eliminate the fraction from the right-hand side of the ratio, we should multiply by 3. To maintain the proper ratio, however, we must multiply the left-hand side by 3 as well. ***Scaling the Ratio*** upward, we get the ratio 6 : 1. This is the **answer**.

Alternately, we could have chosen to express 2 and $\frac{1}{3}$ in terms of a ***Common Denominator*** of 3. Thus:

$$\frac{6}{3} : \frac{1}{3}$$

This quickly simplifies to a ratio of 6 to 1.

Finally, since ratios are equivalent to fractions, we could have written the original ratio as follows:

$$\frac{2}{\frac{1}{3}}$$

Since dividing by a fraction is the same as multiplying by the ***Reciprocal***, we get the following:

$$\frac{2}{\frac{1}{3}} = 2 \times \frac{3}{1} = \frac{6}{1}$$

The fraction $\frac{6}{1}$ is equivalent to a ratio of 6 to 1.

The correct answer is (A).

PS 21. <u>Word Translations</u>: Rates & Work
Difficulty: 300–500   **OG Page:** 155

This ***Rates & Work*** problem does not require a chart. Rather, if we figure out the working rate of each machine, then we can find the effective rate of 10 machines.

When equal machines are ***Working Together***, each machine's rate is an equal fraction of the overall rate. So, if six identical machines produce a total of 270 bottles per minute, then each machine produces 1/6 of that amount every minute, or 270/6 = 45 bottles per minute.

Ten such machines, working together, could produce (10)(45) = 450 bottles per minute.

We now apply the ***Work Formula***, which is simply Rate × Time = Work. In four minutes, the ten machines could produce (450)(4) = 1,800 bottles.

The correct answer is (B).

PS 22. <u>Number Properties</u>: Positives & Negatives
Difficulty: 300–500 **OG Page:** 155

In this problem, we are asked to determine which of five points on a number line has the greatest ***Absolute Value*** of its coordinate. A coordinate is a number that represents a position. On a number line, we need just one coordinate. For instance, the coordinate of point A is −2.

The absolute value of a number is the distance between that number and 0, when the number is plotted on a number line. By definition, absolute values are positive, since there is no such thing as a negative distance. In other words, the farther a number is from zero, the greater its absolute value.

In this case, point A has a coordinate of −2, so the absolute value of its coordinate is $|-2| = 2$.

None of the other points is as far from the origin as point A is. Thus, the absolute values of the other coordinates are all less than 2. Point A's coordinate has the greatest absolute value.

The correct answer is (A).

PS 23. <u>Number Properties</u>: Divisibility & Primes
Difficulty: 300–500 **OG Page:** 155

The simplest and fastest way to solve this problem involving ***Primes*** and ***Remainders*** is simply to ***Pick a Prime Number*** greater than 3 for n.

If $n = 5$, then n^2 is 25. The remainder when 25 is divided by 12 is 1. This is the **answer**.

No more work is needed! The question requires that the remainder be the same, no matter which prime

number greater than 3 is selected for n. Otherwise, there would be more than one right answer. As a result, we can be certain of our answer.

Of course, if we really want to check, we can pick other primes larger than 3. If $n = 7$, then n^2 is 49, and the remainder when 49 is divided by 12 is also 1. If $n = 11$, then $n^2 = 121$, and 121 divided by 12 also yields remainder 1.

While this problem is best solved by simply picking a number, as above, a useful point about ***Number Properties*** may be made here. Several of the answer choices are impossible, according to what we know about n^2.

A remainder of 0 would mean that n^2 is divisible by 12, which cannot be true. For a number to be divisible by 12, it must contain 12's prime factors (2, 2, and 3). However, n^2 contains no primes other than n, which cannot be 2 or 3.

2 can also be easily eliminated: since n must be a prime greater than 3, it is necessarily odd. An odd times an odd is an odd, so n^2 must also be odd. It is not possible for an odd n^2 to yield an even remainder when divided by an even.

Finally, n^2 could only yield a remainder of 3 after being divided by 12 if n^2 were a multiple of 3. This is not possible, since n^2 is the square of a prime greater than 3.

The theoretical approach to this problem is in fact very difficult and should be avoided.

The correct answer is (B).

PS 24. <u>FDPs</u>: Fractions
Difficulty: 300–500 **OG Page:** 155

This problem involves ***Complicated Fractions***, because it contains embedded fractions within larger fractions. The best strategy is to "unravel" the complex fraction by simplifying the embedded parts first and working outward.

$$\frac{1}{1+\frac{1}{3}} - \frac{1}{1+\frac{1}{2}}$$

If our arithmetic went awry at this point and we had to guess, we could use ***Estimation*** and our knowledge of how **Reciprocals** work to eliminate the negative answer choices (A), (B), and (C). Since $1+\dfrac{1}{3}$ is smaller than $1+\dfrac{1}{2}$, the reciprocal of $1+\dfrac{1}{3}$ (that is, "1 over that number") is greater than the reciprocal of $1+\dfrac{1}{2}$. Thus, the subtraction as written will yield a positive number.

Back to **Direct Computation**, we begin by simplifying the expression:

$= \dfrac{1}{\dfrac{3}{3}+\dfrac{1}{3}} - \dfrac{1}{\dfrac{2}{2}+\dfrac{1}{2}}$ Combine terms in the denominator by using a **Common Denominator**.

$= \dfrac{1}{\dfrac{4}{3}} - \dfrac{1}{\dfrac{3}{2}}$ Use the reciprocal rule to "flip" the fractions in the denominators.

$= \dfrac{3}{4} - \dfrac{2}{3}$ Subtract the fractions by using a common denominator.

$= \dfrac{9}{12} - \dfrac{8}{12} = \dfrac{1}{12}$

The correct answer is (D).

PS 25. Geometry: Coordinate Plane
Difficulty: 300–500   OG Page: 155

This problem asks us to find the coordinates of a particular point, V, on the given **Coordinate Plane**.

The coordinates of a point are always written in the form (x, y). The first number, x, refers to the horizontal position of the point along the x-axis. The second number, y, refers to the vertical position of the point along the y-axis.

The origin, where the axes cross, always has coordinates $(0, 0)$. Not all the tick marks are labeled, but the 5 and the −5 on the diagram tell us that the scale is 1. That is, the distance between successive tick marks is 1.

First, find the value of the x-coordinate. Point V is to the right of the origin $(0, 0)$, so the x-value is positive. The point corresponds to the 7th horizontal tick mark, so the x-coordinate is 7.

Next, find the value of the y-coordinate. Point V is below the origin $(0, 0)$, so the y-value is negative.

The point corresponds to the 5th vertical tick mark, so the y-coordinate is −5.

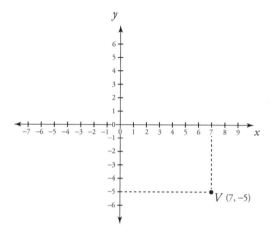

Putting these coordinates together in the proper order, we write the coordinates of point V as $(7, -5)$.

The correct answer is (E).

PS 26. Word Translations: Algebraic Translations
Difficulty: 300–500   OG Page: 156

This **Algebraic Translations** word problem mentions that a piece of rope is cut into 2 pieces. It then gives us a relationship between the lengths of the two pieces. We can use this relationship to establish expressions for each piece of rope. First, we ought to **Name a Variable**:

> Piece 1 (the shorter piece) $= x$
> Piece 2 (the longer piece) $= x + 18$

Naming just one variable (x) will save us time later. Now, we can use these two definitions to create a single equation, since we know that the two pieces together sum to a length of 40.

> $x + (x + 18) = 40$
> $2x + 18 = 40$
> $2x = 22$
> $x = 11$

That means that the length of the shorter piece (x) is 11 and the length of the longer piece $(x + 18)$ is 29. We are asked for the shorter length, 11 feet. This is the **answer**.

In this problem, it's worth taking a look at the wrong answer choices. Notice that there are two pairs of answers that sum to 40: $11 + 29 = 40$ and $18 + 22 = 40$. In such a scenario, answer choice

(A), which does not have a partner, is unlikely to be the correct answer. Also, since we are looking for the length of the shorter piece, the higher number in each pair is also unlikely to be correct, eliminating 22 and 29 as possibilities. 18 is also somewhat unlikely, since it is a number given in the problem (one piece of rope is 18 feet longer than the other).

Finally, note that 29 is a trap answer that results from solving the right equation but reporting the length of the *longer* piece instead of the shorter piece.

The correct answer is (B).

PS 27. <u>Word Translations</u>: Statistics
Difficulty: 500–600 **OG Page:** 156

Like other problems involving the average (arithmetic mean), this problem calls for the *Average Formula*, often written as:

$$\frac{\text{Sum}}{\text{Number of Data Points}} = \text{Average}$$

We rearrange this formula as follows:

(Average) × (Number of Data Points) = Sum.

Using this formula, we first find the sum of the first four test scores, then we write an equation including the 5th test score.

Since the first four test scores average to 78, we can find the sum of these scores:

Average × Number of Data Points = Sum
78 × 4 = 312

We are looking for the 5th score. Let's call it x. Now, we can express the sum of all five scores as $312 + x$. Since we want the average of all five scores to be 80, we use the Average Formula again:

Average × Number of Data Points = Sum
80 × 5 = 312 + x

Thus, we have the following:

400 = 312 + x
88 = x   This is the **answer.**

If it is helpful, we can visualize these steps in the following *Average Chart*:

	Average	× Number	= Sum
First 4 Exams	78	4	312
New Exam	x	1	x
All Exams	80	5	400

The sums add up, since they are total numbers of points. Therefore, $312 + x = 400$ and $x = 88$.

Finally, we could take an intuitive route. Assume that each of the first 4 exam scores is actually 78. Then each score is 2 points short of the average we want (80), leading to a total deficit of 8 points. The fifth score has to make up that 8-point deficit completely, so it must be $80 + 8 = 88$. This method of *Residuals* (overages and deficits) can be fast and effective.

The correct answer is (E).

PS 28. <u>FDPs</u>: Digits & Decimals
Difficulty: 300–500 **OG Page:** 156

A distance is given in inches. This *Digits & Decimals* problem asks us for the equivalent distance in kilometers.

To avoid changing the value, we must multiply the given distance by 1. If 1 kilometer is approximately 3.9×10^4 inches, then $\frac{1 \text{ kilometer}}{3.9 \times 10^4 \text{ inches}} = 1$. This fraction is called a *Conversion Factor*.

Now, multiply the given distance by the conversion factor. Be sure to set up the conversion factor correctly. Since we are given a quantity in inches, put inches in the denominator and cancel:

$$2.3 \times 10^{14} \text{ in} \times \left(\frac{1 \text{ km}}{3.9 \times 10^4 \text{ in}}\right) = \frac{2.3 \times 10^{14}}{3.9 \times 10^4} \text{ km}$$

$$\text{Cancel } \textbf{\textit{Powers of Ten}} = \left(\frac{2.3}{3.9}\right)\left(\frac{10^{14}}{10^4}\right) \text{km}$$

$$= \left(\frac{2.3}{3.9}\right) \times 10^{10} \text{ km}$$

$$= \left(\frac{23}{39}\right) \times 10^{10} \text{ km}$$

Use **Estimation**

$$\approx \left(\frac{24}{40}\right) \times 10^{10} \text{ km}$$

$$= \left(\frac{6}{10}\right) \times 10^{10} \text{ km}$$

$$= 6 \times 10^9 \text{ km}$$

The closest answer choice is 5.9×10^9. This is the **answer**.

Approximating is effective on this problem because the values given in the answer choices are spread out.

Alternatively, we could set up **Proportions**:

$$\frac{x \text{ km}}{2.3 \times 10^{14} \text{ in}} = \frac{1 \text{ km}}{3.9 \times 10^4 \text{ in}}$$

Then **Cross-Multiply** and solve as above.

The correct answer is (B).

PS 29. Number Properties: Positives & Negatives
Difficulty: 300–500   **OG Page:** 156

If the quotient of $\frac{a}{b}$ is positive, a and b must have the **Same Sign** (i.e., they are either both positive or both negative). This **Positives & Negatives** question asks us what else *must* be true.

(A) $a > 0$ *only if* b is also positive. Note that a could be negative, as long as b is negative. INCORRECT

(B) $b > 0$ *only if* a is also positive. As above, both variables could be negative. INCORRECT

(C) $ab > 0$ This *must* be true, as we know that a and b both have the same sign. The product of two variables with the same sign is always positive. **CORRECT**

(D) $a - b > 0$ This does not have to be true, as $a = 3$ and $b = 5$ would demonstrate. The variables just need to have the same sign. We know nothing about their relative size. INCORRECT

(E) $a + b > 0$ Both a and b could be negative, resulting in a negative sum. INCORRECT

We now have the **answer**.

If we only think of positive possibilities, then several of the wrong answers work. Be sure to consider **Negative Possibilities** in questions such as this

one. Any variable (such as a or b) can take on negative values unless the variable itself is specifically restricted to positive values. If a variable is labeled as "positive" or "> 0," or if it represents a number of physical objects, then we know that the variable cannot take on negative values. In this problem, however, no such restrictions apply to a or to b.

The correct answer is (C).

PS 30. Word Translations: Minor Question Types
Difficulty: 300–500   **OG Page:** 156

The problem asks us to **Read a Chart** and determine the number of cars that meet two criteria: a weight of more than 2,500 pounds and a miles-per-gallon rating above 22. So we must count the dots on the chart that fit *both* criteria at once. We should not simply add up the dots that fit each of the criteria independently.

The weight is listed in hundreds of pounds, so any dot that appears to the right of the line at "25" will meet the first criterion. We can count ten dots to the right of the line. We should leave out the dots that lie on the line for "25" itself, as we wish to include only cars weighing "more than" 2,500 pounds.

Now that we have satisfied the first condition, let's consider the second one. The line representing 22 miles-per-gallon appears directly between the lines marking "20" and "24." Five of the dots that met the first criterion fail this test. Thus, of the 10 dots that we counted at first, only 5 remain. This is the **answer**.

Alternately, we could simply examine both criteria at once and then carefully count the dots that appear in the correct portion of the graph (to the right of 25 hundred pounds and above 22 miles-per-gallon). This would yield a total of 5 dots.

The correct answer is (B).

PS 31. EIVs: VICs
Difficulty: 300–500   **OG Page:** 156

We can solve this **Variables In Choices** problem most easily by using **Direct Algebra**.

If John types at the rate of x words per minute, then in m minutes, he can type xm words. This step applies the **Work Formula**, which is simply Rate × Time = Work. Here, work is measured in words.

Since John types a total of *y* words, it must be true that $xm = y$. The question asks for the number of minutes, so to isolate *m*, we divide both sides by *x*, yielding $m = y/x$. This is the **answer**.

Alternatively, we can **Pick Numbers and Calculate a Target**, in which we will pick numbers for *x* and *y*.

Let $x = 2$ (words per minute) and $y = 6$ (words). To type 6 words at the rate of 2 words per minute, John would therefore need 3 minutes, since $(6)/(2) = 3$. Therefore 3 is our **Target Value**. If we plug in 2 for *x* and 6 for *y* in all of the choices, the choice that yields a value of 3 will be our answer:

(A) 2/6 = 1/3   INCORRECT
(B) 6/2 = 3   **CORRECT**
(C) (2)(6) = 12   INCORRECT
(D) ((60)(2))/6 = 120/6 = 20   INCORRECT
(E) 6/((60)(2)) = 6/120 = 1/20   INCORRECT

The correct answer is (B).

PS 32. **Number Properties:** Roots
Difficulty: 600–700   **OG Page:** 156

This **Roots** problem makes us wish for a calculator. First, we should recognize that we cannot break up the given radical into two radicals, because of the plus sign. When we add under a radical sign, we cannot separate the two parts.

The fastest way to simplify this radical expression is to **Factor out the Largest Square** you can from the sum. We have the following sum under the radical:

$$(16)(20) + (8)(32)$$

An initial candidate for a common square factor is 4, but we can do better. Notice that 16 is a factor of the first product *and* of the second product (since 16 is a factor of 32, and the order of multiplication does not matter). So we can rewrite the sum as follows:

$$(16)(20) + (8)(32) = (16)(20) + (8)(2)(16)$$
$$= (16)\big[20 + (8)(2)\big]$$
$$= (16)\big[20 + 16\big]$$
$$= (16)(36)$$

Now, we can put the result under the radical sign:

$$\sqrt{(16)(20) + (8)(32)} = \sqrt{(16)(36)}$$

Because the only operation under the radical is multiplication, we can finally **Split the Radical** and solve:

$$\sqrt{(16)(36)} = \sqrt{16} \times \sqrt{36} = 4 \times 6 = 24$$

This is the **answer**.

In theory we could perform the indicated calculation directly. First, we would compute $(16)(20) + (8)(32) = 576$, and then we would take the square root of 576. However, finding the square root of such a large number can be troublesome. Unless we have memorized a long list of squares, we would need to factor 576 $(= 2^6 \times 3^2)$ and then construct the square root $(= 2^3 \times 3^1 = 8 \times 3 = 24)$. This **Prime Factorization** method will always work, but if we can pull out a large square factor right away, we can get to the right answer faster.

The correct answer is (B).

PS 33. **Geometry:** Circles
Difficulty: 300–500   **OG Page:** 157

This question, about the shaded **Fraction** of a **Circle**, is technically asking us to compare areas (the shaded area versus the overall area of the circle). A simpler approach is to compare central angles. That is, we just need to figure out what fraction of 360° (a whole circle) is included as central angles in the two shaded sectors.

The given angle of 150° makes a straight line with either of the shaded regions. Since the two **Angles** that make up a straight line sum to 180°, each of the shaded regions has a central angle of 30°.

The two central angles of 30° add up to 60°. As a fraction, 60° out of an entire central angle of 360° may be expressed as:

$$\frac{60}{360} = \frac{1}{6}$$

The correct answer is (C).

PS 34. <u>EIVs</u>: VICs
Difficulty: 300–500   **OG Page:** 157

To solve this **Variables In Choices** problem, we will use **Direct Algebra**.

First, we need the **Rate-Time-Distance Formula**, which can be written this way:

$$\text{Rate} = \frac{\text{Distance}}{\text{Time}}$$

Juan's rate for running y yards is:

$$\text{Rate} = \frac{y \text{ yards}}{11 \text{ seconds}}$$

Let's now **Name a Variable**. Using t to represent the seconds it takes to run x yards, we can express the second rate this way:

$$\text{Rate} = \frac{x \text{ yards}}{t \text{ seconds}}$$

Because both rates are the same, we can set these two expressions equal to each other:

$$\text{Rate} = \frac{y}{11} = \frac{x}{t}$$

Finally, we can solve for time t by **Cross-Multiplying** the equation and then dividing by y:

$$yt = 11x$$

$$t = \frac{11x}{y} \quad \text{This is the } \textbf{answer.}$$

Alternately, we can **Pick Numbers and Calculate a Target**. Let's pick $y = 22$ and $x = 44$. If Juan can run 22 yards in 11 seconds, then he can run 44 yards in 22 seconds. Our **Target Value** is 22. Note: normally we do not want to select multiples for the unknowns. However, these values make it easy to calculate the rates.

(A) $\dfrac{11x}{y} = \dfrac{(11)(44)}{(22)} = 22$ **CORRECT**

(B) $\dfrac{11y}{x} = \dfrac{(11)(22)}{(44)} = \dfrac{11}{2}$ INCORRECT

(C) $\dfrac{x}{11y} = \dfrac{(44)}{(11)(22)} = \dfrac{2}{11}$ INCORRECT

(D) $\dfrac{11}{xy} = \dfrac{11}{(44)(22)} = \dfrac{1}{88}$ INCORRECT

(E) $\dfrac{xy}{11} = \dfrac{(44)(22)}{11} = 88$ INCORRECT

The correct answer is (A).

PS 35. <u>Word Translations</u>: Minor Question Types
Difficulty: 300–500   **OG Page:** 157

The problem specifies that John has 10 pairs of matched socks, or 20 individual socks. He loses 7 individual socks. Therefore, he keeps 13 socks. We are asked to determine the maximum number of matching pairs of socks he can still have.

Often, in **Optimization** problems, finding the *maximum* of one quantity entails finding the *minimum* of some other quantity. In this particular problem, if we want to maximize the number of matching pairs remaining, we need to minimize the number of different pairs from which he loses a sock.

In other words, we want John still to have the *most* matching pairs after he loses 7 socks from his 10 pairs. Therefore, we want him to lose the *fewest* matching pairs. Let's imagine that when John loses one sock, he also loses that sock's mate, until he has no socks left to lose.

Now list John's sock pairs in a quick **Table**:

Pair #	Any lost?
1	2 lost
2	2 lost
3	2 lost
4	1 lost, 1 not lost
5	Neither lost
6	Neither lost
7	Neither lost
8	Neither lost
9	Neither lost
10	Neither lost

John lost 3 matching pairs and 1 sock from a 4th pair. Thus, the maximum number of matched pairs John can have left is 6.

The correct answer is (B).

PS 36. <u>Number Properties</u>: Divisibility & Primes
Difficulty: 500–600 **OG Page:** 157

The "lowest positive integer that is divisible" by several numbers is the ***Least Common Multiple***, or LCM, of those numbers.

One easy way to find the LCM of several small numbers is to construct the LCM one step at a time, starting with just two of the numbers.

The LCM of 1 and 2 is 2.
The LCM of 1, 2, and 3 is $2 \times 3 = 6$.
The LCM of 1, 2, 3, and 4 is *not* $2 \times 3 \times 4 = 24$.

Note that $4 = 2 \times 2$ and that we already have one factor of 2 in the previous product, which was 6. Thus, we only need to put in one more factor of 2.

Thus, the LCM of 1, 2, 3, and 4 is $2 \times 3 \times 2 = 12$.
The LCM of 1, 2, 3, 4, and 5 is $2 \times 3 \times 2 \times 5 = 60$.

The LCM of 1, 2, 3, 4, 5, and 6 is still 60, since 60 is divisible by 6. All the ***Prime Factors*** of 6 are already accounted for in $2 \times 3 \times 2 \times 5 = 60$.

Finally, the LCM of 1, 2, 3, 4, 5, 6, and 7 is $2 \times 3 \times 2 \times 5 \times 7 = 60 \times 7 = 420$. This is the **answer**.

Note that if we merely multiply all of the integers from 1 to 7 inclusive we obtain 7!, or 5040, given in choice (E). However, in doing so, we neglect to eliminate duplicate factors.

Alternatively, we could use the ***Prime Columns*** technique to find the LCM. The number 1 cannot contribute anything to the LCM but we can examine the prime factors of the integers 2 through 7.

$2 = 2^1$
$3 = \qquad 3^1$
$4 = 2^2$
$5 = \qquad\qquad 5^1$
$6 = 2^1 \times 3^1$
$7 = \qquad\qquad\qquad 7^1$

To find the LCM, we take the highest power in any column. In other words, we go through every prime factor (in this case, 2, 3, 5, and 7) and search for the highest power of that factor. The highest power of 2 is 2^2, and the highest powers of 3, 5, and 7 are simply 3^1, 5^1, and 7^1. The least common multiple in question is the product of the values we have identified in our table.

$LCM = 2^2 \times 3 \times 5 \times 7 = 420$

The correct answer is (A).

PS 37. <u>FDPs</u>: Fractions
Difficulty: 300–500 **OG Page:** 157

We can use ***Fraction-Decimal Equivalents*** to change this expression into one involving fractions. Specifically, 0.75 equals the fraction 3/4. We make a ***Common Denominator*** by converting 1 to 4/4, as shown below:

$$\frac{1}{\frac{3}{4}-1} = \frac{1}{\frac{3}{4}-\frac{4}{4}}$$

We can proceed by subtracting the two fractions in the denominator of the larger fraction. Finally, we multiply the numerator by the ***Reciprocal*** of the denominator.

$$\frac{1}{\frac{3}{4}-\frac{4}{4}} = \frac{1}{\frac{-1}{4}} = 1 \times \left(\frac{4}{-1}\right) = -4$$

This is the **answer**.

Alternatively, we can multiply the top and bottom of $\dfrac{1}{\frac{3}{4}-\frac{4}{4}}$ by the common denominator of the smaller fractions, which is 4. If we do so, we can get to the right answer as well:

$$\frac{1}{\frac{3}{4}-\frac{4}{4}} \times \frac{4}{4} = \frac{4}{3-4} = \frac{4}{-1} = -4$$

Starting with the original stem, $\dfrac{1}{0.75-1}$, we can perform a decimal computation to yield $1/(-0.25)$. Using fraction-decimal equivalents ($0.25 = 1/4$) or by moving decimal points ($1/0.25 = 100/25$), we can reduce $1/(-0.25)$ to -4.

Last but not least, we can eliminate wrong answers by using **Number-Line Awareness** and the properties of reciprocals. The denominator, −0.25, is a negative fraction between −1 and 0. Therefore, the entire expression, which is the *reciprocal* of −0.25, must be less than −1 (i.e., it is a negative number further away from zero than −1). The only answer choice satisfying this criterion is choice (A).

The correct answer is (A).

PS 38. <u>EIVs</u>: Basic Equations
Difficulty: 300–500   **OG Page:** 157

To solve this **Basic Equations** problem, we can use **Direct Algebra**.

First, we can **Cross-multiply**. Then we can solve for x:

$$\frac{1.5}{0.2 + x} = 5$$
$$1.5 = 5(0.2 + x)$$
$$1.5 = 1 + 5x$$ Don't forget to
                    distribute the 5.
$$0.5 = 5x$$
$$0.1 = x$$

This is the **answer**.

Alternatively, we could use **Algebraic Reasoning** to get the correct answer. If the fraction on the left side of the given equation is equal to 5, the denominator must be 1/5 of the numerator, or 0.3. Therefore, x must be 0.1 to make the sum $(0.2 + x)$ equal to 1/5 of 1.5.

The correct answer is (B).

PS 39. <u>Geometry</u>: Coordinate Plane
Difficulty: 300–500   **OG Page:** 157

This **Coordinate Plane** question asks us to find the point on segment PQ that is twice as far from P as from Q. The **Slope of a Line** describes the relationship between any two points on the line (rise/run) and can be used to find one point from another on the line. By knowing two points on the line, we can calculate the slope of the line segment. Point Q lies at (3, 2) and point P lies at (0, −1).

The slope of $PQ = \frac{2 - (-1)}{3 - 0} = 1$. This means that we can travel up 1 and over to the right 1 to find

points between P and Q. One iteration of the "slope-step" from P brings us to the point (1, 0), two iterations brings us to the point (2, 1), and three iterations brings us to the point Q (3, 2).

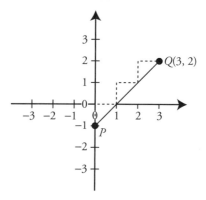

The point twice as far from P as from Q is two steps up from P and one step down from Q. The point we find is (2, 1). This is the **answer**.

Alternatively, since PQ is a straight line segment, we can solve the problem by looking at x and y separately. First, we focus on the horizontal dimension (left-right position) and ask what x-coordinate is twice as far from P's x-coordinate (0) as from Q's x-coordinate (3). In other words, what number between 0 and 3 is twice as far from 0 as from 3? The answer is 2.

In a similar fashion, we now focus on the vertical dimension (up-down position) and ask what y-coordinate is twice as far from P's y-coordinate (−1) as from Q's y-coordinate (2). In other words, what number between −1 and 2 is twice as far from −1 as from 2? The answer is 1. Putting these two answers together, we get the point (2, 1).

The correct answer is (B).

PS 40. <u>Number Properties</u>: Odds & Evens
Difficulty: 300–500   **OG Page:** 158

We are told that n is an integer and then asked which of the given terms must be even. The key word in this **Odds & Evens** problem is "must." The correct choice will be an even integer in every possible case, whether or not n itself is even.

A quick scan might reveal the answer right away, if we recognize **Algebraic Forms of Odds & Evens**. The expression $2n$ means 2 times n. Any integer, when multiplied by an even integer, will result in an even integer. Since 2 is even, $2n$ will be even in all cases. In fact, the general way to represent a random even integer is $2n$ (using n to represent any integer). So $2n$ is the **answer**.

Alternatively, we can use **Arithmetic Rules of Odds and Evens**. To test both n = odd and n = even, make a **Table**:

Answer Choice	n = even	n = odd
$n + 1$	E + 1 = O	O + 1 = E
$n + 2$	E + 2 = E	O + 2 = O
$2n$	2(E) = E	2(O) = E
$2n + 1$	2(E) + 1 = O	2(O) + 1 = O
n^2	(E)(E) = E	(O)(O) = O

The only answer choice that always yields an even is the third choice, $2n$.

Finally, we can also **Test Numbers**. We must be sure to test both an odd number and an even number for n. If we test both $n = 3$ and $n = 4$, we will see that only $2n$ yields an even number in both cases.

The correct answer is (C).

PS 41. EIVs: Quadratic Equations
Difficulty: 500–600   **OG Page:** 158

The most direct way to tackle this **Quadratic Equations** problem is to plug 4 into the equation (since 4 is given as a solution value for x) and solve for the **Unknown Constant** k:

$$(4)^2 + (3)(4) + k = 10$$
$$16 + 12 + k = 10$$
$$28 + k = 10$$
$$k = -18$$

Since $k = -18$, the original equation can now be solved as follows:

$$x^2 + 3x - 18 = 10$$
$$x^2 + 3x - 28 = 0$$
$$(x - 4)(x + 7) = 0$$
$$x = 4 \text{ or } x = -7$$

We know that we can **Factor the Quadratic** into $(x - 4)(x + 7)$ because we need two numbers that

add to 3 but multiply to −28. Since 4 was the solution given in the problem, the solution the question seeks is −7. This is the **answer**.

Alternatively, we might spot another path to the answer by applying **Properties of Quadratics**. First, we subtract 10 from both sides of the original equation: $x^2 + 3x + (k - 10) = 0$. Since the 4 is given as a solution to the equation, we know that this quadratic will factor into $(x - 4)(x \pm ?)$. Since the middle coefficient of the quadratic is 3, we know that the two numbers in the parentheses above, −4 and the question mark, must sum to 3. (The two numbers in the parentheses always sum to the middle coefficient of a quadratic, as we can show by **FOIL**ing the product.)

We need a number which will yield 3 when added to −4: this number turns out to be 7. Therefore, we can factor the quadratic as $(x - 4)(x + 7)$, and the second value of x must be −7.

The correct answer is (A).

PS 42. EIVs: Formulas & Functions
Difficulty: 300–500   **OG Page:** 158

This problem asks us to use a **New Function** to figure out the value of the same function when certain numbers, not variables, are used. This calls for **Substituting Numbers** for the variables in the function. Pay particular attention to the signs used to avoid any arithmetic errors:

$$\begin{vmatrix} 3 & 5 \\ -2 & 4 \end{vmatrix} = (3)(4) - (5)(-2)$$
$$= (3)(4) + (5)(2)$$
$$= 12 + 10 = 22 \quad \text{This is the \textbf{answer}.}$$

Note that two negatives make a positive in the second term. This is a trap built into the problem. If we had instead written $(3)(4) - (5)(2) = -2$, we would have obtained wrong answer choice (B).

The correct answer is (E).

PS 43. FDPs: Fractions
Difficulty: 500–600   **OG Page:** 158

In this **Fractions** problem, it is not necessary to find a common denominator and add 7/8 and

1/9—instead, note that the answers are expressed in ranges. Thus, we can solve the problem with efficient *Estimation*.

7/8 is close to 1. In fact, 7/8 would actually *be* 1 if it weren't missing precisely 1/8. If adding 1/8 to 7/8 would produce 1, then adding 1/9 (which is smaller than 1/8) to 7/8 will produce something slightly less than 1. At the same time, the result must be larger than 7/8, since we are adding a positive number to 7/8.

Only one answer choice offers a range that includes values between 7/8 and 1.

The correct answer is (B).

PS 44. EIVs: Basic Equations
Difficulty: 300–500   **OG Page:** 158

In this *Basic Equations* problem, we are trying to find the value of t for which $x = y$. Since we know x in terms of t, and we also know y in terms of t, we can set the two expressions equal to each other and solve for t.

$x = 1 - 3t \qquad y = 2t - 1$

$1 - 3t = 2t - 1 \quad$ Set x equal to y.

$1 - 5t = -1 \quad$ Subtract $2t$ from both sides.

$-5t = -2 \quad$ Subtract 1 from both sides.

$t = \dfrac{-2}{-5} = \dfrac{2}{5} \quad$ Divide both sides by -5.

2/5 is the **answer**.

Alternatively, we could plug in answer choices for t, but in this case, plugging answer choices is slower and more prone to error.

The correct answer is (D).

PS 45. FDPs: Fractions
Difficulty: 300–500   **OG Page:** 158

This *Fractions* problem asks us to subtract several quantities. In order to perform the calculation correctly, we need to follow the *Order of Operations*, which we can remember using the acronym *PEMDAS*. In the context of this problem, PEMDAS means that we have to perform the operation inside the Parentheses (which happens to be a subtraction) before doing the first Subtraction.

Begin with the portion inside the parentheses. First, manipulate each fraction to get a *Common Denominator*. Once that is done, subtract the numerators.

$$\frac{1}{2} - \frac{2}{3} = \frac{3}{6} - \frac{4}{6} = \frac{-1}{6} = -\frac{1}{6}$$

Next, insert the result from above into the full equation. Don't forget about the negative sign, and remember that subtracting a negative number is equivalent to adding a positive number.

$$1 - \left(-\frac{1}{6}\right) = 1 + \frac{1}{6} = \frac{6}{6} + \frac{1}{6} = \frac{7}{6}$$

The correct answer is (B).

PS 46. Number Properties: Exponents
Difficulty: 300–500   **OG Page:** 158

Recall the *Exponent Rule of Division*: when we divide two terms with the same base, we subtract exponents.

$$\frac{(0.3)^5}{(0.3)^3} = (0.3)^{5-3} = (0.3)^2 = 0.09$$

This is the **answer**.

Note that 0.09 can be easily confused with 0.9, as in choice (D). Be careful with *Decimals* in this problem.

Also, do not cancel the bases out before combining the exponents. We should *not* set the expression equal to $\dfrac{1^5}{1^3}$ or any other incorrect variation.

Combine the exponents first, as shown above. In this way, we follow the *Order of Operations*.

The correct answer is (C).

PS 47. FDPs: Percents
Difficulty: 300–500   **OG Page:** 158

This problem requires us to use the *Percents* of each plot to calculate the percent of the whole. In plot I, the number of seeds that germinated was $(0.57)(200) = 114$.

By the way, a fast way to do this computation is to *Trade Decimals*: $(0.57)(200) = (57)(2) = 114$. We move the decimal point of 0.57 two places to the *right* (making 57), and to compensate, we move the decimal point of 200 two places to the *left* (making 2).

In plot II, the number of seeds that germinated was (0.42)(300) = (42)(3) = 126. Therefore, the total number of seeds that germinated in both plots was 114 + 126 = 240. Expressed as a percentage of the total number of seeds, the result is 240/500 = 0.48, or 48 percent. This is the **answer**.

We can additionally look at this problem in terms of **Weighted Averages**. The final answer, 48%, is in fact a weighted average of 57% and 42%, the original percents. However, we should only use weighted-average insights as a double-check, since the computations in the first approach above provide a quick and straightforward path to the right answer.

If we recognize the desired percentage as a weighted average, we would expect the answer (48%) to be closer to the percent for the plot with *more* seeds (42%) and further away from the percent for the plot with *fewer* seeds (57%). This expectation is correct. However, it only allows us to eliminate D and E.

The correct answer is (C).

PS 48. <u>Geometry:</u> Triangles & Diagonals
Difficulty: 300–500   **OG Page:** 159

To solve this **Triangles** problem, we should **Draw the Figure** on our paper, including any additional information that can be inferred from the wording of the question.

Since $\overline{AB}$ is parallel to $\overline{EC}$, segment $\overline{BD}$ crosses both $\overline{AB}$ and $\overline{EC}$ at the same angle. (In other words, $\overline{BD}$ is a **Transversal of Parallel Lines**.) Thus, angles $\angle ABD$ and $\angle ECD$ are equal to each other and can both be represented by $x°$. By similar reasoning, we can conclude that angle $\angle BAD$ is 45°.

If two sides of a triangle are equal, their opposite angles are equal. Since $CE = DE$ within **Isosceles Triangle** CDE, we can infer that angles $\angle ECD$ and $\angle CDE$ are also equal to each other and there-

fore both equal to $x°$.

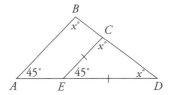

Note that the triangle as shown in the problem is NOT to scale. CE does not look equal to DE, but we are told that they are equal, so we must trust the rules, not our eyes, and draw the proper implication (i.e., that the opposite angles are also equal).

The **Sum of the Angles** in any triangle is 180. From either triangle BDA or triangle CDE, we can set up the following equation and solve:

$$x + x + 45 = 180$$
$$2x = 135$$
$$x = 67.5$$

The correct answer is (C).

PS 49. <u>EIVs:</u> Inequalities
Difficulty: 500–600   **OG Page:** 159

When manipulating **Compound Inequalities,** we must perform **Direct Algebra** on *every term* of the inequality. Begin by subtracting 5 from each term in the inequality to isolate $5n$:

$$1 < 5n + 5 < 25$$
$$-4 < 5n < 20$$

Divide all of the terms by 5 to isolate n:

$$-\frac{4}{5} < \frac{5n}{5} < \frac{20}{5}$$
$$-\frac{4}{5} < n < 4$$

Since n must be an integer, n can be 0, 1, 2 or 3, so there are four possible integers. This is the **answer**.

The method above is the surest and quickest path to the goal. Alternatively, we can **Test Numbers,** plugging various integer values into the original inequality to see how many integers satisfy the inequality. If we start with $n = 0$, the center expression becomes 5(0) + 5 = 5, which is both greater than 1 and less than 25. Since this value is greater than 1, we should try $n = -1$ to make sure that zero is the smallest value of n that works. -1 turns the center expression to 0, which is NOT greater than 1.

In this way we can continue testing increasingly larger values for n until the value of the center expression is no longer less than 25. We find that n values of 0, 1, 2 and 3 all work. However, this method takes more time, and we also run the risk of missing values or over-including values at either end of the defined range.

The correct answer is (B).

**PS 50. <u>Number Properties</u>: Positives & Negatives
Difficulty:** 600–700   **OG Page:** 159

At first, we might be tempted to say that the least possible value for the given *Absolute Value* is 3. This seems sensible enough because when $y = 4$, then $5y = 20$, and $23 - 5y = 23 - 20 = 3$. Certainly, if y is anything less than 4, then $5y$ will be less than 20, and the absolute value will be larger than 3.

However, what happens when y is an integer larger than 4? When $y = 5$, then $5y = 25$, and $23 - 5y = 23 - 25 = -2$. Now, -2 has an absolute value of 2, which is *less* than 3. We can test larger values for y, but the absolute value of the outcome will grow. For instance, if $y = 6$, then $|23 - 5y| = |23 - 5(6)| = |23 - 30| = |-7| = 7$, which is larger than 2.

As a result, when y is 5, we minimize the absolute value of $23 - 5y$. This minimum value, 2, is the **answer**.

We should expect tricks with absolute values. After all, absolute value converts negatives to positives. When we see absolute values, we need to be aware of *Negative Possibilities*. At the very least, we should examine the first y value that makes the term inside the absolute value negative, just to see what happens. This y value, 5, leads us to the answer, which is 2.

We could also look at this problem from the perspective of *Divisibility*. "$5y$," where y is an integer, just means "some multiple of 5." We are looking for the multiple of 5 that, when subtracted from 23, leaves the lowest possible absolute value.

Absolute value expresses distance on a number line. So we are looking for the multiple of 5 that is closest to 23. This turns out to be the fifth multiple of 5, or 25. When $y = 5$, the distance between 23 and $5y$ will be as small as possible: 2.

Finally, remember to answer the right question. The question is not which value of y leads to the smallest absolute value, *but what that smallest absolute value is.*

The correct answer is (B).

**PS 51. <u>Number Properties</u>: Exponents & Roots
Difficulty:** 500–600   **OG Page:** 159

This *Exponents & Roots* problem asks us to examine the expression $(\sqrt{7} + \sqrt{7})^2$, which is equivalent to $(2\sqrt{7})^2$. To *Square a Radical* that has a coefficient (here, 2 is the coefficient), we can square the coefficient and the radical separately and then multiply the results:

$2^2 = 4$ and $(\sqrt{7})^2 = 7$

$4 \times 7 = 28$ This is the **answer**.

Alternatively, we can *FOIL* the expression:

$(\sqrt{7} + \sqrt{7})(\sqrt{7} + \sqrt{7}) =$
$(\sqrt{7})(\sqrt{7}) + (\sqrt{7})(\sqrt{7}) + (\sqrt{7})(\sqrt{7}) + (\sqrt{7})(\sqrt{7}) =$
$7 + 7 + 7 + 7 = 28$

The correct answer is (C).

**PS 52. <u>Word Translations</u>: Ratios
Difficulty:** 500–600   **OG Page:** 159

This problem requires us to compute the *Ratio* of people 21 or under to the total population.

We are told that there are 3 times as many people aged 21 or under as there are people over 21. Note that these two subgroups ("21 or under" and "over 21") together make up the entire population. In other words, we have two parts that make a whole.

Since we are not asked for an actual number, but only for a ratio, we can pick a *Smart Number* for one of the subgroups. We should pick a number for the group being compared *to* (that is, the "over 21" group). Let's say that there are 10 people over

21. Since there are 3 times as many people aged 21 or under, there are 30 such people. Therefore, we have 40 people in all. The ratio of "21 or unders" to the whole population is 30 to 40, or 3 to 4. This is the **answer**.

Alternatively, we can introduce the idea of an *Unknown Multiplier* to account for the fact that the actual number of individuals is unknown. Suppose that the number of those 21 and over is x. The problem tells us that the number of people 21 and under is three times as many, or $3x$. Because the two groups collectively account for everyone, the total population is $x + 3x = 4x$. The desired ratio is therefore:

$$\frac{3x}{4x} = \frac{3}{4},$$ which can also be written as 3 to 4.

By the way, we should never do math with the ages in this problem. "Over 21" and "21 and under" are just labels for groups. We may as well use "Old" and "Young."

The correct answer is (E).

PS 53. <u>Geometry</u>: Lines & Angles
Difficulty: 300–500   **OG Page:** 159

We can't immediately solve for y in this problem, because any equation we could set up would also have an x. But we do have a way to solve for x.

The two *Angles* labeled $3x$ and $2x$ make up a *Straight Line* and therefore sum to 180°. Thus:

$3x + 2x = 180$
$5x = 180$
$x = 36$

Now that we have a value for x, we can solve for y. $2x$ and $(y + 30)$ are *Alternate Angles* and are therefore equal. Thus:

$2x = y + 30$

Substitute 36 for x and solve for y:

$2(36) = y + 30$
$72 = y + 30$
$42 = y$ This is the **answer**.

Alternatively, note that $3x$ and $y + 30$ must also sum to 180°, as they together form a straight line.

$3x + y + 30 = 180$
$3(36) + y + 30 = 180$
$108 + y + 30 = 180$
$y = 42$

The correct answer is (E).

PS 54. <u>Number Properties</u>: Roots
Difficulty: 300–500   **OG Page:** 159

This problem asks us to find the *Sum of Roots*.

Because $\sqrt{80}$ and $\sqrt{125}$ do not have the same number underneath the root symbol, we cannot directly add them together. However, we can *Simplify Each Root,* decreasing the number that remains under the radical.

First, express the number under the radical as the product of *Prime Factors*. Because pairs of factors under the radical form a perfect square, we can take that factor outside the radical.

$$\sqrt{80} = \sqrt{2 \times 2 \times 2 \times 2 \times 5} = 2 \times 2 \times \sqrt{5} = 4\sqrt{5}$$
$$\sqrt{125} = \sqrt{5 \times 5 \times 5} = 5 \times \sqrt{5} = 5\sqrt{5}$$

We can now add the two terms together because they contain the same root:

$$4\sqrt{5} + 5\sqrt{5} = 9\sqrt{5}$$ This is the **answer**.

As an alternative, we can *Estimate* the answer. $\sqrt{80}$ is just under 9 ($= \sqrt{81}$), and $\sqrt{125}$ is just over 11 ($= \sqrt{121}$). Thus, the sum we are looking for is approximately 20.

Among the answer choices, we see $\sqrt{5}$, which is a little more than 2 ($= \sqrt{4}$), and $\sqrt{205}$, which is between 14 ($= \sqrt{196}$) and 15 ($= \sqrt{225}$).

Only answer choice (A) is close to 20, since $9\sqrt{5} \approx 9(2) = 18$, rounding down.

The correct answer is (A).

PS 55. <u>Word Translations</u>: Ratios
Difficulty: 500–600   **OG Page:** 159

Kelly and Chris each packed some boxes with books. The problem specifies that Chris packed 60% of the total number of boxes. Kelly, therefore, must have packed the remaining 40% of boxes. Given these *Percents,* we are asked to find the *Ratio* of the number Kelly packed to the number Chris packed.

\# boxes packed by Kelly : \# boxes packed by Chris

Because the problem never specifies any actual numbers of boxes, we can pick our own *Smart Number* to solve. When a problem uses percentages, 100 is a Smart Number to pick for that problem.

Let's assume there are 100 boxes total. Chris packed 60% of the total, or 60 boxes. Kelly therefore packed the remaining 40 boxes.

Now we plug these numbers into the desired ratio, making sure to order the information correctly.

\# boxes packed by Kelly : \# boxes packed by Chris
         40   :   60

Now, we can *Simplify the Ratio* by dividing both sides by common factors. We can first divide both sides by 10, removing a zero from each number as follows.

$$40 : 60 = 4 : 6$$

Finally, we can divide both sides by 2.

$$4 : 6 = 2 : 3 = 2 \text{ to } 3$$ This is the **answer**.

By the way, we could have written these ratios as *Fractions.* The calculations would be identical.

The correct answer is (E).

PS 56. <u>FDPs</u>: FDP Connections
Difficulty: 300–500   **OG Page:** 160

Whenever a problem uses words such as "closest" or "approximation," it is best to *Estimate*. Use more convenient numbers than the ones provided in this problem, which involves both *Fractions* and *Decimals*. Changing 50.2 to 50, 0.49 to 0.5, and 199.8 to 200, we have a much simpler problem:

$$\frac{50 \times 0.5}{200} = \frac{25}{200} = \frac{1}{8}$$

The correct answer is (B).

PS 57. <u>Word Translations</u>: Statistics
Difficulty: 300–500   **OG Page:** 160

The most straightforward way to solve this problem is to use the *Average Formula:*

$$\text{Average} = \frac{\text{Sum}}{\text{Number of Data Points}}$$

We are seeking an unknown quantity. Let's *Name a Variable* and call that unknown quantity x.

Use *Algebraic Translation* to turn the question into the following equation:

$$\frac{10 + 30 + 50}{3} = \frac{20 + 40 + x}{3} + 5$$

Multiply both sides by 3:

$$10 + 30 + 50 = 20 + 40 + x + 15$$
$$90 = 75 + x.$$

Hence $x = 15$.   This is the **answer**.

Notice that the first average is 5 more than the other average. This is not the same as saying that the *sum* of the first set of numbers is 5 more than the other sum. If we had made this mistake, we would have picked 25 as the answer.

The correct answer is (A).

PS 58. <u>EIVs</u>: Basic Equations
Difficulty: 300–500   **OG Page:** 160

In this *Basic Equations* problem, we are told that $y = kx + 3$, where k is a constant. In other words, x and y can vary, but k is always the same. Although we do not know the value of k, in this circumstance k is *not* a variable. Rather, k is an *Unknown Constant.*

We know from the question that when $x = 2$, $y = 17$. Having a set of values for x and y allows us to determine the unknown constant k. Plug these values into the given equation and solve for k:

$$y = kx + 3$$
$$(17) = (2)k + 3$$
$$14 = 2k$$
$$7 = k$$

Now we know that $y = 7x + 3$.

Thus, when $x = 4$, $y = 7(4) + 3 = 28 + 3 = 31$.

The correct answer is (B).

PS 59. <u>Word Translations</u>: Algebraic Translations
Difficulty: 500–600   **OG Page:** 160

This ***Algebraic Translations*** problem presents an ***Hourly Wage Relationship.*** Harry and James both have a regular pay rate of x dollars per hour, and they have overtime pay rates of $1.5x$ and $2x$ dollars per hour, respectively. Harry receives his overtime rate for hours in excess of 30, while James receives his overtime rate for hours in excess of 40.

We know that James worked 41 hours last week, so we can find an exact expression for James' salary last week in terms of x. Finally, we are told that Harry and James were both paid the *same* amount last week. This is the key to forming a relationship between the two and figuring out how many hours Harry worked last week.

First, let's figure out how much James was paid last week. Since James worked 41 hours, he received x dollars per hour for 40 hours and $2x$ dollars per hour for the 1 hour that is in excess of 40. Thus, he received $40x + 2x$ dollars, or $42x$ dollars. If necessary, use a ***Pay Chart*** to think through the reasoning, as follows.

James' salary:

	Rate ($/hr)	×	*Hours*	=	*Salary ($)*
Regular	x		40		$40x$
Overtime	$2x$		1		$2x$
Total			41		$42x$

Now, we need to write an expression for Harry's salary last week. We don't know how many hours Harry worked last week. However, we do know that his total salary will be equal to that of James. Since James earned $42x$, it is clear that Harry must have worked more than 30 hours (in 30 hours, Harry would only have made $30x$ dollars).

We can save a lot of time on this problem by focusing only on the overtime hours. We know that James earned $30x$ dollars for his first 30 hours of work. In order to have earned the same amount

of money as Harry, he would have needed to earn $42x - 30x = 12x$ dollars in overtime. We also know he earned $1.5x$ dollars per hour. Therefore, if t represents the number of hours of overtime he worked, then:

$$1.5x(t) = 12x$$
$$t = 8$$

If he worked 8 hours overtime, and 30 hours at regular pay, then he worked 38 hours total. This is the **answer**.

Of course, we could also ***Pick a Number*** for x. Since the answer is a fixed number, it does not depend on x. So our result will be the same, no matter what x we pick.

The correct answer is (D).

PS 60. <u>FDPs</u>: Successive Percents & Percent Change
Difficulty: 500–600   **OG Page:** 160

We begin with 10 ounces of water. However, we lose 0.01 ounces per day for 20 days, for a total loss of $0.01 \times 20 = 0.2$ ounces. We must now determine a ***Percent Change:*** what percent of the original amount was lost in total. In other words, 0.2 is what percent of 10?

Let's use a simple ***Percent Table***:

	Numbers	Percentage Fraction
PART	0.2	x
WHOLE	10	100

$$\frac{0.2}{10} = \frac{x}{100}$$

$$20 = 10x$$

$$x = 2$$

The correct answer is (D).

PS 61. <u>FDPs</u>: Percents
Difficulty: 500–600   **OG Page:** 160

If the solution contains 15 grams of glucose per 100 cubic centimeters of solution, then the ***Ratio*** of glucose to solution is $\dfrac{15}{100} = \dfrac{3}{20}$.

We can *Name a Variable* to represent the grams of glucose in 45 cubic centimeters of solution. Let's call this amount x.

To determine x, we can now set up a *Proportion* and *Cross-Multiply*:

$$\frac{3}{20} = \frac{x}{45}$$
$$135 = 20x$$
$$\frac{135}{20} = x$$
$$\frac{27}{4} = x$$
$$x = 6.75 \quad \text{This is the \textbf{answer}.}$$

Alternatively, we could express the concentration of glucose as a *Percent*. The algebra works essentially the same way as above.

The correct answer is (E).

PS 62. <u>**Geometry:**</u> Lines & Angles
Difficulty: 500–600 **OG Page:** 160

We can look at a parallelogram as a pair of *Parallel Lines* intersected by another pair of parallel lines. Redraw the diagram, extending the lines past the corners of the parallelogram.

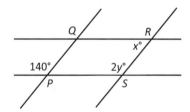

Remember that if we cross two parallel lines with another line (called a *transversal*), then we create equal angles. The acute angles (smaller than 90 degrees) will all be the same, and the obtuse angles (larger than 90 degrees) will all be the same as well. As a result, the corresponding acute angles inside or bordering a parallelogram will all be equal. The same is true for corresponding obtuse angles inside or bordering a parallelogram.

In this case, the angle labeled $2y°$ corresponds to the angle labeled 140°. Because corresponding angles are equal, $2y = 140$. Thus, $y = 70$.

Moreover, in the diagram above, any acute angle

plus any obtuse angle equals 180°. This is because we can always put one of the acute angles next to one of the obtuse angles and form a *Straight Line:*

Thus, we know that x and $2y$ sum to 180:

$$x + 2y = 180$$
$$x + 2(70) = 180$$
$$x + 140 = 180$$
$$x = 40$$

Alternatively, we could have used the fact that *Adjacent Angles of a Parallelogram* add up to 180°, if we remembered that fact.

Either way, the desired answer is given by

$$y - x = 70 - 40 = 30$$

The correct answer is (A).

PS 63. <u>**Word Translation:**</u> Ratios
Difficulty: 300–500 **OG Page:** 161

A *Proportion* will solve this *Ratios* problem most efficiently:

$$\frac{1 \text{ km}}{0.6 \text{ miles}} = \frac{x \text{ km}}{2 \text{ miles}}$$

Note that it is helpful to label units when setting up a proportion to insure that the proportion is correct. However, once we have set up the proportion, it is often easier to drop the units.

Cross-multiply: $2 = 0.6x$

Since the answer choices are given in fraction form, multiply both sides of the equation by 10 to eliminate the decimal:

$$20 = 6x$$

Divide by 6: $\frac{20}{6} = x$

Simplify the fraction: $\frac{10}{3} = x$

The correct answer is (A).

PS 64. <u>FDPs</u>: Successive Percents & Percent Change
Difficulty: 500–600   **OG Page:** 161

We can approach this **_Successive Percents_** problem by calculating the change in value each year to find the new balance. In other words, when you see **_Compound Interest_,** be sure to **_Follow the Money_** step by step.

Original Investment: $10,000
At the end of Year One: 10% increase = (0.10)($10,000) = $1,000 New balance = $10,000 + $1,000 = $11,000
At the end of Year Two: 5% increase = (0.05)($11,000) = $550 New balance = $11,000 + $550 = $11,550
At the end of Year Three: 10% decrease = (0.10)($11,550) = $1,155 New balance = $11,500 − $1,155 = $10,395

We can also approach this problem by using the following **_Formulas for Percent Increase/Decrease_**:

To find the amount after a x% increase,

$$\text{Original Amount} \times \left(1+\frac{x}{100}\right) = \text{New Amount}$$

To find the amount after a x% decrease,

$$\text{Original Amount} \times \left(1-\frac{x}{100}\right) = \text{New Amount}$$

We can multiply these changes to the original amount to find the final value after three years:

$$(\$10,000)\left(\frac{110}{100}\right)\left(\frac{105}{100}\right)\left(\frac{90}{100}\right)$$

10% decrease in Year 3
5% increase in Year 2
10% increase in Year 1
Original balance

We can now simplify this product:

$$(\$10,000)\left(\frac{110}{100}\right)\left(\frac{105}{100}\right)\left(\frac{90}{100}\right)$$

$$\$(110)(105)\left(\frac{90}{100}\right)$$

$$\$(11)(105)(9)$$

= $10,395   This is the **answer**.

By the way, we should never simply add or subtract successive percents. In other words, a 10% increase, followed by a 5% increase and then a 10% decrease, is *never* equivalent to a simple 5% increase. Answer choice C, which represents this simple 5% increase, is a trap.

The correct answer is (B).

PS 65. <u>Word Translations</u>: Algebraic Translations
Difficulty: 600–700   **OG Page:** 161

This **_Algebraic Translation_** problem specifies that a fruit stand sold apples for $0.70 each and bananas for $0.50 each. A customer purchased at least one of each and spent a total of $6.30. We are asked to determine the total number of pieces of fruit the customer purchased.

Let's first **_Name Variables_** and represent the number of apples as A and the number of bananas as B. In value equations involving decimal dollars (cents), it is often easier to convert to whole numbers of cents. In cents, the value of the apples that were purchased is $70A$. Likewise, the value of the bananas is $50B$. We can write an equation for the total value:

$$70A + 50B = 630$$

Dividing through by 10, we get

$$7A + 5B = 63$$

Now, since there are two variables and one equation, we normally could not solve for A and B. However, each variable must be a positive whole number. We are told that the customer bought some of both types of fruit, and we can assume that the customer did not buy fractional pieces of fruit. This **_Hidden Constraint_** on A and B means that there must be a unique pair of integers that make this equation work.

Often, a good way to find the ultimate solution is to look for a **_Partial Solution_**. Often, a partial solution that meets *some* constraints but violates *others* is easier to find. Looking at 63, we should think 7×9. Since we have $7A$ up front, a partial solution is 9 apples and 0 bananas:

$$7(9) + 5(0) = 63$$

We know that the customer bought *some* bananas, so this solution is not right, but it is a starting point. Now, we have to increase the number of bananas and therefore reduce the number of apples. Should we exchange these 1 for 1? No, because apples are worth more than bananas, and the equation we have expresses value. In other words, we cannot simply take away 1 apple and add 1 banana, because the equation will no longer be true:

$$7(8) + 5(1) \neq 63$$

However, if we remove a certain number of apples and add an *equal value* of bananas, we will maintain equality. Since apples are worth 70 cents each and bananas are worth 50 cents each, we know that 5 apples are worth the same as 7 bananas (they are both worth 350 cents, or $3.50). So we should take away 5 apples from our partial solution and add 7 bananas:

$$7(9 - 5) + 5(0 + 7) = 63$$

We can confirm that $7(4) + 5(7) = 63$. Thus, the customer bought 4 apples and 7 bananas, for a total of 11 pieces of fruit.

The correct answer is (B).

PS 66. <u>Word Translations</u>: Ratios
Difficulty: 500–600   **OG Page:** 161

When we have **Multiple Ratios** among many quantities, we can **Make Common Terms**. That is, change the ratios so that the same number, or term, corresponds to the same quantity. We change the terms by multiplying both parts of the ratio by the same number (just as we can multiply top and bottom of a fraction by the same number). Once we have common terms, we can combine the ratios and find the answer.

This process is easiest to see in a **Table**. First, list the three given ratios on separate lines:

	1st	:	2nd	:	3rd	:	4th
(a)			8	:		:	5
(b)	3	:	4				
(c)					3	:	2

Now, we multiply each ratio to make the numbers corresponding to each quantity the same. For

instance, the number of 4th graders must be a multiple of 5, according to ratio (a). It must also be a multiple of 2, according to ratio (c). To unify these ratios, multiply ratio (a) by 2 and ratio (c) by 5, so that we have 10 in both rows for the number of 4th graders.

	1st	:	2nd	:	3rd	:	4th
2 × (a)			16	:		:	10
(b)	3	:	4				
5 × (c)					15	:	10

Finally, we multiply ratio (b) by 4, so that we have 16 in both rows for the number of 2nd graders.

	1st	:	2nd	:	3rd	:	4th
2 × (a)			16	:		:	10
4 × (b)	12	:	16				
5 × (c)					15	:	10

As a result, we can form a combined ratio of all grades, which is 12 : 16 : 15 : 10. The ratio of 1st to 3rd graders is 12 : 15. After we remove a factor of 3 from both sides of the ratio, we get 4 : 5. This is the **answer**.

This problem can also be done algebraically, by assigning variables to all grades and setting up proportions. However, that method is much more difficult.

The correct answer is (E).

PS 67. <u>Word Translations</u>: Probability
Difficulty: 500–600   **OG Page:** 161

We can solve this problem by either of the two fundamental approaches to probability: by the basic formula or by combining probabilities of component events.

We can use the **Basic Probability Formula**,

$$\text{Probability} = \frac{\text{\# of successful outcomes}}{\text{total \# of outcomes}},$$ as long as we are careful to define "outcomes" so that they are equally likely. In this case, an "outcome" consists of a choice of exactly one number from each set. Since set A has four elements and set B has five, the total number of outcomes is $4 \times 5 = 20$.

Of these outcomes, exactly four are successful:

Outcome	Set A		Set B
Choose	2	and	7
Choose	3	and	6
Choose	4	and	5
OR Choose	5	and	4

The probability in question is therefore 4/20, or 0.2. This is the **answer**.

We can also use the *Domino Effect*, which tells us to multiply successive independent probabilities. First, we calculate, separately, the probability of *each* of the four events listed above (2 and 7, 3 and 6, 4 and 5, 5 and 4). For each of these cases, the chance of picking the "correct" first number (from set A) is 1/4, and the chance of picking the "correct" second number (from set B) is 1/5. Therefore, the probability of *each* of these outcomes is $\frac{1}{4} \times \frac{1}{5}$, or 1/20.

Since the four outcomes are mutually exclusive (that is, no two of them can happen at the same time), we add together the four probabilities to get 4/20 = 0.2.

The correct answer is (B).

PS 68. <u>EIVs</u>: Formulas & Functions
Difficulty: 300–500   **OG Page:** 161

The question asks for N. We are given this

Complicated Formula: $N = \dfrac{20Ld}{600 + s^2}$, where

L = # of lanes in the same direction = 2
d = length of highway in feet (we are given 1/2 mile, which seems rather short for a highway!)
s = average speed in mph = 40

We need to convert d to the correct units (feet) before plugging into the formula for N. If 1 mile is 5,280 feet, then 1/2 a mile is 1/2 of 5,280 feet, or 2,640 feet. So d = 2,640 feet.

Now we plug the values of L, d, and s into the function for N and simplify. We should avoid computing products before *Canceling* as many factors as possible.

$$
\begin{aligned}
N &= \frac{20Ld}{600 + s^2} \\
&= \frac{20(2)(2,640)}{600 + (40)^2} \\
&= \frac{(40)(2,640)}{600 + 1,600} \\
&= \frac{(4)(264)(100)}{2,200} \\
&= \frac{(4)(264)}{22} \\
&= \frac{(2)(264)}{11} = (2)(24) = 48
\end{aligned}
$$

The correct answer is (D).

PS 69. <u>Word Translations</u>: Statistics
Difficulty: 600–700   **OG Page:** 162

This *Statistics* question asks for the *Median* annual number of shipments of manufactured homes in the United States for the years 1990–2000. The graph of this 10 year period shows the annual number of shipments for manufactured homes for each of the 11 years in this period (1990 and 2000 are both included in the set, so the number of years is 2000 − 1990 + 1 = 11).

To answer the question, we need to *Read the Graph* correctly. The median of a set with an odd number of terms is the middle term when the set is arranged in increasing order. For a set of 11 terms arranged in ascending order, the 6th term will be the median. It might be tempting to identify 1995 as the median term, since 1995 is the middle year for the sequence of 11 years starting with 1990. However, it is the *values* of the statistics themselves that must be placed in ascending order, not the years in which they occurred.

As we figure out the order of the values, we should avoid copying down the graph on our paper or estimating every value. One way to save time and avoid mistakes is to make a quick *Left-to-Right Graph:*

90 1 2 3 4 5 6 7 8 9 00

Now, working *vertically* from smallest to largest, we mark the heights in order, using the gridlines as demarcations. Start at the shortest column. Our marks should mimic the vertical positions of the columns on the original graph. In this way, we can easily spot errors. Once we reach the 6th smallest column, we can stop.

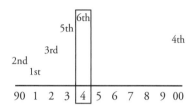

It may be difficult to distinguish the 4th smallest column (year 2000) and the 5th smallest column (year 1993). Notice, however, that that distinction doesn't matter, because they are both clearly smaller than the 6th smallest column (year 1994), which is just slightly above the 300,000 gridline.

Likewise, some of the larger columns may be difficult to tell apart, but we can clearly tell that the 1994 column is smaller than all of them. Moreover, we do not need to mark these larger columns at all.

Using the answer choices, we see that the closest approximation of the number of shipments in 1994 is 310,000.

The correct answer is (C).

PS 70. <u>EIVs</u>: Basic Equations
Difficulty: 300–500   **OG Page:** 162

This ***Basic Equations*** problem tells us that $y \neq 0$, so we know that it is "legal" to divide both sides by y. Remember, dividing by 0 leaves an undefined result, which is unacceptable. ***Dividing by a Variable*** is always a method to apply with care.

Since we know that y is *not* equal to 0, we can divide both sides of the equation by y right away. This leaves us with a much simpler equation with only one variable:

$$\frac{3x-5}{2} = 1$$

From here, we can solve for x:

$$3x - 5 = 2$$
$$3x = 7$$
$$x = 7/3$$

The correct answer is (C).

PS 71. <u>EIVs</u>: Inequalities
Difficulty: 300–500   **OG Page:** 162

In order to solve this ***Inequalities*** problem, we need to isolate x in each inequality by ***Direct Algebra:***

$$x + 5 > 2$$
$$x > 2 - 5$$
$$x > -3$$

$$x - 3 < 7$$
$$x < 7 + 3$$
$$x < 10$$

Combining these two inequalities into a ***Compound Inequality*** yields:

$$-3 < x < 10$$

Thus, x must be between -3 and 10.

The correct answer is (A).

PS 72. <u>Number Properties</u>: Divisibility & Primes
Difficulty: 300–500   **OG Page:** 162

This ***Divisibility*** problem specifies that the people in a gym class can be evenly divided into either 8 or 12 teams. This implies that the number of people is a ***Multiple*** of both 8 and 12. Because we are asked to find the lowest possible number of people satisfying this condition, we must determine the ***Least Common Multiple*** (LCM) of 8 and 12.

For two relatively simple numbers such as 8 and 12, we can just ***List Multiples*** of each number, looking for the smallest number on both lists.

8:      8, 16, 24, 32…
12:     12, 24, 36…

Since 24 is the first number on both lists, 24 is the LCM. This is the **answer**.

We can also find the LCM using the ***Venn Diagram Method for LCM***. The prime factorizations of the two numbers in question are $8 = 2 \times 2$

× 2 and 12 = 2 × 2 × 3 As shown below, we write the common factors of two 2's into the shared area and the remaining factors into the non-shared areas.

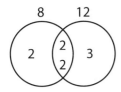

The LCM is the product of all primes in the diagram:

LCM = 2 × 2 × 2 × 3 = 24

The smallest possible number of people in the gym class is 24.

The correct answer is (B).

PS 73. <u>Number Properties</u>: Exponents & Roots
Difficulty: 300–500   **OG Page:** 162

The most efficient way to solve this tricky ***Exponents & Roots*** problem is to recognize that the particular value 0.345 that appears in *r*, *s*, and *t* is not important. The same principles would hold for any positive ***Proper Fraction*** (or decimal between 0 and 1). This recognition requires ***Number Line Awareness:*** in particular, what is special about numbers between 0 and 1.

When a proper fraction is squared, it gets smaller. This result is often referred to as the diminishing effect of fractions. For instance, if we square 1/4, we get $(1/4)^2 = 1/16$, which is smaller than 1/4.

Conversely, when we take the square root of a proper fraction, it gets larger. For instance, if we take the square root of 1/4, we get 1/2, which is larger than 1/4.

Thus, in relation to the given quantities, the square will be the smallest of the three numbers, and the square root will be the largest.

As a result, we have $s < r < t$. This is the **answer**.

If we tried to actually compute or even just estimate the square of 0.345 or the square root of 0.345, we would be wasting time and effort.

The correct answer is (D).

PS 74. <u>FDPs</u>: Fractions
Difficulty: 500–600   **OG Page:** 162

This ***Variables In Choices*** problem also involves ***Fractions***. One approach is to use ***Direct Algebra***.

First, we should ***Name Variables***: C = number of cars, T = number of trucks, and P = number of pickup trucks on the lot.

Now we can ***Algebraically Translate*** the statements in the problem:

(1) *A total of* n *trucks and cars* $C + T = n$

(2) *Number of cars =* $\frac{1}{4}$*number of trucks* $C = \frac{1}{4}T$

(3) $\frac{2}{3}$ *of the trucks are pickups* $P = \frac{2}{3}T$

We can substitute (2) into (1) to find T in terms of *n*:

$$n = C + T = \frac{1}{4}T + T = \frac{5}{4}T, \text{ so } T = \frac{4}{5}n$$

Since we are finding the number of pickups, P, we can plug this equation into (3):

$$P = \frac{2}{3}T = \left(\frac{2}{3}\right)\left(\frac{4}{5}n\right) = \frac{8}{15}n$$

This is the **answer**.

If necessary, a ***Tree Diagram*** can help us visualize the subsets along the way:

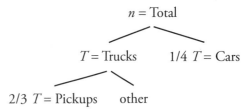

We can also use ***Pick Numbers and Calculate a Target***. The fractions in the problem relate to the number of trucks, so we can use 12 (the product of the two denominators, 3 and 4) as a ***Smart Number*** to represent the number of trucks on the lot. We can also find the other quantities:

Number of cars = $\frac{1}{4}(12) = 3$

Number of pickups = $\frac{2}{3}(12) = 8$

Total vehicles = 3 cars + 12 trucks = 15 = *n*

Furthermore, if there are 12 trucks, and 2/3 of the trucks are pickup trucks, then there are 2/3 of 12 = 8 pickup trucks on the lot.

If we let n = 15, we want the answer choice that will give us the number of pickups, or 8, which is our **Target Value**.

(A) $\frac{1}{6}n = \left(\frac{1}{6}\right)(15) = \frac{5}{2}$ INCORRECT

(B) $\frac{5}{12}n = \left(\frac{5}{12}\right)(15) = \frac{25}{4}$ INCORRECT

(C) $\frac{1}{2}n = \left(\frac{1}{2}\right)(15) = \frac{15}{2}$ INCORRECT

(D) $\frac{8}{15}n = \left(\frac{8}{15}\right)(15) = 8$ **CORRECT**

(E) $\frac{11}{12}n = \left(\frac{11}{12}\right)(15) = \frac{55}{4}$ INCORRECT

The correct answer is (D).

PS 75. Word Translations: Minor Question Types
Difficulty: 500–600   **OG Page:** 162

This **Optimization** problem specifies that there are 40 members on a committee and that, in order for a resolution to pass, at least 2/3 of those 40 members have to vote "yes."

$40 \times (2/3) = 80/3 = 26\,{}^{2}/_{3}$

We cannot, of course, have a fraction of a person, and at least $26\,{}^{2}/_{3}$ must have voted "yes," so at least 27 people must vote in favor of the resolution in order for it to pass. That is, Minimum Yes's = 27. We need to be careful when we **Round** to meet a **Hidden Constraint,** such as the condition that we must have whole numbers of people.

The question asks us to determine the maximum number of members who could vote against the resolution and still have the resolution pass. We already know that Minimum Yes's = 27 and Minimum Yes's plus Maximum No's equals the total 40. So we have at most 40 − 27 = 13 members who could vote against the resolution and still have it pass. This is the **answer**.

Alternatively, if at least 2/3 must vote yes for the resolution to pass, then no more than 1/3 can vote against it.

$40 \times (1/3) = 40/3 = 13\,{}^{2}/_{3}$

Again, we cannot have a fraction of a person, and since no more than $13\,{}^{2}/_{3}$ can vote against the resolution, a maximum of 13 people can vote against it. Be sure not to round $13\,{}^{2}/_{3}$ up to 14, which is a trap answer.

The correct answer is (E).

PS 76. Word Translations: Ratios
Difficulty: 500–600   **OG Page:** 163

We are told that the dollar amounts allocated to household expenses, food, and miscellaneous items are in the ratio 5 : 2 : 1, respectively. We are also told that the total amount allocated to these three categories is $1,800. When we are given a three-part **Multiple Ratio** and the total for all three quantities, it is often best to use the **Unknown Multiplier** strategy.

Make a quick **Table:**

Household Expenses	Food	Misc. Items
5x	2x	1x

Now create an equation that shows that the total amount of money allocated is $1800:

$5x + 2x + 1x = 1800$
$8x = 1800$
$x = 225$

Now that we know the value of the unknown multiplier, x, we can substitute to obtain the desired quantity: the amount allocated for food.

Food = $2x$
Food = $2(225) = 450$

The correct answer is (D).

PS 77. Word Translations: Algebraic Translations
Difficulty: 300–500   **OG Page:** 163

We can use **Direct Algebra** to solve this **Algebraic Translations** problem. First, to represent the numbers of men and women, we should **Name a Variable** and create expressions:

\# women = x
\# men = $x − 4$

The expression for the number of men incorporates the constraint that there are 4 more women than men. Thus, there are 4 fewer men than women.

(We could have chosen x to be the number of men, but the above choices are more convenient since the problem calls for the number of women.)

Since the total number of people on the board is 10, we know that $x + (x - 4) = 10$. Therefore, $2x - 4 = 10$, so $x = 7$. This is the **answer**.

Alternatively, if we name two variables (such as w and m), we will need to do just a little more algebra to solve the problem.

> \# women = w
> \# men = m

Then we have two equations:

> $w = m + 4$ 4 more women than men
> $w + m = 10$ Total of 10 people

Now solve for w, using **Substitution**:

> $w - 4 = m$ Write m in terms of w
> $w + (w - 4) = 10$ Substitute
> $2w - 4 = 10$ Simplify
> $2w = 14$
> $w = 7$

Be sure to choose the number of *women* as the answer. The correct number of *men* is an *incorrect* answer choice.

The correct answer is (D).

PS 78. FDPs: Successive Percents & Percent Change
Difficulty: 500–600   **OG Page:** 163

To solve a **Compound Interest** problem such as this, we should **Follow the Money** step by step.

"An annual rate of 8 percent compounded semiannually" means two payments in one year, each payment for half of the annual rate. Thus, Leona's certificate of deposit pays 4% interest at the end of the 6th month, which increases the principal in the certificate of deposit. Then another 4% interest will be paid on that new principal balance at the end of the 12th month. In other words, we have these transactions:

> $ 10,000 Leona deposits $10,000 initially
> + ____400 4% of $10,000 = 1st semiannual payment
> $ 10,400   Resulting principal
> + ____416 4% of $10,400 = 2nd semiannual payment
> $ 10,816   Final value

Note that the second interest payment is calculated on $10,400, not $10,000. To compute 4% of $10,400, write $(0.04)(10,400)$. In a product involving decimals, we can simplify the computation by **Trading Decimal Places.** That is, we can move the decimal place of 0.04 two places to the right, and to compensate, we move the decimal place of 10,400 two places to the left: $(0.04)(10,400) = (4)(104) = 416$. The extra $16 is the "interest on the interest": 4% of the first 4% of $10,000.

At the end of a year, Leona had $816 more than she originally deposited. The total interest paid was $816. This is the **answer**.

Note that $800 = 8% of $10,000 is a trap answer. We must not only know the definition of "compounded semiannually," but also remember to include in our computation the interest paid on the interest already earned.

The correct answer is (C).

PS 79. FDPs: Digits & Decimals
Difficulty: 500–600   **OG Page:** 163

When we see **Fractions with Decimals** in the numerator and the denominator, we should first try to **Get Rid of Decimals**. In order to convert these decimals into whole numbers, we should multiply by a **Power of 10** (the same power of 10 for both the top and the bottom of the fraction).

Multiplying by a power of 10 is the same as moving the decimal point. Thus, we can just move the decimal points—as long as we move the top and bottom decimals the same total number of places, and in the same direction.

To convert $(0.0036)(2.8)$ to $(36)(28)$, we have to move the decimal points a total of 5 places to the right. We need to move 4 places for 0.0036 and 1 place for 2.8. This is equivalent to multiplying by 100,000, or 10^5.

To convert $(0.04)(0.1)(0.003)$ to $(4)(1)(3)$, we have to move the decimal points a total of 6 places to the right. We need to move 2 places for 0.04, 1 place for 0.1, and 3 places for 0.003. This is equivalent to multiplying by 1,000,000, or 10^6.

To take care of all the decimals, we should choose to move the decimal points 6 places in both the numerator and the denominator. The extra place in the numerator becomes an extra zero on one number:

$(0.0036)(2.8)$ becomes $(36)(280)$ or $(360)(28)$.

Again, this is equivalent to multiplying top and bottom by 1,000,000, or 10^6.

$$\frac{(0.0036)(2.8)}{(0.04)(0.1)(0.003)} \times \left(\frac{10^6}{10^6}\right)$$

$$= \frac{(36)(280)}{(4)(1)(3)}$$

$$= \frac{(\overset{3}{\cancel{36}})(280)}{(\cancel{4})(1)(\cancel{3})}$$

$$= (3)(280)$$

$$= 840 \qquad \text{This is the } \textbf{answer}.$$

Alternatively, we can eliminate the decimals in the original by expressing each term with powers of ten.

$$\frac{(36 \times 10^{-4})(28 \times 10^{-1})}{(4 \times 10^{-2})(1 \times 10^{-1})(3 \times 10^{-3})}$$

$$= \frac{(36)(28)}{(4)(3)} \times \frac{10^{-5}}{10^{-6}}$$

$$= 84 \times 10^1$$

$$= 840$$

The correct answer is (A).

PS 80. Word Translations: Rates & Work
Difficulty: 500–600 **OG Page:** 163

This is a ***Working Together*** problem. Let's begin by writing down the given rates for each machine. These rates are expressed in words in the first sentence. "120 bolts every 40 seconds" means 120 bolts per 40 seconds, or 120 bolts divided by 40 seconds. Thus, perform the divisions to simplify the rates.

$$r_a = \frac{120 \text{ bolts}}{40 \text{ sec}} = 3 \text{ bolts/sec}$$

$$r_b = \frac{100 \text{ bolts}}{20 \text{ sec}} = 5 \text{ bolts/sec}$$

Now, because the machines are working together, we ***Add the Rates.***

3 bolts/sec + 5 bolts/sec = 8 bolts/sec

This 8 bolts/sec represents the machines' combined rate. Working together, the two machines can make 8 bolts every second.

Now, we want to determine how long it will take for the machines to create 200 bolts. Having already determined the combined rate, we create an ***Rate-Time-Work Chart:***

Rate	×	Time	=	Work
8 bolts/sec		t sec		200 bolts

$8t = 200$
$t = 200/8 = 25$ This is the **answer**.

If necessary, include the labels (in this problem "bolts" and "seconds") in the table. In the end, the labels should cancel properly, leaving the right label for the answer.

The correct answer is (B).

PS 81. Word Translations: Rates & Work
Difficulty: 500–600 **OG Page:** 163

This ***Population Growth*** question states that the amount of bacteria increases by the same factor every three hours. When the GMAT says "increases by the same factor," it means we multiply whatever the current amount of bacteria is by the same number every three hours. For example, if the original amount of bacteria is 20 grams and increases by a factor of 2 every three hours, then after three hours, there will be $(2)(20) = 40$ grams of bacteria. After another three hours, there will be $(2)(40) = 80$ grams of bacteria. Notice that $(2)(2)(20) = (2^2)(20) = 80$.

In the problem, we are told that the initial amount of bacteria is 10.0 grams. Since we don't know the value of the factor by which the amount will increase, let's ***Name a Variable*** and call the factor z. After the first three hours, we will have $10z$ bacteria. After another three hours, we will have $z(10z) = 10z^2$ bacteria. We know from the chart that after the two three-hour periods we have 14.4 grams of bacteria. Therefore,

$$10z^2 = 14.4$$
$$z^2 = \frac{14.4}{10}$$
$$z^2 = 1.44$$

We now have to take the **Square Root** of a **Decimal**, but the problem gives us a number (1.44) very related to a perfect square we should know (144 is the square of 12).

$$z = \sqrt{1.44} = 1.2$$

We now know that the amount of bacteria increases by a factor of 1.2 every three hours. Thus, after the first three-hour period, there will be $10(1.2) = 12.0$ grams of bacteria. This is the **answer**.

Note that the right answer is NOT the simple average of 10.0 and 14.4. 12.2 is a trap answer choice.

The correct answer is (A).

✐ **PS 82. Number Properties:** Divisibility & Primes
Difficulty: 600–700   **OG Page:** 163

This difficult **Divisibility** problem asks us to determine which one of five generic products of integers must always be divisible by 3, regardless of the value of integer n (which we are told is greater than 6).

The only way that the product of three integers will be divisible by 3 is if one of the numbers being multiplied together is a multiple of 3. This question is really asking, "Which of the following groups of numbers is guaranteed to contain a multiple of 3?"

To **Test Possible Cases**, imagine a **Number Line** without numbers, on which every third tick mark is larger than the others.

On this number line, the large tick marks represent multiples of 3. Every integer n is in one of three positions on this number line:

   (a) On a large tick, if n is a multiple of 3 (e.g., 3, 6, 9, and so on).
   (b) One unit to the right of a large tick, if n is 1 more than a multiple of 3 (e.g., 4, 7, 10, and so on).
   (c) Two units to the right of a large tick, if n is 2 more than a multiple of 3 (e.g., 5, 8, 11, and so on).

The correct answer will contain a multiple of 3 no matter which position n is on the number line.

If n is a multiple of 3, the product will automatically be divisible by 3. Let's see what happens to the answer choices when n is in one of the other two positions. Let's first try making n a number one greater than a multiple of 3. We put the parts of each answer choice on a number line.

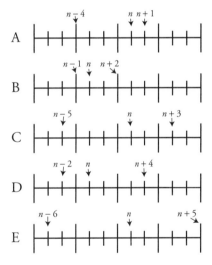

Of the answer choices, only A, B and E contain a multiple of 3. C and D are out, because no expression lands on a big tick. Now we can test the remaining three answer choices if n is two larger than a multiple of 3.

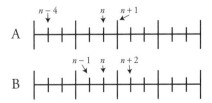

Now the only answer choice that contains a multiple of 3 is A. We can now see that, no matter what integer n is, one of these three expressions will definitely be a multiple of 3: n, $n + 1$, and $n - 4$. As a result, the quantity $n(n + 1)(n - 4)$ will always contain a multiple of 3 and *must* be divisible by 3.

The correct answer is (A).

PS 83. Word Translations: Algebraic Translations
Difficulty: 500–600   **OG Page:** 163

This *Algebraic Translations* problem involves a typical *Cost Relationship.*

The cost to produce a batch of tools is $10,000 plus $3 per tool. While the natural next step seems to be to construct an equation such as $C = 10,000 + 3t$, a glance at the answers shows very small numbers. The question asks for the profit *per tool,* so we can save time if we avoid calculating large numbers when they are not needed. Instead, let's move forward by figuring out costs and revenues on a per-tool basis.

20,000 tools are produced. The cost of each tool is $3 plus each tool's "share" of the fixed $10,000 cost.

$10,000 divided by 20,000 tools yields $0.50 per tool, for a total cost per tool of $3.50.

The tools are sold for $8 each, so the profit per tool is:

$8 – $3.50 = $4.50

The correct answer is (C).

PS 84. EIVs: VICs
Difficulty: 500–600   **OG Page:** 164

This *Variable in Choices* problem involving a *Profit Relationship* asks for the price at which each battery was sold. We can first approach this problem using the *Direct Algebra* method.

If 100 batteries were purchased for a total cost of q dollars, each battery costs $q/100$ dollars.

The selling price for each battery is 50% above the cost of purchasing the battery. We can use the following *Formula for Percent Increase*:

To find the amount after a $x\%$ increase,

$$\text{Original Amount} \times \left(1 + \frac{x}{100}\right) = \text{New Amount}$$

The selling price for the battery is therefore

$$\left(\frac{q}{100}\right)\left(1 + \frac{50}{100}\right) = \left(\frac{q}{100}\right)\left(\frac{150}{100}\right) = \left(\frac{q}{100}\right)\left(\frac{3}{2}\right) = \frac{3q}{200}$$

This is the **answer**.

Alternatively, we could **Pick Numbers and Calculate a Target**. If we let $q = 400$, then each battery costs $4.00. To calculate the selling price of the battery, we need to find the amount of markup.

Cost of Battery:	$4.00
50% Markup: (0.50)(4) =	$2.00
Selling price: $4.00 + $2.00=	$6.00

We want to see which answer choice will result in our **Target Value** of 6 when we plug in $q = 400$.

(A) $\dfrac{3q}{200} = \dfrac{(3)(400)}{(200)} = 6$ **CORRECT**

(B) $\dfrac{3q}{2} = \dfrac{(3)(400)}{(2)} = 600$ INCORRECT

(C) $150q = (150)(400) = 60,000$ INCORRECT

(D) $\dfrac{q}{100} + 50 = \dfrac{(400)}{(100)} + 50 = 54$ INCORRECT

(E) $\dfrac{150}{q} = \dfrac{(150)}{(400)} = \dfrac{3}{8}$ INCORRECT

The correct answer is (A).

PS 85. Number Properties: Consecutive Integers
Difficulty: 600–700   **OG Page:** 164

The problem indicates that there is a sequence of 10 *Consecutive Integers.* However, we do not know any of the specific numbers in the sequence. The problem then tells us that the sum of the first 5 integers in the sequence is 560, and asks us to calculate the sum of the last 5 integers in the sequence.

We can answer the question efficiently if we **Recognize the Pattern** between the first five elements of the set and the next five. If we label the first number in the set x, then the second number is $(x + 1)$, the third number is $(x + 2)$, etc. The tenth and final number is $(x + 9)$.

x	$x+1$	$x+2$	$x+3$	$x+4$
$x+5$	$x+6$	$x+7$	$x+8$	$x+9$

To go from the 1st number in the top row to the 1st number in the bottom row, we add 5. To go from the 2nd number in the top row to the 2nd number in the bottom row, we add 5, and so on. There are five numbers in the top row, and each counterpart in the bottom row is 5 greater, so the sum of the entire bottom row is 25 greater than the sum of the entire top row:

x	$x+1$	$x+2$	$x+3$	$x+4$	= 560
↓ (+5)	↓ (+5)	↓ (+5)	↓ (+5)	↓ (+5)	
$x+5$	$x+6$	$x+7$	$x+8$	$x+9$	= 585

585 is the **answer**.

Alternatively, we can apply **Properties of Consecutive Integer Sets.** Specifically, the median and the average of any such set will be equivalent. If the first 5 numbers sum to 560, then their average is $A = \dfrac{560}{5} = 112$. That means the median of the 5 numbers is 112, so the first 5 numbers in the overall set are 110, 111, 112, 113 and 114.

That means that the next 5 numbers in the list are 115, 116, 117, 118 and 119. We can use the same shortcut to quickly find the sum of these 5 numbers. The median of this list is 117, so the average is also 117. Since $117 = $ Sum/5, the sum of these 5 numbers is 585.

The correct answer is (A).

PS 86. <u>Word Translations</u>: Rates & Work
Difficulty: 500–600 **OG Page:** 164

We are told in this **Rates & Work** problem that Machine A produces 100 parts twice as fast as Machine B does. This means that Machine A's rate is twice the rate of Machine B. Since the problem states that Machine B can produce 100 parts in 40 minutes, we can use the **Rate–Time–Work**

Formula $W = RT$ to calculate Machine B's rate:

100 parts = $R \times$ 40 min

R = 100 parts / 40 min = 2.5 parts/min

Now that we know Machine B's rate, we can simply double it to obtain Machine A's rate.

$2 \times 2.5 = 5$ parts/min

Finally, we are asked how many parts Machine A can produce in 6 minutes. We know Machine A's rate, so we can plug this figure and the given time into the work formula:

$R \times T = W$
5 parts/min $\times$ 6 min = 30 parts

The correct answer is (A).

PS 87. <u>Number Properties</u>: Divisibility & Primes
Difficulty: 500–600 **OG Page:** 164

This problem, like many other problems involving repeating cycles, is a disguised problem about **Remainders.**

The pattern is red (R), green (G), white (W), blue (B), yellow (Y). Since the pattern continues this way, RGWBY, every five beads, we know that the 5th, 10th, 15th, … beads are all yellow. These positions are the **Multiples** of 5. The 6th, 11th, 16th, … beads are red. Since these beads come immediately after the yellow ones, they are all 1 more than a multiple of 5. Therefore, the position of any red bead will give a remainder of 1 upon division by 5. For the same reasons, green beads, upon division by 5, will give a remainder of 2; white beads, 3; and blue beads, 4.

Since our necklace ends with a white bead, we are looking for an answer choice that yields a remainder of 3 upon division by 5. Only answer choice E, 68, divided by 5 yields a remainder of 3. Thus, 68 is the **answer.**

Alternatively, we can use **Pattern Recognition.** Remember that obvious patterns tend to emerge quickly in most problems involving remainders and repeating sequences. Therefore, we can write out a series of examples until the pattern becomes clear.

Red beads: 1, 6, 11, 16, 21, 26, …

Green beads: 2, 7, 12, 17, 22, 27, …

White beads: 3, 8, 13, 18, 23, 28, …

Blue beads: 4, 9, 14, 19, 24, 29, …

Yellow beads: 5, 10, 15, 20, 25, 30, …

The pattern is clear: we can tell the color of any particular bead by looking at its **Units Digit.** The white beads have units digit 3 or 8. The only such number in the answer choices is 68.

The correct answer is (E).

PS 88. Geometry: Coordinate Plane
Difficulty: 500–600   **OG Page:** 164

In this **Coordinate Plane** problem, we use the

Slope of a Line, defined as $\dfrac{\text{rise}}{\text{run}} = \dfrac{\text{change in } y}{\text{change in } x}$

$= \dfrac{y_2 - y_1}{x_2 - x_1}$.

If the line passes through (a, b) and $(a + 3, b + k)$,

then slope $= \dfrac{\text{change in } y}{\text{change in } x} = \dfrac{(b+k)-b}{(a+3)-a} = \dfrac{k}{3}$.

We can best understand lines by using the conventional **Equation for a Line** $y = mx + b$, in which m is the slope and b is the y-intercept. We can write an equation for this line in standard form, using the information given to us in the question stem:

$$x = 3y - 7$$
$$3y - 7 = x$$
$$3y = x + 7$$
$$y = \frac{1}{3}x + \frac{7}{3}$$

Thus, the slope of the line is 1/3. Now we match the expression we found earlier for the slope, $k/3$, to this value.

$$\frac{1}{3} = \frac{k}{3}$$
$$k = 1 \quad \text{This is the \textbf{answer}.}$$

Alternatively, we can solve this problem by **Plugging in Coordinates:** that is, by putting the given coordinates (a, b) and $(a + 3, b + k)$ into the

given equation. Be sure to put in the coordinates in the right order, since the given equation is not a standard form of a line. Instead of expressing y in terms of x, as is typical, the given equation expresses x in terms of y. Remember also that the x-coordinate always comes first in the pair (a, b).

$$x = 3y - 7$$
$$a = 3b - 7 \quad \text{and} \quad a + 3 = 3(b + k) - 7$$

Through either **Substitution** or **Elimination,** we can now solve for k. Taking the second route, we subtract the a equation from the $a + 3$ equation. First, simplify the second equation.

$$a + 3 = 3b + 3k - 7$$

$$
\begin{aligned}
a + 3 &= 3b + 3k - 7 \\
-\{\, a &= 3b \qquad\; -7 \,\} \\
\hline
3 &= \qquad 3k \\
1 &= k
\end{aligned}
$$

The correct answer is (D).

PS 89. EIVs: VICs
Difficulty: 700–800   **OG Page:** 164

Although this problem involves **Variables In Choices**, we *must* use **Direct Algebra** to solve. Picking numbers is impossible, because s and t are actually defined.

According to the question, s is the product of the integers from 100 to 200, and t is the product of the integers from 100 to 201. We are not tested on our ability to physically compute such large products. Therefore, there must be a way to compare the values of s and t directly. Write out a few terms of each definition and line up the two equations to compare them.

$$s = 100 \times 101 \times 102 \times 103 \times \ldots 200$$
$$t = 100 \times 101 \times 102 \times 103 \times \ldots 200 \times 201$$

Notice that t is identical to s, EXCEPT for the fact that t includes 201. That is to say, t must be equal to s times 201:

$$t = s \times 201 \qquad s = \frac{t}{201}$$

The answers are given in terms of t, so we want to get rid of the s in the final equation. We can do this by replacing s with $\dfrac{t}{201}$.

$$t = s \times 201 \qquad s = \dfrac{t}{201}$$

$$\dfrac{1}{s} + \dfrac{1}{t} = \dfrac{1}{t/201} + \dfrac{1}{t} \qquad \text{(substituting into the expression)}$$

$$= \dfrac{201}{t} + \dfrac{1}{t}$$

$$= \dfrac{202}{t}$$

The correct answer is (D).

PS 90. <u>Word Translations</u>: Algebraic Translations
Difficulty: 300–500 **OG Page:** 164

This is a standard **Algebraic Translations** problem that we can solve by **Direct Algebra**. These problems reward neat work and an organized approach. Start by **Naming Variables** to represent Jake's weight and his sister's weight. Let's use j and s. Note that these variables represent the individuals' *current* weights.

Next, we need to create equations. In this case, our first equation should read as follows:

$j - 8$	$=$	$2s$
"If Jake loses 8 pounds	he will weigh	twice as much as his sister."

The second equation is a simple sum and should read:

$$j + s = 278$$

We must solve for j. While we would normally manipulate the equations to get rid of s, doing so in this case will force us to work with fractions. For sake of ease, we begin by putting j in terms of s in the first equation:

$$j - 8 = 2s$$
$$j = 2s + 8$$

We can then insert $2s + 8$ in the second equation, in place of j:

$$(2s + 8) + s = 278$$
$$3s + 8 = 278$$
$$3s = 270$$
$$s = 90$$

From here, we can solve for j in the first equation:

$$j - 8 = 2(90)$$
$$j - 8 = 180$$
$$j = 188 \quad \text{This is the } \textbf{answer.}$$

We can easily double-check by using the second equation:

$$188 + 90 = 278$$

The correct answer is (E).

PS 91. <u>Word Translations</u>: Algebraic Translations
Difficulty: 500–600 **OG Page:** 165

In this **Algebraic Translations** problem, we have a **Cost Relationship** between two items.

First, we can **Name Variables**, using M to represent the price of 1 map and B to represent the price of 1 book. If the store sold 12 maps and 10 books for \$38.00, we can write the following equation:

$$12M + 10B = 38$$

Likewise, if 20 maps and 15 books were sold for \$60.00, we can set up a second equation to equate the dollars spent:

$$20M + 15B = 60$$

At this point, we have **Two Unknowns** (M and B) and **Two Different Linear Equations** (each equation would represent a line in a coordinate plane). Thus, we can solve for M and B. If this were a Data Sufficiency problem, we could stop right here. However, on Problem Solving, we need to find an actual number.

Note that we are asked for how much less a map sells for than a book. In other words, we are ultimately looking for the quantity $B - M$, not the prices B and M themselves. The easiest path forward is to solve for the variables individually, then subtract them to find the answer.

We can take either of two approaches to solve the system of equations: **Substitution** or **Elimination**. If we use substitution, we solve one equation for one variable, then plug into the other equation. Unfortunately, we will also end up with equations that involve a lot of fractions.

For this reason, elimination is probably the faster route, if we can learn to use it. We can solve for M and B by subtracting one equation from the other. The goal is to cancel out one of the unknowns so that we will be left with a single unknown. In order to ensure that one of the unknowns will cancel out, we need to make that unknown's coefficient the same in both equations. To do so here, we can multiply $12M + 10B = 38$ by 1.5, turning the coefficient of B into 15:

$$1.5(12M + 10B = 38)$$
$$18M + 15B = 57$$

Note that multiplying 38 by 1.5 is equivalent to adding 1/2 of 38 to 38: $19 + 38 = 57$.

Now we can subtract and solve for M:

$$20M + 15B = 60$$
$$-(18M + 15B = 57)$$
$$\overline{2M + 0B = 3}$$

Therefore, $2M = 3$ and $M = 1.5$. If $M = 1.5$, we can determine the value of B:

$$12(1.5) + 10B = 38$$
$$18 + 10B = 38$$
$$10B = 20$$
$$B = 2$$

If $B = 2$ and $M = 1.5$, then the difference is $0.50.

The correct answer is (B).

PS 92. FDPs: Successive Percents & Percent Change
Difficulty: 300–500   **OG Page:** 165

This *Percent Change* problem asks us to express a year-to-year increase in sales from $320 million to $385 million in terms of an approximate percentage. In order to evaluate the answer, we must first calculate the dollar increase, and then relate it to the original figure. This yields the following:

$$\frac{\text{Percent Increase}}{100} = \frac{\$385M - \$320M}{\$320M}$$
$$\frac{\text{Percent Increase}}{100} = \frac{385 - 320}{320}$$
$$\frac{\text{Percent Increase}}{100} = \frac{65}{320}$$

Then we solve for the percent increase:

$$\text{Percent Increase} = \frac{65}{320} \times 100 = \frac{65 \times 100}{320} = \frac{650}{32}$$

We could do long division at this point but, because the question asks us for an approximate value, we can simply **Estimate.** Specifically, we look for multiples of the denominator that are close in value to the numerator. Since 64 is 2 times 32, we can see that 640 is 20 times 32. Thus, our increase is just over 20%. Looking at the answer choices, we know that 20% is the **answer**.

An alternative approach is to use the **Benchmarking** technique. We can see that a 50% year-to-year increase from an original value of $320 million would correspond to an increase of $160 million (half of $320 million), resulting in a final sales figure of $320 million + $160 million = $480 million. This figure is clearly too high, so we can tell that the answer cannot be (D) or (E). Likewise, 10% year-to-year increase would correspond to an increase of $32 million, resulting in a final sales figure of $320 million + $32 million = $352 million. As this is figure is too small, we can eliminate choice (A). Of the remaining two choices, 20% is the easier to calculate, resulting in a final sales figure of $320 million + $64 million = $384 million. This value is very nearly equal to the actual sales figure of $385 million.

The correct answer is (C).

PS 93. Word Translations: Statistics
Difficulty: 300–500   **OG Page:** 165

For an ordered list with an even number of elements, the **Median** is the average (arithmetic mean) of the middle two terms. Thus, the list 3, 6, 8, 19 has a median of 7, the average of 6 and 8. Notice that the median of this set is not actually in the set.

Since the medians of both lists are equal, the list x, 3, 6, 8, 9 must also have a median of 7.

For an ordered list with an odd number of terms, the median is simply the middle term—that is, the median is always one of the elements of the list.

Since no 7 appears in List II, x itself must be 7.

The correct answer is (B).

PS 94. FDPs: Successive Percents & Percent Change
Difficulty: 600–700   **OG Page:** 165

In this problem, all registered voters are either Democrats or Republicans. Moreover, all registered voters are expected either to vote for or not to vote for Candidate A. Because the problem gives us **Percents,** we can use 100 as a **Smart Number** to be the number of registered voters.

If we take an **Overlapping Sets** approach, we can fill out a **Double-Set Matrix** to organize the information in the problem. The shaded box answers the question.

	Vote for Candidate A?		
	Yes	No	Total
Republican			40
Democrat			60
Total	?		100

The problem states that 75% of the Democrats are expected to vote for Candidate A. If there are 60 Democrats, the number of Democrats expected to vote for Candidate A is:

$$(0.75)(60) = 45$$

The problem also states that 20% of the Republicans are expected to vote for Candidate A. If there are 40 Republicans, the number of Republicans expected to vote for Candidate A is:

$$(0.20)(40) = 8$$

We can fill in our Double-Set Matrix with the number of people from each party expected to vote for Candidate A.

	Vote for Candidate A?		
	Yes	No	Total
Republican	8		40
Democrat	45		60
Total	?		100

The total number of registered voters expected to vote for Candidate A is $8 + 45 = 53$. Since the number of all registered voters is 100, 53 also corresponds to the percent we are looking for. 53% is the **answer**.

Notice that we did not need the No column, so the full machinery of the Double-Set Matrix was not used. Several other approaches can work. However, the computations all wind up looking much the same.

The correct answer is (B).

PS 95. FDPs: Fractions
Difficulty: 600–700   **OG Page:** 165

This **Fractions** problem asks us to add, subtract, multiply, or divide various quantities. In order to do so correctly, we need to follow the **Order of Operations,** which we can remember using the acronym **PEMDAS:**

Parentheses
Exponents
Multiplication
Division
Addition
Subtraction

$$\frac{1}{2} + \left[\left(\frac{2}{3} \times \frac{3}{8} \right) \div 4 \right] - \frac{9}{16} = ?$$

Begin with the multiplication inside the round parentheses. Look to **Cancel Common Factors:**

$$\frac{2}{3} \times \frac{3}{8} = \frac{{}^1\cancel{2}}{\cancel{3}_1} \times \frac{\cancel{3}^1}{\cancel{8}_4} = \frac{1}{4}$$

and then divide inside the square brackets:

$$\frac{1}{4} \div 4 = \frac{1}{4} \times \frac{1}{4} = \frac{1}{16}$$

The problem now reads:

$$\frac{1}{2} + \frac{1}{16} - \frac{9}{16}$$

When given only addition and subtraction with no parentheses, we can work from left to right. Start by converting $\frac{1}{2}$ to $\frac{8}{16}$ so that we can work with **Common Denominators**:

$$\frac{8}{16} + \frac{1}{16} - \frac{9}{16} = \frac{9}{16} - \frac{9}{16} = 0$$

The correct answer is (E).

PS 96. <u>Word Translations</u>: Ratios
Difficulty: 500–600   **OG Page:** 165

We are told that the **Ratio**, by mass, of hydrogen to oxygen is 2 : 16. We are then asked to determine the number of grams of oxygen in 144 grams of water. Since 144 grams is the total mass of hydrogen and oxygen combined, it is best to use the **Unknown Multiplier** strategy.

First, we can make a **Table**:

Hydrogen	Oxygen
$2x$	$16x$

Create an equation that shows that the total combined mass of hydrogen and oxygen is 144 grams:

$2x + 16x = 144$
$18x = 144$
$x = 8$

Now that we know the value of the unknown multiplier, x, we can substitute to determine the number of grams of oxygen:

Oxygen = $16x$
Oxygen = $16(8) = 128$

The correct answer is (D).

PS 97. <u>EIVs</u>: Quadratic Equations
Difficulty: 300–500   **OG Page:** 165

This problem presents two **Quadratic Equations**, both of which are already set to zero and factored. The solutions to these quadratics will be the numbers that cause one of the two factored parts to equal zero.

In the first equation, $x(2x + 1) = 0$, the factors are x and $2x + 1$. If the former is equal to zero, then $x = 0$. If the latter is equal to zero, then $x = -1/2$.

In the second equation, $(x + 1/2)(2x - 3) = 0$, the factors are $x + 1/2$ and $2x - 3$. If the former is equal to zero, then $x = -1/2$. If the latter is equal to zero, then $x = 3/2$.

Since both of the equations are true, x can only be equal to $-1/2$. This is the **answer**.

This problem can also be solved by **Plugging In Answer Choices**. We simply try the answer choices one by one, and we stop when we find the number that solves both equations.

(A) is incorrect because $(-3)(2(-3) + 1)$ is not equal to zero. There's no need to try the second equation if the first doesn't work.

If we try (B), we find that $(-1/2)(2(-1/2) + 1) = 0$ in the first equation. We also find that $(-1/2 + 1/2)[2(-1/2) - 3] = 0$ in the second equation.

The correct answer is (B).

PS 98. <u>EIVs</u>: Formulas & Functions
Difficulty: 500–600   **OG Page:** 166

The question concerns a measurement scale and the corresponding intensity readings. To keep track of the scale definition and the various readings mentioned in the question text, we can use a **Population Chart**. Population Charts are typically used for tracking growth of a population. In this problem, the intensity readings grow "exponentially," just like a population. Each successive reading is some factor *times* the previous reading.

First, translate the words to be sure we understand the scale definition. If a reading of $n + 1$ corresponds to an intensity *10 times* that which corresponds to a reading of n, then higher readings correspond to higher intensities. More specifically, we can start to create the chart. Let's **Name a Variable** and call the first intensity x:

Reading	Intensity
n	x
$n + 1$	$10x$

For relating readings that differ by 1, this definition is great. However, we are asked to relate the intensities for readings of 3 and 8, a difference of 5 steps. We should go step by step, relating the readings of 3 to 4, then 4 to 5, then 5 to 6, and so on.

Let's continue the previous chart, making n equal to 3:

Reading	Intensity
$n = 3$	x
4	$10x$
5	$10(10x) = 100x = 10^2x$
6	$10(100x) = 1,000x = 10^3x$
7	$10(1,000x) = 10,000x = 10^4x$
8	$10(10,000x) = 100,000x = 10^5x$

Thus, the intensity corresponding to a reading of 8 (10^5x) is 10^5 greater than the intensity corresponding to a reading of 3. This is the **answer**.

As is typical on population or growth problems, a **Pattern** emerged: the exponent on the 10 in the intensity measurement increases by 1 as the reading increases by 1. We might save work if we notice this pattern right away and realize that

$$\frac{\text{intensity for reading 8}}{\text{intensity for reading 3}} = 10^{8-3} = 10^5$$

Separately, we might note that adding 1 to the reading is the same as multiplying the intensity by 10. Adding 2 to a reading is the same as multiplying the intensity by 100 (which is 1 followed by 2 zeros). Extrapolating this pattern, we can conclude that adding 5 to a reading is the same as multiplying the intensity by 100,000 (1 followed by 5 zeros).

The correct answer is (C).

PS 99. Word Translations: Statistics
Difficulty: 500–600   **OG Page:** 166

We are given a set of 5 positive integers listed in increasing order:

$$n, n + 1, n + 2, n + 4, n + 8$$

In a set containing an *odd* number of values, the **Median** is the value that appears in the middle when the data is arranged in increasing order. In this case, $n + 2$ is the middle term and is therefore the median.

The **Mean** (average) can be calculated using the **Average Formula:**

$$\text{Average} = \frac{\text{Sum}}{\# \text{ of terms}}$$
$$= \frac{n + (n+1) + (n+2) + (n+4) + (n+8)}{5}$$
$$= \frac{5n + 15}{5}$$
$$= n + 3$$

The question asks how much greater the mean is than the median:

$$\text{mean} - \text{median} = (n + 3) - (n + 2) = 1$$

This is the **answer.**

Alternatively, since this question involves **Variables In Choices,** we could have opted to **Pick a Value** for n. If $n = 2$, the 5 numbers in the set would be 2, 3, 4, 6 and 10.

The median would be 4, the middle number.

The mean would be $\frac{2+3+4+6+10}{5} = \frac{25}{5} = 5$.

The mean would be $5 - 4 = 1$ greater than the median, so our **Target Value** would be 1.

Testing each answer choice, we can see that only (B) gives the target value.

(A)	0	INCORRECT
(B)	1	**CORRECT**
(C)	$2 + 1$	INCORRECT
(D)	$2 + 2$	INCORRECT
(E)	$2 + 3$	INCORRECT

The correct answer is (B).

PS 100. EIVs: Basic Equations
Difficulty: 300–500   **OG Page:** 166

This **Basic Equations** problem involves standard **Algebraic Translations.** In this case, we are given an actual value for one of our variables. As a result, we can use **Direct Algebra.** Insert the known value in place of the variable in the first equation:

$$290 = \frac{5}{9}(K - 32)$$

Next, multiply the whole equation by $\frac{9}{5}$ to remove the fraction from the right-hand side:

$$\frac{9}{5}(290) = K - 32$$

It may help to break 290 into two separate factors, 29 and 10, so that we can cancel more easily:

$$\frac{9}{5}(29)(10) = K - 32$$
$$(9)(29)(2) = K - 32$$
$$(18)(29) = K - 32$$
$$522 = K - 32$$
$$554 = K$$

The correct answer is (D).

PS 101. <u>Word Translations:</u> Rates & Work
Difficulty: 500–600   **OG Page:** 166

In this *Rates & Work* problem, we can choose a *Smart Number* for the size of the pool to simplify the computations. Since we are given times of 9 hours and 5 hours, we should choose a size that is divisible by both 9 and 5. Let's pick 45 gallons. Using the relationship Rate × Time = Work, we can create an *Rate–Time–Work Chart* and solve for each outlet's rate of work.

	Rate (gal/hr)	×	Time (hours)	=	Work (gallons)
First Outlet	5		9		45
Second Outlet	9		5		45
Together					

The first outlet pumps 5 gallons per hour (= 1/9 of the pool), and the second outlet pumps 9 gallons per hour (= 1/5 of the pool). Together, then, they pump 5 + 9 = 14 gallons per hour. We are ultimately looking for t, the time it takes both outlets to fill the pool.

	Rate (gal/hr)	×	Time (hours)	=	Work (gallons)
First Outlet	5		9		45
Second Outlet	9		5		45
Together	5 + 9 = 14		t		45

Now, write an equation to represent the last row of the table:

$$14\,t = 45$$
$$t = 45 \div 14 = \frac{45}{14}$$

At this point, we can either perform long division or estimate, noting that the answer choices are relatively far apart. If the calculation were 45 ÷ 15, we would get exactly 3. The real answer is slightly bigger than 3, because the real denominator is slightly smaller than 15. Of the answer choices, only 3.21 fits. This is the **answer**.

There is a shortcut for straightforward *Working Together* problems, in which the task is the same for each machine and for the machines working together:

$$\frac{1}{9 \text{ hours}} + \frac{1}{5 \text{ hours}} = \frac{1}{\text{Time working together}}$$

This formula gets us to $\dfrac{45}{14 \text{ hours}}$ quickly.

However, we should understand the formula as a special case of adding rates.

The correct answer is (D).

PS 102. <u>Geometry:</u> Polygons
Difficulty: 500–600   **OG Page:** 166

In this *Polygons* problem, we are asked to determine approximately the perimeter of a *Square* that has a diagonal of length 20. We should *Name a Variable* now to represent the key metric for any square: the length of any side. If we let x stand for the length of a side of the square, then the perimeter equals $4x$.

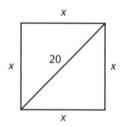

From the right triangle formed by the diagonal and two sides of the square, we can use the *Pythagorean Theorem* to write the following:

$$x^2 + x^2 = 20^2$$

$$2x^2 = 400$$

$$x^2 = 200$$

$$x = \sqrt{200} = \sqrt{100 \times 2} = \sqrt{100} \times \sqrt{2} = 10\sqrt{2}$$

Alternatively, we can observe that the triangle in question is a **45–45–90** triangle. We can solve for x using the side ratios of this special triangle:

$$x\sqrt{2} = 20$$

$$x = \frac{20}{\sqrt{2}} = \frac{20\sqrt{2}}{2} = 10\sqrt{2}$$

The square root of 2 is approximately equal to 1.4. Now we can ***Estimate***: $x \approx 14$ and $4x \approx 56$. The closest answer choice is 60. This is the **answer**.

We may also note that in this case, with the choices so far apart, we can find the right answer by ***Testing Answer Choices*** and applying reasonable geometric constraints. If the perimeter were equal to 40, as in answer choice (A), then each side of the square would have to equal 10. However, in that case, the sum of the lengths of two sides would equal the length of the diagonal, which is not possible. Likewise, if the perimeter were equal to 80, as in answer choice (C), then each side of the square would have to equal 20, making the length of the diagonal equal to the length of a side. This is also unreasonable. The diagonal of a square would be longer than any of its sides. The only sensible answer available to us is 60.

The correct answer is (B).

PS 103. <u>Word Translations:</u> Ratios
Difficulty: 600–700   **OG Page:** 166

The ***Ratio*** of students to teachers is 30 to 1, while adding 50 students and 5 teachers changes the ratio to 25 to 1. To solve this problem, we can use the ***Unknown Multiplier*** strategy.

The present student/teacher ratio of 30 to 1 can be written as this ***Proportion***:

$$\frac{30x}{(1)x}$$

where the real number of students is the 30th mul-

tiple of some number x (the Unknown Multiplier) and the real number of teachers is simply x. Adding 50 students and 5 teachers to create a new 25 to 1 ratio can therefore be written as:

$$\frac{30x + 50}{x + 5} = \frac{25}{1}$$

Now we can do ***Direct Algebra*** and solve for x:

$$30x + 50 = 25x + 125$$
$$5x = 75$$
$$x = 15$$

This value for x is not only the Unknown Multiplier but the actual number of teachers right now. x teachers = 15 teachers. This is the **answer**.

Note that in this case x is equal to our final answer, but this is only because a 1 happens to be part of the first ratio (30 to 1). Generally speaking, the Unknown Multiplier is not itself the final answer to the question.

The correct answer is (E).

PS 104. <u>EIVs:</u> Equations with Exponents
Difficulty: 500–600   **OG Page:** 166

Because the problem involves an ***Inequality*** between ***Exponents*** with different bases, we cannot compare the numbers directly.

$$25^n > 5^{12}$$

To simplify the problem, replace 25 with 5^2, so both sides have a ***Common Base.***

$$(5^2)^n > 5^{12}$$

Now we can apply the ***Rule of Multiplying Exponents***: $(a^x)^y = a^{xy}$

$$5^{2n} > 5^{12}$$

Because the bases are the same, we can compare the exponents:

$$2n > 12$$
$$n > 6$$

The smallest integer for which $n > 6$ is 7. This is the **answer**.

Technically, by the way, we cannot compare exponents when the base is either 0 or 1, but those special cases do not apply here.

The correct answer is (B).

PS 105. <u>Word Translations:</u> Probability
Difficulty: 600–700   **OG Page:** 166

This *Probability* problem discusses a group but specifies only *Percents* when describing characteristics of the group. No real numbers are used. Use a *Smart Number* to make the work easier. Because this is a percentage problem, 100 is a Smart Number. Assume that there are 100 people in the study group.

The problem specifies that 60% of the members are women, so 60 out of the 100 people are women. The problem further specifies that 45% *of the (60) women* are lawyers.

So the number of female lawyers is 0.45×60. An easy way to do this calculation is to first convert 0.45 to a fraction, and then to cancel common factors.

$$\frac{45}{100} \times 60 = \frac{45}{{}_5\cancel{100}} \times \cancel{60}^3 = 9 \times 3 = 27$$

27 of the women are lawyers.

The problem asks us to determine the probability that the random member selected will be a female lawyer. We can calculate this probability with the **Basic Probability Formula:** taking the number of desired outcomes and dividing by the total possible outcomes.

The desired outcome is a female lawyer. Because there are 27 female lawyers, there are 27 ways to select one female lawyer. There are 100 people total, so there are 100 ways to select one person from the group. The probability is $27/100 = 0.27$.

The correct answer is (C).

PS 106. <u>Number Properties:</u> Divisibility & Primes
Difficulty: 600–700   **OG Page:** 167

In this *Divisibility* problem, we need to recognize that, in an expression such as $x/y = 96.12$, the *Remainder* is equal to $0.12y$. In other words, the

remainder must be equal to the decimal part of the quotient times the divisor, which in this case is y.

For example, $32/5 = 6.4$ as a *Decimal*. In remainder notation, $32/5 = 6$, with remainder 2. Notice that the remainder (2) must be equal to the decimal portion (0.4) times the divisor (5). In other words, $2 = 0.4 \times 5$.

Since our remainder must be equal to $0.12y$ and we are also told that the remainder is 9, set $0.12y$ equal to 9 and solve for y. To reduce the fraction quickly, move decimal points.

$$0.12y = 9$$

$$y = \frac{9}{0.12} = \frac{900}{12} = \frac{300}{4} = \frac{150}{2} = 75$$

The correct answer is (B).

PS 107. <u>Number Properties:</u> Divisibility & Primes
Difficulty: 500–600   **OG Page:** 167

This *Divisibility* problem expresses the integer x as $x = 2^i 3^k 5^m 7^i$, where the exponents themselves are also integers. Since 2, 3, 5, and 7 are prime numbers, the expression $2^i 3^k 5^m 7^i$ represents the **Prime Factorization** of x. Therefore, the crux of the problem consists of finding the prime factorization of x.

Since x is already expressed as a product, simply express each part of the product in terms of primes:

$x = 1 \times 2 \times 3 \times 4 \times 5 \times 6 \times 7 \times 8$

$\quad = (2)(3)(2^2)(5)(2 \times 3)(7)(2^3)$

Note that we can ignore the "1" at the beginning of the factorization, since multiplication by 1 does not contribute to the value of a product.

Combine the terms with like bases:

$(2 \times 2^2 \times 2 \times 2^3)(3 \times 3)(5)(7) = (2^7)(3^2)(5^1)(7^1)$

Therefore $i = 7$, $k = 2$, $m = 1$, and $p = 1$, so the desired sum is $7 + 2 + 1 + 1 = 11$.

The correct answer is (D).

PS 108. <u>FDPs</u>: Digits & Decimals
Difficulty: 500–600   **OG Page:** 167

One straightforward approach to this *Digits &*
Decimals question is to convert t to simple fractional form as follows.

$$t = \frac{1}{2^9 \times 5^3} = \frac{1}{512 \times 125} = \frac{1}{64,000}$$

Multiplying 512 by 125 directly is cumbersome. A
more elegant approach is to group 2's and 5's to
make *Powers of 10:*

$$t = \frac{1}{2^9 \times 5^3} = \frac{1}{(2^6 \times 2^3) \times 5^3} = \frac{1}{2^6 \times (2^3 \times 5^3)}$$

$$= \frac{1}{2^6 \times 10^3} = \frac{1}{64 \times 10^3} = \frac{1}{64,000}$$

At this point, we have a few options.

(1) We can simply do *Long Division* of 64,000
into 1, counting the zeros after the decimal place
and stopping once we get to a non-zero digit:

$$64,000\overline{)1.00000000...}^{0.0000156...}$$

Therefore, t has 4 zeros between the decimal point
and the first nonzero digit to the right of the decimal point. This is the **answer.**

(2) Alternatively, we can compare t in this fractional form to some *Benchmark* fractions:

$$\frac{1}{100,000} < \frac{1}{64,000} < \frac{1}{10,000}$$

$$0.00001 < \frac{1}{64,000} < 0.0001$$

All numbers greater than 0.00001 and less than
0.0001 (such as 0.000011, 0.00002, 0.000078) all
have 4 zeroes between the decimal point and the
first nonzero digit.

(3) Finally, we can notice the following partial
Power of Ten:

$$\frac{1}{64,000} = \frac{1}{64} \times 10^{-3}$$

Using either long division or benchmarks as above,
we can determine that 1/64 in decimal form has one

zero between the decimal point and the first nonzero
digit. The factor of 10^{-3} moves the decimal to the
left, increasing the number of zeros by 3. Thus, t
has $1 + 3 = 4$ zeros between the decimal point and
the first nonzero digit after the decimal point.

The correct answer is (B).

PS 109. <u>FDPs</u>: Successive Percents & Percent Change
Difficulty: 600–700   **OG Page:** 167

This *Percent Change* question breaks the pharma-
ceutical company's sales into two parts, giving the
corresponding royalties for each part: the first $20
million with $3 million in royalties and the next
$108 million with $9 million in royalties. List the
parts in a *Table.*

	First	*Second*
Royalties	$3 million	$9 million
Sales	$20 million	$108 million
Royalties/Sales	3/20	9/108 = 1/12

The question then asks for the approximate percent decrease in the ratio of royalties to sales from
the first part to the second part.

$$\text{Percent change} = \frac{\text{New} - \text{Original}}{\text{Original}} \times 100\%$$

The Original here is the *Ratio* of royalties to sales
for the first part, and the New is the ratio of royalties to sales for the second part. We get a
Complicated Fraction that we can reduce using a
Common Denominator:

$$\frac{\text{New} - \text{Original}}{\text{Original}} = \frac{\text{Second} - \text{First}}{\text{First}}$$

$$= \frac{\frac{1}{12} - \frac{3}{20}}{\frac{3}{20}} = \frac{\frac{5}{60} - \frac{9}{60}}{\frac{9}{60}} = \frac{-\frac{4}{60}}{\frac{9}{60}}$$

$$-\frac{4}{60} \times \frac{60}{9} = \frac{-4}{9} = -0.\overline{44}$$

To convert to a percent, we multiply this value by
100%, so the percent change is approximately
45% (and the negative sign simply means that the
value went down, not up).

The correct answer is (C).

PS 110. <u>Number Properties</u>: Divisibility & Primes
Difficulty: 600–700   **OG Page:** 167

p is the product of all of the integers from 1 to 30, or 30! (30 factorial). We are asked for the greatest integer k for which 3^k is a factor of p. In other words, in this **Divisibility** problem, we need to find how many 3's are factors of p.

Using the **Factor Foundation Rule**, we can see that each multiple of 3 from 1 to 30 will contribute factors of 3 to the overall product. The non-multiples of 3 will not contribute factors of 3 and can thus be ignored.

$$3 = \mathbf{3} \times 1$$
$$6 = \mathbf{3} \times 2$$
$$9 = \mathbf{3} \times \mathbf{3}$$
$$12 = \mathbf{3} \times 2 \times 2$$
$$15 = \mathbf{3} \times 5$$
$$18 = \mathbf{3} \times \mathbf{3} \times 2$$
$$21 = \mathbf{3} \times 7$$
$$24 = \mathbf{3} \times 2 \times 2 \times 2$$
$$27 = \mathbf{3} \times \mathbf{3} \times \mathbf{3}$$
$$30 = \mathbf{3} \times 5 \times 2$$

We can see that, collectively, the multiples of 3 between 1 and 30, inclusive, contribute 14 factors of 3 to p. Therefore, 14 is the **answer**.

A different way to add up the 3's is to count by powers of 3. First, count all the multiples of 3 just once. There are 10 multiples of 3 between 3 and 30, inclusive. Now, add 1 for each multiple of 9, since each multiple of 9 contains at least one more 3. We have 3 multiples of 9 (9, 18, and 27) in the range. Finally, add 1 more for 27, since 27 contains three 3's, as shown above.

We get $10 + 3 + 1 = 14$ factors of 3.

The correct answer is (C).

PS 111. <u>FDPs</u>: Successive Percents & Percent Change
Difficulty: 500–600   **OG Page:** 167

In this **Percent Change** problem, the regular price of a candy bar is $0.40, so two bars at the regular price would cost $0.80. Since the bars are on sale at two for $0.75, there is a savings of $0.05 on the purchase of two bars.

This savings represents $0.05/0.80 = 5/80 = 0.0625 = 6.25\%$ of the original purchase price. This is the **answer**.

We can also use **Fractions** to avoid having to deal with decimals:

$$\frac{\frac{5}{100}}{\frac{80}{100}} = \left(\frac{5}{100}\right)\left(\frac{100}{80}\right) = \frac{5}{80} = \frac{1}{16} = 6.25\%$$

We should be careful to avoid common errors. If we divide the total 5-cent saving by 40 cents (the price of *one* bar), we get answer choice (E). Also, the 5-cent saving is $2\frac{1}{2}$ cents per bar, but this is not a percent discount of the price (as in answer choice (A).

The correct answer is (B).

PS 112. <u>EIVs</u>: VICs
Difficulty: 300–500   **OG Page:** 167

In this **Variables In Choices** problem, which also involves **Roots**, we are asked to solve for r in terms of s. This means that we need to manipulate the equation to get r by itself on one side of the equals sign. On the other side of the equation, there should be an expression involving s. In other words, we want this equation:

$r = $ something involving s

One potential complication to the problem might have involved the sign of s, but we are told that s is, in fact, positive. This makes the algebra straightforward, and we can solve this problem using **Direct Algebra**.

First, **Square Both Sides** to eliminate the square root:

$$\left(\sqrt{\frac{r}{s}}\right)^2 = s^2$$
$$\frac{r}{s} = s^2$$

Next, multiply both sides by the denominator of the left side, in order to eliminate the fraction and isolate r:

$$r = s \times s^2 = s^3 \quad \text{This is the } \textbf{answer.}$$

An alternative approach is to **Pick Numbers**. First, pick a simple number for *s*. Say *s* = 2. Then we solve for *r* as follows:

$$\sqrt{\frac{r}{s}} = s$$

$$\sqrt{\frac{r}{2}} = 2$$

$$\left(\sqrt{\frac{r}{2}}\right)^2 = 2^2 = 4$$

$$\frac{r}{2} = 4$$

$$r = 8$$

Note that we still have to perform the algebraic steps to isolate *r* (such as squaring both sides). Now, we match the **Target Value** of 8 to the answer choices.

(A) $\frac{1}{s} = \frac{1}{2} \neq 8$ INCORRECT

(B) $\sqrt{s} = \sqrt{2} \neq 8$ INCORRECT

(C) $s\sqrt{s} = 2\sqrt{2} \neq 8$ INCORRECT

(D) $s^3 = 2^3 = 8$ **CORRECT**

(E) $s^2 - s = 2^2 - 2 = 2 \neq 8$ INCORRECT

The correct answer is (D).

PS 113. <u>Geometry</u>: Polygons
Difficulty: 500–600   **OG Page:** 168

In this **Polygons** problem, we are asked what **Fraction** of the door's surface is covered by the trim. To rephrase, we are looking for this **Ratio of Areas:**

$$\frac{\text{Area of Trim}}{\text{Total Area of Door}}$$

It is clear that the total area of the door is simply 6 × 8 = 48 square feet. Therefore, the desired quantity is now:

$$\frac{\text{Area of Trim}}{48}$$

Because the trim is irregularly shaped, it may be easier to find the area of the two rectangles that are NOT covered by trim and subtract that area from the total area of the door in order to find the area of the trim. This is an application of the **1 − x Principle:**

What we want = Everything − What we don't want

If the trim is one foot wide, then the three strips of trim running horizontally take up 3 vertical feet. Since the height of the door is 8 feet, 5 feet of vertical distance is taken up by the non-trim areas.

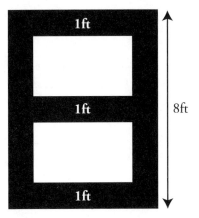

Since the width of the door is six feet and two strips of trim running vertically are each 1 foot wide, 4 feet of horizontal distance is taken up by the non-trim areas.

Therefore, the area of the door that is NOT covered by trim is 5 × 4 = 20 square feet. Note that it does not matter that the two non-trim areas are not touching—we have simply calculated their area as though they were sitting on top of one another, forming a single rectangle.

If the area of the non-trim portion of the door is 20 square feet, the area covered by trim is 48 − 20

= 28 square feet. Finally, we compute the fraction of the door covered by the trim:

$$\frac{28}{48} = \frac{7}{12}$$

The correct answer is (D).

PS 114. <u>FDPs</u>: Digits & Decimals
Difficulty: 500–600   **OG Page:** 168

This **Decimals** problem asks us to compare a, a^2, and a^3, if we know that $a = -0.3$.

The particular value of a is not important. What we need is **Number Line Awareness**. Specifically, we need to recognize that -0.3 is a negative proper fraction (a decimal between -1 and 0).

Without performing any computations, we can observe **Positive & Negative Rules** for **Exponents** to eliminate answer choices.

A negative number taken to an even power results in a positive number.

A negative number taken to an odd power results in a negative number.

From this observation, a^2 will be positive. On the other hand, both a and a^3 will be negative. Thus, a^2 is larger than both a and a^3. Any positive number is larger than any negative number (that is, any positive number is to the right of any negative number on a number line), since 0 is greater than any negative but less than any positive.

We can eliminate (A), (C), and (D) because a^2 is not the largest value in those answer choices.

Now we can apply additional knowledge about negative proper fractions. Specifically, when we raise a number such as -0.3 to an *odd* power, it gets closer to zero. In other words, it gets *larger*.

$a^3 = (-0.3)^3 = -0.027$, and $-0.027 > -0.3$

Remember that the larger of two negative numbers is closer to zero. For instance, $-8 < -2 < 0$. So we know that $a < a^3 < 0$, and we also know that $0 < a^2$.

Putting the inequalities together, we have $a < a^3 < a^2$.

The correct answer is (B).

PS 115. <u>FDPs</u>: Successive Percents & Percent Change
Difficulty: 600–700   **OG Page:** 168

This **Successive Percents** problem discusses a group but specifies only percentages when describing characteristics of the group. No real numbers are used. Use a **Smart Number** to make the work easier.

Pick a real number for one of the three people (Mary, Tim, or Juan) and then calculate the appropriate value for the other two. We can start with any person, but because the question asks for a percentage of Juan's income, it's a good idea to pick a number for Juan. Let's pick 100, an easy number to deal with in terms of percentages.

The problem specifies that Tim's income is 40% less than Juan's income. We can **Name Variables** and use **Direct Algebra** to write $T = J - 0.4J$. If Juan's income is 100, then Tim's income is $100 - 40 = 60$.

The problem specifies that Mary's income is 60% more than Tim's income. That is, $M = T + 0.6T = 60 + (0.6)60 = 60 + 36 = 96$.

So, if Juan's income is 100, then Tim's income is 60, and Mary's income is 96.

Since Mary's income is 96 and Juan's income is 100, Mary's income is 96% of Juan's.

The correct answer is (C).

PS 116. <u>Number Properties</u>: Consecutive Integers
Difficulty: 600–700   **OG Page:** 168

One way to solve this problem is to use an essentially **Geometric** argument by studying the **Pattern** in the table. In the given table, we can see that we do not need to place entries along the diagonal of the table, since the distance from any city to itself is 0. Also, since the distance from City A to City B is equal to the distance from City B to City A, we need only represent this distance once in our table. This means we can omit all of the boxes below the diagonal, since they will contain duplicate entries.

In a 30×30 table for 30 cities, there would be a total of $30(30) = 900$ boxes. Eliminating the 30 boxes along the diagonal, we are left with 870 boxes. Since there are an equal number of boxes above and below the diagonal, and since we only need to place entries in the boxes above the diagonal, we can cut the remaining number of boxes in half: 870/2 = 435. We need a total of 435 entries. This is the **answer**.

Alternatively, we can recognize this problem as an example of **Disguised Combinatorics**. Many word problems involving the words "how many" are combinatorics problems. This problem essentially asks how many unique pairings of two cities exist out of a pool of 30 cities. We can use the

Combination Formula $\left(\dfrac{n!}{r!(n-r)!} \right)$ to determine

the number of combinations of 2 items chosen from a pool of 30 items:

$$\frac{30!}{2!(30-2)!} = \frac{30!}{2!\,28!} = \frac{30 \times 29}{2} = 15 \times 29 = 435$$

A way to remember the combination formula is that when we're picking from a pool, we have this

many in-groups: $\dfrac{\text{Pool!}}{\text{In's!\ Out's!}}$

One final alternative is to solve the problem by **Counting** the number of dots (●'s). There are no ●'s in the first column, one ● in the second column, two ●'s in the third column and so on. This pattern will continue until there are 29 ●'s in the 30th column. In order to add up all the ●'s in all the columns, therefore, we simply need to add up the numbers 1 through 29. We can use the sum formula for **Consecutive Integers**:

Sum = (Average)×(Number of terms)

$$\text{Sum} = \left(\frac{1+29}{2} \right) \times (29) = 435$$

The correct answer is (B).

PS 117. Number Properties: Roots
Difficulty: 500–600   **OG Page:** 168

Notice that only one answer choice in this **Roots** problem contains a denominator. This problem is very specialized: it demands the ability to rationalize a denominator containing a sum or difference of square roots. To get this particular difference out of the denominator, we must multiply by the

Conjugate. The conjugate of a difference of roots is the sum of roots, and vice versa. The conjugate of $\sqrt{n+1} - \sqrt{n}$ is $\sqrt{n+1} + \sqrt{n}$, so we multiply both the top and the bottom of the fraction by this sum:

$$\frac{1}{\sqrt{n+1} - \sqrt{n}} \left(\frac{\sqrt{n+1} + \sqrt{n}}{\sqrt{n+1} + \sqrt{n}} \right)$$

To find the new denominator, we need to **FOIL**.

$$\frac{\sqrt{n+1} + \sqrt{n}}{(\sqrt{n+1})(\sqrt{n+1}) - (\sqrt{n})(\sqrt{n+1}) + (\sqrt{n})(\sqrt{n+1}) - (\sqrt{n})(\sqrt{n})}$$

We can simplify this expression. Notice the middle two terms in the denominator cancel each other out. This cancellation happens because multiplying a difference of two things by the sum of the same two things gives us the **Difference of Squares** of those two things. In fact, this is the whole purpose of multiplying by this strange conjugate: to cause the middle terms to cancel.

The result is this:

$$\frac{\sqrt{n+1} + \sqrt{n}}{(n+1) - (n)} = \frac{\sqrt{n+1} + \sqrt{n}}{1} = \sqrt{n+1} + \sqrt{n}$$

This is the **answer**.

Although the problem contains **Variables In Choices**, we probably want to avoid picking numbers as a strategy in this case. No matter what numbers we pick, we will get messy roots that we will need to approximate in both the stem and the answer choices. We can eliminate a couple of answer choices this way, but it may be difficult to get all the way to the right answer.

The correct answer is (E).

PS 118. Word Translations: Ratios
Difficulty: 500–600   **OG Page:** 168

For questions that ask for the "approximate length," we do not need to solve the problem completely. In fact, we probably should not bother to solve, since **Estimation** is likely to be faster.

Drawing a Picture of the rectangular display may be helpful:

$L = ?$

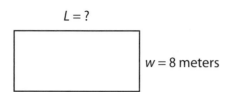

$w = 8$ meters

We have drawn the rectangle to make L a little more than 50% longer than w, since we are told that the ratio of length to width is 3.3 to 2. (If the ratio were exactly 3 to 2, the length would be exactly 50% longer, since $3/2 = 1.5 = 1 + 50/100$.) This observation alone allows us to eliminate answer choice A (7 is shorter than 8) and answer choice B (11 is not quite 50% longer than 8).

If 3.3 is a little more than 50% greater than 2, the length will be a little more than 50% greater than 8. That is, $L \approx 8 + $ (a little more than 4) $\approx$ a little longer than 12. The closest value among the answer choices is 13. This is the **answer**.

To actually solve, set up an **Proportion** for the **Ratio** and substitute $w = 8$:

$$\frac{L}{w} = \frac{3.3}{2}$$
$$L = \frac{3.3w}{2}$$
$$L = \frac{(3.3)(8)}{2}$$
$$L = (3.3)(4) = 13.2$$

Note that even though we solved precisely, we are still required to estimate, since the exact length of L is not listed among the choices.

The correct answer is (C).

PS 119. <u>EIVs</u>: Inequalities
Difficulty: 300–500   **OG Page:** 169

Each of the given **Inequalities** can be simplified with **Direct Algebra**:

$x + 6 > 10$ $x - 3 \leq 5$
$x > 4$ $x \leq 8$

We can combine these two inequalities into one **Compound Inequality** by turning the inequality signs in the same direction and merging the x's.

$4 < x$ $x \leq 8$
$4 < x \leq 8$

The correct answer is (D).

PS 120. <u>EIVs</u>: VIC
Difficulty: 500–600   **OG Page:** 169

For a **Variables In Choices** problem such as this one, we have two routes to a correct answer: **Direct Algebra** or a **Tracking Chart** with actual numbers.

Using **Direct Algebra**, we begin by setting up equations. Translating directly from the text, we find:

$$d = 3j = \frac{1}{2}p$$

We are asked for the total number of books, in terms of d. So let's simply put j and p each in terms of d:

Since $d = 3j$, we know that $j = \frac{1}{3}d$.

Since $d = \frac{1}{2}p$, we also know that $p = 2d$.

Finally, we add the three sets of books together:

$$d + j + p$$
$$= d + \frac{1}{3}d + 2d = \left(3\frac{1}{3}\right)d = \frac{10}{3}d$$

This is the **answer**.

Alternately, we can **Pick Numbers and Calculate a Target**. First, we should pick **Smart Numbers** for d, j, and p. Since these variables are bound by certain ratios, the numbers that we pick must agree with these ratios. It would also be wise to pick a number for d that is a multiple of 3, because $d = 3j$. Let's pick numbers:

$d = 6$
$j = 2$
$p = 12$

According to our Smart Numbers, the total number of books is 20. Thus, 20 is our **Target Value**.

Next, plug in 6 for *d* in each of the answer choices, in order to find one that matches our target value of 20.

(A) $\frac{5}{6}(6) = 5$ INCORRECT

(B) $\frac{7}{3}(6) = 14$ INCORRECT

(C) $\frac{10}{3}(6) = 20$ **CORRECT**

(D) $\frac{7}{2}(6) = 21$ INCORRECT

(E) $\frac{9}{2}(6) = 27$ INCORRECT

The correct answer is (C).

PS 121. <u>Word Translations</u>: Combinatorics
Difficulty: 500–600   **OG Page:** 169

We need to know how many pairs of teams we can select from a pool of 8. We can solve this *Combinatorics* problem using the *Anagram Method.* In essence, whenever we select two teams to play each other, we are saying "yes" to 2 and "no" to the remaining 6. For example,

A	B	C	D	E	F	G	H
Y	Y	N	N	N	N	N	N

In the above scenario, we say "yes" to teams A and B and "no" to the remaining 6. Every time we rearrange these 2 Y's and 6 N's, we are saying "yes" to a different pair and "no" to a different group of 6 teams. So if we knew the number of ways we could arrange 2 Y's and 6 N's, we would know the number of ways we can select 2 teams out of 8.

To count the ways we can do so, we divide the factorial of the total number of teams by the factorial of the number of teams we are choosing and by the factorial of the number of teams we are excluding. We divide by 2! and 6! to take into account that the 2 N's and 6 Y's are identical.

$$\frac{8!}{2!6!} = \frac{{}^4\cancel{8} \times 7 \times \cancel{6 \times 5 \times 4 \times 3 \times 2 \times 1}}{\cancel{2} \times 1 \times \cancel{6 \times 5 \times 4 \times 3 \times 2 \times 1}} = \frac{4 \times 7}{1} = 28$$

Thus, there are 28 different pairs of teams that could play each other. This is the **answer.**

Alternatively, using a *Geometric* argument, we can imagine an 8×8 *Table* that lists all the possible pairs of teams. Let's study the pattern on entries in this table.

	A	B	C	D	E	F	G	H
A	X	same						
B	same	X						
C			X					
D				X				
E					X			
F						X		
G							X	
H								X

There are 8 × 8 = 64 boxes in the table. We subtract 8 for the 8 "X" boxes in the diagonal , which would represent a team playing itself. We are left with 64 − 8 = 56 boxes. Finally, every possible game is double-counted by the remaining boxes. For instance, the game between A and B corresponds to either box labeled "same." Thus, we divide 56 by 2 to get 28 unique games.

Finally, we could do a summation. Team A plays 7 other teams. Team B plays 7 other teams as well, but we have already counted the A–B match, so we just count 6 new games. Likewise, Team C plays 5 games that we have not counted yet, and so on to Team H. The sum 7 + 6 + 5 + 4 + 3 + 2 + 1 equals 28, as we can compute longhand or find by *Consecutive Integer* techniques. The average number is 4, and there are 7 terms. The sum is 4 × 7 = 28.

The correct answer is (C).

PS 122. <u>EIVs</u>: VICs
Difficulty: 500–600   **OG Page:** 169

This *Variables In Choices* problem defines a *New Function* and gives us a relation based on that function. We are asked to determine the value of one of the variables in terms of the other.

We need to solve for *c* in terms of *a*, given that $a\,\theta\,c = 0$.

First, we *Substitute a* and *c* into the formula for the function, which is defined in terms of *a* and *b*. The variable *a* is in the same position as before, but c takes the place of b. Thus, we can write the following:

$$a \theta c = \frac{a-c}{a+c} = 0$$

Note that a fraction equals zero if its numerator equals zero. For example, $0/5 = 0$. Therefore, we must have

$$a - c = 0$$
or
$$c = a \quad \text{This is the \textbf{answer}.}$$

It is important to note that a fraction *will not* equal zero when the denominator is equal to zero. Dividing by zero results in an undefined expression. Thus, it is not possible for $c = -a$. In fact, we are even told that a does *not* equal $-c$, to prevent division by zero, so answer choice (A) cannot be the right answer.

The correct answer is (E).

PS 123. <u>FDPs:</u> Percents
Difficulty: 600–700 **OG Page:** 169

In this ***Percents*** problem, the price of lunch for 15 people was \$207, including 15% gratuity. Since the question asks us for a cost per person excluding gratuity, use the following equation to find the total price excluding gratuity, where x is that pre-tip price:

$$x(1.15) = 207$$

$$x = \frac{207}{1.15}$$

We can simplify this fraction by multiplying top and bottom by 100 to eliminate the decimal:

$$x = \frac{20,700}{115}$$

Now ***Cancel Factors.*** We start with 5, which obviously goes into both top and bottom:

$$x = \frac{20,700 \div 5}{115 \div 5} = \frac{4,140}{23}$$

Since 23 is a prime and we want a precise number, we now have to resort to long division:

$$\begin{array}{r} 180 \\ 23\overline{)4140} \\ \underline{23} \\ 184 \\ \underline{184} \end{array}$$

Thus, \$180 was the total pre-tip price. Dividing this amount equally across 15 people, we get \$180 ÷ 15 = \$12 exactly. This is the **answer**.

This final step is a specific application of the ***Average Formula***:

$$\frac{\text{Total Price}}{\text{Number of People}} = \text{Average Price per Person}$$

The correct answer is (B).

PS 124. <u>Word Translations:</u> Overlapping Sets
Difficulty: 600–700 **OG Page:** 169

In this ***Overlapping Sets*** problem, people in Town X are either male or female, and they are either employed or not employed. Because the problem gives us percentages, we can use 100 as a ***Smart Number*** to represent the population of Town X.

We can fill out a ***Double-Set Matrix*** to organize the information in the problem. The shaded box helps to answer the question.

	Employed?		
	Yes	**No**	**Total**
Male	48		
Female	**?**		
Total	64		100

From the Double-Set Matrix, we can determine the number of employed females in Town X:

$$64 - 48 = 16 \text{ employed females}$$

To compute the percent of employed people who are female, we need to evaluate this expression:

$$\frac{\text{number of employed females}}{\text{total employed people}} \times 100\%$$

$$= \frac{16}{64} \times 100\% = 25\% \quad \text{This is the \textbf{answer}.}$$

Pay careful attention to the wording in problems such as this one. For instance, we want to calculate the percent of *employed* people who are females. Thus, we should divide the number of employed females (16) by the total number of *employed* people (64), not the overall total (100).

The correct answer is (B).

PS 125. <u>EIVs:</u> Inequalities
Difficulty: 600–700   **OG Page:** 169

This **Inequalities** problem, which also involves **Variables In Choices,** specifies that p and q are both positive integers. We also know that $p/q < 1$. We are asked to determine which expression in the answer choices *must* be greater than 1.

To solve, we can **Pick Numbers and Calculate a Target.** In fact, because of the **Exponents & Roots,** we do not even need to set a specific target value. We simply need to figure out whether the result is larger or smaller than 1.

This is a good problem for picking numbers. There are only two variables, with well-defined constraints. If $p/q < 1$, and p and q are both positive, then $p < q$. We can try $p = 2$ and $q = 3$.

(A) $\sqrt{\dfrac{p}{q}} = \sqrt{\dfrac{2}{3}} =$ less than 1   INCORRECT

(B) $\dfrac{p}{q^2} = 2/9 =$ less than 1   INCORRECT

(C) $\dfrac{p}{2q} = 2/6 =$ less than 1   INCORRECT

(D) $\dfrac{q}{p^2} = 3/4 =$ less than 1   INCORRECT

(E) $\dfrac{q}{p} = 3/2 = 1.5 =$ greater than 1 **CORRECT**

Thus, we have the **answer**.

Alternatively, we can use **Number Properties** to solve this problem. If positive integer p divided by positive integer q is less than 1, then p must be smaller than q. Go through the answer choices and note down how each expression behaves when positive p is less than positive q.

(A) $\sqrt{\dfrac{p}{q}} = \sqrt{\text{number} <1} < 1$ INCORRECT

(B) $\dfrac{p}{q^2} = \dfrac{\text{original } p}{\text{even larger } q} < 1$ INCORRECT

(C) $\dfrac{p}{2q} = \dfrac{\text{original } p}{\text{even larger } q} < 1$ INCORRECT

(D) $\dfrac{q}{p^2} = \dfrac{\text{original } q}{\text{even larger } p}$ is < 1 or > 1 INCORRECT

(E) $\dfrac{q}{p} = \dfrac{\text{original } q}{\text{original } p} > 1$ **CORRECT**

The correct answer is (E).

PS 126. <u>Word Translations:</u> Rates & Work
Difficulty: 500–600   **OG Page:** 170

In this **Working Together** problem, we are told that one machine can complete a production order in 4 hours, working alone, and that another machine can complete the same job in 3 hours, working alone. We must now determine how many hours it would take both machines working simultaneously to complete the order. Remember, if two or more agents are performing simultaneous work, we can **Add The Rates.**

The first machine's rate is 1 order every 4 hours, or 1/4 orders per hour. Similarly, the second machine's rate is 1/3 orders per hour. Add these rates to get the combined rate:

$1/4 + 1/3 = 3/12 + 4/12 = 7/12$ orders per hour.

To determine the time to complete 1 order working together, we can create an **Rate–Time–Work Chart:**

R (orders/hour)	$\times$	T (hours)	$=$	W (orders)
7/12	$\times$	T	$=$	1

$$\left(\dfrac{7}{12}\right)T = 1$$

$$T = \dfrac{12}{7} \text{ hours, or } 1\dfrac{5}{7} \text{ hours.}$$

This is the **answer.**

There is a shortcut for straightforward **Working Together** problems, in which the task is the same for each machine and for the machines working together:

$$\dfrac{1}{4 \text{ hours}} + \dfrac{1}{3 \text{ hours}} = \dfrac{1}{\text{time working together}}.$$

This formula can get us to 12/7 hours quickly, However, we should understand the formula as a special case of adding rates.

The correct answer is (C).

PS 127. <u>EIVs</u>: VICs
Difficulty: 500–600   **OG Page:** 170

We should begin this *Variables In Choices* question by determining whether it will be cheaper to ship the packages separately or combined. Since the *first* pound is *more* expensive, it must be *cheaper to ship the combined package* (since the more expensive "first pound" is only paid once, rather than twice). We can use this sort of *Algebraic Reasoning* to gut-check our answer.

If we continue down the *Direct Algebra* road, we need to determine the cost to mail each package separately and the cost to mail them together. We'll begin with the cost to mail the packages separately. The first package weighs 3 pounds. The cost to ship the first pound is x cents/pound, for a total of x cents. The cost to ship the remaining 2 pounds is y cents/pound, for a total of $2y$ cents. So the cost to ship the 3 pound package is $x + 2y$ cents. The second package weighs 5 pounds. The cost to mail the first pound is x cents, and the cost to mail the remaining 4 pounds at y cents per pound is $4y$ cents for a combined cost of $x + 4y$ cents. That means that to ship both packages separately costs $(x + 2y) + (x + 4y) = 2x + 6y$ cents.

If the packages are mailed together, the total weight will be 8 pounds. The cost to mail the first pound is x cents and the cost to mail the remaining 7 pounds is $7y$ cents, for a total of $x + 7y$ cents. The cost of shipping the packages separately is $2x + 6y$. The cost of shipping them together is $x + 7y$. Since the latter is cheaper, the savings is $(2x + 6y) - (x + 7y)$, which reduces to $x - y$. This is the **answer**.

Alternatively, we can *Pick Numbers and Calculate a Target*, choosing specific values for the per-pound rates x and y. Let $x = 3$ and $y = 2$, so that all the answer choices will be different.

First we have to figure out how much it will cost to mail the packages separately. The cost to ship the 3 pound package will be 3 cents to ship the first pound and 2 cents/pound for the remaining 2

pounds, for a total cost of 7 cents. The cost to ship the 5 pound package will be 3 cents to ship the first pound and 2 cents/pound to ship the remaining 4 pounds, for a total cost of 11 cents. The cost to ship the packages separately is $7 + 11 = 18$ cents.

If the packages are mailed together the total weight is 8 pounds. It will cost 3 cents to mail the first pound and 2 cents/pound to ship the remaining 7 pounds, for a total cost of 17 cents. Therefore, it is cheaper by 1 cent to ship them together. This is our *Target Value*.

Testing each answer choice, we can see that only (A) gives the target value.

(A) $3 - 2 = 1$ **CORRECT**
(B) $2 - 3 = -1$ INCORRECT
(C) 3   INCORRECT
(D) Separately   INCORRECT
(E) Separately   INCORRECT

The correct answer is (A).

PS 128. <u>FDPs</u>: Percents
Difficulty: 600–700   **OG Page:** 170

We are told that an investment doubles approximately every $70/r$ years, where r is the percent interest, compounded annually. Do not worry about where this *Special Formula* comes from. We are simply asked to use it. In fact, although the problem involves compound interest, we should not use the typical compound interest formula, which is unnecessary.

For this particular investment, $r = 8$, so this investment doubles every $70/r = 70/8 = 8.75$ years.

Now, we can use a *Population Chart* to track the growth of the investment.

Time	Investment Amount
now	$5,000
8.75 years from now	$10,000
17.5 years from now	$20,000

Notice that we track two stages of doubling. In 18 years, the initial investment has time to double twice.

When Pat is ready for college 18 years from now, the amount of the investment will be a little more than $20,000. The greatest (and therefore, closest) value among the answer choices is exactly $20,000. This is the **answer**.

Alternatively, we could have rounded 8.75 years right away to 9 years. Of course, there would still be two rounds of doubling.

The correct answer is (A).

PS 129. <u>FDPs</u>: Digits & Decimals
Difficulty: 600–700   **OG Page:** 170

On this problem, which involves both *Decimals* and *Rates,* Cindy's distance of travel (*d*) was 290 miles when rounded to the nearest 10 miles. Thus, her actual distance could have been any value that satisfies the following *Inequality:* $285 \le d < 295$.

Notice that the 285 is included in the range (285 rounds up to 290), whereas the 295 is NOT. 295 rounds up to 300.

If Cindy used 12 gallons of gasoline, rounded to the nearest gallon, then her gallon usage, *g*, must satisfy the following inequality:

$$11.5 \le g < 12.5$$

To find the possible range of values for Cindy's miles per gallon (*mpg*) for the trip, we must take the distance (*d*) and divide by the gallon usage (*g*). Since we are looking for a range, we must find both the smallest and largest possible values for her *mpg*. To *Optimize* the value of *mpg* in both directions, we should consider *Extreme Values* of *d* and *g*.

Since *mpg* = *d*/*g*, the *smallest* value for *mpg* can be found by taking the *smallest d* and dividing by the *largest g*: 285/12.5.

Conversely, the *largest* value for *mpg* can be found by taking the *largest d* and dividing by the *smallest g*: 295/11.5.

If we combine these two findings, the *mpg* must satisfy the following inequality:

$$\frac{285}{12.5} < mpg < \frac{295}{11.5}$$ This is the **answer**.

Note that the endpoints are technically NOT included here because each contains either a value

of *d* (295) or of *g* (12.5) that was not included in the original inequalities. This is consistent with the word *between* in the question. *Between* is used to express an inequality for which the endpoints are NOT included.

The correct answer is (D).

PS 130. <u>EIVs</u>: Inequalities
Difficulty: 600–700   **OG Page:** 170

The number line shows that *x* ranges from −5 to 3, inclusive. We need to choose the algebraic form of an *Absolute Value Inequality* that defines this range.

First, notice that answer choices (A) and (B) list only *x* inside the absolute value bars. If we were to graph these inequalities, the midpoint of the range for each (A) and (B) would be zero. This is because nothing within the equation has shifted the shaded section of the number line.

Within each of the final three answer choices, however, there is either addition or subtraction inside the absolute value bars, after the *x*. In each case, this change would *Shift the Midpoint* of the range from zero. The given range has a midpoint of −1. Thus, we can say that the midpoint has been shifted down one unit from zero. In order to compensate for this change, we will need to add 1 to *x*. Only answer choice (E) shows the proper form: $|x + 1|$. Thus, we know that (E) is the **answer**.

Another approach makes use of the fact that absolute value expressions that define continuous intervals have a common form.

We need to know two values to correctly define the range: the center of the range and the distance each of the endpoints lies from the center. The center of the range is simply the average of the endpoints:

$$\frac{-5+3}{2} = \frac{-2}{2} = -1$$

Both −5 and 3 are 4 units away from the center. We now have what we need to define the interval.

Both endpoints are 4 units away from the center. That means that any point on the interval will be at most 4 units away from the center. So the absolute value of the expression will have to be less than or equal to 4.

$$|\ ?\ | \le 4$$

Now we need to figure out what goes in the absolute value. Imagine what would happen if we put x inside the absolute value:

$$|\ x\ | \le 4$$

This expression would cover the interval −4 to 4, with a center of 0. But we need the center to be −1. We can recenter this expression by adding 1 to x.

$$|x+1| \le 4$$

Now when we plug in −1, we get 0. This should make sense because −1 is the center, and hence 0 units away from the center. Moreover, plugging either −5 or 3 into the equation gives us 4, which makes sense because both endpoints are 4 units away from the center.

One final approach is to *Focus on the End Points* of the given range. Specifically, test −5 and 3 in each of the answer choices. When inserted for x, these numbers should set the two sides of the inequality equal to each other. This only works for the final answer choice. When x equals −5, $|(-5) + 1| = 4$. When x equals 3, $|(3) + 1| = 4$.

Note that answer choice (B) satisfies both end points. However, when we plug in 3 for x in (B), the two sides of the inequality are not equal. This means that 3 is not a proper end point of (B). Instead, the graph for (B) would extend beyond 3, including values that are not defined by the given number line.

The correct answer is (E).

PS 131. FDPs: Percents
Difficulty: 500–600   **OG Page:** 170

In this *Percents* problem, there are currently 500 employees, 15% of whom are women. Thus, there are $(0.15)(500) = 75$ women at the company. If 50 more workers are hired, there will be a total of 550 workers. The question asks how many of the 50

will have to be women in order to raise the percentage of women at the company to 20%.

Since we know that we will have 550 total workers, the goal percentage, 20%, is equivalent to $(0.20)(550) = 110$ women.

We already have 75 women, so we must hire $110 - 75 = 35$ women. This is the **answer**.

If it is helpful, we can use a *Change Table* to keep track of our thinking:

	Old	Change	New
Women	75 (15%)	+35	110 (20%)
Men			
Total	500	+50	550

Alternatively, we can *Name a Variable* and call the number of new women x. Then we can set up the following equation, using the fraction 1/5 as an *Equivalent* of 20%:

$$\frac{75 + x}{550} = 20\% = \frac{1}{5}$$

We can now *Cross-Multiply* and solve for x:

$$375 + 5x = 550$$
$$5x = 175$$
$$x = 35$$

Thus, 35 of the 50 new workers will have to be women in order to increase the percentage of women to 20%.

The correct answer is (E).

PS 132. Word Translations: Statistics
Difficulty: 600–700   **OG Page:** 171

This *Statistics* problem asks us to determine the average value of a subset of numbers, given the averages of the full set and of the other subset of numbers. The best approach is to use the *Average Law* separately on each set and on each subset. The average of a set is given by the sum of the terms, divided by the number of terms:

$$A = \frac{S}{N}$$

Then, we can solve for the sum as *Sum = Average × Number*. Let S_{10} denote the sum of the revenues for all 10 days. Likewise, let S_6 denote the sum of the revenues for the first 6 days and S_4 denote the sum of the revenues for the last 4 days. Using the above relation, we can write:

$$S_{10} = 10 \times \$400 = \$4,000$$
$$S_6 = 6 \times \$360 = \$2,160$$

Now, note that $S_{10} = S_6 + S_4$. Therefore,

$$S_4 = S_{10} - S_6 = \$4,000 - \$2,160 = \$1,840.$$

The desired average of the last 4 days is

$$A = \frac{S_4}{4} = \frac{\$1,840}{4} = \$460.$$

An alternative approach is to use **Weighted Averages**. The first 6 days represent 60% of the total of 10 days, while the last 4 days represent the remaining 40%. These percentages constitute the weights carried by the subset averages in terms of their contribution to the overall average. If we let A stand for the average of the last 4 days, then

$$\$400 = (60\%) \times \$360 + (40\%) \times A$$
$$\$400 = \$216 + 0.4A$$
$$0.4A = \$400 - \$216 = \$184$$
$$A = \$184 / 0.4 = \$460.$$

Finally, we can use the method of **Residuals**. Imagine that on each of the first 6 days, the shop actually makes only $360, but it needs to make $400. Then the shop is short $40 on each of those days. (Each $40 shortfall is the residual.) The total shortfall in the first 6 days is then 6 days × $40 = $240. In the last 4 days, the shop must make $400 every day, plus an extra $240 over the 4 days to make up the shortfall. The extra $240 over 4 days = $240 ÷ 4 = $60 per day, so the shop must make $400 + $60 = $460 per day (on average) over the last 4 days.

The correct answer is (D).

PS 133. FDPs: Digits & Decimals
Difficulty: 500–600   **OG Page:** 171

In this **Digits & Decimals** problem, "Per capita" means "per person." To find the per capita expen-

diture, we need to divide the total expenditure by the total population. That is, we need to calculate 1.2×10^{12} dollars divided by 240 million people. One million is 10^6, so we can use **Powers of Ten** to write the following **Fraction:**

$$\frac{1.2 \times 10^{12}}{240 \times 10^6}$$

Notice that the nonzero portions of the numerator and denominator, 12 and 24, have a special relationship: 24 is 2 × 12. Thus, 12/24 = 1/2. However, we can avoid fractions or decimals (and thereby reduce our potential for error) by noting that 120/24 = 5. Let's therefore manipulate the numerator and denominator using powers of ten to yield 120 and 24. Since $120 = 1.2 \times 10^2$, we take 2 powers of 10 from the 10^{12} part of the numerator to write 120. Likewise, since $240 = 24 \times 10^1$, we convert 240 to 24 by moving 1 power of 10 into the 10^6 part of the denominator.

$$\frac{1.2 \times 10^{12}}{240 \times 10^6} = \frac{1.2 \times 10^2 \times 10^{10}}{24 \times 10^1 \times 10^6} = \frac{120 \times 10^{10}}{24 \times 10^7}$$

Finally, we simplify, using rules for **Dividing Exponents:**

$$\frac{120 \times 10^{10}}{24 \times 10^7} = \frac{120}{24} \times \frac{10^{10}}{10^7} = 5 \times \frac{10^{10}}{10^7}$$
$$= 5 \times 10^3 = 5,000$$

Since the units of the original numbers were dollars and people, the unit of the answer is "dollars per person." In per capita calculations, the "per person" unit is often implied at the end. We simply say that the per capita expenditure is $5,000.

The correct answer is (E).

PS 134. Geometry: Polygons
Difficulty: 500–600   **OG Page:** 171

This **Polygons** problem gives us information about a rectangular window. If the window's length is twice its width, we can **Name a Variable** as follows:

w = the window's width
$2w$ = the window's length

Draw a Picture to visualize the information.

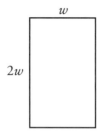

The ***Perimeter*** is the distance around the figure, so we can add the lengths of all four sides:

$$P = w + 2w + w + 2w = 10$$
$$6w = 10$$
$$w = \frac{10}{6} = \frac{5}{3}$$
$$2w = (2)\left(\frac{5}{3}\right) = \frac{10}{3}$$

The window has dimensions by $\frac{5}{3}$ by $\frac{10}{3}$.

The correct answer is (B).

PS 135. <u>Word Translations</u>: Combinatorics
Difficulty: 600–700   **OG Page:** 171

This ***Combinatorics*** problem gives a complicated diagram and asks us to determine the total number of different paths from point X to point Y.

A fast approach makes use of the ***Fundamental Counting Principle*** of Combinatorics.

The total number of paths is equal to the *product* of the number of options at each decision point, or fork in the road.

Start along the path from X until we get to the first fork. There are 2 different paths to choose, so we have 2 options for our first decision.

At the second fork, we also have 2 different options, and at the third and final fork, we have 3 different options. Therefore, the total number of paths is $2 \times 2 \times 3 = 12$. This is the **answer**.

Alternatively, we can count paths by literally ***Drawing Pictures,*** laying out the different paths. One possible path is:

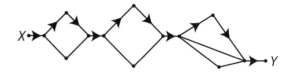

A second possible path is:

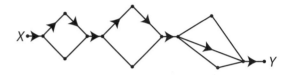

If we continued to draw out all the separate paths, we would find 12 unique paths. However, this approach is time-consuming and prone to error.

The correct answer is (C).

PS 136. <u>EIVs</u>: Formulas & Functions
Difficulty: 500–600   **OG Page:** 171

In this ***Strange Symbol*** problem, which also involves ***Roots,*** we must follow the procedure defined by the symbol while also paying attention to order of operations. We should simplify the expression in parentheses first:

$$5 \odot 45 = \sqrt{5 \times 45} = \sqrt{(5) \times (5 \times 3 \times 3)} = 5 \times 3 = 15$$

Now we can proceed from left to right and evaluate $15 \odot 60$:

$$15 \odot 60 = \sqrt{15 \times 60}$$
$$\sqrt{15 \times 60} = \sqrt{(3 \times 5) \times (2 \times 2 \times 3 \times 5)} = 2 \times 3 \times 5 = 30$$

This is the **answer**.

We have computed the roots using ***Prime Factors***. Of course, we can also use ***Direct Computation:***

$$\sqrt{5 \times 45} = \sqrt{225} = 15$$
$$\sqrt{15 \times 60} = \sqrt{900} = 30$$

The correct answer is (A).

PS 137. <u>Number Properties</u>: Exponents
Difficulty: 500–600   **OG Page:** 171

In this tricky problem, which involves ***Repeating Decimals*** and ***Powers of Ten,*** it is tempting to try to combine $10^4 - 10^2$ into 10^2. However, the only time that we can subtract exponents is when we are dividing exponential terms.

$10^4 - 10^2$ actually yields a rather unruly number:

10,000 − 100 = 9,900

In this case, the better approach is to **Distribute** the repeating decimal term:

$(10^4 - 10^2)(0.001212...)$

$= (10^4)(0.001212...) - (10^2)(0.001212...)$

Multiplication by 10^4 moves the decimal point four places to the right, yielding 12.1212...

Multiplication by 10^2 moves the decimal point two places to the right, yielding 0.121212...

Now we can line up the two terms vertically

12.121212...
− .121212...

We can see that all the digits beyond the decimal point cancel upon subtraction, yielding a difference of 12. This is the **answer**.

Since the answer choices are generally far apart, **Estimation** is also a good way to solve this problem. Since $10^2 = 100$ is so small relative to $10^4 = 10,000$, the left-hand term can be estimated as 10,000. Also, the right-hand term can be estimated as 0.12. With these estimates, the product is $10,000 \times 0.12$, which is exactly 12.

The correct answer is (E).

PS 138. <u>FDPs</u>**:** Fractions
Difficulty: 600–700   **OG Page:** 171

In this **Fractions** problem, we are told about two work shifts: day and night. For each shift, we are also told about the number of workers and the number of boxes per worker. Since there is a lot of information, we need to keep it all organized. A great way to do so is with a **Table,** in which we calculate the number of boxes loaded by each shift.

	# of workers	Boxes per worker	Boxes Loaded
Day Crew			
Night Crew			
Total			

We can make the problem easier by selecting **Smart Numbers**. We are free to do so, since the question provides no actual numbers (such as the number of workers), but only relationships between variables (such as the ratio of one variable to another).

Each night worker loaded 3/4 as many boxes as each day worker. A Smart Number for the number of boxes per worker on the day crew is 4, the denominator of this ratio. In other words, if we simply say that each day worker loads 4 boxes, then each night worker loads (3/4) × 4 = 3 boxes.

The night crew has 4/5 as many workers as the day crew. A Smart Number for the number of day workers is 5, the denominator of this ratio. In other words, if we simply say that there are 5 day workers, then there are (4/5) × 5 = 4 night workers. Now, fill in the chart, multiplying across to get the number of boxes loaded on each shift. Notice that this problem is similar to a **Rate** problem. Here, the rate is boxes *per worker*, so we multiply by *workers* (not by time) to get total boxes.

	# of workers	Boxes per worker	Boxes Loaded
Day Crew	5	4	(5)(4) = 20
Night Crew	(4/5)5 = 4	(3/4)4 = 3	(4)(3) = 12
Total			20 + 12 = 32

The day crew loaded 20 of the 32 boxes, or 20/32 = 5/8 of all the boxes loaded.

The correct answer is (E).

PS 139. <u>FDPs</u>**:** Percents
Difficulty: 500–600   **OG Page:** 172

This **Percents** question provides us with a minimum and maximum tip percentage for a meal that costs $35.50.

The minimum tip percentage is 10%, which would amount to a tip of 0.1 × $35.50 = $3.55. (The easiest way to take 10% of any number is to move the decimal point to the left one place.)

The maximum tip percentage is 15%, which would amount to a tip of 0.15 × $35.50 = $5.33, rounded to the nearest cent. (Another way to take 15% of a number is to take 1.5 times the 10% benchmark, which was found in the last step.)

The total amount paid for the meal must satisfy the following *Inequality:*

$$\$35.50 + \$3.55 < \text{meal} < \$35.50 + \$5.33$$
$$\$39.05 < \text{meal} < \$40.83$$

Looking at the answer choices, we can see that the test writers decided to round this range "outward" to $39 and $41. This rounding is legitimate because a value between $39.05 and $40.84 *must* be between $39 and $41. The range $39 to $41 is the **answer**.

Note that there are limits to rounding an inequality's endpoints. We must round *outward* to ensure that we safely include the original inequality. For instance, if the actual maximum were $40.4 and we rounded *down* to $40, we would be cutting off part of the original inequality.

Alternatively, we could *Estimate* the range. $35.50 plus 10%, or $3.55, is $39.05. An additional 5% on the tip is half of 10%, or half of $3.55, which is less than $2—let's say approximately $1.75. Since the answer choices give $2 ranges, we know that the top end will be $39.05 + $1.75, or just below $41. Thus, $39 to $41 is the only safe range.

The correct answer is (B).

PS 140. Word Translations: Algebraic Translations
Difficulty: 300–500   **OG Page:** 172

This is a standard *Algebraic Translations* problem. We can begin by *Naming Variables* for the two unknown lifts. In this case, let's use f and s to represent the first and second lifts, respectively.

Next, translate the given information to create equations. We are told that the sum of the lifts equals 750 pounds. We can create our first equation as follows:

$$f + s = 750$$

The second equation comes from the second sentence, which states that "twice the weight of his first lift was 300 pounds more than his second lift."

$$2f = s + 300$$

By the way, the phrase "more than" technically places the "+ 300" *after* the s. For addition, this distinction doesn't matter, but if the problem read "300 pounds *less* than his second lift," we would write $s - 300$.

We are asked for f, so we want to make s disappear:

$$f + s = 750$$
$$s = 750 - f$$

$$2f = (750 - f) + 300 \quad \textbf{Substitute } (750 - f) \text{ for}$$
$$\qquad\qquad\qquad\qquad\qquad s \text{ in the second equation.}$$
$$2f = 1050 - f$$
$$3f = 1050$$
$$f = 350$$

The correct answer is (D).

PS 141. Word Translations: Minor Question Types
Difficulty: 500–600   **OG Page:** 172

This *Optimization* question asks us to determine the greatest number of members the club could have, given the fact that the club collected at least $12 from each of its members and took in a total of $599.

In order to *maximize the number* of members, we want to *minimize the amount* that each contributed. Since each contributed at least $12, let's say that each member gave the minimum of $12. We should find a number close to $599 that is a multiple of 12. $600 fits: $12 \times 50 = 600$. However, if the club really had 50 members and each member gave the minimum of $12, then we cannot make the total any smaller than $600. To make $599 a possibility, there must be fewer than 50 members.

Let's try 49 members. If each contributes the minimum, then we have $12 \times 49 = 600 - 12 = \$588$. To reach $599, one or more of the members contributes more than the minimum.

Alternatively, we can also simply divide 599 by 12, yielding $49\frac{11}{12}$. If partial members were allowed, then $49\frac{11}{12}$ members could contribute the minimum of $12 for a total of $599. The key is to know whether to round down or up. Because we cannot have a partial member, we round the fractional result down. The most memberships we can have is 49.

The correct answer is (C).

PS 142. <u>Number Properties</u>: Divisibility & Primes
Difficulty: 600–700   **OG Page:** 172

In this ***Divisibility*** problem, we are asked to find the smallest possible positive integer y such that $3{,}150y$ is the square of an integer, i.e., a perfect square.

The wrong way to do this problem is to test values of y, since that will take a very long time. The key is to focus on ***Prime Factors*** and to be aware that, in any perfect square, all of the prime factors will "pair up." That is, all prime factors will appear an even number of times. For instance, the perfect square 36 contains a pair of 2's and a pair of 3's in its prime factorization.

We must first find the prime factors of 3,150 to determine which ones are "single." Although 3,150 is a rather large number, it is clearly divisible by 10, making the factorization easier:

$$3{,}150 = 315 \times 10 = 63 \times 5 \times 10 = 7 \times 9 \times 5 \times 10$$

Breaking the numbers down further, and ordering the factors from smallest to largest, we finally obtain

$$3{,}150 = 2 \times 3 \times 3 \times 5 \times 5 \times 7$$

Therefore, the ***Prime Box*** of 3,150 contains two 3's and two 5's, but only one each of 2 and 7. We need the prime box of $3{,}150y$ to contain only pairs of primes if $3{,}150y$ is to be a perfect square. Single primes are not allowed. This means that y must provide at least one 2 and one 7. Also, because we are looking for the smallest possible y, those two factors should be all that y provides. This leads to $y = 2 \times 7 = 14$. This is the **answer**.

The figure below illustrates the prime box.

Prime box of $3{,}150y$

3	5	2	7
3	5	2	7

y provides the second 2 and the second 7.

The correct answer is (E).

PS 143. <u>FDPs</u>: Digits & Decimals
Difficulty: 500–600   **OG Page:** 172

This ***Decimals*** question tells us "$[x]$ is the greatest integer less than or equal to x." A good way to rephrase this ***New Function*** is simply, "Round down." That is, if x is a positive integer, leave it alone. If it is positive but not an integer, delete the decimal portion.

So let's compute the function for the positive values first:

$$[3.4] = 3$$
$$[2.7] = 2$$

Be careful with the negative value. When we "round down" any number, we must move to the left on a number line. For negative numbers, this is *not* equivalent to just dropping the decimal portion. -1.6 rounds down to -2, not to -1.

$$[-1.6] = -2$$

Therefore,

$$[-1.6] + [3.4] + [2.7] = -2 + 3 + 2 = 3$$

This is the **answer**.

By the way, if we confuse the new bracket symbol $[x]$ with the absolute value $|x|$, we will choose the wrong answer. We should NOT make the value of $[-1.6]$ positive.

The correct answer is (A).

PS 144. <u>EIVs</u>: Quadratic Equations
Difficulty: 600–700   **OG Page:** 172

In this ***Quadratic Equations*** problem, we are given the equation $\dfrac{4-x}{2+x} = x$ and are asked to find $x^2 + 3x - 4$.

We do not want to solve the equation for x. In fact, when we rearrange the equation with ***Direct Algebra*** into a standard quadratic, it looks like the expression we want to find.

Start by multiplying the entire equation by the denominator of the fraction.

$$(2+x)\left(\frac{4-x}{2+x}\right) = x(2+x)$$

Distribute. $\quad\quad\quad\quad\quad\quad\quad\quad\quad 4 - x = 2x + x^2$

Add x to both sides. $\quad\quad\quad\quad\quad 4 = x^2 + 3x$

Subtract 4 from both sides. $\quad\quad 0 = x^2 + 3x - 4$

The expression that the problem asks for, $x^2 + 3x - 4$, has a value of 0. This is the **answer**.

Remember, we are solving for the value of the expression $x^2 + 3x - 4$, *not* for x itself. Do not factor the quadratic! If we solve for x, we will run into a trap. Both valid solutions for x, −4 and 1, are given as answer choices.

The correct answer is (C).

PS 145. <u>Geometry</u>: Triangles & Diagonals
Difficulty: 600–700 $\quad\quad$ **OG Page:** 172

This **Triangles** problem provides a diagram. Redraw this diagram and label it completely. We are given values for the two parallel sides: 2 and 5 feet, respectively. We are also told that line *AB* is 13 feet.

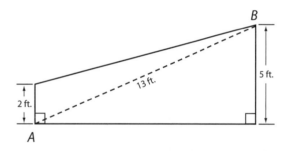

The formula for the **Area of a Trapezoid** is $A = \dfrac{(b_1 + b_2)h}{2}$.

The bases are the two parallel sides, so in this problem, $b_1 = 2$ and $b_2 = 5$. Note that a base is not necessarily the side that is on the ground. In this case, the bases are vertical. The height is the length of a perpendicular line drawn between the two bases. Thus, the bottom of the trapezoid is actually the height.

Line *AB*, which has length 13, represents the hypotenuse of a **Right Triangle**. One leg of this triangle has length 5. The other leg is the unknown bottom of the trapezoid.

This is a common right triangle: the **5–12–13**. Therefore, we know that the missing leg of the tri-

angle is 12. (This length can also be found using the **Pythagorean Theorem**.)

Since this length is also the height of the trapezoid, we now have all the numbers needed in the formula for the trapezoid's area:

$$A = \frac{(2 + 5)12}{2} = 7 \times 6 = 42 \text{ square feet}$$

This is the **answer**.

Alternatively, we can **Split the Figure** into a triangle and a rectangle and then add the two areas.

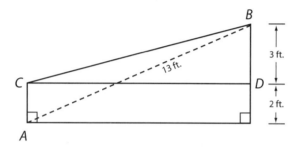

The base of the triangle, *CD*, is 12 (as calculated above) and its height is 3.

$$A = \frac{1}{2}bh = \frac{1}{2}(12)(3) = 18$$

For the rectangle, the length is 12 and the width is 2. $A = lw = 12 \times 2 = 24$.

Area of triangle + Area of rectangle = 18 + 24 = 42.

The correct answer is (C).

PS 146. <u>EIVs</u>: Formulas & Functions
Difficulty: 500–600 $\quad\quad$ **OG Page:** 172

This problem involves a **Recursive Sequence,** in which each item of the sequence is defined in terms of the values of previous items in the sequence.

We are asked for the value of x_3, so substitute 3 for the value of n in the formula:

$$x_3 = 2x_2 - \frac{1}{2}x_1$$

The value of x_3 depends on the values of x_2 and x_1. We are told that $x_1 = 2$, but we do not yet know the value of x_2, so we will have to determine this value first.

$$x_2 = 2x_1 - \frac{1}{2}x_0 = 2(2) - \frac{1}{2}(3) = 4 - 1.5 = 2.5$$

We can now use the values of x_2 and x_1 to determine the value of x_3:

$$x_3 = 2x_2 - \frac{1}{2}x_1 = 2(2.5) - \frac{1}{2}(2) = 5 - 1 = 4$$

This is the **answer**.

A **Sequence Diagram** can keep us organized as we work. Draw blanks for each term, and fill in what we know. We are given two values, x_0 and x_1:

$$\underline{3} \ \ \underline{2} \ \ \underline{\ \ } \ \ \bigcirc$$

These two values give us $x_2 = 2.5$, so we can write:

$$\underline{3} \ \ \underline{2} \ \ \underline{2.5} \ \ \bigcirc$$

Finally, we take the middle values (x_1 and x_2) and produce the target x_3:

$$\underline{3} \ \ \underline{2} \ \ \underline{2.5} \ \ \underline{(4)}.$$

The correct answer is (C).

PS 147. Geometry: Triangles & Diagonals
Difficulty: 500–600   **OG Page:** 173

This **Triangles** problem describes a distance VR but does not actually show this distance in the given diagram. Thus, we should **Draw a Picture** that shows VR. We should also name the point at the right angle. Let's call it Q:

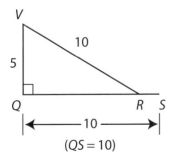

$(QS = 10)$

Knowing that $QS = 10$, we need to find RS to answer the question. We can use the triangle VQR

to find QR and then subtract QR from the overall distance of 10.

VQR is a **Right Triangle**. Since it contains a leg and hypotenuse in a 1 : 2 ratio, it must be a **30–60–90** right triangle.

The sides of a 30–60–90 right triangle fit the following ratio:

Short side: x

Long side: $x\sqrt{3}$
Hypotenuse: $2x$

We know that the short side is 5, so $x = 5$. This means that the long side (QR) must be $5\sqrt{3}$.

Alternatively, we can use the **Pythagorean Theorem** to solve for QR:

$$QR^2 + 5^2 = 10^2$$
$$QR^2 + 25 = 100$$
$$QR^2 = 75$$
$$QR = \sqrt{75} = \sqrt{25}\sqrt{3} = 5\sqrt{3}$$

The last step uses **Roots**. Now that we have found QR, we can subtract it from the total distance QS. We get $RS = QS - QR = 10 - 5\sqrt{3}$.

The correct answer is (A).

PS 148. Word Translations: Statistics
Difficulty: 700–800   **OG Page:** 173

In this difficult **Statistics** problem, we are given an equation with three unknowns (x, y, and k) and certain **Inequality Constraints** on those unknowns (all are positive, and $x < y$). We are asked for a number that *could* be a value of k. Thus, we cannot solve for k as a single number (in fact, the given equation is *already* solved for k).

One approach is to manipulate the equation using **Direct Algebra** so that we can more easily plug in k and examine the consequences for x and y. We want single occurrences of x and y, so multiply through by $x + y$, then set one side equal to zero, grouping the coefficients of x and y.

$$\left(\frac{x}{x+y}\right)(10)+\left(\frac{y}{x+y}\right)(2)=k$$
$$10x+20y=k(x+y)$$
$$10x+20y=kx+ky$$
$$(10-k)x+(20-k)y=0$$

At this point, we can ***Test the Answer Choices*** and compare the results to the given constraints.

(A) $(10-10)x+(20-10)y=0$
$10y=0$
$y=0$

Incorrect: We are told that y is positive.

(B) $(10-12)x+(20-12)y=0$

$-2x+8y=0$
$8y=2x$
$y=\frac{1}{4}x$
$y<x$ (since x is positive)

Incorrect: We are given the constraint that $x<y$.

(C) $(10-15)x+(20-15)y=0$
$-5x+5y=0$
$5y=5x$
$y=x$

Incorrect: We are given the constraint that $x<y$.

(D) $(10-18)x+(20-18)y=0$
$-8x+2y=0$
$2y=8x$
$y=4x$

$y>x$

CORRECT: We are given the constraint that $x<y$.

At this point, we know that 18 is the **answer**. For the sake of completeness, though, we should generally finish testing all the choices.

(E) $(10-30)x+(20-30)y=0$
$-20x-10y=0$
$-10(2x+y)=0$

But since x and y are positive,
$-10(2x+y)=$ neg(pos) = neg

Incorrect: Using ***Positive & Negative Rules,*** we should recognize that it is impossible for a negative multiplied by a positive to equal zero.

Alternatively, we might recognize that the original equation is in the form of a ***Weighted Average***.

$$\left(\frac{x}{x+y}\right)(10)+\left(\frac{y}{x+y}\right)(20)=k$$

$$\underbrace{\frac{\text{Weight}}{\text{Sum of weights}}}(\text{Data point})+\underbrace{\frac{\text{Weight}}{\text{Sum of weights}}}(\text{Data point})$$
= Weighted Average

Thus, the equation has this meaning: k is the weighted average of a set with x number of 10s and y number of 20's, where x and y are the so-called weights. For instance, if $x=2$ and $y=3$, then the set has two 10's and three 20's in it, and the weighted average could be written as follows:

$$\left(\frac{2}{2+3}\right)(10)+\left(\frac{3}{2+3}\right)(20)=k$$
$$=\left(\frac{2}{5}\right)(10)+\left(\frac{3}{5}\right)(20)$$
$$=4+12=16$$

A property of any weighted average is that it will always fall between the two values being averaged: in this case, between 10 and 20. Furthermore, the weighted average of two values will fall closer to whichever value is more heavily weighted. In this question $x<y$, so the 20's are more heavily weighted. (In other words, there are more 20's than 10's in the set being averaged.) Thus, the correct answer must be between 15 and 20. Among the answer choices, 18 is the only number that falls in this range.

Finally, we might try to ***Test Numbers.*** By plugging a series of positive x's and y's, with $x<y$, we would get k's that fall between 15 and 20. We might not be able to produce 18 exactly with our particular test numbers, but we should be able to eliminate more distant answer choices.

The correct answer is (D).

➤**PS 149. <u>Word Translations</u>:** Rates & Work
Difficulty: 700–800 **OG Page:** 173

Because this question involves both **Variable In Choices** and **Average Rates**, we have two ways to plug in numbers: **Pick A Number** for VICs and use a **Smart Number** for average rate questions.

Taking the average rate approach first, we can choose a Smart Number of 100 for the total distance traveled by Francine.

The **Rate–Time–Distance Chart** below represents the rates, times and distances for the two legs of Francine's trip. If we use a Smart Number of 100 for the total distance, the distance covered by the first leg equals x. The distance traveled in the second leg is $100 - x$. Here is the chart so far:

	Rate	Time	Distance
1st Leg	40		x
2nd Leg	60		$100 - x$
TOTAL	?		100

To calculate the times for each leg, we divide the distance by the rate. The total time is the sum of the times of the two legs.

	Rate	Time	Distance
1st Leg	40	$x/40$	x
2nd Leg	60	$(100-x)/60$	$100 - x$
TOTAL	?	$x/40 + (100-x)/60$	100

Finally, we can compute the average rate by dividing the total distance by the total time. This is not the same as taking the simple average of the two rates (which is a mistake).

We can simplify the expression for the total time by finding a common denominator:

$$\frac{x}{40} + \frac{100-x}{60} = \frac{3x}{120} + \frac{200-2x}{120} = \frac{x+200}{120}$$

We can now write the average speed for the trip:

$$\text{Avg speed} = \frac{\text{TOTAL distance}}{\text{TOTAL time}} = \frac{100}{\frac{x+200}{120}}$$
$$= \frac{12000}{x+200}$$

This is the **answer**.

In addition plugging in 100 as the Smart Number for the total distance, we can also **Pick A Number** for x. A value of 40 is a good pick since it can be nicely divided by the rate on the first leg (40 miles per hour).

If $x = 40$, then in the first leg of the trip, Francine traveled 40% of 100 miles, or 40 miles. In the second leg of the trip, she traveled the remaining 60 miles. The time for each leg works out to exactly 1 hour. Fill in the chart:

	Rate	Time	Distance
1st Leg	40	1	40
2nd Leg	60	1	60
TOTAL	?	2	100

The **Target Value** is the average speed = 100/2 = 50.

Testing each answer choice, we can see that only (E) gives the target value when we plug in 40 for the value of x.

(A) $\dfrac{180-40}{2} = 70$ INCORRECT

(B) $\dfrac{40+60}{4} = 25$ INCORRECT

(C) $\dfrac{300-40}{5} = 52$ INCORRECT

(D) $\dfrac{600}{115-40} = 8$ INCORRECT

(E) $\dfrac{12,000}{40+200} = 50$ **CORRECT**

The correct answer is (E).

PS 150. <u>Number Properties</u>: Equations w/ Exponents
Difficulty: 300–500 **OG Page:** 173

In this problem involving **Equations with Exponents,** we are given the value of x. Thus, simply **Plug This Value** into the equation and solve. Straightforward questions like this often carry a high risk for making arithmetic errors. We should first write down the equation as given, to make sure that our transcription is correct:

$$\frac{x^4 - x^3 + x^2}{x-1}$$

Next, plug in (−1) for x in each case. We should add parentheses around the −1 in order to deal with signs correctly. This extra precaution is especially important when we have **Powers of Negative Numbers.** Thus, we now have:

$$\frac{(-1)^4 - (-1)^3 + (-1)^2}{(-1) - 1}$$

From here, we can solve with **Direct Computation.** Let's simplify each component individually:

$$\frac{(1) - (-1) + (1)}{(-1) - 1}$$

$$\frac{1 + 1 + 1}{-1 - 1}$$

$$\frac{3}{-2} = -\frac{3}{2}$$

The correct answer is (A).

PS 151. FDPs: Successive Percents & Percent Change
Difficulty: 500–600   **OG Page:** 173

In this **Successive Percents** problem, we want the lowest possible price. So we should first apply the greatest possible discount of 40% and then take another 25% off from that new price.

First, find 40% of 16. We can use **Decimal Equivalents** of percents. 40% = 0.4, so (0.4)(16) = 6.40. Therefore, the regular discounted price will be $16.00 − $6.40 = $9.60.

Now we need to find 25% of 9.60. 25% = 0.25, so (0.25)(9.60) = 2.40. Therefore, the final price will be $9.60 − $2.40 = $7.20. This is the **answer**.

Alternatively, we could do the following calculation. Taking a 40% discount is equivalent to taking 60% of the price. That is, we can multiply the price by 6/10, or by 3/5 using **Fraction Equivalents** of percents. Likewise, taking a 25% discount is equivalent to taking 75% of the price. That is, we can multiply by 75/100, or 3/4. These multiplications work in succession. Thus, we can figure out the final price as follows.

3/5 of 3/4 of $16 =

$$\left(\frac{3}{5}\right)\left(\frac{3}{4}\right)(16) = \left(\frac{3}{5}\right)\left(\frac{3}{1}\right)(4) = \frac{36}{5} = 7.2 = \$7.20$$

Choice (A) here is meant to be a trap. $5.60 is what we would get if we subtracted 25% of the *original* price from the discounted price.

The correct answer is (B).

PS 152. Geometry: Triangles & Diagonals
Difficulty: 600–700   **OG Page:** 174

In this **Triangles** problem, the shaded portion of the figure is a **Right Triangle** with legs x and y and hypotenuse z. Given the area of this triangle and a further relation between the lengths of the legs, we are asked for the length of the hypotenuse. First, we should note that if we want to compute the **Area of a Right Triangle,** we can use the perpendicular legs of the triangle as a base and a altitude (or height). Therefore, we can write

$$A = \frac{1}{2}bh = \frac{1}{2}xy = 24$$

or

$$xy = 48$$

Furthermore, we are given the relation

$$x = y + 2$$

Substituting this expression for x into the equation above yields a **Quadratic Equation:**

$$y(y + 2) = 48$$
$$y^2 + 2y - 48 = 0$$

Factor the quadratic expression:

$$(y + 8)(y - 6) = 0$$

The two roots of the quadratic equation are $y = -8$ and $y = 6$ However, the first of these is not a valid length for the side of a triangle. Lengths are not negative. Therefore, $y = 6$ and $x = 6 + 2 = 8$.

Notice that in factoring, we are asking "what two numbers multiply together to yield −48 and add up to 2?" In fact, we can directly solve $xy = 48$ and $x = y + 2$ by simply asking "what two numbers multiply together to 48 and differ by 2?" A quick check of the factors of 48 yields 6 and 8.

At this point, the easiest way to determine the value of z is to recognize that 6 and 8 are the legs of a **3–4–5** right triangle scaled up by a factor of 2. Therefore, z is also scaled up by the same factor. $z = 2 \times 5 = 10$. This is the **answer**.

Alternatively, we may solve for z using the *Pythagorean Theorem*:

$$z^2 = x^2 + y^2 = 64 + 36 = 100$$
$$z = 10$$

The correct answer is (E).

PS 153. <u>**Word Translations:**</u> Algebraic Translations
Difficulty: 500–600   **OG Page:** 174

This ***Algebraic Translations*** question asks us to solve a system of equations. If Jack is now 14 years older than Bill, then we can ***Name Variables*** and represent this relationship as follows:

$$J = B + 14 \quad \text{OR} \quad J - 14 = B$$

Note that J and B represent the current ages of Jack and Bill, respectively. The next equation states the relationship between the two ages "in ten years." Keep in mind that both people need to age ten years: thus, we need to write $J + 10$ and $B + 10$ to represent Jack's and Bill's future ages.

In 10 years, Jack will be twice as old as Bill:

$$(J + 10) = 2(B + 10)$$
$$J + 10 = 2B + 20$$

Since we want Jack's age in 5 years, we can ***substitute*** for B. To save time on systems of equations, we substitute for the variable that is NOT the one we ultimately want.

$$J + 10 = 2(J - 14) + 20$$
$$J + 10 = 2J - 28 + 20$$
$$J + 10 = 2J - 8$$
$$18 = J$$

Add 5 to get $18 + 5 = 23$, Jack's age in 5 years.

This is the **answer.**

Alternatively, we can organize our thinking in an ***Age Chart***. Fill in the chart using the first relationship between Jack's and Bill's age (Jack is now 14 years older) and moving forward in time within each row by adding 5 or 10 years. In this way, we can avoid using more than one variable.

	Now	*+ 5 yrs*	*+ 10 yrs*
Jack	J	$J + 5 = ?$	$J + 10$
Bill	$J - 14$		$J - 14 + 10$ $= J - 4$

Finally, write the second relationship outside the chart and solve. The algebra is essentially the same as above.

In 10 years, Jack will be twice as old as Bill:

$$J + 10 = 2(J - 4) = 2J - 8$$
$$18 = J$$

Again, we must remember to add 5 years to Jack's current age to find his age in 5 years' time. Jack will be $18 + 5 = 23$.

The correct answer is (D).

PS 154. <u>**Word Translations:**</u> Rates & Work
Difficulty: 500–600   **OG Page:** 174

We are told in this ***Rates & Work*** problem that it takes 8 hours to fill $\frac{3}{5}$ of a pool. We are asked to find how long it takes to fill the remaining $\frac{2}{5}$ of the pool at the same rate. In general, with Work problems, we use the ***Rate-Time-Work Formula***, which can be written this way:

$$\text{Rate} = \frac{\text{Work}}{\text{Time}}$$

However, this formula is unnecessary in this situation. The rate at which the pool is being filled is constant, so we can just set up a ***Ratio*** to solve for the remaining time. The time it took to fill 3/5 of the pool is ***Directly Proportional*** to the time it will take to fill the remaining 2/5 of the pool.

Naming a Variable, we can let t be the time it takes to fill 2/5 of the pool. Then we set up a ***Proportion:***

$$\frac{8}{t} = \frac{3/5}{2/5} \qquad \text{Now solve for } t.$$
$$\frac{8}{t} = \frac{3}{5} \times \frac{5}{2}$$
$$\frac{8}{t} = \frac{3}{2}$$
$$16 = 3t$$

$$\frac{16}{3} = t$$

$$t = 5\frac{1}{3} \text{ hours.}$$

$\frac{1}{3}$ of an hour is 20 minutes. The time it takes to fill the remaining volume of the pool is 5 hours 20 minutes.

The correct answer is (B).

PS 155. EIVs: Quadratic Equations
Difficulty: 600–700   **OG Page:** 174

This **Quadratic Equations** problem specifies a series of mathematical operations to perform on the variable x. The words can be **Algebraically Translated** into an equation containing the variable x.

The first sentence can be translated as: $\frac{2x}{3}$

The second sentence can be translated as: $\sqrt{\frac{2x}{3}} = x$

Notice the phrase "*positive* square root." This may seem redundant at first, since the GMAT almost never refers to negative square roots, and the square root symbol ($\sqrt{}$) always means the positive square root. However, the modifier is actually a subtle clue that zero is not an option.

Now we can solve the equation for x.

$$\sqrt{\frac{2x}{3}} = x$$

$$\frac{2x}{3} = x^2$$

$$2x = 3x^2$$

$$0 = 3x^2 - 2x$$

$$0 = x(3x - 2)$$

$$x = 0 \text{ or } x = 2/3$$

Because the problem tells us that x is positive, and the square root is positive, x cannot be zero. Therefore, x equals 2/3. This is the **answer**.

Alternatively, we can use **Algebraic Reasoning** to solve the problem more quickly once we reached

$\frac{2x}{3} = x^2$. Since $x \neq 0$, we can divide by x to get

$$\frac{2}{3} = x.$$

The correct answer is (D).

PS 156. FDPs: Percents
Difficulty: 500–600   **OG Page:** 174

In this **Percents** problem, we are first told that a tank contains 10,000 gallons of a solution that is 5 percent sodium chloride. We can use the **Percent Formula** to determine how much sodium chloride is present in the tank. To fill in the formula, we can **Name a Variable** and call this unknown amount of sodium chloride x.

$$\frac{\text{PART}}{\text{WHOLE}} = \frac{\text{PERCENT}}{100}$$

$$\frac{x}{10,000} = \frac{5}{100}$$

$$100x = 50,000$$
$$x = 500$$

There are 500 gallons of sodium chloride in the tank.

2,500 gallons of water evaporate from the tank, leaving us with 7,500 gallons of total solution. Since only water evaporated, the amount of sodium chloride has not changed and is still 500 gallons. We are asked what percent of the remaining solution is sodium chloride, or "500 is what percent of 7,500?" Again, we can use the percent formula and name another variable, letting p equal the unknown percentage:

$$\frac{500}{7,500} = \frac{p}{100}$$

$$50,000 = 7,500p$$
$$50,000/7,500 = p$$
$$500/75 = p$$
$$20/3 = p$$

$$p = 6\frac{2}{3} \text{ or } 6.67\%$$

The correct answer is (D).

➤**PS 157. <u>Number Properties</u>:** Consecutive Integers
  Difficulty: 600–700   **OG Page:** 174

The easiest way to solve this *Consecutive Integers* problem is to ignore the given formula entirely and to use the *Average Formula:*

(Average)(Number of Terms) = Sum.

The problem asks for the sum of 100 + 102 + 104 + ... + 298 + 300. Since this is an *Evenly Spaced Set,* the average of *all* of the numbers is the same as the average of the first and last numbers, or $\frac{100+300}{2}=200$. To find *how many* numbers are in the set, note that 100 is the 50th even integer and that 300 is the 150th even integer. We are counting from the 50th even integer through the 150th even integer. The result is the same if we *Count Consecutive Integers* from 50 through 150. Therefore, we have 150 − 50 + 1 = 101 integers. The sum of the set is therefore

(200)(101) = 20,200   This is the **answer**.

Since the answer choices are so far apart, we can also simply *Estimate* that there are 100 integers in the series, giving a sum of approximately (200)(100) = 20,000. From this approximation, it is still clear that (B) is the correct answer.

Notice that 301 − 99 = 202. The even integers between 99 and 301 do NOT include the endpoints given. The interval between 100 and 300 is 200. Dividing by 2 (to count only the even integers) and "adding 1 before we're done," we get 101 even integers in the interval.

The correct answer is (B).

PS 158. <u>EIVs</u>: VICs
  Difficulty: 700–800   **OG Page:** 174

We are given information about men and women on a committee, as well as changes to the membership of that committee. We can organize the variables in a *Change Table:*

	Before	*After ("enlarged committee")*
Men	m	$m + 2$
Women	w	$w + 3$
Total	$m + w$	$m + w + 5$

If we randomly select one person from the committee *after members are added* (i.e., the right column of our chart), the ***Probability*** of selecting a woman is $\frac{\#\text{of women}}{\text{total \# of people}} = \frac{w+3}{m+w+5}$.

This is the **answer**.

EVERY other answer choice is a trap, in which the numerators and denominators appear somewhere in the chart or (in the case of $w + m + 3$) include the incorrect sum of expressions from the chart. As we set up the probability fraction, we have to use the expressions representing the "After" situation (after members are added), not the "Before" situation.

The correct answer is (E).

PS 159. <u>Number Properties</u>: Divisibility & Primes
  Difficulty: 500–600   **OG Page:** 175

This *Divisibility & Primes* question asks how many unique prime factors between 1 and 100 the number 7,150 has. We can break 7,150 down into primes using *Prime Factorization*. To expedite the process, start with the largest recognizable factor (in this case, start with 10). 7,150 = 715 × 10.

Continuing with the 715, we can see that 715 is divisible by 5. We can find that 715/5 = 143, so 7,150 = 143 × 5 × 10.

The final, tricky step in this prime factorization involves factoring 143. Using the *Rules of Divisibility by Certain Integers*, we can see that there is no prime factor less than or equal to 10 that is a factor of 143. 143 is, however, divisible by 11, which goes in 13 times. We have to be sure to check every prime up to the square root of the number 143, which is just under 12.

By the way, an abridged version of a divisibility rule for 11 holds that for all *three-digit integers*, if the units digit and the hundreds digit sum to the tens digit, the number is divisible by 11 (e.g., in the case of 143, 3 + 1 = 4, so 11 goes into 143).

We now have the full prime factor tree of 7,150:

7150

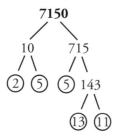

We can express 7,150 as the product of primes: $7{,}150 = 2 \times 5^2 \times 11 \times 13$.

Thus 7,150 has four unique prime factors—2, 5, 11 and 13—all of which are between 1 and 100. This is the **answer**.

Note that if we had mistakenly thought 143 was a prime, we would have identified only two unique primes between 1 and 100.

The correct answer is (D).

PS 160. Geometry: Circles & Cylinders
Difficulty: 500–600   **OG Page:** 175

In order to find the area of the ***Circular*** path, we must find the area of the flowerbed and subtract it from the area of the larger circle, which includes the flowerbed and the path. We ***Subtract Areas*** to find the area of a figure, such as the circular path, that represents the difference between two simpler shapes (the two circles shown).

After re-creating the drawing, we must insert the information that the path is 3 feet wide. We show this as follows:

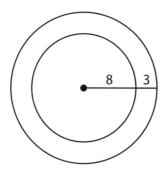

The ***Area of a Circle*** is simply πr^2. Note that the radius of the larger circle is $8 + 3$, or 11. Thus, we can write out our equation as follows:

$$\text{Area}_{\text{path}} = \text{Area}_{\text{large circle}} - \text{Area}_{\text{small circle}}$$

$$\text{Area}_{\text{path}} = \pi(11)^2 - \pi(8)^2$$

$$\text{Area}_{\text{path}} = 121\pi - 64\pi$$

$$\text{Area}_{\text{path}} = 57\pi$$

The correct answer is (D).

PS 161. EIVs: Inequalities
Difficulty: 600–700   **OG Page:** 175

We can solve this ***Inequalities*** problem using ***Direct Algebra.*** First, we know that $\sqrt{n} > 25$. We want to find a possible value of $\dfrac{n}{25}$, so we need to manipulate the given inequality so that we get $\dfrac{n}{25}$ on one side. To go from $\sqrt{n}$ to $\dfrac{n}{25}$, we should first square the inequality, then divide by 25.

If both sides of an inequality are positive, we are allowed to square it, because we do not have to worry about negative values.

$$\sqrt{n} > 25$$
$$(\sqrt{n})^2 > 25^2$$
$$n > 25^2$$

We should know that 25^2 is 625, but since we are not finished with the problem, we can avoid needless computation. Now we divide both sides by 25:

$$\frac{n}{25} > \frac{25^2}{25}$$
$$\frac{n}{25} > 25$$

Note that $25^2/25$ equals 25 again.

As a result, our target expression $\dfrac{n}{25}$ must be greater than 25. The only choice that is greater than 25 is 26. This is the **answer**.

Alternatively, we can plug an ***Extreme Value*** into the expression we are looking for, $\dfrac{n}{25}$. As soon as we write $n > 25^2$, we know that n is greater than 25^2. Thus, we can plug the phrase "greater than 25^2" into $\dfrac{n}{25}$:

$$\frac{n}{25} = \frac{\text{greater than } 25^2}{25}$$

$$= \text{greater than } \frac{25^2}{25}$$

$$= \text{greater than } 25$$

Thus, $\frac{n}{25}$ is greater than 25, and the only possibility among the answer choices is 26.

The correct answer is (E).

PS 162. <u>Word Translations</u>: Ratios
Difficulty: 600–700   **OG Page:** 175

In this **Ratios** problem, we are given the **Multiple Ratio** 6 : 5 : 2, which indicates the relative weight of apples, peaches and grapes in a fruit salad. The ratio itself does not indicate the absolute quantity of any of the ingredients, but rather only the relative quantities. Therefore, we should introduce an **Unknown Multiplier** x in order to obtain the actual quantities. With this definition, the actual weights of apples, peaches and grapes in the salad are $6x$, $5x$, and $2x$, respectively. The total weight of the salad is given by

$$W = 6x + 5x + 2x = 13x = 39$$

We can now solve for x:

$$x = 3$$

The weight of the apples is $6x = 18$ pounds, and the weight of the grapes is $2x = 6$ pounds. Therefore, there are $18 - 6 = 12$ more pounds of apples than grapes.

The correct answer is (B).

PS 163. <u>EIVs</u>: VICs
Difficulty: 700–800   **OG Page:** 175

The key to solving this **Variables In Choices** problem is to translate the lengthy story into a single equation. We will take the **Direct Algebra** route in our first solution.

The first task is to **Name Variables.** Since "save" and "spend" both begin with the same letter, we can avoid confusion by using "v" for "amount saved." We can then define "amount spent" in terms of v:

I = income
v = amount saved
$I - v$ = amount spent

We are asked what fraction of his income Henry will need to save this year. Therefore, in the end we want the ratio of savings to income this year: $\frac{v}{I}$.

We can write down "$\frac{v}{I} = ?$" to remind ourselves what we are ultimately solving for.

Next year, Henry will have an amount to spend equal to the amount he saved multiplied by $(1 + r)$. Thus, the amount he will have to spend next year can be written as $v(1 + r)$.

We are also told that this amount will be equal to one-half of the amount he spends this year (which we have already defined as $I - v$). Therefore, we can write

$$v(1 + r) = \tfrac{1}{2}(I - v)$$

Because there are two variables, we are not looking for a numerical solution. Instead, manipulate the equation to yield v/I:

$$2v(1 + r) = I - v$$
$$2v + 2vr = I - v$$
$$3v + 2vr = I$$
$$v(3 + 2r) = I$$
$$3 + 2r = \frac{I}{v}$$

Since we want $\frac{v}{I}$, simply "flip" both sides of the equation (that is, take the reciprocal of both sides):

$$\frac{v}{I} = \frac{1}{3 + 2r} \qquad \text{This is the **answer**.}$$

Alternatively, we can **Pick Numbers and Calculate a Target.** Because the given condition is so complicated, we need to choose numbers carefully to fit the condition. Notice, also, that if we pick $r = 0$ or $r = 1$ as very simple test numbers, more than one answer choice gives us the same result.

First, let's choose $60 as Henry's income this year, since 60 is divisible by many small integers (2, 3, 4, 5, and 6). Now, rather than choose a value of r and try to find the corresponding amount saved (by trial and error), we should choose an amount saved and compute the corresponding value of *r*. This will save us time.

Imagine that Henry saves $30 (1/2 his income) and spends $30. Next year, he will have $30 (1 + *r*) available to spend. We want this amount to equal half the amount he spends this year, or $30 × 1/2 = $15. Set the two amounts equal and solve for *r*, as follows:

$$30(1 + r) = 15$$
$$1 + r = 1/2$$
$$r = -1/2$$

In real life, we expect a positive *r* for money we save, but since the condition forces Henry's money to shrink in this case, we get a negative *r*. Do not let this result slow you down. Now, compute the **Target Number** and test each answer choice, using the value of *r* we found:

Target = $30 saved / $60 income = 1/2

(A) $\dfrac{1}{r+2} = \dfrac{1}{-\frac{1}{2}+2} = \dfrac{1}{1\frac{1}{2}} = \dfrac{1}{\frac{3}{2}} = \dfrac{2}{3}$; INCORRECT

(B) $\dfrac{1}{2r+2} = \dfrac{1}{2(-\frac{1}{2})+2} = \dfrac{1}{-1+2} = \dfrac{1}{1} = 1$; INCORRECT

(C) $\dfrac{1}{3r+2} = \dfrac{1}{3(-\frac{1}{2})+2} = \dfrac{1}{-\frac{3}{2}+2} = \dfrac{1}{\frac{1}{2}} = 2$; INCORRECT

(D) $\dfrac{1}{r+3} = \dfrac{1}{-\frac{1}{2}+3} = \dfrac{1}{2\frac{1}{2}} = \dfrac{1}{\frac{5}{2}} = \dfrac{2}{5}$; INCORRECT

(E) $\dfrac{1}{2r+3} = \dfrac{1}{2(-\frac{1}{2})+3} = \dfrac{1}{-1+3} = \dfrac{1}{2}$; **CORRECT**

The correct answer is (E).

PS 164. Number Properties: Exponents
Difficulty: 500–600   **OG Page:** 175

This **Exponents** problem tells us $m^{-1} = -\dfrac{1}{3}$ and asks us to find the value of m^{-2}.

One way to solve this problem is to first find the value of *m* and then evaluate m^{-2}. We know that a **Negative Exponent** is just the reciprocal:

$$x^{-1} = \dfrac{1}{x}$$

If $m^{-1} = -\dfrac{1}{3}$, then $m = -3$. Now, we can evaluate m^{-2}:

$$m^{-2} = (-3)^{-2} = \left(-\dfrac{1}{3}\right)^2 = \dfrac{1}{9}$$

This is the **answer**.

Another approach to this problem is to use the following **Rule of Multiplying Exponents**:

$$(a^x)^y = a^{xy}$$

If we notice that $m^{-2} = (m^{-1})^2$, then we can answer the question simply by squaring both sides of the given equation:

$$m^{-1} = -\dfrac{1}{3}$$
$$(m^{-1})^2 = \left(-\dfrac{1}{3}\right)^2$$
$$m^{-2} = \dfrac{1}{9}$$

The correct answer is (D).

PS 165. EIVs: VICs
Difficulty: 600–700   **OG Page:** 176

This **Variables In Choices** problem specifies that Lois has *x* dollars more than Jim has and that they have a total of *y* dollars together. We can determine the number of dollars Jim has using the **Direct Algebra** method.

First, we translate the word problem into algebra. We can **Name Variables** to represent Lois's and Jim's amounts of money. Let's use *L* and *J*. Then we can relate those variables.

$$L = J + x$$
$$L + J = y$$
$$J = ?$$

The answer choices show only *x* and *y*, so we want to express *J* in terms of only those two variables. To do so, we will also need to get rid of *L*. We can manipulate the equations and add them together so that we cancel out *L*. Begin by isolating *J* in each equation.

$$J = L - x$$
$$J = -L + y$$

Now we can add the equations and solve for *J*.

$$J = L - x$$
$$\underline{J = -L + y}$$
$$2J = y - x \quad \rightarrow \quad J = \frac{y - x}{2}$$

This is the **answer**.

Alternatively, we can ***Pick Numbers and Calculate a Target***. Pick easy numbers and remember to follow any constraints given in the problem.

If $L = 10$ and $J = 6$, then Lois has $x = 4$ more dollars than Jim has, and together they have $y = 16$ dollars. Since we are asked to solve for *J*, we want an answer choice that equals 6, the number we chose, given that $x = 4$ and $y = 16$.

(A) $\frac{y - x}{2} = \frac{16 - 4}{2} = \frac{12}{2} = 6$ **CORRECT**

(B) $y - \frac{x}{2} = 16 - \frac{4}{2} = 16 - 2 = 14$ INCORRECT

(C) $\frac{y}{2} - x = \frac{16}{2} - 4 = 8 - 4 = 4$ INCORRECT

(D) $2y - x = 2(16) - 4 =$ too big   INCORRECT

(E) $y - 2x = 16 - 2(4) = 16 - 8 = 8$ INCORRECT

The correct answer is (A).

PS 166. <u>FDPs</u>: Percents
Difficulty: 600–700   **OG Page:** 176

This ***Algebraic Translations*** problem involves several calculations. We can find the solution efficiently by organizing the information in a ***Table*** and setting up equations.

The rows correspond to the first 100 games, the remaining games, and the total number of games. The columns are the "Win %," "Games Played," and "Games Won" (with Games Won = Win % × Games Played). Just as with an Rate-Time-Distance Table, the final column is equal to the product of the first two.

	Win %	Games Played	Games Won
First 100 games			
Remaining games			
Total			

The first step is to input the information provided in the problem. We know all of the winning percentages, and we know that there were 100 games originally played. Let's ***Name a Variable*** and call the number of remaining games *n*.

Fill in the table, multiplying across to get an expression or number for Games Won in each row.

	Win %	Games Played	Games Won
First 100 games	0.80	100	0.80(100) = 80
Remaining games	0.50	*n*	0.50*n*
Total	0.70	100 + *n*	0.70(100 + *n*)

Now we use the "Games Won" column to create an equation. The games won in the first two rows must add up to total games won in the third row.

$$80 + 0.50n = 0.70(100 + n)$$
$$80 + 0.50n = 70 + 0.70n$$
$$10 = 0.20n$$
$$50 = n$$

Since $n = 50$, the number of remaining games was 50. The problem asks for the total number of games played, which is $100 + n$.

$100 + 50 = 150$ total games played.

The correct answer is (D).

PS 167. <u>Word Translations</u>: Overlapping Sets
Difficulty: 500–600   **OG Page:** 176

This standard ***Overlapping Sets*** problem presents two binary splits: four years of experience vs. less than four years of experience, and degree vs. no degree. Construct a ***Double-Set Matrix*** according to these criteria, filling in the information from the prompt and indicating the desired quantity with a question mark:

	At Least 4 Yrs	Less than 4 Yrs	Total
Degree	?		18
No Degree		3	
Total	14		30

Remembering that the first two elements of every row and column must add to the third element, we can fill in the rest of the chart:

	At Least 4 Yrs	Less than 4 Yrs	Total
Degree	**5**	*13*	18
No Degree	*9*	3	*12*
Total	14	*16*	30

There are 5 candidates with at least four years of experience and a degree.

The correct answer is (E).

PS 168. <u>EIVs</u>: Basic Equations
Difficulty: 500–600 **OG Page:** 176

To solve this **Basic Equations** problem, we will use **Direct Algebra.** We can tackle the algebra in several ways. For instance, we can cancel the denominators by multiplying both sides by x:

$$1 + \frac{1}{x} = 2 - \frac{2}{x}$$

$$\left(1 + \frac{1}{x} = 2 - \frac{2}{x}\right)x$$

$$x + 1 = 2x - 2$$

$$3 = x \qquad \text{This is the } \textbf{answer.}$$

Alternatively, we could subtract 1 from each side and add $2/x$ to each side. Note that $1/x$ and $2/x$ have the same denominator, so they add up to $3/x$.

$$1 + \frac{1}{x} = 2 - \frac{2}{x}$$

$$\frac{1}{x} = 1 - \frac{2}{x}$$

$$\frac{3}{x} = 1$$

$$3 = x$$

We could also use x as a common denominator. This approach requires a little more fraction work:

$$1 + \frac{1}{x} = 2 - \frac{2}{x}$$

$$\frac{x}{x} + \frac{1}{x} = \frac{2x}{x} - \frac{2}{x}$$

$$\frac{x + 1}{x} = \frac{2x - 2}{x}$$

$$x + 1 = 2x - 2$$

$$3 = x$$

The correct answer is (E).

PS 169. <u>Word Translations</u>: Ratios
Difficulty: 500–600 **OG Page:** 176

The first piece of information gives the **Ratio** of the number of vehicle accidents to the number of vehicles that traveled on a certain highway last year. This ratio can be used to calculate the actual number of accidents since we are given the actual number of vehicles that traveled on that highway. We can set up a proportion to do so:

$$\frac{96 \text{ accidents}}{100 \text{ million vehicles}} = \frac{x}{3 \text{ billion vehicles}}$$

We can simplify the calculations by using **Powers of 10.** 100 million = 100,000,000 = 10^8. 1 billion = 1,000,000,000 = 10^9.

$$\frac{96}{10^8} = \frac{x}{3 \times 10^9}$$

$$96(3 \times 10^9) = (10^8)x$$

$$\frac{96(3 \times 10^9)}{10^8} = x$$

$$96(3 \times 10) = x$$

$$2880 = x \qquad \text{This is the } \textbf{answer.}$$

Alternatively, we can solve this problem using **Mental Calculation.** 1 billion is ten times 100 million, so the number of accidents for 1 billion motorists would be $96 \times 10 = 960$. The number of accidents then for 3 billion motorists would be $3 \times 960 = 2,880$.

The correct answer is (C).

PS 170. <u>Word Translations</u>: Overlapping Sets
Difficulty: 600–700   **OG Page:** 176

This ***Overlapping Sets*** problem calls for a ***Double-Set Matrix***. We recognize this problem type from the outset, since it presents two criteria for the group, each of which splits the group in two. In this case, we have those who passed the test or did not and those who took the course or did not.

Begin by creating the Double-Set Matrix. It does not matter which yes/no option is on top and which is on the side.

	Passed test	*Did not*	*Total*
Took course			
Did not			
Total			

Next, insert the information from the problem carefully, keeping an eye out for internal algebra. Because real numbers are given, we cannot call the total 100. In fact, we are solving for this total. So we should ***Name a Variable*** and call the total t. "Thirty percent of the members" will be shown as $0.3t$. We can fill in the "Did Not Pass" column as well.

	Passed test	*Did not*	*Total*
Took course		12	
Did not		30	
Total	$0.3t$	42	$t = ?$

We can create an equation by summing across the bottom row. Then we solve algebraically.

$$0.3t + 42 = t$$
$$42 = 0.7t$$
$$42 = \frac{7}{10}t$$
$$42 \left(\frac{10}{7}\right) = t$$
$$60 = t$$

The correct answer is (A).

PS 171. <u>EIVs</u>: Formulas & Functions
Difficulty: 600–700   **OG Page:** 176

The nth term of the given ***Sequence*** is $n + 2^{n-1}$, in which n represents that term's placement in the sequence. We are asked for the difference between the 6th and the 5th terms of the sequence. Because these terms are not numbered too high, the ***Exponents*** that we have to deal with are small.

Thus, the best way to solve this problem is to find the needed terms by ***Direct Computation***, then subtract.

For the fifth term, $n = 5$. The term itself is $5 + 2^{5-1}$ $= 5 + 2^4 = 5 + 16 = 21$.

For the sixth term, $n = 6$. The term itself would be $6 + 2^{6-1} = 6 + 2^5 = 6 + 32 = 38$.

The question is asking for the difference between 38 and 21. $38 - 21 = 17$. This is the **answer**.

Often, in sequence problems, we extrapolate a pattern. However, the GMAT has set a trap pattern in this problem. The difference between the first and second terms is 2. The difference between the second and third terms is 3. If we thought that the differences simply grow with the integers 2, 3, 4, 5, 6, etc., then our answer would be 6 (choice C), which is incorrect.

The correct answer is (E).

PS 172. <u>EIVs</u>: Equations with Exponents
Difficulty: 600–700   **OG Page:** 176

In this ***Quadratic Equation,*** both the left side and the right side are perfect squares. Therefore, the simplest solution method is to ***Take the Square Root*** of both sides. We should remember that there will be two valid solutions, one positive and the other negative. This approach yields:

$$x - 1 = \pm\sqrt{400} = \pm 20$$

Positive solution: $x - 1 = 20$, in which case $x = 21$. Negative solution: $x - 1 = -20$, in which case $x = -19$.

The question asks not for x itself, but for $x - 5$. The positive solution, $x = 21$, leads to $21 - 5 = 16$. This number is not among the available choices.

However, the negative solution $x = -19$ leads to $-19 - 5 = -24$. This is the **answer**.

Note that the negative solution is what leads to the correct answer here. The GMAT knows that we often forget about this solution. When we unsquare both sides of an equation, we must remember to **Test the Negative Possibility.** After all, unsquaring $y^2 = 9$ yields two possibilities: $y = 3$ and $y = -3$.

An alternative approach for finding x is to multiply out the left side, collect all terms on that side, and then **Factor** the resulting quadratic. Indeed, if the given equation had not involved perfect squares, this approach would have been the only option. In this case, however, it requires cumbersome arithmetic, since we have to factor 399 into two numbers that differ by 2. We might think to try 21 and 19, since they are close to 20 (the square root of 400), but these numbers are much clearer in hindsight. The details are shown below for the sake of completeness:

$$(x-1)^2 = x^2 - 2x + 1 = 400$$
$$x^2 - 2x - 399 = 0$$
$$(x-21)(x+19) = 0$$

The correct answer is (C).

PS 173. EIVs: Inequalities
Difficulty: 500–600 **OG Page:** 176

In this **Inequalities** problem, we need to find the range of all values for which $1 - x^2 \geq 0$. First, simply add x^2 to both sides:

$$1 \geq x^2$$

If we prefer, we can flip the inequality around and write $x^2 \leq 1$.

Now we can make use of **Number Line Awareness.** Numbers whose squares are less than 1 are positive or negative proper fractions, and the numbers whose squares are actually equal to 1 are -1 and 1. Thus, the numbers we want are between -1 and 1, inclusive. We can write this range as a **Compound Inequality**:

$$-1 \leq x \leq 1 \quad \text{This is the \textbf{answer}.}$$

Another method is to **Test Values** that are inside or outside the ranges presented in the answer choices. For instance, we can try 2. Since 2 doesn't work (because 2^2 is NOT ≤ 1), we can eliminate answer choices A and D, which allow 2.

Next, we can try -2. It also does not work, so we can eliminate B, which allows -2.

Only C and E are left. Pick a value allowed by one of the answer choices but not by the other. For example, try $-1/2$. Since $(-1/2)^2 = 1/4$, which is less than 1, $-1/2$ must be included in the range of answers for x. Thus, we can eliminate C, which does not include $-1/2$.

The correct answer is (E).

PS 174. Word Translations: Probability
Difficulty: 600–700 **OG Page:** 177

This problem asks us to find the **Probability** of getting at least one tails when you flip a coin three times. The **Basic Probability Formula** is:

$$\text{Probability} = \frac{\text{Desired Outcomes}}{\text{Total Outcomes}}$$

One approach is to **List All the Possibilities** for the three tosses:

HHH HHT HTH THH
TTH THT HTT TTT

Out of the eight possible outcomes, seven of them show at least one tails. Thus, the probability of getting at least one tails in three tosses is $\frac{7}{8}$. This is the **answer**.

Another approach to this problem is to use the **1 – x Principle**. The idea is to focus on the failures, not the successes, when the failures are easier to count or otherwise measure. The question can be rephrased in this way: "*What is the probability of NOT showing ALL heads?*"

Since $P(\text{HHH}) + P(\text{not HHH}) = 1$, we can answer this question by finding $1 - P(\text{HHH})$.

If the probability of showing one head is $\frac{1}{2}$, then the probability of showing heads on the first toss, heads on the second toss and heads on the third toss is:

$$\left(\frac{1}{2}\right)\left(\frac{1}{2}\right)\left(\frac{1}{2}\right) = \frac{1}{8}.$$

Thus, the answer to the problem is

$$1 - \frac{1}{8} = \frac{7}{8}.$$

The correct answer is (D).

PS 175. FDPs: Fractions
Difficulty: 600–700   **OG Page:** 177

The problem specifies the **Fraction** of students in a certain class who received A's, B's, and C's. The problem further specifies the actual number of students who received D's. The question asks us to determine the total number of students in the class. We can **Name Variables** and represent the unknown total as x and the unknown fraction of D students as y.

Let's organize the information in a **Table:**

Grade	Fraction	Actual #
A	1/5	
B	1/4	
C	1/2	
D	y	10
Total	1	x

We can determine y, the fractional amount represented by D, because the fractions of all four grades must add up to 1. We can either use common denominators or **Percentage Equivalents**. Let's take the second approach:

Grade	Fraction	Percentage	Actual #
A	1/5	20%	
B	1/4	25%	
C	1/2	50%	
D	y	z	10
Total	1	100%	x

Determine the percentage represented by a D grade:

$$20 + 25 + 50 + z = 100$$

$$z = 5$$

Therefore, 5% of the total equals 10 students, or

$$\frac{5}{100}x = 10$$

$$x = 10 \times \frac{100}{5} = {}^{2}\cancel{10} \times \frac{100}{\cancel{5}_1} = 200$$

The correct answer is (D).

PS 176. FDPs: Fractions
Difficulty: 500–600   **OG Page:** 177

This problem provides three expressions in terms of x and asks us to determine whether the value must increase for each of these as x increases from 165 to 166. The properties of **Linear Equations** and of **Fractions** can help to answer the question.

I. $2x - 5$
This expression is straightforward, so we can simply **Plug In the Values** 165 and 166 and see which one is bigger.

$$2(165) - 5 = 330 - 5 = 325$$
$$2(166) - 5 = 332 - 5 = 327$$

If we apply **Algebraic Reasoning**, we can avoid computation. If x goes up, so does $2x$, and so does $2x - 5$.

327 is bigger than 325, so $2x - 5$ increases.

II. $1 - 1/x$
The key here is to grasp numerator and denominator rules for fractions. We are dealing with positive values of x, and as the denominator of a positive fraction increases, the value of the fraction decreases. Therefore, as positive x increases, $1/x$ decreases. Since we are subtracting a smaller value from 1 as x increases, $1 - 1/x$ must increase.

III. $\dfrac{1}{x^2 - x}$

Factoring the denominator into $x(x - 1)$, we notice that as long as x is greater than 1, we are multiplying two positive consecutive integers in the denominator. Therefore, as x increases the value in the denominator must also increase, and the overall value of the fraction must decrease.

The only two expressions that must increase are I and II. This is the **answer**.

Note that we could also directly **Substitute Values** for x in this problem. The numbers 165 and 166 are arbitrary. As long as we choose numbers greater than 1, the fractions in Expressions II and III will remain positive. The same properties used above will hold. Thus, we can simplify the computations by using small numbers, such as $x = 2$ and $x = 3$.

The correct answer is (C).

PS 177. <u>Geometry</u>: Triangles & Diagonals
Difficulty: 600–700   **OG Page:** 177

The distance called for in this **Diagonals** problem is the main diagonal of the box, the diagonal that stretches between two opposite corners, through the interior of the box. Be sure to **Draw a Picture**:

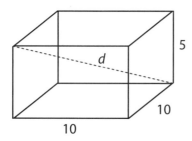

This problem can be solved most quickly and easily with the **Deluxe Pythagorean Theorem**, which is especially designed to find distances like this one. That theorem states that, for any rectangular box with length l, width w, and height h, we know that $l^2 + w^2 + h^2 = d^2$, in which d is the length of the main diagonal.

Substituting the given length, width, and height into this formula yields $10^2 + 10^2 + 5^2 = d^2$, or $225 = d^2$. Therefore, $d = 15$ inches. This is the **answer**.

The other approach to this problem is to use the standard **Pythagorean Theorem** twice. Since d is not currently the hypotenuse of a triangle, construct *another* right triangle, in the *base* of the box, by drawing a diagonal across that base:

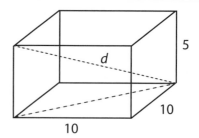

First, find the length of this new base diagonal. The fastest way to find its length is to realize that it creates a **45–45–90** triangle with the two sides of length 10.

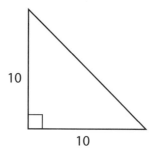

Since the ratio of side to hypotenuse in a 45°–45°–90° triangle is $1 : \sqrt{2}$, this triangle's sides are 10, 10, and $10\sqrt{2}$.

Alternately, we can use the Pythagorean Theorem: $10^2 + 10^2 = (\text{new diagonal})^2$. Therefore, new diagonal $= \sqrt{200}$, or $10\sqrt{2}$.

Once this base diagonal has been found, consider the triangle that it forms with the main diagonal, d, and the height of the box (which is 5).

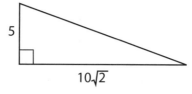

We can use the Pythagorean Theorem to solve for d:

$$5^2 + (10\sqrt{2})^2 = d^2 \quad (\text{or, } 5^2 + (\sqrt{200})^2 = d^2)$$
$$25 + 200 = d^2$$
$$225 = d^2$$
$$15 = d$$

The correct answer is (A).

PS 178. <u>Word Translations</u>: Overlapping Sets
Difficulty: 700–800   **OG Page:** 177

In this **Overlapping Sets** problem, there are three clubs, and some students are in more than one club. Since there are *three* clubs, each with an "In or Out" decision, we should use 3-circle **Venn Diagram** to keep track of the students.

Chess = 40 total

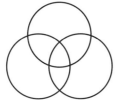

Drama = 30 total   Math = 25 total

Any student can now be placed in a specific location to represent exactly which clubs he or she is in.

Notice that we have written the number of students from the given chart *next to* the circles, not *in* the circles. The 40 students in Chess club may be in Chess club only, Chess and Drama, Chess and Math, or in all three clubs. These facts are represented by different zones of the "Chess" circle. While we know that the Chess circle should hold a total of 40 students, we do not know how many students are in each zone of that circle.

We start filling in the circles with the numbers given for students who are in more than one club. Notice that no one is in all three clubs, so the central overlap contains a zero.

Chess = 40 total

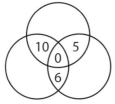

Drama = 30 total   Math = 25 total

The only students left over are those in one club only. Subtracting the multiple-club students from the total in each club, we can now put the remaining students in the non-overlapping zones of the circles.

Chess = 40 total

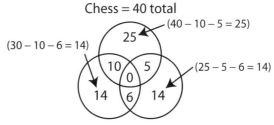

Drama = 30 total   Math = 25 total

Each number within the circles now represents a set of unique students. In essence, we have corrected for the overlap (i.e., we will not count the 5 students in both Math and Chess as 10 different students). Thus, we can add each separate set of students to get the total number of different students in the three clubs:

$$(25 + 14 + 14) + (10 + 5 + 6) + 0 = 53 + 21 = 74.$$

This is the **answer**.

Alternatively, we could add up the number of students in each club, then subtract the number of students who are in *two* clubs in order to eliminate the overlap correctly. Since no student is in all three clubs, we do not have to worry about any further overlap.

$$(40 + 30 + 25) - (10 + 5 + 6) = 95 - 21 = 74.$$

The correct answer is (C).

PS 179. <u>Word Translations</u>: Ratios
Difficulty: 300–500   **OG Page:** 177

Since the two quantities have a **Ratio** of 3 to 4, we can use an **Unknown Multiplier** to represent the two quantities as $3x$ and $4x$, where x could represent any value. If each quantity is increased by 5, the ratio of the new values can be expressed algebraically:

$$\frac{3x+5}{4x+5}$$

However, this expression has no fixed numerical value. Depending upon what we choose as a value for x, we will get different values for the relationship:

If $x = 1$, $\dfrac{3(1)+5}{4(1)+5} = \dfrac{8}{9}$

If $x = 2$, $\dfrac{3(2)+5}{4(2)+5} = \dfrac{11}{13}$

Thus, we cannot determine the value of the expression from the information given. This is the **answer**.

We can illustrate the same concept in a less algebraic manner by simply **Picking Numbers** that fit the 3 : 4 ratio, such as (3, 4) and (6, 8). Adding 5 to each of the first set of values gives new values of 8 and 9, which would have a ratio of 8/9. Adding 5 to each of the second set of values gives new values of 11 and 13, which would have a ratio of 11/13. These ratios are different, so the answer cannot be determined from the given information.

Incidentally, addition and subtraction are both operations that have unpredictable effects on a ratio. Multiplication and division, however, affect ratios in a predictable manner.

The correct answer is (E).

PS 180. Word Translations: Statistics
Difficulty: 500–600   **OG Page:** 178

Before we attempt to solve this **Statistics** problem, let's create equations from the given information using the **Average Formula:**

$$\frac{x+y}{2} = 60$$

$$\frac{y+z}{2} = 80$$

Next, we can simplify each of these equations:

$x + y = 120$

$y + z = 160$

We are asked for $z - x$, which is a **Combined Expression**, or *Combo*. The most direct approach to find this Combo is to subtract the first equation from the second equation. This is the **Elimination** route. We can line up the common terms vertically and subtract to eliminate y:

$$
\begin{array}{rrrr}
 & y & + z & = 160 \\
- [\; x & + y & & = 120] \\
\hline
-x & & + z & = 40
\end{array}
$$

The y's have been cancelled out. Since $-x + z$ is the same as $z - x$, we have $z - x = 40$. This is the **answer**.

Alternatively, we could solve via **Substitution**. We want to eliminate y. So we rewrite y in terms of x in the first equation:

$$y = 120 - x$$

Next, plug this value in for y in the second equation:

$$
\begin{aligned}
y + z &= 160 \\
(120 - x) + z &= 160 \\
120 + z - x &= 160 \\
z - x &= 40
\end{aligned}
$$

The correct answer is (B).

PS 181. FDPs: Fractions
Difficulty: 600–700   **OG Page:** 178

The key to this **Fractions** problem is to read carefully and make sure that we are answering the right question. The question asks for the fraction of the original amount of air that has been removed after 4 strokes of the pump. We can approach this several ways.

Perhaps the easiest way to approach this mathematically is to determine the fraction of air that remains in the tank after 4 strokes and then subtract this fraction from 1. This approach takes advantage of the **1 − x Principle:** to find what we want, we can find what we *don't* want and subtract it from the total.

We can *Name a Variable* and call the original amount of air in the tank x. After 1 stroke there will be $(1/2)x$ remaining in the tank. With each subsequent stroke, we multiply by 1/2:

$$\frac{1}{2}\left(\frac{1}{2}\left(\frac{1}{2}\left(\frac{1}{2}x\right)\right)\right) = \left(\frac{1}{2}\right)^4 x = \frac{1}{16}x.$$ Thus, after 4 strokes, there will 1/16 remaining in the tank. Therefore, the pump must have removed

$$1 - \frac{1}{16} = \frac{15}{16}$$ of the air in the tank. This is the **answer**.

Alternatively, we can ***Pick a Value*** for the amount of air in the tank and determine what fraction would remain after 4 strokes. To pick a number, we can use the choices for guidance. Since all of the denominators in the choices seem to be based on 16 or its factors, let's choose 16 as our value for a full tank.

After 1 stroke, there will be 8 units left in the tank.

After 2 strokes, there will be 4 units left in the tank. After 3 strokes, there will be 2 units left in the tank. After the fourth stroke, there will be only 1 unit left.

Therefore, 15 out of the 16 units have been removed.

Notice that choice (E) is the fraction that *remains* in the tank after 4 strokes. We must remember to subtract 1/16 from 1 to get the right answer.

The correct answer is (A).

PS 182. <u>FDPs</u>: Digits & Decimals
Difficulty: 700–800   **OG Page:** 178

This ***Digits*** problem concerns the possible sums of two 2-digit integers that have the same digits in reverse order, such as 15 and 51.

One option is to use ***Direct Algebra.*** Although an algebraic approach can be harder than working with concrete numbers, in this case it provides valuable insight.

First, we have to ***Name Variables.*** Let's call the two digits in question x and y, so that x is the tens digit and y the units digit of M. Because N has the same digits in reverse order, its tens digit is y and its units digit is x.

The place value of a digit in the tens place is equal to the value of the digit times 10. For instance, in the integer 45, the 4 in the tens place actually contributes 40 to the overall value of the integer, whereas the units digit of 5 contributes just the value of the digit itself. In other words, we can write

$$45 = 40 + 5$$
$$45 = 4 \times 10 + 5$$

In this light, we can write expressions for M and N in terms of the digits x and y, as follows:

$$M = 10x + y$$
$$N = 10y + x$$

The sum of the two numbers is:

$$M + N = 10x + y + 10y + x$$
$$= 11x + 11y = 11(x + y)$$

Because x and y are integers, $M + N$ has to be a multiple of 11. Of the choices given, all but 181 are multiples of 11, and therefore possible values for $M + N$. Thus, 181 *cannot* equal $M + N$. This 181 is the **answer.**

A less abstract approach is to ***Test the Answer Choices.*** Starting with the smallest answer choice, we can ask ourselves whether the sum of two "mirror image" integers could equal that total.

$$44 = 13 + 31$$
$$99 = 63 + 36$$
$$121 = 65 + 56$$
$$165 = 96 + 69$$

181 is the only value that can't be attained by adding two "mirror image" integers.

The correct answer is (A).

PS 183. <u>Word Translations</u>: Rates & Work
Difficulty: 500–600   **OG Page:** 178

A ***Rate–Time–Distance Chart*** is helpful in solving this ***Rates*** problem. Fill in the givens:

	Rate	Time	Distance
Car A		2	80
Car B		?	80

Notice that the distance is the same for each car. Since A traveled 80 miles in 2 hours, its rate is 80/2 = 40 miles per hour.

B's rate is 50 percent faster than A's. 150% of 40 = 1.5(40) = 60.

	Rate	Time	Distance
Car A	40	2	80
Car B	60	?	80

We want B's time. Since Rate × Time = Distance, we can write the following:

$$60t = 80$$

$$t = \frac{80}{60} = \frac{4}{3} = 1\frac{1}{3} \text{ hours}$$

The correct answer is (C).

PS 184. Word Translations: Statistics
Difficulty: 600–700   **OG Page:** 178

We can use the *Average Formula* to solve this *Statistics* problem:

$$\text{Average} = \frac{\text{Sum of terms}}{\text{Number of terms}}$$

$$63 = \frac{(K) + (2K + 3) + (3K - 5) + (5K + 1)}{4}$$

$$(63)(4) = K + 2K + 3 + 3K - 5 + 5K + 1$$

$$252 = 11K - 1$$

$$253 = 11K$$

$$K = \frac{253}{11} = 23$$

The correct answer is (D).

PS 185. Number Properties: Odds & Evens
Difficulty: 500–600   **OG Page:** 178

The *Odds & Evens* problem specifies that p is an even integer and q is an odd integer. The question asks which of the answer choices must be an odd integer.

Let's start by applying *Properties of Odds & Evens.*

(A) $\dfrac{p}{q} = \dfrac{\text{even}}{\text{odd}} =$ not guaranteed to be an integer

    INCORRECT

(B) $pq = \text{even} \times \text{odd} = \text{even}$ INCORRECT

(C) $2p + q = 2(\text{even}) + \text{odd} = \text{even} + \text{odd} = \text{odd}$

    CORRECT

(D) $2(p + q) = 2(\text{even} + \text{odd}) = 2(\text{odd}) = \text{even}$

    INCORRECT

(E) $\dfrac{3p}{q} = \dfrac{\text{even}}{\text{odd}} =$ not guaranteed to be an integer

    INCORRECT

Thus, we have the **answer.**

Alternatively, we can *Test Numbers.* Let $p = 2$ and $q = 3$ (remember that p has to be even and q has to be odd).

(A) $\dfrac{p}{q} = \dfrac{2}{3} =$ not an integer   INCORRECT

(B) $pq = 2(3) = 6$ INCORRECT

(C) $2p + q = 2(2) + 3 = 4 + 3 = 7$ **CORRECT**

(D) $2(p + q) = 2(2 + 3) = 2(5) = 10$ INCORRECT

(E) $\dfrac{3p}{q} = \dfrac{(3)2}{3} = 2$ INCORRECT

The correct answer is (C).

PS 186. FDPs: Fractions
Difficulty: 500–600   **OG Page:** 178

In this problem, Drum X and Drum Y are filled to *Fractions* of their capacities, with no specific amounts given. To make the computations easier, choose *Smart Numbers* equal to common multiples of the denominators of the fractions in the problem and assign these numbers as the total capacities of Drum X and Drum Y. It will then be much easier to determine how full Drum Y is after emptying Drum X's contents into it.

The denominators in this problem are 2 and 3. A Smart Number here would be the least common denominator, which is 6. Therefore, assign Drum X a capacity of 6. Since Drum Y has twice the capacity of Drum X, it has a capacity of 12.

Drum X is 1/2 full of oil, so it currently contains 1/2 of 6, which is 3 units of oil.

Drum Y is 2/3 full of oil, so it currently contains 2/3 of 12, which is 8 units of oil.

If the 3 units of oil in Drum X are poured into Drum Y, Drum Y will then contain 8 + 3 = 11 units of oil.

The question asks the fraction of its capacity to which Drum Y is now filled. Drum Y now contains 11 units of oil out of a total capacity of 12, so it is 11/12 full. This is the **answer**.

Note that if we simply add 1/2 and 2/3 we obtain 7/6, given in answer choice (D). If we add 1/2 and 2 × (2/3) (since Drum Y has twice the capacity of Drum X) we get 3/6 + 8/6 = 11/6, given in choice (E). Picking Smart Numbers is an excellent way to avoid the trap answers in this type of problem.

The ***Direct Algebra*** approach, which is harder, involves a combination of equations:

$y = 2x$, therefore $x = (1/2)y$

$(1/2)x + (2/3)y$ = fraction of capacity

We can ***Substitute*** and solve:

$(1/2)(1/2)y + (2/3)y =$
$(1/4)y + (2/3)y =$
$(3/12)y + (8/12)y =$
$(11/12)y$

The correct answer is (C).

PS 187. FDPs: FDP Connections
Difficulty: 500–600   **OG Page:** 179

We can solve this problem, which involves ***Connection Between Fractions and Percents,*** by combining the fractions and converting the result to a percent, or by converting into percentages first and then combining.

$$\frac{x}{25}+\frac{x}{50}=\frac{2x}{50}+\frac{x}{50}=\frac{3x}{50}=\frac{6}{100}x$$

$\frac{6}{100}$ is equivalent to 6%. This is the **answer**.

Alternatively, since 1/50 = 0.02 and 1/25 = 0.04, we can rewrite the given expression as 0.02x + 0.04x, or 0.06x. Therefore, the expression is 6 percent of x.

One final way to solve this problem is to ***Pick a Number and Create a Target***. Since the problem discusses percents of x, a natural choice is x = 100. With this choice of x, the expression in the problem becomes $\frac{100}{50}+\frac{100}{25}=2+4=6$, which is our

Target Number. Since 6 is 6% of 100, the expression is equal to 6% of x.

The correct answer is (A).

PS 188. EIVs: Formulas & Functions
Difficulty: 700–800   **OG Page:** 179

For formulas involving **Strange Symbols,** you need to carefully follow directions. Additionally, because we have a ***Nested Formula*** with two levels, we need to deal with the formulas inside the parentheses first.

If $a \otimes b = \frac{a^2 b}{3}$, then to evaluate $3 \otimes -1$, we have to substitute 3 everywhere we see an a, and substitute -1 everywhere we see a b.

$$3 \otimes -1 = \frac{(3)^2(-1)}{3} = \frac{-9}{3} = -3.$$

Next, replace the result in the parentheses and perform the remaining operation. The function now reads $2 \otimes -3$. Now substitute 2 for a and substitute -3 for b.

$$2 \otimes -3 = \frac{(2)^2(-3)}{3} = 4\left(\frac{-3}{3}\right) = -4.$$

The correct answer is (E).

PS 189. Geometry: Circles & Cylinders
Difficulty: 600–700   **OG Page:** 179

All ***Rectangular Boxes*** have six faces. Each pair of opposite faces is a set of identically sized rectangles. The rectangular wooden box in this ***Cylinders*** question, with dimensions of 6, 8 and 10, has one pair of oppositely positioned 6 × 8 faces, another pair of 6 × 10 faces, and a third pair of 8 × 10 faces. To maximize the volume of a cylindrical canister that will stand upright on one of the six faces of this wooden box, we must decide which of the three different-sized faces to stand the canister up on. In other words, we must ***Test Scenarios.***

The first thing to realize is that whichever of the three different sized faces is chosen, the other dimension will become the maximum height of the cylinder. The picture below shows one of three total possibilities. We see that the base of the canister is on the 6 × 8 face, so the canister has a maximum height of 10. We should be sure to **Draw a Picture** on our own page. In fact, for **3-D Geometry** problems, we often ought to wind up with several.

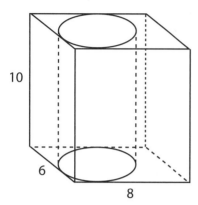

The maximum diameter (and thus radius) of the cylinder will be determined by the dimensions of the side of the rectangle chosen for the cylinder to stand on. The base of a cylinder is a circle, and the maximum diameter for a circle contained inside a rectangle is determined by the shorter of the two dimensions of the rectangle. This is because a circle expands equally in all directions and thus fits perfectly inside a square, not a rectangle. We can see this from the figure below. In 3-D geometry problems, it is often helpful to draw 2-D overhead or side views.

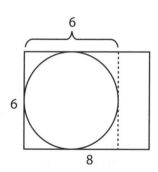

This means that there are three different scenarios for the maximum-sized canister that can be placed in this box, as outlined in the **Table** below.

Canister upright on face	Max Diameter	Max Radius	Height
6 × 10 (I)	6	3	8
6 × 8 (II)	6	3	10
8 × 10 (III)	8	4	6

The formula for the **Volume of a Cylinder** is function of two variables: the radius (r) and the height (h).

$$V = \pi r^2 h$$

To maximize the value of the volume, it is necessary to maximize the value of the variable that is *squared*, i.e. the radius. Option III above should achieve the maximum volume. We can quickly calculate the volumes to verify:

$$V_{(I)} = \pi(3)^2(8) = 72\pi$$
$$V_{(II)} = \pi(3)^2(10) = 90\pi$$
$$V_{(III)} = \pi(4)^2(6) = 96\pi$$

The correct answer is (B).

PS 190. <u>FDPs</u>: Digits & Decimals
Difficulty: 500–600   **OG Page:** 179

In this **Digits** problem, it would be difficult to actually multiply these numbers together and arrive at an answer within two minutes. Fortunately, we can use the **Units Digit Shortcut** instead. By the way, the units digit is the last digit of an integer. For instance, the units digit of 1,273 is 3.

To calculate the units digit of a product, we only need to consider the units digit of each of the numbers we are multiplying. Therefore, if we are asked to calculate the units digit of 13^4, we only need to figure out the units digit of 3^4. Likewise, for 17^2, we only need to consider 7^2, and for 29^3, 9^3.

13^4 has the same units digit as $3^4 = 81$ = units digit 1.

17^2 has the same units digit as $7^2 = 49$ = units digit 9.

29^3 has the same units digit as $9^3 = 729$ = units digit 9.

We can use these individual units digits to compute the units digit of the entire product:

$1 \times 9 \times 9 = 81$ = units digit 1.

The correct answer is (E).

⟿ PS 191. <u>Word Translations</u>: Combinatorics
Difficulty: 600–700   **OG Page:** 179

This is a ***Disguised Combinatorics*** problem. The key to identifying disguised Combinatorics is to look for language, such as "how many," that asks us to determine the number of ways in which an event can occur.

Here, we are asked to determine the number of ways in which Pat can walk from X to Y without backtracking. It would be extremely cumbersome to try to trace all the possible routes by hand. Instead, we can use the ***Anagram Method*** to determine the number of ways.

Notice that Pat must walk 2 blocks to the right and then 3 blocks up in order to get from X to Y, regardless of the particular route. So if we could determine the number of ways in which Pat could arrange the 2 "Rights" and the 3 "Ups" in any sequence, we could figure out all the routes from X to Y. In other words, how many arrangements, or anagrams, are possible for RRUUU?

Since there are repetitions of the R's and U's, we must divide the factorial of the total number (5!) by the factorials of each group of repetitions (2! and 3!):

$$\frac{5!}{2!3!} = \frac{5 \times 4 \times \cancel{3 \times 2 \times 1}}{2 \times 1 \times \cancel{3 \times 2 \times 1}} = \frac{20}{2} = 10$$

Thus, there are 10 possible routes of minimum length between X and Y. This is the **answer.**

To remember the formula, we can make an ***Anagram Chart:***

1	2	3	4	5
R	R	U	U	U

The repeated letters on the bottom remind us to divide 5! by 2! and 3! when we count the anagrams of RRUUU.

The correct answer is (C).

⟿ PS 192. <u>Word Translations</u>: Ratios
Difficulty: 700–800   **OG Page:** 179

In this ***Ratio*** problem, we are given a ***Multiple Ratio*** involving three ingredients in a solution.

The problem further states that some of the ratios are altered from the original situation. We can write the original ratio of soap to alcohol to water as

$$(S:A:W)_{original} = 2:50:100.$$

Multiple ratios with more than two parts, such as this one, are a convenient way of expressing the relative sizes of more than two quantities. One way to attack this problem is to ***Break Up the Multiple Ratio*** into 2 typical two-part ratios. For example, the ratio of soap to alcohol, as well as the ratio of soap to water, can be extracted from the multiple ratio above:

$$(S:A)_{original} = 2:50$$
$$(S:W)_{original} = 2:100$$

Notice that the 2 is the same for the soap in the two ratios above. Now, we are told that the ratio of soap to alcohol is doubled, while that of soap to water is halved:

$$(S:A)_{new} = 2 \times (2:50) = 4:50$$
$$(S:W)_{new} = \tfrac{1}{2} \times (2:100) = 1:100$$

In order to actually ***Alter a Ratio,*** we change *just one* number in the ratio. To double the ratio of soap to alcohol, for instance, we change the ratio from 2 : 50 to 4 : 50. We should not double *both* numbers. If we do, we end up with 4 : 100, which is exactly the same as 2 : 50. This works just like fractions. Doubling 2/50 gives us 4/50, not 4/100.

Now that we have the new ratios 4 : 50 and 1 : 100, we need to ***Scale the Ratios*** before re-assembling them into a new multiple ratio. That is, we need the common ingredient (soap) to have the same number in both ratios. To scale a ratio, we change *both* numbers by the same factor. For instance, we can scale 1 : 100 to 2 : 200 or 4 : 400. Since soap appears as 4 in one ratio and as 1 in the other, we scale 1 : 100 to 4 : 400. Now we can ***Recombine the Two-Part Ratios*** into a new multiple ratio:

$$(S:A)_{new} = 4:50$$
$$(S:W)_{new} = 4:400$$
$$(S:A:W)_{new} = 4:50:400 = 2:25:200$$

At this point, we can introduce an **Unknown Multiplier** x in order to go from relative to absolute quantities of the ingredients. Rewriting the ratio with this multiplier, we have:

$$(S : A : W)_{new} = 2x : 25x : 200x$$

If the amount of alcohol will be 100, then

$$A = 100 = 25x$$
$$4 = x$$

Thus, the amount of water in the solution will be

$$W = 200x = 200 \times 4 = 800 \text{ cubic centimeters}$$

This is the **answer**.

Alternatively, as we become more comfortable with multiple ratios, we can avoid breaking the multiple ratio down into typical two-part ratios. We simply adjust one number at a time in a table, keeping track of what happens to the two-part ratios $S : A$ and $S : W$.

First, we try to double $S : A$, as follows.

	S	A	W
old	2	50	100
	×↓2		
	4	50	100

We have successfully doubled $S : A$. But we have also doubled $S : W$. That's bad. To fix the issue, we should leave S alone and change W. We want to reduce $S : W$, so we should make W bigger (as we would a denominator, which W effectively is). Let's try doubling W.

	S	A	W
	4	50	100
			×↓2
	4	50	200

This step brings $S : W$ back to where it was originally (4 : 200 is the same as 2 : 100), but we need to cut the original ratio $S : W$ in half. So we keep going, doubling W again.

	S	A	W
	4	50	200
			×↓2
	4	50	400

Now we are all set with the two-part ratios. $S : A$ is double what it was, and $S : W$ is half what it was. Now we just need to scale the whole ratio up, so that there are actually 100 cubic centimeters of alcohol.

	S	A	W
new	4	50	400
	×↓2	×↓2	×↓2
	8	100	800

We are looking for the final amount of water, which is 800 cubic centimeters.

The correct answer is (E).

PS 193. FDPs: Percents
Difficulty: 600–700   **OG Page:** 179

In this **Overlapping Sets** problem that also involves **Percents,** students in a class are categorized by how they answered two questions on a test. Some students (75%) got the first question right, and the rest did not. Likewise, some students (55%) got the second question right, and the rest did not. Some students (20%) got neither question right. We are asked for the percentage of students who got both questions right.

One approach is to use a **Double-Set Matrix**. Since we are dealing with percents only (no actual numbers of students), we choose the **Smart Number** 100 for the total number of students in the class. Shade the box we want.

	Q1 Right	Q1 Wrong	Total
Q2 Right			
Q2 Wrong			
Total			100

Now we fill in the numbers we know. Since 75 students got Q1 right, without regard to whether they got Q2 right, we put 75 at the bottom of the first column. Similarly, the 55 students who got Q2 right are placed in the first row's Total column. We also know that if 75 students got Q1 right, then $100 - 75 = 25$ students got it wrong. Likewise, $100 - 55 = 45$ students got Q2 wrong. Finally, the 20 students who got both questions wrong go in the middle box (Q1 Wrong and Q2 Wrong):

	Q1 Right	*Q1 Wrong*	*Total*
Q2 Right			55
Q2 Wrong		20	45
Total	75	25	100

Now, we fill in the rest of the table, making sure that all the rows and all the columns add up:

	Q1 Right	*Q1 Wrong*	*Total*
Q2 Right	50	5	55
Q2 Wrong	25	20	45
Total	75	25	100

50 students out of 100, or 50% of the class, got both questions right. This is the **answer**.

Alternatively, we can use a ***Quick Formula for Overlapping Sets:***

Total = Group 1 + Group 2 − Both + Neither

The logic behind this formula is that, since those who are in both groups have been counted twice, subtracting them once will count them correctly. Moreover, since those in neither group have not been counted at all, they are simply added.

Again, our total is 100 students. Thus:

$$100 = 75 + 55 - B + 20$$
$$100 = 150 - B$$
$$B = 50$$

The correct answer is (D).

PS 194. <u>**Geometry:**</u> Coordinate Plane
Difficulty: 600–700 **OG Page:** 180

This ***Coordinate Plane*** problem tells us that point *A* has coordinates (2, 3), that the line $y = x$ is the perpendicular bisector of *AB*, and that the *x*-axis is the perpendicular bisector of *BC*. We are asked to find the coordinates of point *C*.

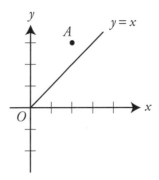

If $y = x$ is the ***Perpendicular Bisector*** of *AB*, then the line is perpendicular to *AB*, and intersects *AB* at its midpoint. This means the distance from point *A* to the line is equal to the distance from the line to point *B*. In other words, *B* is the ***Reflection*** of *A* through the line $y = x$. The word reflection is no accident: if *A* represents a person and the line $y = x$ represents a mirror, then *B* is the image of *A* "in the mirror."

We can sketch point *B* to lie to the right of and lower than point *A*, with coordinates of about (3, 2). We can prove that these indeed are the coordinates of point *B*, since we know that perpendicular lines have slopes that are the negative reciprocal of one another. The slope of $y = x$ is 1. The slope of segment *AB* must be −1. However, in order to solve this problem, we do not need to take such a formal approach involving slopes.

If the *x*-axis is the perpendicular bisector of *BC*, we can also say that point *C* is the reflection of point *B* through the *x*-axis. We can sketch point *C* with coordinates of (3, −2).

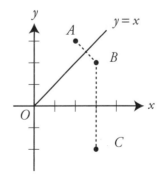

Thus, (3, −2) is the **answer**.

Even if we were unsure about the precise coordinates, using our reflection process we can ***Estimate*** the correct answer. With this analysis, we know that point C must be in quadrant IV, which eliminates (A), (B), and (E). We also know that point C must be to the right of point A, which eliminates (C).

The correct answer is (D).

PS 195. Word Translations: Algebraic Translations
Difficulty: 700–800   **OG Page:** 180

This problem specifies that a store charges the same price for each towel that it sells and that a certain (unspecified) number of towels can be purchased for $120. If the current price of each towel were to increase by $1, however, then ten fewer towels could be bought for that same $120. The question asks for the current price of one towel.

Let's take a **Direct Algebra** approach and set up a **Change Table** to organize the information. We need to **Name Variables**. Let x be the current price per towel, and let y be the current number of towels we can buy for $120.

	Current	New
Price per towel	x	$x + 1$
# of towels for $120	y	$y - 10$

We can now express the **Cost Relationships** that we know.

Current Total Cost: $xy = 120$

New Total Cost: $(x + 1)(y - 10) = 120$

The two equations are not linear, so solving for the variables will involve quadratics. It will take a fair amount of work to solve this way.

Instead, notice that the answers are almost all very small (1, 2, 3, 4, and 12). Let's switch approaches and try **Testing the Answer Choices**.

Begin with the middle number. If 3 is the current price of each towel, then we could buy 120/3 = 40 towels for $120. The new price would be 3 + 1 = $4 per towel, and we could buy 120/4 = 30 towels for $120. This fits the data, as we can see in our table.

	Current	New
Price per towel	$x = 3$	$x + 1 = 4$
# of towels for $120	$y = 40$	$y - 10 = 30$

Thus, the current price of each towel is in fact $3. This is the **answer**.

If (C) did not work out, we would be able to determine if we needed a larger or smaller number and would then test a corresponding answer choice.

Although it may seem hard to switch approaches mid-stream, this is a good overall strategy for certain tough problems. If the first path looks like a lot of work, we should see whether we can switch lanes to where the traffic is flowing faster.

If we had continued with the algebraic approach, we would have gotten the following:

$$xy = 120$$
$$y = 120 / x$$
$$(x + 1)(y - 10) = 120$$
$$(x + 1)(120/x - 10) = 120$$
$$(x + 1)(120 - 10x) = 120x$$
$$120x - 10x^2 + 120 - 10x = 120x$$
$$-10x^2 - 10x + 120 = 0$$
$$x^2 + x - 12 = 0$$
$$(x + 4)(x - 3) = 0$$
$$x = 3 \text{ (must be >0)}$$

The correct answer is (C).

PS 196. EIVs: Basic Equations
Difficulty: 600–700   **OG Page:** 180

This difficult **Basic Equations** problem asks for the number of green marbles in Jar R. We are therefore looking for the value of z. We can use the information in each row to create an equation corresponding to each jar:

Jar P:	$x + y = 80$	[1]
Jar Q:	$y + z = 120$	[2]
Jar R:	$x + z = 160$	[3]

In general, systems of three equations and three unknowns are painful to solve, but the GMAT tends to keep the work under control. We should look for shortcuts or **Symmetries** in the form of the equations to reduce the number of steps needed to solve.

In the given table of equations, we can see that x, y, and z each appear two times. Therefore, we can save time by *Adding Equations.*

If we add our original three equations, we obtain $2x + 2y + 2z = 360$. Divide both sides by 2 and obtain $x + y + z = 180$. Now, since Equation [1] tells us that $x + y = 80$, we can substitute 80 for the *Combined Expression* $x + y$ in our equation:

$$(x + y) + z = 180$$
$$80 + z = 180$$
$$z = 100 \quad \text{This is the } \textbf{answer.}$$

Alternatively, we can always utilize *Substitution and Combination.* Ultimately we need the value of z, so let's first isolate one of the variables in Equation [1] and substitute it into another equation. For example, we can solve for y in Equation [1]: $y = 80 - x$

Now replace y in Equation [2] with $80 - x$: $(80 - x) + z = 120$. Subtract 80 from both sides, obtaining $-x + z = 40$. We'll call this equation [4].

Now we can see that combining Equations [3] and [4] using addition would cause the x terms to cancel, leaving an equation with only z:

$$x + z = 160 \quad [3]$$
$$+ \quad -x + z = 40 \quad [4]$$
$$\overline{ 2z = 200} \quad \text{Divide by 2}$$
$$z = 100$$

The correct answer is (D).

PS 197. <u>Geometry</u>: Circles & Cylinders
Difficulty: 500–600 **OG Page:** 180

First, we can change the time units in this Circles problem to make them compatible: 15 seconds = 1/4 minute. Since the fan runs at the rate of 300 revolutions per minute, it rotates $(1/4)(300) = 75$ times in the given 15-second period.

To understand the path followed by the point, we should *Draw a Picture:*

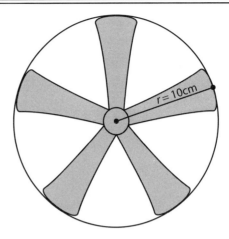

From this diagram, we should see that the point is moving along the circumference of a circle with radius 10 centimeters, or 10 cm. During each revolution, the point travels a distance equal to the circumference of the circle, which is $2\pi r = 2\pi(10) = 20\pi$ cm. Since the blade revolves 75 times, the total distance traveled by the point is $(75)(20\pi) = 1500\pi$ cm.

The correct answer is (B).

PS 198. <u>Number Properties</u>: Divisibility & Primes
Difficulty: 700–800 **OG Page:** 180

One approach to this *Divisibility & Primes* problem is to set up a *Prime Box* for n, which holds all of the prime factors of n, including repeats.

First, we can take the prime factorization of n, remembering that p is a prime number greater than 2 (i.e., 3, 5, 7, 11, etc.) and therefore an odd prime. We can use a *Factor Tree:*

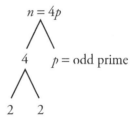

Therefore, n's prime box contains the following:

$$\boxed{2, 2, p}$$

The "divisors of n" are the same as the "factors of n".

A complete list of the factors of n includes 1, the

unique prime factors of *n*, and every possible product of the prime factors of *n*.

The factors of *n* are thus 1, 2, 4, *p*, 2*p*, and 4*p*. Of these, the odd factors of *n* are 1 and *p*. The even factors of *n* are 2, 4, 2*p*, and 4*p*.

There are four different positive even divisors of *n*. This is the **answer**.

Another, less theoretical, approach is to **Pick a Value** for *p* that follows the constraint that *p* is a prime number greater than 2.

Say that *p* = 3, so *n* = 4*p* = (4)(3) = 12.

The divisors of *n* = 12 are 1, 2, 3, 4, 6, and 12. There are four even divisors in this list (2, 4, 6, and 12).

The number picking approach is not only easy, but also mathematically safe. The answer *cannot* depend on which *p* we pick. No matter what prime number greater than 2 we choose, the answer must be the same. Thus, we are free to choose *any* convenient *p* and work out an answer.

The correct answer is (C).

PS 199. Word Translations: Statistics
Difficulty: 600–700   **OG Page:** 180

The formula for **Standard Deviation** is quite complicated: standard deviation = the square root of the average of the squares of the differences between each term and the mean. Fortunately, GMAT questions tend to test only our conceptual understanding of standard deviation, rather than our computational skills.

Conceptually speaking, standard deviation is a way to measure, for a set of numbers, the typical distance between any one of those numbers and the average for that set. A set of numbers close to one another will have a smaller standard deviation than a set of numbers that differ greatly from one another.

If we consider these three sets conceptually, we can see that Set II must have the smallest standard deviation: since all the numbers are equal to one another, they are all equal to the average, and so the standard deviation is actually 0.

Set I has the second smallest standard deviation. The average of the set is 74, and all the terms are 0, 1, or 2 units away from 74.

Set III has the greatest standard deviation. Though three of the terms are very close to the average (74.6), two of the terms, 62 and 89, stray far.

Thus, the ordering of sets from greatest standard deviation to least must be III, I, II.

The correct answer is (D).

PS 200. Word Translations: Overlapping Sets
Difficulty: 600–700   **OG Page:** 181

This **Overlapping Sets** problem is best solved with a **Double-Set Matrix**. In this case, the total group is the 50 researchers. The first categorization is "Assigned to A" vs. "Assigned to B." The second categorization is "Prefer A" vs. "Prefer B."

Begin by filling in the known information.:

	Assigned to A	Assigned to B	Total
Prefer A			35
Prefer B			15
Total	20	30	50

We are looking for the lowest possible number of researchers who will NOT be assigned to the team they prefer. In other words, this is an **Optimization** problem as well. We want the lowest possible sum of the "Prefer A but in B" and "Prefer B but in A" boxes:

	Assigned to A	Assigned to B	Total
Prefer A			35
Prefer B			15
Total	20	30	50

In order to minimize the numbers in each of these boxes, we must maximize the numbers in each of the other two unfilled boxes. This method of maximizing one value to minimize another is characteristic of optimization problems.

	Assigned to A	Assigned to B	Total
Prefer A	20		35
Prefer B		15	15
Total	20	30	50

Note that, although we want to maximize the number of people in the top-left and middle boxes, we are constrained by the totals. Because only 15 people prefer B, the maximum number of people who can be assigned to the middle box is 15. A **Hidden Constraint** is at work here: the number of people in any box cannot be negative. Similarly, only 20 people are assigned to A, so 20 is the maximum number of people who can be in the top-left box. We now have enough information to fill in the two cells we need to know.

	Assigned to A	*Assigned to B*	*Total*
Prefer A	20	15	35
Prefer B	0	15	15
Total	20	30	50

0 + 15 = 15 represents the minimum number of people assigned to a team other than the one they prefer. This is the **answer**.

Notice that one box contains zero people—the minimum possible. If negative values were allowed in some boxes, we could increase the desired maximum further, so we should expect the non-negative constraint to come into play.

The correct answer is (A).

PS 201. Number Properties: Consecutive Integers
Difficulty: 600–700   **OG Page:** 181

In an **Evenly-Spaced Set,** the **Mean** and the **Median** will always be the same. Since the multiples of any integer are evenly spaced (in this case, by 5), it must be true that $m = M$. Thus, $M - m$ must equal 0. This is the **answer**.

Alternatively, we can handle this question by **Direct Computation.** List out the first 10 positive multiples of 5: 5, 10, 15, 20, 25, 30, 35, 40, 45, 50.

Since these numbers are evenly spaced, the average of the whole set will be the average of the smallest and largest terms in the set. Use the **Average Formula.** (5 + 50)/2 = 55/2 = 27.5. Therefore, m = 27.5.

Since we have an even number of terms in the set, the median of the set will be the average of the two middle terms: (25 + 30)/2 = 55/2 = 27.5.

Therefore, M = 27.5.

$M - m = 27.5 - 27.5 = 0$.

The correct answer is (B).

PS 202. EIVs: VICs
Difficulty: 600–700   **OG Page:** 181

This **Variables In Choices** problem, which also involves **Percents,** asks us to express y as a percentage of x, if we know x as a percentage of y.

One option is to approach the problem using **Direct Algebra.** Knowing that "of" means times and "percent" means division by 100, we can **Algebraically Translate** the first relation as:

$$x = \frac{m}{100} \times y$$

We are asked to answer the question, "what percent of x is y?" The best approach is to **Name a Variable** w to stand for the "what" in "what percent." We can then answer the question by solving for w. Accordingly:

$$y = \frac{w}{100} \times x$$

Substituting for x from the first relation yields

$$y = \frac{w}{100} \times \frac{m}{100} \times y$$

Divide both sides by y and solve for w:

$$1 = \frac{w}{100} \times \frac{m}{100}$$

$$1 = \frac{wm}{10,000}$$

$$\frac{10,000}{m} = w \qquad \text{This is the **answer**.}$$

An alternative approach is to **Pick Numbers and Calculate a Target.** Suppose we pick $m = 50$. In that case, x is 50%, or half, of y, and so y must be twice x, or 200% of x. Our **Target Value** is therefore 200.

We must be careful not to misinterpret "twice x" to mean that the target value is 2. Likewise, we must not think that $m = 0.50$. If we get confused on these points, we could pick incorrect answers.

We can now substitute $m = 50$ into each answer choice to determine which one yields a value of 200.

(A) $100m = 100 \times 50 = 5,000$ INCORRECT

(B) $\dfrac{1}{100m} = \dfrac{1}{100 \times 50} = \dfrac{1}{5,000}$ INCORRECT

(C) $\dfrac{1}{m} = \dfrac{1}{50}$ INCORRECT

(D) $\dfrac{10}{m} = \dfrac{10}{50} = \dfrac{1}{5}$ INCORRECT

(E) $\dfrac{10,000}{m} = \dfrac{10,000}{50} = 200$ **CORRECT**

The correct answer is (E).

PS 203. FDPs: Digits & Decimals
       Difficulty: 500–600   **OG Page:** 181

In this *Digits & Decimals* problem, we are asked for the 25th digit to the right of the decimal point when 6 is divided by 11. The GMAT does not require more calculation than is reasonable in two minutes (the approximate amount of time available per problem on the exam). In this case, we should expect to find a *Pattern* that we can easily extend to the 25th decimal place *without* calculating every digit in between.

Thus, we can begin *Long Division,* preparing to stop when the pattern becomes apparent:

$$
\begin{array}{r}
0.54\overline{54} \\
11\overline{)6.0000} \\
-55 \\
\hline
50 \\
-44 \\
\hline
60 \\
-55 \\
\hline
50 \\
\end{array}
$$

The pattern we notice is an alternating cycle of 5's and 4's.

We want to know the 25th digit after the decimal. Note that odd places (1st, 3rd, 5th...) after the decimal are the digit 5, and even places after the decimal (2nd, 4th, 6th...) are the digit 4.

$$0.54\overline{54}$$

odd places   even places

Thus, we can infer that the 25th place is the digit 5.

The correct answer is (C).

PS 204. EIVs: VICs
       Difficulty: 600–700   **OG Page:** 181

We can summarize the information given in this *Variables In Choices* problem in the following *Pay Table:*

	Hours Worked	*Total Earned*
John	10 hours	$x + y$
Mary	8 hours	$x - y$

The problem essentially asks us to find x in terms of y. We can approach the problem using the *Direct Algebra* method.

First, we can express the hourly wage as:

$$\text{Hourly Wage} = \frac{\text{Total Earned}}{\text{Hours Worked}}$$

Since John's and Mary's hourly wages are the same, we can write an equation as follows:

$\dfrac{x+y}{10} = \dfrac{x-y}{8}$	Cross-multiply
$8(x+y) = 10(x-y)$	Distribute
$8x + 8y = 10x - 10y$	Subtract $8x$ and add $10y$
$18y = 2x$	Divide by 2
$x = 9y$	

In this problem, it would be hard to *Pick Numbers and Calculate a Target,* because we have to select values for x and y that result in equal ratios. If we pick a value for y (say, $y = 1$), it is not immediately evident what value of x will result in an equal wage for both Mary and John. At this point, we would need to set up an equation:

$$\frac{x+1}{10} = \frac{x-1}{8}$$

This equation is not that much easier to solve than the equation that includes both *x* and *y*. Still, this approach will work.

The correct answer is (E).

PS 205. <u>Geometry:</u> Triangles & Diagonals
Difficulty: 600–700   **OG Page:** 181

The problem specifies that the area of *Triangle ORP* equals 12. This triangle lives in the *Coordinate Plane*. Point *R* is not drawn, but we are told that *R* is located somewhere on the *y*-axis. Point *R*'s *x*-coordinate is therefore 0, but we do not know *R*'s *y*-coordinate. We are asked to find it.

We should begin by *Redrawing the Figure*, including point *R*. We should also draw the triangle specified by the question.

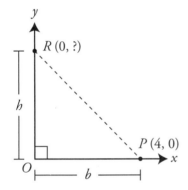

We know that the area of the triangle is 12. We also know that the base of the triangle has a length of 4. What we are missing is the height. The base and the height of any triangle are perpendicular. *OP*, the base of the triangle, runs along the *x*-axis. *OR*, which runs along the *y*-axis, is perpendicular to *OP*, so *OR* is the height of the triangle. This is true for any *Right Triangle:* the two shorter legs can be taken as a base and a height. And if *OR* is the height of the triangle, then the distance from the origin to point *R* is the height.

The *Area of a Triangle* is given by the formula $A = \frac{1}{2}bh$, where *b* and *h* are the base and height, respectively. Plug in the two givens and solve:

$$12 = \frac{1}{2}(4)h$$
$$6 = h$$

If the length of the height is 6, then the distance from the origin to point *R* must be 6. That means the *y*-coordinate of point *R* must be 6.

The correct answer is (B).

PS 206. <u>Word Translations:</u> Rates & Work
Difficulty: 600–700   **OG Page:** 181

This *Rates* problem asks us to determine how many hours it will take for Car A to overtake and drive 8 miles ahead of Car B, starting from 20 miles behind. Recall that when two bodies are traveling in the same direction, we subtract their rates. This gives us the effective rate at which Car A is gaining on Car B. We can use the following formula for *Relative Rates:*

$$(\text{Rate}_A - \text{Rate}_B) \times t = (\text{difference in distance})$$

We are told that Car A is traveling at 58 mph and Car B is traveling at 50 mph. Car A must drive the same distance as Car B, plus the extra 20 miles to make up for the head start and the extra 8 miles after it overtakes Car B, as specified in the question. Therefore, Car A must drive 20 + 8 = 28 miles further than Car B. Substitute the known values into the formula and solve for *t*:

$$(58 - 50)\, t = 28$$
$$8t = 28$$
$$t = 28/8$$
$$t = 3.5 \text{ hours}$$ This is the **answer.**

We can also solve this problem using an *Rate–Time–Distance Chart.*

Since the cars must travel for the same amount of time, we place a *t* in the Time for Car A and Car B. Car B will travel some distance *d*, and Car A will travel that same distance plus an extra 28 miles.

	Rate	*Time*	*Distance*
Car A	58	*t*	*d* + 28
Car B	50	*t*	*d*
Total			

We can now set up two equations:

$$58t = d + 28$$
$$50t = d$$

Use **Substitution** to replace *d* in the first equation with 50*t*:

$$58t = (50t) + 28$$
$$8t = 28$$
$$t = 3.5 \text{ hours}$$

The correct answer is (E).

PS 207. <u>Word Problems</u>: Statistics
Difficulty: 600–700   **OG Page:** 182

In this **Statistics** problem, we are told that the average production for a company was 50 units over *n* days. If we **Name a Variable** and assign *t* to total production over this period, we can represent this scenario using the **Average Formula.**

$$\frac{t}{n} = 50$$

Today's production adds 90 units to the total production, 1 to the number of days, and 5 units to the average production.

$$\frac{t+90}{n+1} = 55$$

We are asked to solve for *n*. To do so, we can isolate *t* in the first equation, **Substitute** for it in the second equation, and solve:

$$t = 50n$$
$$\frac{(50n)+90}{n+1} = 55$$
$$50n + 90 = 55(n+1)$$
$$50n + 90 = 55n + 55$$
$$35 = 5n$$
$$7 = n \qquad \text{This is the **answer**.}$$

Alternatively, we can solve this problem by **Testing Answer Choices**. Let's test answer choice (C). If *n* = 10, the average production over those 10 days was 50 units, so 50 × 10 represents the total number of units produced. 500 units were produced. The next day, 90 units were produced, so after 11 days, 590 units were produced. If the average production at that point was 55 units, then $\frac{590}{11}$ should equal 55. It doesn't, so (C) can't be the

right answer. Doing the same calculations for the other answer choices reveals that (E) works.

The correct answer is (E).

PS 208. <u>EIVs</u>: VICs
Difficulty: 700–800   **OG Page:** 182

Although this question can be solved using **Direct Algebra**, this method is inadvisable. The algebra is messy and prone to error, given the **Negative Signs** and **Even Exponents**.

Moreover, we could perform the algebra correctly but be forced to go further, in order to match the particular form in the right answer choice.

As a result, this question is best treated as a **Variables In Choices** question. The most efficient and reliable approach is to **Pick Numbers** and **Calculate a Target**.

Let *x* = 2. Replace *x* with $1/x$ (i.e., 1/2) in the expression given and compute the **Target Number:**

$$\left(\frac{x+1}{x-1}\right)^2 = \left(\frac{\frac{1}{2}+1}{\frac{1}{2}-1}\right)^2 = \left(\frac{\frac{3}{2}}{-\frac{1}{2}}\right)^2 = \left(\frac{3}{-1}\right)^2 = 9$$

The answer choice that yields a value of 9 when we plug in 2 for *x* is the correct answer.

(A) $\left(\frac{x+1}{x-1}\right)^2 = \left(\frac{2+1}{2-1}\right)^2 = \left(\frac{3}{1}\right)^2 = 9$

(B) $\left(\frac{x-1}{x+1}\right)^2 = \left(\frac{2-1}{2+1}\right)^2 = \left(\frac{1}{3}\right)^2 = \frac{1}{9}$

(C) $\frac{x^2+1}{1-x^2} = \frac{2^2+1}{1-2^2} = \frac{4+1}{1-4} = \frac{-5}{3}$

(D) $\frac{x^2-1}{x^2+1} = \frac{2^2-1}{2^2+1} = \frac{4-1}{4+1} = \frac{3}{5}$

(E) $-\left(\frac{x-1}{x+1}\right)^2 = -\left(\frac{2-1}{2+1}\right)^2 = -\left(\frac{1}{3}\right)^2 = -\frac{1}{9}$

The correct answer is (A).

PS 209. <u>Geometry</u>: Lines & Angles
Difficulty: 600–700   **OG Page:** 182

As there seems to be no direct relationship between *x* and *y*, which measure **Angles,** we must find the individual values of these variables and then sum them to answer the question.

As with any *Geometry* question that involves a picture, we should begin by *Redrawing the Figure* and filling in any known information. For ease of explanation, points in the figure have been labeled.

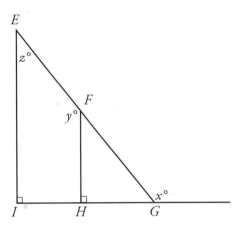

There are two ways we can find the value of y. We know that shape *EFHI* is a *Quadrilateral,* and the internal angles of any quadrilateral must sum to 360. We also know that $\angle EIH$ and $\angle IHF$ are right angles. Therefore $90 + 90 + 50 + y = 360$. Solving for y gives us $y = 130$.

Alternatively, we can recognize that $\overline{EI}$ and $\overline{HF}$ are *Parallel* to each other. We know this because they are both perpendicular to $\overline{IG}$. $\overline{EG}$ acts as a *Transversal.* We know that $\angle IEF$ and $\angle HFG$ must be equal, which means $\angle HFG = 50$. We also know that $\angle EFH$ and $\angle HFG$ must sum to 180. So $y + 50 = 180$, and $y = 130$.

To find the value of x, we must think about how x relates to the rest of the figure. x is an *Exterior Angle* to the triangle *EIG*. Since the exterior angle of a triangle is equal to the sum of the two non-adjacent interior angles, we can solve. $\angle EIH$ is a right angle and $\angle IEF$ is 50.

$$x = 90 + 50$$
$$x = 140$$

$$x + y = 140 + 130 = 270$$

The correct answer is (D).

PS 210. <u>Geometry</u>: Coordinate Plane
Difficulty: 500–600   **OG Page:** 182

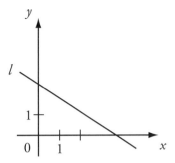

The primary way to solve this Coordinate Plane problem is to come up with the equation of the line. One way to do this is to use the *Slope-Intercept Equation,* $y = mx + b$, where m represents the slope of the line, and b the y-intercept.

This line has a y-intercept of 2, where the line crosses the y-axis. It has a slope of $-2/3$, because, as the line goes from left to right, it goes down by 2 units as it goes across by 3 units.

Therefore, we can write the equation as:

$$y = (-2/3)x + 2$$

Notice that none of the equations in the answer choices contain fractions. Therefore we need to do *Direct Algebra*. Multiply the equation by 3 in order to eliminate the fraction $-2/3$.

$$3y = -2x + 6$$
$$2x + 3y = 6 \qquad \text{This is the \textbf{answer}.}$$

Alternatively, we can *Test Answer Choices* by plugging in the two points on the line that we know of, namely (3, 0) and (0, 2), into the answer choices. This approach could take more time, but if we are organized, it will definitely work.

Note that both sets work for the equation in answer choice (B):

$$2(3) + 3(0) = 6$$
$$2(0) + 3(2) = 6.$$

None of the other equations work for both of the points.

The correct answer is (B).

PS 211. <u>FDPs</u>: Digits & Decimals
Difficulty: 600–700   **OG Page:** 182

In this **Digits** problem, we can take a **Direct Algebra** approach if we **Name Variables,** in this case, the digits of the two-digit number mentioned.

We can call the first two-digit number *XY* and the second two-digit number *YX*, where *X* and *Y* are the digits (NOT the product of *X* and *Y*). In the first number, *X* is in the 10's place and *Y* is in the 1's place. We can thus express *XY* as $10X + Y$. We can similarly express *YX* as $10Y + X$.

To illustrate with an actual number, consider the number 36. We can express 36 as $3(10) + 6(1)$, because 3 is in the 10's place and 6 is in the 1's.

We know that the difference between *XY* and *YX* is 27. Therefore, $XY - YX = 27$. We can substitute using the expressions above and simplify:

$$(10X + Y) - (10Y + X) = 27$$
$$9X - 9Y = 27$$
$$9(X - Y) = 27$$
$$X - Y = 3$$

Therefore, *X* and *Y* differ by 3.

We can also **Test Numbers.** This approach will take longer, because we have to find a number that fits the criterion by trial and error. However, once we hit upon any number that fits the criterion (e.g., 14), we can easily solve the problem.

The correct answer is (A).

PS 212. <u>EIVs</u>: VICs
Difficulty: 600–700   **OG Page:** 182

In this **Variables In Choices** problem, we are told that a **Circle** in the **Coordinate Plane** with center *C* is tangent to both the *x* and *y* axes, such that the distance from the origin *O* to point *C* equals *k*. We are asked for the radius of the circle.

In order to solve for the radius, it is helpful to **Redraw the Picture**, adding lines where necessary. Draw line segments from *C* to the points of tangency with the axes, as shown below:

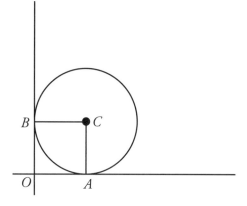

Because points *A* and *B* are on the circle, the distance from either of them to *C* must equal the radius *r*. Furthermore, a radius drawn to a point of tangency is perpendicular to the tangent at that point. Therefore, since all angles of quadrilateral *OACB* equal 90°, and the side lengths are equal, *OACD* is a **Square,** with *OC* as its diagonal. The length of the **Diagonal of a Square** is $\sqrt{2}$ times the side length:

$$k = r\sqrt{2}$$

Solving for *r* yields $r = \dfrac{k}{\sqrt{2}}$. This is the **answer**.

We could also have obtained this result by noticing that *OAC* and *OBC* are **45–45–90** triangles, or by using the **Pythagorean Theorem** on either of those right triangles:

$$r^2 + r^2 = 2r^2 = k^2 \qquad \text{Square root both sides.}$$
$$r\sqrt{2} = k \qquad \text{Solve for } r.$$
$$r = \frac{k}{\sqrt{2}}$$

The correct answer is (B).

PS 213. <u>EIVs</u>: VICs
Difficulty: 600–700   **OG Page:** 183

Notice that the verbal wind-up to this **Variables In Choices** problem—everything having to do with resistors and circuits —is irrelevant. The question is simply, "The reciprocal of *r* is equal to the sum of the reciprocals of *x* and *y*. What is *r* in terms of *x* and *y*?"

The **Reciprocals** of r, x, and y are simply 1/r, 1/x, and 1/y, respectively. Thus we can **Algebraically Translate** the words as follows:

$$\frac{1}{r}=\frac{1}{x}+\frac{1}{y}$$

If we take a **Direct Algebra** approach, it is tempting to simply "flip everything over" and conclude that r = x + y. However, this would be an illegal move: we can only invert both sides when each side consists entirely of a single fraction. That is, before we can "flip everything over," we must combine the right side into a single fraction. Multiply 1/x and 1/y by "convenient" forms of 1 in order to get a common denominator:

$$\frac{1}{r}=\frac{1}{x}\times\frac{y}{y}+\frac{1}{y}\times\frac{x}{x}$$

$$\frac{1}{r}=\frac{y}{xy}+\frac{x}{xy}$$

$$\frac{1}{r}=\frac{x+y}{xy}$$

NOW, we are permitted to do the "big flip":

$$r=\frac{xy}{x+y}\qquad\text{This is the **answer**.}$$

Don't forget the final flip! One of the wrong answers is the correct expression for 1/r.

We could also **Pick Numbers and Calculate a Target,** but the algebraic route is relatively fast and straightforward, once we learn to avoid the traps.

Finally, if we were really stuck, we could eliminate some wrong answers by **Units Analysis**. The correct answer must have the units of resistance. Since x and y have these same units, the formula for r in terms of x and y must yield these units.

Let's take an analogy. If x and y were lengths in feet, then r would need to be a length in feet as well. Which answer choices give us lengths in feet (not square feet, not 1/feet, etc.)? The only choices that actually give us lengths in feet are (B) and (D). The same holds true for units of resistance.

Moreover, we should avoid (B) because the result is too simplistic. If r equals x plus y, then all the talk of reciprocals would be pointless.

The correct answer is (D).

PS 214. <u>Word Translations</u>: Probability
Difficulty: 600–700   **OG Page:** 183

In this **Probability** problem, we want to find the probability that:

Xavier solves the problem
   AND
Yvonne solves the problem
   AND
Zelda does *not* solve the problem.

This problem involves **Multiple Outcomes.** When we want outcomes A AND B both to happen, and A and B are independent events, we can multiply the probability of A by the probability of B to find the probability that both outcomes occur. (In probability problems, the word AND usually means to multiply, while the word OR usually means to add.)

We are given the probabilities of Xavier and Yvonne solving the problem, but not of Zelda NOT solving the problem. To find the probability of Zelda NOT solving the problem, we will use the **1 − x Principle.** We know that:

$$P\left(\begin{array}{c}\text{Zelda solves}\\\text{the problem}\end{array}\right)+P\left(\begin{array}{c}\text{Zelda does NOT}\\\text{solve the problem}\end{array}\right)=1$$

so,

$$P\left(\begin{array}{c}\text{Zelda does NOT}\\\text{solve the problem}\end{array}\right)=1-P\left(\begin{array}{c}\text{Zelda solves}\\\text{the problem}\end{array}\right)$$

$$=1-\frac{5}{8}=\frac{3}{8}$$

In other words, if Zelda has a 5/8 chance of success, she has a 3/8 chance of failure.

Now we can answer the question by multiplying:

$$\left[P\left(\begin{array}{c}\text{Xavier}\\\text{solves the}\\\text{problem}\end{array}\right)\right]\left[P\left(\begin{array}{c}\text{Yvonne}\\\text{solves the}\\\text{problem}\end{array}\right)\right]\left[P\left(\begin{array}{c}\text{Zelda does}\\\text{NOT solve}\\\text{the problem}\end{array}\right)\right]$$

$$= \left(\frac{1}{4}\right)\left(\frac{1}{2}\right)\left(\frac{3}{8}\right) = \frac{3}{64}$$ This is the **answer**.

Notice that if we had used Zelda's chance of *success* instead, we would have come up with wrong answer choice (D).

The correct answer is (E).

PS 215. <u>EIVs</u>: Quadratic Equations
Difficulty: 700–800   **OG Page:** 183

This problem specifies an equation and then asks what x "could" be. Note the word "could": this means that there is more than one possible value for x, but only one of the possible values will appear among the answer choices. As we will see, we will wind up with a ***Quadratic Equation.***

$$\frac{1}{x} - \frac{1}{x+1} = \frac{1}{x+4}$$

Combine the two fractions on the left by creating a ***Common Denominator***, which is $x(x+1)$:

$$\frac{1}{x} - \frac{1}{x+1} = \frac{x+1}{x(x+1)} - \frac{x}{x(x+1)} =$$

$$\frac{x+1-x}{x(x+1)} = \frac{1}{x(x+1)}$$

Initially, this may seem complicated, but notice step 2: the x variables cancel each other out in the numerator.

Now we have the following:

$$\frac{1}{x(x+1)} = \frac{1}{x+4}$$

Take the reciprocal of each side and solve:

$$x(x+1) = x+4$$
$$x^2 + x = x+4$$
$$x^2 + x - x - 4 = 0$$
$$x^2 - 4 = 0$$
$$(x+2)(x-2) = 0$$
$$x = -2 \ or \ 2$$

Only -2 is among the choices. This is the **answer**.

Alternatively, we can answer this question by ***Testing Answer Choices.*** This may initially seem like a lot of work, but there is a shortcut. We know that the denominators of fractions cannot equal 0 because we ***Cannot Divide by Zero.*** If we look at the three fractions in this equation, we see that x cannot equal 0, −1 or −4, respectively. But 0, −1 and −4 are all answer choices, which means there are only two possible values of x: −2 or −3.

Testing the surviving answer choices gives us:

(C) $\dfrac{1}{-2} - \dfrac{1}{-2+1} = \dfrac{1}{-2+4}$ → $-\dfrac{1}{2} - (-1) = \dfrac{1}{2}$

$$\frac{1}{2} = \frac{1}{2}$$

(D) $\dfrac{1}{-3} - \dfrac{1}{-3+1} = \dfrac{1}{-3+4}$ → $-\dfrac{1}{3} - \left(-\dfrac{1}{2}\right) = 1$

$$\frac{1}{6} = 1$$

The equation is true when $x = -2$.

The correct answer is (C).

PS 216. <u>Number Properties</u>: Exponents & Roots
Difficulty: 600–700   **OG Page:** 183

When we simplify ***Exponential Expressions***, we should look for a ***Common Base***. Notice that all of the denominators are powers of 2. Start by breaking each base down into its ***Prime Factors***:

$$\left(\frac{1}{2}\right)^{-3}\left(\frac{1}{4}\right)^{-2}\left(\frac{1}{16}\right)^{-1} = \left(\frac{1}{2}\right)^{-3}\left(\frac{1}{2^2}\right)^{-2}\left(\frac{1}{2^4}\right)^{-1}$$

To simplify the given expression, remember that an expression with a negative exponent is the reciprocal of what the expression would be with a positive exponent. When we see ***Negative Exponents***, we should immediately think about ***Reciprocals***. Now apply the negative exponents by taking the reciprocal of each term and making the exponent positive. Then we add exponents:

$$(2)^3 \, (2^2)^2 \, (2^4)^1 = 2^3 \times 2^4 \times 2^4 = 2^{3+4+4} = 2^{11}$$

Because all of the answer choices have negative exponents, we can perform the same transformations on them—simply take the reciprocal of each and change the exponent to a positive. Our answer matches that in choice (B):

$$2^{11} = \left(\frac{1}{2}\right)^{-11}$$ This is the **answer**.

Alternatively, we can solve the problem without changing the exponents to their positive forms. We can bring the outside exponent inside and apply it to both numerator and denominator:

$$\left(\frac{1}{2}\right)^{-3}\left(\frac{1}{2^2}\right)^{-2}\left(\frac{1}{2^4}\right)^{-1} =$$

$$\left(\frac{1}{2^{-3}}\right)\left(\frac{1}{2^{-4}}\right)\left(\frac{1}{2^{-4}}\right) =$$

$$\left(\frac{1}{2^{-11}}\right)$$

The correct answer is (B).

PS 217. <u>Number Properties</u>: Divisibility & Primes
Difficulty: 600–700   **OG Page:** 183

This problem, which presents a large product of prime numbers (2's, 3's, 5's, and 7's, multiplying to 147,000), can be identified as a *Prime Factorization* problem once we understand the strange rules of the bead game. If we factor the given product, 147,000, into primes, then we will be able to determine what beads were pulled.

$$147,000 = 147 \times 1,000$$

1,000 is easy to factor, but 147 is a less common number. However, we can use *Divisibility Rules* to find the factors of 147. The digits of 147 add up to a multiple of 3 ($1 + 4 + 7 = 12$), so 147 is divisible by 3.

$$147 \times 1,000 = (3 \times 49) \times (10 \times 10 \times 10)$$
$$= 3 \times 7 \times 7 \times 2 \times 5 \times 2 \times 5 \times 2 \times 5$$
$$= 2^3 \times 3 \times 5^3 \times 7^2$$

We know that prime factorizations are unique. In other words, the above factorization ($2^3 \times 3 \times 5^3 \times 7^2$) is the only way of breaking down the number 147,000 into 2's, 3's, 5's, and 7's—indeed, the only way of breaking that number down into primes at all.

Therefore, since the bead values correspond to these primes, we know that three blue beads (the

2's), one green bead (the 3), three yellow beads (the 5's), and two red beads (the 7's) must have been drawn. We only care about the red beads in the end, but we should complete the prime factorization to ensure there are no lurking 7's anywhere.

Thus, two red beads were removed from the container.

The correct answer is (D).

PS 218. <u>EIVs</u>: Basic Equations
Difficulty: 600–700   **OG Page:** 183

This *Basic Equations* question asks us to solve for y. This problem tests our ability to manipulate a *Complicated Fraction*. First we should *Cross multiply*, then solve for y:

$$\frac{2}{\left(1+\frac{2}{y}\right)} = 1$$

$$2 = \left(1+\frac{2}{y}\right)$$

$$1 = \frac{2}{y}$$

$$y = 2$$ This is the **answer**.

Alternatively, we can use *Algebraic Reasoning* to "think" our way to a correct answer. If the fraction on the left side of the given equation is equal to 1, the numerator and denominator must be equal, and therefore the sum in the denominator must equal 2. That means that $1 + 2/y = 2$. Solving for y, we get $2/y = 1$, which means that $y = 2$.

The correct answer is (D).

PS 219. Number Properties: Consecutive Integers
Difficulty: 600–700   **OG Page:** 184

The set of three integers $\{a, b, c\}$ is defined as a set of consecutive positive integers in ascending order. Using our rules for *Consecutive Integers* and *Divisibility,* we can tackle scenarios I, II and III.

I. $c - a = 2$ ALWAYS TRUE

By definition, a set of three consecutive integers is one that can be expressed as n, $n + 1$, $n + 2$. The third member of the set, which, in this case, is c, must be 2 more than the first member of the set, a.

$(n + 2) - (n) = 2$

II. *abc* is an even integer   ALWAYS TRUE

Any product of integers that includes at least one even number will always be even. A set of three consecutive numbers must contain at least one even, and therefore will always have an even product.

III. $\dfrac{a+b+c}{3}$ is an integer   ALWAYS TRUE

This statement is asserting that the sum of three consecutive integers is divisible by 3. For any set of consecutive integers with an odd number of items, the sum of all of the integers is ALWAYS a multiple of the number of items. Since this is the sum of 3 consecutive integers, it will be divisible by 3. This could also be proven algebraically:

$\dfrac{n+(n+1)+(n+2)}{3} = \dfrac{3n+3}{3} = n+1$, which is not only an integer, but also the middle term of the sequence, *b*.

Thus, all three statemens are definitely true. This is the **answer**.

It is also possible to **Plug in Numbers** to prove each of the three statements. However, since we must find which statement(s) MUST be true, it is important to try more than one case. With consecutive integers, it makes the most sense to at least try both a case that begins with an odd integer and a case that begins with an even. Set up a **Table** to track these cases.

a, b, c	c − a = 2?	abc is even ?	(a + b + c)/3 = integer?
2, 3, 4	4 − 2 = 2	(2)(3)(4) = 24	(2 + 3 + 4)/3 = 3
3, 4, 5	5 − 3 = 2	(3)(4)(5) = 60	(3 + 4 + 5)/3 = 4

The questions can all be answered Yes in both cases.

The correct answer is (E).

PS 220. FDPs: Successive Percents & Percent Change
Difficulty: 600–700   **OG Page:** 184

This **Percent Change** problem also involves **Algebraic Translations.** Thus, we begin by deter-

mining the unknowns (the original hourly wage and the original number of hours worked) and **Naming Variables** (*w* and *h*, respectively). The product of the wage and the number of hours, *wh*, will represent the original amount of money earned. This is a typical **Wage Relationship.**

Because the hourly wage was increased by 25%, the new hourly wage will be 125% of the original wage, or 1.25*w*. We know that the number of hours will decrease, but we do not know by how much. We need to name one more variable. Use *x* to indicate the coefficient that should be placed in front of *h* to indicate the new hourly total.

We know that the total amount of money earned will remain the same. Thus:

$wh = (1.25w)(xh)$

We can divide both sides by *w* and *h*, because we know neither of them equals 0.

$1 = 1.25x$

At this stage, the easiest way to solve for *x* is to convert 1.25 to a fraction. 5/4 is equivalent to 1.25.

$1 = \dfrac{5}{4}x$ Multiply by the reciprocal $\dfrac{4}{5}$

$\dfrac{4}{5} = x = 80\%$ Convert $\dfrac{4}{5}$ to a percent

We are asked for the percentage decrease in the number of hours worked. 100% − 80% = 20%. This is the **answer**.

We could also use **Smart Numbers** to represent the original hourly wage and hours. Pick an hourly wage that is easy to increase by 25%. Let's say that this wage is $8/hr. The new wage will then be $10/hr. A Smart Number of hours originally worked could be 10, giving a total salary of $80. To earn the same amount at $10/hr, the number of hours would have to fall to 8, for a 20% decrease.

Finally, a **Percent Shortcut** relates 25% and 20% together. A 25% increase followed by a 20% decrease brings a number back to its original value. This is because 5/4 (1.25 = 25% increase) and 4/5 (0.80 = 20% decrease) are reciprocals. If hourly wages go up by 25%, we should drop hours 20% to compensate.

The correct answer is (B).

PS 221. <u>Word Translations</u>: Overlapping Sets
Difficulty: 600–700 **OG Page:** 184

This ***Overlapping Sets*** question asks us to determine both the minimum and maximum numbers of students who could be majoring in both chemistry and biology. We must therefore consider both cases as we think about ***Optimization*** both ways.

The maximum number of students who could be majoring in both subjects cannot be greater than the number majoring in the less numerous group. In other words, if 130 students major in chemistry and 150 in biology, the maximum number who could be majoring in both cannot be greater than 130. It could equal 130 (if all chemistry majors are also biology majors), but it cannot be greater.

Determining the minimum number requires a bit more thought. The question tells us that at least 30 students of the 200 total major in neither subject, then at most 200 − 30 = 170 students are majoring in one or the other or both. Since the sum of 130 and 150 is greater than 170, the "extra" students must have been counted in both groups. Thus, at least (130 + 150) − 170 = 110 students must be majoring in both subjects.

Thus, we conclude that the number of double-majors can be any integer between 110 and 130. This is the **answer**.

Notice that we've used a ***Hidden Constraint***: the number of people in any category cannot be less than zero.

A less theoretical approach to calculating the minimum involves the use of a ***Double-Set Matrix***.

We can define the sets as

(1) those who major in chemistry/those who don't
(2) those who major in biology/those who don't

and fill in the matrix with the given information as follows (and shade the box in question):

	Chem	No Chem	Total
Bio			150
No Bio		≥ 30	
Total	130		200

Because every row and column must add up to the total, we have enough information to figure out what can go in the rest of the boxes.

For the sake of the explanation, let's fill in the remaining information in phases. The newly added terms are indicated using **bold**.

	Chem	No Chem	Total
Bio			150
No Bio		≥ 30	**50**
Total	130	**70**	200

	Chem	No Chem	Total
Bio		**≤ 40**	150
No Bio	**≤ 20**	≥ 30	50
Total	130	70	200

Now we can use either the "Chem" column or the "Bio" row to calculate the minimum number of those who majored in both:

	Chem	No Chem	Total
Bio	**≥ 110**	≤ 40	150
No Bio	≤ 20	≥ 30	50
Total	130	70	200

If we wanted to calculate the maximum using the matrix, we could do so by considering the minimums (0) for the "No Chem/Bio" and "No Bio/Chem" boxes:

	Chem	No Chem	Total
Bio	**≤ 130**	≥ 0	150
No Bio	≥ 0	≥ 30	50
Total	130	70	200

The number of students majoring in both subjects must be between 110 and 130.

The correct answer is (D).

PS 222. <u>EIVs</u>: Quadratic Equations
Difficulty: 500–600 **OG Page:** 184

In this ***Algebra*** problem, we are asked to determine the number of possible values of x that satisfy a given equation. We can begin by multiplying the entire equation by x in order to eliminate the fraction. This turns the equation into a ***Quadratic:***

$$5 - \frac{6}{x} = x$$
$$5x - 6 = x^2$$

We can **Factor** this quadratic after bringing all terms to one side:

$$x^2 - 5x + 6 = 0$$
$$(x - 2)(x - 3) = 0$$

The solutions to the equation are 2, and 3, which are distinct. Therefore, x has two possible values. This is the **answer**.

Even if we were unable to factor the quadratic equation correctly, we would still be able to determine how many solutions are possible for x. As a secondary method, we can use the piece of the **Quadratic Formula** know as the **Discriminant**—$b^2 - 4ac$. This is the part under the square root in the formula. If the discriminant is positive, there are 2 solutions for x. If it's 0, there is 1 solution, and if it's negative there are no solutions.

We assign the coefficient of the x^2 term the variable a, assign the coefficient of the x term the variable b, and the coefficient of the constant term the variable c. For this equation, $a = 1$, $b = -5$ and $c = 6$. So $b^2 - 4ac = (-5)^2 - 4(1)(6) = 25 - 24 = 1$. The discriminant is positive so there are two possible solutions for x.

The correct answer is (C).

PS 223. <u>FDPs:</u> Percents
Difficulty: 700–800   **OG Page:** 184

In this **Percents** problem, we are told that **Mixture** X is 40% ryegrass, mixture Y is 25% ryegrass, and a mixture of X and Y is 30% ryegrass. We are asked to find what percent of the mixture by weight comes from mixture X.

Using **Algebraic Translations**, we want to write an equation to relate the amounts of ryegrass. **Naming Variables,** we can let x be the amount of mixture X, while y can be the amount of mixture Y. Converting **Percents to Decimals,** we can write $0.40x$ as the amount of ryegrass in mixture X. Similarly, $0.25y$ is the amount of ryegrass in mix-

ture Y, and $0.30(x + y)$ is the amount of ryegrass in the combined mixture.

$$0.40x + 0.25y = 0.30(x + y)$$
$$0.40x + 0.25y = 0.30x + 0.30y$$
$$0.10x = 0.05y$$

We can multiply both sides by 100 to get rid of the decimals:

$$10x = 5y$$
$$2x = y$$

Now we can find the ratio of x to y:

$$\frac{x}{y} = \frac{1}{2}$$

If x and y are in a 1 to 2 ratio, then x is 1/3 of the total and y is 2/3 of the total. Since the total is 100%, x is therefore 33^1/₃%. This is the **answer**.

Alternatively, we can look at this problem as a **Weighted Averages** problem. The percent of ryegrass in the combined mixture of X and Y, 30%, is between the ryegrass percents in the separate mixtures (40% and 25%). This should make sense: if we mix 2% milk with 0%(nonfat) milk, we get milk with a fat percentage *between* 2% and 0%. The exact number depends on the relative proportion of the original amounts. If we have a lot more nonfat milk than 2% milk in the mixture, the overall fat percentage will be closer to 0%, whereas if we have a lot more 2% milk than nonfat milk in the mixture, the overall fat percentage will be closer to 2%. We can see this on a spectrum:

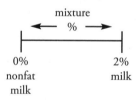

In the Official Guide problem, we are mixing 25% ryegrass with 40% ryegrass. We should expect a number in between, which is what we get (30%). Because the resulting 30% is closer to 25% that to 40%, we must have more of the 25% ryegrass (Y) than of the 40% ryegrass (X). This intuition can help us confirm our answer (that we have ^{1}/₃x and ^{2}/₃y).

The algebra in the first approach is quick enough and straightforward enough to master. Algebra is the way we ought to generate the actual number, but we should also understand the result conceptually using weighted averages.

The correct answer is (B).

PS 224. Number Properties: Consecutive Integers
Difficulty: 700–800   **OG Page:** 184

This ***Consecutive Integers*** problem asks us about the product $n(n + 1)(n + 2)$ which is the product of three consecutive integers. Looking at our answer choices, we want to know whether the product will be odd or even.

We should first consider ***Even & Odd Rules***. If we have consecutive integers, at least one will be even. Also, any product with an even number will be even.

> If n is even, then (even)(odd)(even) = even
> If n is odd, then (odd)(even)(odd) = even

We see that the product is even regardless of whether n is odd or even, so we can eliminate (A) and (B). (Notice that in (A) and (B) the key word *only* means that the product cannot be even in any other situation.) We can also eliminate (C) because the product is never odd.

We can also ***Test Values*** for n and see whether we spot any patterns.

> Suppose $n = 2$ (here, n is an even integer),
> (2)(3)(4) = 24   This is an even product.
> Suppose $n = 3$ (here, n is an odd integer),
> (3)(4)(5) = 60   This is an even product.

In (D), we want to find whether the product is divisible by 3. By ***Consecutive Integer Rules,*** the product of p or more consecutive integers is always divisible by p. This is true because in a group of p consecutive integers, at least one is a multiple of p. Thus, the product of 3 consecutive integers will always be divisible by 3, whether n is even or odd. So we can eliminate (D), which demands that the product be divisible by 3 *only* when n is odd.

Looking at (E), we cannot automatically conclude that the product of 3 consecutive integers is divisible by 4. However, when n is even, $n + 2$ is also even. Because two of the factors in the product are

divisible by 2, the entire product is definitely divisible by 4 whenever n is even. This is the **answer**.

Again, we can test values for n to confirm. Reusing the examples above, we see that the output numbers (24 and 60) are *both* divisible by 3, whether n is even or odd. Thus, (D) cannot be correct, and we are left with only one choice.

The correct answer is (E).

PS 225. FDPs: Fractions
Difficulty: 700–800   **OG Page:** 184

This ***Fractions*** problem specifies that a straight pipe is 1 yard long and is marked off in fourths and thirds. Start by drawing a diagram:

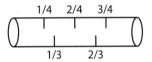

Remember that 1/3 > 1/4, so 1/3 should be placed to the right of 1/4. To clarify, think of the ***Decimal Equivalents:*** 1/3 is approximately 0.33 and 1/4 is 0.25.

The pipe is then cut at each of the above marks. We need to calculate a complete list of the lengths of pipe that result. Calculate one length and use ***Process of Elimination*** to get rid of any choices that do not include that length. Repeat until only one answer choice remains.

We can see immediately that one piece runs from the beginning to the first mark: 1/4. So one piece must be 1/4 in length. Eliminate answer (E).

Next, there is a length between the 1/4 mark and the 1/3 mark. The length is equal to the distance between these two numbers: 1/3 − 1/4 = 4/12 − 3/12 = 1/12. Eliminate (A), (B), and (C). Only (D) remains. This is the **answer**.

Alternatively, we could consider all possible lengths. To do so, we can think of thirds and fourths in terms of their ***Common Denominator,*** 12: 1/3 = 4/12, and 1/4 = 3/12. Then we can mark off every 3/12th and every 4/12th.

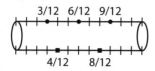

We can see that the differences are 3/12 (= 1/4), 1/12, and 2/12 (= 1/6).

The correct answer is (D).

PS 226. <u>FDPs</u>: Digits & Decimals
Difficulty: 700–800   **OG Page:** 184

In this difficult ***Digits & Decimals*** problem, we are asked to determine the value of $m - k$. Since m and k are both located on the left side of the equation, we must simplify this side. When dividing powers with the same base, we subtract exponents, so dividing 10^m by 10^k will result in 10^{m-k}.

However, we must also divide 0.0015 by 0.03, which is more easily accomplished if we convert these numbers to the integers 15 and 3. In order to do so, we can ***Trade Decimal Places for Powers of Ten.***

In the numerator, we move the decimal point four places to the right in order to change 0.0015 to 15. We compensate for shift by decreasing the exponent of 10 by 4. Our new numerator is thus $15 \times 10^{m-4}$.

Similarly, to convert 0.03 to the integer 3, we move the decimal point two places to the right. We trade these two places for two powers of 10 by decreasing the exponent by 2. Our new denominator is $3 \times 10^{k-2}$.

The problem now reads:

$$\frac{15 \times 10^{m-4}}{3 \times 10^{k-2}} = 5 \times 10^7$$

$$\frac{15}{3} \times \frac{10^{m-4}}{10^{k-2}} = 5 \times 10^7 \quad \text{Subtract exponents}$$

$$5 \times 10^{(m-4)-(k-2)} = 5 \times 10^7 \quad \text{Divide by 5}$$

$$10^{(m-4)-(k-2)} = 10^7$$

Since both sides of this equation share the same base (10), we can set the exponents equal to each other.

$(m - 4) - (k - 2) = 7$ Distribute the negative sign

$m - 4 - k + 2 = 7$ Combine like terms

$m - k - 2 = 7$ Add 2 to both sides

$m - k = 9$

The correct answer is (A).

PS 227. <u>EIVs</u>: VICs
Difficulty: 500–600   **OG Page:** 185

This tough ***Variables in Choices*** problem asks us to solve for $2xy$ in terms of a and b.

We can solve this problem by ***Picking Numbers and Calculating a Target.*** For this problem, Picking Numbers is faster, easier, and more reliable for most people than a purely algebraic approach.

If we let $x = 3$ and $y = 2$, then $2xy = 2(3)(2) = 12$. Thus, 12 is the ***Target Value.***

Use the values of x and y to find the values of a and b: $(3) + (2) = a = 5$ and $(3) - (2) = b = 1$. We now plug $a = 5$ and $b = 1$ into each answer choice to see which yields a value of 12:

(A) $\dfrac{a^2 - b^2}{2} = \dfrac{(5)^2 - (1)^2}{2} = \dfrac{24}{2} = 12$ **CORRECT**

(B) $\dfrac{b^2 - a^2}{2} = \dfrac{(1)^2 - (5)^2}{2} = -\dfrac{24}{2} = -12$ INCORRECT

(C) $\dfrac{a - b}{2} = \dfrac{5 - 1}{2} = \dfrac{4}{2} = 2$ INCORRECT

(D) $\dfrac{ab}{2} = \dfrac{(5)(1)}{2} = \dfrac{5}{2}$ INCORRECT

(E) $\dfrac{a^2 + b^2}{2} = \dfrac{(5)^2 + (1)^2}{2} = \dfrac{26}{2} = 13$ INCORRECT

Only answer choice (A) yields the target value of 12. This is the **answer**.

Alternatively, using a "textbook" ***Direct Algebra*** approach, we can solve for x by ***Elimination***. That is, we add the equations to cancel y:

$$\begin{array}{r} x + y = a \\ +(x - y = b) \\ \hline 2x = a + b \\ x = \dfrac{a+b}{2} \end{array}$$

We can use elimination to solve for y as well. This time, we subtract the equations to cancel x:

$$x + y = a$$
$$\underline{-(x - y = b)}$$
$$2y = a - b$$
$$y = \frac{a - b}{2}$$

Finally, we substitute these expressions for x and y into $2xy$. Notice the ***Difference of Squares*** that results. This is a favorite case of a ***Special Product***.

$$2xy = 2\left(\frac{a+b}{2}\right)\left(\frac{a-b}{2}\right) = \frac{2}{4}(a+b)(a-b) = \frac{a^2 - b^2}{2}$$

The correct answer is (A).

PS 228. <u>EIVs</u>: Formulas & Functions
Difficulty: 700–800   **OG Page:** 185

As stated in the problem, an ***Arithmetic Sequence*** is one in which each term after the first is equal to the sum of the preceding term and a constant. Since we can relate each term to its preceding term, ultimately we can relate each term to the first term by ***Direct Algebra.***

For the arithmetic sequence p, r, s, t, u, we can ***Name a Variable*** to express the constant difference between terms. Let's call this difference k.

$$r = p + k$$
$$s = r + k = (p + k) + k = p + 2k$$
$$t = s + k = (p + 2k) + k = p + 3k$$
$$u = t + k = (p + 3k) + k = p + 4k$$

Thus, the initial sequence in terms of p and k is:

$$p, r, s, t, u = p, p + k, p + 2k, p + 3k, p + 4k$$

Now we can plug in these terms to test the given sequences. Keep in mind that, for an arithmetic sequence, the difference between successive terms must be constant. This difference does not have to equal k, however.

I. $2p$, $2r$, $2s$, $2t$, $2u$
$= 2p, 2(p + k), 2(p + 2k), 2(p + 3k), 2(p + 4k)$
$= 2p, 2p + 2k, 2p + 4k, 2p + 6k, 2p + 8k$

The difference between successive terms is constant. Each time, we add $2k$.

   YES: this is an arithmetic sequence.

II. $p - 3$, $r - 3$, $s - 3$, $t - 3$, $u - 3$
$= p - 3, (p + k) - 3, (p + 2k) - 3,$
$\quad (p + 3k) - 3, (p + 4k) - 3$
$= p - 3, p - 3 + k, p - 3 + 2k,$
$\quad p - 3 + 3k, p - 3 + 4k$

The difference between successive terms is constant. Each time we add k.

   YES: this is an arithmetic sequence.

III. p^2, r^2, s^2, t^2, u^2
$= p^2, (p + k)^2, (p + 2k)^2, (p + 3k)^2, (p + 4k)^2$
$= p^2, (p^2 + 2pk + k^2), (p^2 + 4pk + k^2), \text{etc.}$

The difference between the first and second terms is $(p^2 + 2pk + k^2) - p^2 = 2pk + k^2$. The difference between the second and third terms is $(p^2 + 4pk + k^2) - p^2 + 2pk + k^2 = 2pk$. This is only an arithmetic sequence if $2pk + k^2 = 2pk$. If $k \neq 0$, then $2pk + k^2 \neq 2pk$.

   NO: This is not an arithmetic sequence, unless $k = 0$ (in which case all the numbers in the sequence are the same).

We can also surmise that this last group is not a sequence by knowing something about exponents. Exponents increase larger bases faster than they do smaller bases. They do not operate with consistent rates. Thus, it would be impossible for the squares of evenly spaced nonzero terms to be evenly spaced themselves.

Thus, the only two sequences that must be arithmetic are I and II. This is the **answer**.

Alternatively, we can solve this problem by ***Picking Numbers.*** We must be sure that the numbers we pick create an arithmetic sequence:

$$p = 3$$
$$r = 5$$
$$s = 7$$
$$t = 9$$
$$u = 11$$

Using these terms, the three sequences would look like this:

    I. 6, 10, 14, 18, 22
    II. 0, 2, 4, 6, 8
    III. 9, 25, 49, 81, 121

The first two sequences have a constant difference between the terms, and are therefore arithmetic. The third sequence is not spaced evenly, however, and is therefore not arithmetic.

The correct answer is (D).

PS 229. Geometry: Coordinate Plane
Difficulty: 700–800   **OG Page:** 185

To construct a possible **Triangle** PQR in the **Coordinate Plane,** we must make three selections/decisions: the point P, the point Q, and the point R. Because we need to count up triangles, we are dealing with a **Disguised Combinatorics** problem.

According to the **Fundamental Counting Principle**, we can find the number of ways to make each individual decision and multiply those to find the total number of triangles that can be constructed.

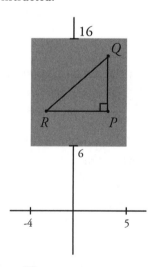

Since $\overline{PR}$ is parallel to the x-axis and the right angle is at P, the triangles formed must resemble the triangle pictured above. Note that point Q can be above point P (as pictured) or below point P, and point R can be left of point P (as pictured) or right of point P.

The number of potential points for P can be found using the Fundamental Counting Principle (also known as the **Slot Method**).

# of potential P points = (number of potential x-coordinates for P) × (number of potential y-coordinates for P)

The x-coordinate of P can be any integer between -4 and 5, inclusive, so there are $5 - (-4) + 1 = 10$ possibilities for x. We "add 1 before we're done" because we are **Counting a Consecutive Integer Set,** namely, -4 through 5.

The y-coordinate of P can be any integer between 6 and 16, inclusive, so there are $16 - 6 + 1 = 11$ possibilities for y. Now we can count possible positions for P:

# of possible P points = $10 \times 11 = 110$

To find the number of potential R points, given a particular P, we simply need to count the number of possible x-coordinates for R, since the y-coordinate for R must be the same as the y-coordinate for P. (We know this because $\overline{PR}$ must be parallel to the x-axis.)

Since R cannot occupy the same space as P, there is one fewer possibility for the x-coordinate of R than there were possibilities for P. Thus, there are $10 - 1 = 9$ possible x-coordinates for R, but only 1 possible y-coordinate. As a result, there are $9 \times 1 = 9$ possible positions for R.

# of possible R points = 9

To find the number of potential Q points, given a particular P and a particular R, we simply need to count the number of possible y-coordinates for Q since the x-coordinate for Q must be the same as the x-coordinate for P (as the right angle must be at point P).

Q cannot occupy the same space as P, because then if it did, PQR would not be a triangle. So Q has one fewer possibility for its y-coordinate than P had. There are $11 - 1 = 10$ possible y-coordinates for Q, but only 1 possible x-coordinate. As a result, there are $10 \times 1 = 10$ possible positions for Q.

# of possible Q points = 10

The total number of triangles can be found by using the Fundamental Counting Principle one additional time:

# of possible Triangles = (# of possible P points) × (# of possible R points) × (# of possible Q points)

# of possible Triangles = $110 \times 9 \times 10 = 9{,}900$

The correct answer is (C).

PS 230. <u>Number Properties</u>: Exponents & Roots
Difficulty: 700–800   **OG Page:** 185

We must begin this complicated *Exponents* and *Fractions* problem by properly simplifying the sum in the numerator. We approach this sum by finding a *Common Factor* of the various terms and placing that factor outside parentheses. The remaining factors of each element of the sum will then be added together.

This question wants to know how many times 2^{-17} the fraction is. Moreover, each term in the numerator a power of 2 near 2^{-17}. If we factor out 2^{-17} from each term we will have 2^{-17} in the numerator, which will help us make a direct comparison. Notice that this problem is more straight forward if we keep the *Negative Exponents* as they are, rather than change them to a positive exponent and move them to the other part of the fraction.

Factoring out 2^{-17} gives us:

$$\frac{2^{-17}(2^3 + 2^2 + 2^1 + 2^0)}{5}$$

We can now simplify the interior of the parentheses:

$$\frac{2^{-17}(8 + 4 + 2 + 1)}{5} = \frac{2^{-17}(15)}{5}$$

We can further reduce this to $2^{-17}(3)$. In other words, our fraction is 3 times 2^{-17}.

The correct answer is (C).

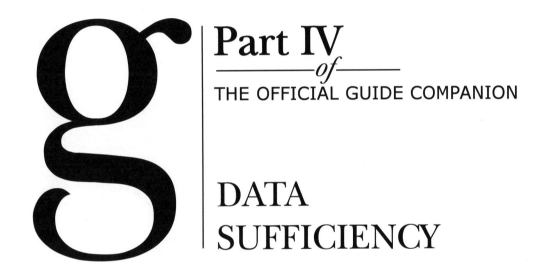

g | Part IV
of
THE OFFICIAL GUIDE COMPANION

DATA
SUFFICIENCY

DS 1. EIVs: Basic Equations
Difficulty: 300–500   **OG Page:** 273

In this problem involving **Basic Equations** and **Absolute Value,** we are asked to determine the value of $|x|$. There is no need to rephrase this question, so we can go straight to the statements.

(1): INSUFFICIENT. If $x = -|x|$, then we know that x must be negative or zero, since it equals the negation of an absolute value, which will always be positive or zero. This does not tell us anything about the specific numeric value of $|x|$, however.

(2): SUFFICIENT. If $x^2 = 4$, then x must equal either 2 or −2. Since $|2| = 2$ and $|-2| = 2$, it must be true that $|x| = 2$. This is sufficient to answer the question. If you know a variable's **Square,** you know its absolute value.

Note that the trap in this question is to think that both statements are needed in order to determine whether $x = 2$ or $x = -2$. Since the absolute value of either solution is the same, and we are asked only about the absolute value, we do not need to know the exact value of x.

The correct answer is (B): Statement (2) ALONE is sufficient, but statement (1) alone is not sufficient.

DS 2. FDPs: Percents
Difficulty: 500–600   **OG Page:** 273

In this **Percents** problem, we are asked to determine the percentage of red-haired women in a group of people.

$$\frac{\text{red-haired women}}{\text{number of people in group}}(100) = ?$$

We would be able to answer this question if we knew the number of red-haired women and the total number of people in the group. Also, we could answer the question if we are given the relevant proportion directly.

(1): INSUFFICIENT. Even if we know that 5% of the women in the group have red hair, we do not know how many women there are, nor do we know how many people there are in the group as a whole.

(2): INSUFFICIENT. This statement tells us nothing about women with red hair.

(1) and (2): INSUFFICIENT. Even with these combined pieces of information, we do not know the number of women with red hair, the number of people in the group as a whole, or the fraction of red-haired women in the group.

The correct answer is (E): Statements (1) and (2) TOGETHER are not sufficient.

DS 3. Word Translations: Probability
Difficulty: 300–500   **OG Page:** 273

The probability that a boy will be selected to read is equal to the number of boys divided by the total number of students. The **Rephrased** question is therefore "What is B/T?"

We will have sufficient information if we are given the actual amounts, or told the proportion directly.

(1): SUFFICIENT. If boys are two-thirds of the class, $B/T = 2/3$. The probability of selecting a boy is 2/3.

(2): INSUFFICIENT. Knowing that 10 students are girls does not tell us the number of boys or the total number of students.

The correct answer is (A): Statement (1) ALONE is sufficient, but statement (2) alone is not sufficient.

DS 4. Word Translations: Overlapping Sets
Difficulty: 500–600   **OG Page:** 273

In this **Overlapping Sets** problem, students are enrolled in chemistry and/or biology. Some students may be enrolled in both courses, and some students may be enrolled in neither course.

If we use a **Double-Set Matrix**, we can let x be the number of students enrolled in both biology and chemistry, and y be the number of students enrolled in neither class.

		Chemistry?		
		Yes	No	Total
Biology?	Yes	x		
	No		y	
	Total			

We can *Rephrase* this question as, "What is $x - y$?"

(1): INSUFFICIENT. Knowing 60 people took chemistry does not provide enough information to find $x - y$.

Biology?		Chemistry?		
		Yes	No	Total
	Yes	x		
	No		y	
	Total	60		

(2): INSUFFICIENT. Knowing 85 people took biology does not provide enough information to find $x - y$.

Biology?		Chemistry?		
		Yes	No	Total
	Yes	x		85
	No		y	
	Total			

(1) and (2): INSUFFICIENT. Even with the total enrollment numbers for both biology and chemistry, we still cannot find $x - y$.

Biology?		Chemistry?		
		Yes	No	Total
	Yes	x		85
	No		y	
	Total	60		

The correct answer is (E): Statements (1) and (2) TOGETHER are not sufficient.

DS 5. Word Translations: Minor Question Types
Difficulty: 300–500   **OG Page:** 273

The problem, which involves *Number Line* thinking, specifies that an expressway has the following four exits in order: J, K, L, and M. The problem asks for the value of the distance from K to L. There is no simple rephrasing of this question. We have to know something about the relationship between K and L.

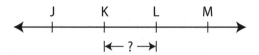

(1): INSUFFICIENT. We can add this information to our diagram, but we cannot calculate the distance from K to L.

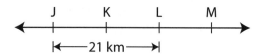

(2): INSUFFICIENT. We can add this information to our diagram, but we cannot calculate the distance from K to L.

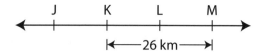

(1) AND (2): INSUFFICIENT. Even with both statements, there are multiple possible values for the distance from K to L. Here are two possibilities:

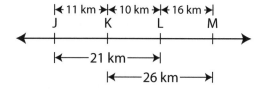

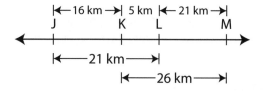

In essence, the fixed distances (21 and 26 km) can slide past each other, changing the K-to-L distance.

The correct answer is (E): Statements (1) and (2) TOGETHER are not sufficient.

DS 6. Number Properties: Odds & Evens
Difficulty: 300–500   **OG Page:** 273

This *Odds & Evens* question asks whether $n + 1$ is odd. Since the integer n must be even in order for $n + 1$ to be odd, we can *Rephrase* the question as "Is n even?"

(1): SUFFICIENT. If $n + 2$ is an even integer then n must also be even. Only an even integer added to another even (2, in this case) can equal another even integer. Here, we are applying *Properties of Odds & Evens*.

(2): SUFFICIENT. Since odds and evens alternate, we know that if $n - 1$ is odd, n must be even.

The correct answer is (D): EACH statement ALONE is sufficient.

DS 7. <u>FDPs:</u> Percents
Difficulty: 300–500   **OG Page:** 273

This *Percents* problem requires an understanding of the term "rate of return," which refers to the average return, in dollars, of the investment *per dollar invested*. (Remember that all rates are expressed as one unit *per* another unit.) This type of rate may be expressed either as a *Fraction* or as a *Percent*.

(1): SUFFICIENT. The annual rate of return for investment type J is $115 per $1,000, or $(115/1,000)$ per dollar invested. Likewise, the annual rate of return for investment type K is $300 per $2,500, or $(300/2,500)$ per dollar invested. Since these are both definite numerical figures, we will be able to determine which of them is greater. No further calculation is necessary.

(2): INSUFFICIENT. This statement provides the rate of return of investment type K. However, we know nothing about investment type J.

The correct answer is (A): Statement (1) ALONE is sufficient, but statement (2) alone is not sufficient.

DS 8. <u>Word Translations:</u> Algebraic Translations
Difficulty: 300–500   **OG Page:** 273

In this *Algebraic Translations* problem, we can first *Name Variables:*

r = # of crates of oranges
g = # of crates of grapefruit

We are told the prices of crates of oranges and grapefruit, and we need to find the number of crates containing oranges. In other words, we are looking for the value of r.

(1): INSUFFICIENT. This statement translates into the following equation:

$r = 2g + 20$

Using only this equation, we cannot figure out the value of r.

(2): INSUFFICIENT. Since we are given a total cost, we can combine it with the information in the question stem about price to set up the following equation, which expresses a *Cost Relationhip:*

$15r + 18g = 38,700$

Using only this equation, we cannot figure out the value of r.

(1) and (2): SUFFICIENT. Using *Direct Algebra* to manipulate both equations, we can find the value of both variables. We can *Substitute* for r and solve for g:

$15(2g + 20) + 18g = 38,700$

or substitute for g and solve for r:

$15r + 18(r - 20)/2 = 38,700.$

In either equation, we have one variable and no exponents, so we will be able to find unique values for both variables. We can solve for r.

In fact, even before substituting, we should recognize that when we have *Two Different Linear Equations* and *Two Unknowns,* we can solve for the unknowns.

The correct answer is (C): BOTH statements TOGETHER are sufficient, but NEITHER statement ALONE is sufficient.

DS 9. <u>FDPs:</u> Fractions
Difficulty: 300–500   **OG Page:** 273

This question involves both *Fractions* and *Algebraic Translations*. To get started, we can *Name Variables* representing various quantities.

s = amount that Pat saved last month
e = amount that Pat earned last month

From the given information, we know that $s = \$600$.

We are asked to find e.

(1): SUFFICIENT. Knowing that Pat spent 1/2 of his earnings last month for living expenses while saving 1/3 of the remainder means that Pat saved 1/3 of the remaining 1/2 of his earnings or $\left(\frac{1}{3}\right)\left(\frac{1}{2}\right) = \frac{1}{6}$ of his earnings.

We can use this information, in conjunction with the given to solve for e:

$$s = \frac{1}{6}(e)$$
$$600 = \frac{1}{6}(e)$$
$$e = 3600$$

(2): INSUFFICIENT. We know that Pat paid twice as much in taxes as he saved, so he paid $1,200 in taxes. However, this tells us nothing about his earnings.

The correct answer is (A): Statement (1) ALONE is sufficient, but statement (2) alone is not sufficient.

DS 10. <u>Word Translations</u>: Rates & Work
Difficulty: 300–500   **OG Page:** 273

This problem describes a tank of water into which water is being pumped and out of which water is being drained. This is actually a variation of the **Working Together: Add the Rates** problem type. In this case, the two pipes are working *against* each other, so we **Subtract the Rates.** The inlet rate minus the outlet rate will give us the effective rate. We need both the inlet and outlet rates, or the difference between the two, in order to solve.

(1): INSUFFICIENT. This statement does not provide us with either the inlet or the outlet rate. Moreover, knowing the original amount of water in the tank is of no use whatsoever, as we are only concerned with the rate of increase, not with any actual amount in the tank.

(2): SUFFICIENT. This statement alone gives us both of the rates that we need. We do not need to actually subtract to find the overall rate of increase, as we know that we have enough information to do so.

The correct answer is (B): Statement (2) ALONE is sufficient, but statement (1) alone is not sufficient.

DS 11. <u>EIVs</u>: Inequalities
Difficulty: 300–500   **OG Page:** 273

In this **Inequalities** problem, we are asked whether x is negative. There is no need to rephrase this question, so we can proceed directly to the statements.

(1): SUFFICIENT. If $9x > 10x$, it must be true that x is negative.

One way to verify this is to subtract $9x$ from both sides, using **Direct Algebra:**

$$9x > 10x$$
$$9x - 9x > 10x - 9x$$
$$0 > x$$

If 0 is greater than x, then x is negative by definition.

Alternatively, we can **Test Possibilities:** specifically, both a positive value for x and a negative value. Then we can contrast the outcomes. For example, if $x = 2$, then $9x = 18$ and $10x = 20$. It is NOT true that $9x > 10x$ if $x = 2$, so this case does not fit the statement.

However, if $x = -2$, then $9x = -18$ and $10x = -20$. In this case, it is true that $9x > 10x$. We can see that only negative values of x will fit this statement.

(2): INSUFFICIENT. Here, knowing that $x + 3$ is positive does not tell us whether x itself is positive or negative.

We can express this statement as $x + 3 > 0$ and then subtract 3 from both sides: $x > -3$. There are both positive and negative values that will satisfy this inequality.

The correct answer is (A): Statement (1) ALONE is sufficient, but statement (2) alone is not sufficient.

DS 12. <u>Number Properties</u>: Odds & Evens
Difficulty: 300–500   **OG Page:** 273

In this **Odds & Evens** problem, we are asked if the sum of the two integers i and j is even. The sum of two even integers would be even, as would the sum of two odd integers. Therefore, a good **Rephrasing** of the question is, "Are i and j both even or both odd?"

(1): INSUFFICIENT. This statement does not allow us to determine if *i* is even or odd. Moreover, it tells us nothing about *j*.

(2): SUFFICIENT. If *i = j*, then either both variables will be even or both will be odd. The sum will be even in either case. Notice that we must *Test All Cases,* but we wind up at the same destination.

The correct answer is (B): Statement (2) ALONE is sufficient, but statement (1) alone is not sufficient.

DS 13. Word Translations: Algebraic Translations
Difficulty: 300–500   **OG Page:** 273

A call costs $0.42 for each of the first 3 minutes ($1.26 total) and $0.18 for each additional minute. How long was the call? This *Algebraic Translations* situation can be rephrased as an equation. We can *Name a Variable* and let *C* stand for the total cost of the call. We also use *x* for the full number of minutes, as was already defined in the problem. Notice that we only start paying 18 cents per minute after 3 minutes:

$$C = 1.26 + 0.18(x - 3)$$

This is a fairly typical kind of *Cost Relationship.* Since we have a *Linear Equation* with two variables, it is clear that knowing *C* will allow us to solve for *x*, and knowing *x* will allow us to solve for *C*. Therefore, we can further *Rephrase* the question as, "What is the total cost *C*, or what is the number of minutes *x*?"

(1): SUFFICIENT. We already know that the charge for the first three minutes of the call is $1.26. If this is $0.36 less than the charge for the remainder of the call, then the remainder of the call costs $1.62. Therefore, the entire call costs $1.26 + $1.62, or $2.88. Thus, *C* is $2.88, and we know we can solve for *x*.

(2): SUFFICIENT. *C* = $2.88. Therefore, we know that 2.88 = 1.26 + 0.18(*x* − 3). It is now possible to solve for *x* (of course, we do not need to actually do so).

The correct answer is (D): EACH statement ALONE is sufficient.

DS 14. Word Translations: Rates & Work
Difficulty: 600–700   **OG Page:** 274

In this *Rates* problem, we are asked to find the time it takes for Car X to cross a bridge that is 1/2 mile long. We can use the *Rate–Time–Distance Formula* to find the time:

$$\text{Time} = \frac{\text{Distance}}{\text{Rate}}$$

$$\text{Time} = \frac{(\frac{1}{2} \text{ mile})}{\text{Rate}}$$

Given that we are looking for time, there are three legitimate *Rephrasings* of the question that we can consider:

What is Car X's rate?

What is Car X's time?

What is another relationship between Car X's rate and time?

(1): INSUFFICIENT. All we know from this statement is that Car X was on the bridge one second less than Car Y. Without knowing how long Car Y was on the bridge, we do not know how long Car X was on the bridge. This does not answer any of our rephrased questions.

(2): INSUFFICIENT. With Car Y's rate, we can find how long Car Y was on the bridge.

$$\text{Time} = \frac{\text{Distance}}{\text{Rate}} = \frac{(\frac{1}{2} \text{ mile})}{(30 \text{ miles per hour})}$$

$$= \frac{1}{60} \text{ hour} = 1 \text{ minute}$$

Knowing how long Car Y was on the bridge tells us nothing about Car X, thus this statement is insufficient.

(1) and (2): SUFFICIENT. With both statements, we know Car Y was on the bridge for 1 minute, or 60 seconds, and Car X was on the bridge for 1 second less than Car Y, or 59 seconds.

The correct answer is (C): BOTH statements TOGETHER are sufficient, but NEITHER statement ALONE is sufficient.

DS 15. <u>EIVs</u>: Basic Equations
Difficulty: 300–500   **OG Page:** 274

This ***Basic Equations*** problem tells us that $n + k = m$ and asks for the value of k. This is a ***Combined Expression*** or Combo problem in disguise. We do not need the values of the individual variables, but rather a value for an arithmetic combination of them. For Combo problems, we should determine everything that would be sufficient before looking at the statements.

In this case, solve the given equation for the desired variable, k. If $n + k = m$, then $k = m - n$. Determining the value of k is sufficient, but it is also sufficient to determine the value of $m - n$. We can ***Rephrase*** the question as "What is k, or what is $m - n$?"

(1): INSUFFICIENT. This does not provide us with values for either k or $m - n$.

(2): SUFFICIENT. The given equation, $m + 10 = n$, does not contain k at all, but it does contain both m and n. It can be rearranged to yield a value for $m - n$. We get $m - n = -10$. Therefore $k = -10$.

The correct answer is (B): Statement (2) ALONE is sufficient, but statement (1) alone is not sufficient.

DS 16. <u>Number Properties</u>: Divisibility & Primes
Difficulty: 300–500   **OG Page:** 274

No rephrasing is required. We are asked whether x is an integer. As we shall see, this problem requires knowledge of ***Integer Properties*** and ***Divisibility Rules.***

(1): SUFFICIENT. $x/2$ is an integer. We can ***Name a Variable*** to represent this integer. Let's call it m. Then $x/2 = m$.

The question asks about x, so let's solve this equation for x. We get $x = 2m$. So x is equal to 2 times some integer m. Doubling any integer must produce a new integer.

(2): INSUFFICIENT. $2x$ is an integer. Let $2x = n$. Solving for x, we get $x = n/2$. So x is equal to some integer n divided by 2.

Do we get an integer whenever we divide an integer by 2? Not always. If n is even, $n/2$ will be an integer. If n is odd, $n/2$ will not be an integer.

The correct answer is (A): Statement (1) ALONE is sufficient, but statement (2) alone is not sufficient.

DS 17. <u>Number Properties</u>: Odds & Evens
Difficulty: 300–500   **OG Page:** 274

No rephrase is necessary. This ***Odds & Evens*** question asks whether P is odd.

(1): SUFFICIENT. Add the given quantities to create one expression $(3P + 15)$ that we are told is an even number. $3P + 15 =$ even. 15 is odd, so if we subtract it from both sides, we know that $3P$ is odd. The reason is that Even − Odd = Odd, by ***Properties of Odds & Evens.*** Furthermore, the only way for a product of integers such as $3P$ to be odd is for all the integers to be odd. Therefore, P itself must be odd.

(2): SUFFICIENT. Add the given quantities to create one expression $(3P + 8)$ that we are told is an odd number. $3P + 8 =$ odd. 8 is even, so if we subtract 8 from both sides, we know that $3P$ must be odd, because Odd − Even = Odd. Furthermore, the only way for a product of integers such as $3P$ to be odd is for all the integers to be odd. Therefore, P itself must be odd.

The correct answer is (D): EACH statement ALONE is sufficient.

DS 18. <u>Geometry</u>: Polygons
Difficulty: 300–500   **OG Page:** 274

In this ***Polygons*** problem, we are given the dimensions of a certain rectangular block. We are asked how many of these blocks could fit in a certain rectangular box.

If we think about this ***3-D Geometry*** problem in real life terms, we realize that if we know the dimensions of the box, we will be able to figure out how many blocks fit in the box. So our ***Rephrased*** question is "What are the dimensions of the box?"

(1): INSUFFICIENT. Knowing that there are 25 blocks on the bottom layer does not tell us how many blocks there are total.

(2): SUFFICIENT. If we know the dimensions of the box, we can calculate the number of blocks that can fit in it.

Remember, at this stage, it would actually be a waste of time to figure out how many blocks can fit in the box.

The correct answer is (B): Statement (2) ALONE is sufficient, but statement (1) alone is not sufficient.

DS 19. EIVs: Formulas & Functions
Difficulty: 300–500   **OG Page:** 274

We know from the given information that there are 200 terms in **Sequence** S. However, we are not given any of the values of the terms in the sequence or the rule about how the terms relate to one another. The question asks for the 192nd term. Remember, since this is Data Sufficiency, we do not have to find the *actual* value. We simply have to know that we *could* get it, in theory.

(1): INSUFFICIENT. Knowing that the first term of S is −40 tells us nothing about the 192nd term since we do not know how the terms relate to one another.

(2): INSUFFICIENT. Knowing that each term of S after the first term is 3 less than the preceding term tells us how the terms are related to one another. This can be used to generate one term from another, but this is not enough to tell us the 192nd term, because we still need the value of one of the terms.

(1) and (2): SUFFICIENT. Statement (1) gives us the value of one of the terms and statement (2) gives us a way to find every term from the preceding. It is possible to find the 192nd term by subtracting 3 from the first term 191 times.

A sequence can often be seen as a series of dominoes. Statement (1) gives us the first domino in the sequence but doesn't tell us how the dominoes are connected. Statement (2) connects each domino to its predecessor but doesn't give us any actual

domino. We need the two statements together to knock down every domino, including the 192nd.

Of course, we could use a **Direct Sequence** formula and solve:

$$S_2 = -40 - 3$$
$$S_3 = -40 - 3(2)$$
$$\vdots$$
$$S_n = -40 - 3(n-1)$$
$$S_{192} = -40 - 3(191) = -613$$

However, we should avoid carrying out this calculation, or at least we should stop as soon as we recognize that we can find the 192nd term.

The correct answer is (C): BOTH statements TOGETHER are sufficient, but NEITHER statement ALONE is sufficient.

DS 20. Geometry: Triangles & Diagonals
Difficulty: 300–500   **OG Page:** 274

In this **Triangles** problem, we can begin by **Drawing the Picture** described:

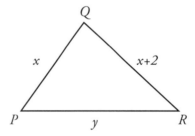

Note that, because we don't know actual values, the triangle cannot be drawn to scale.

We are asked which angle has the greatest measure. This will be the angle across from the longest side. We know that x can't be longest side, because it must be smaller than $x + 2$. Either the y side or the $x + 2$ side must be longest.

In order to find the longest side, and therefore the largest angle, we can ask the **Rephrased** question: "Is $y > x + 2$?"

(1): SUFFICIENT. $y = x + 3$. We can show this information in the drawing:

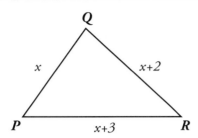

Although we do not know the value of *x*, we know that $\overline{PR}$ is longer than the other two side lengths. Thus, $\angle PQR$, which is opposite side length $\overline{PR}$, will be the largest angle.

(2): INSUFFICIENT. Although this statement gives us a value for *x*, we still do not know the value of *y*. Thus, we cannot determine whether the side of length *y* is longer or shorter than either of the other two sides.

The correct answer is (A): Statement (1) ALONE is sufficient, but statement (2) alone is not sufficient.

DS 21. Word Translations: Overlapping Sets
Difficulty: 300–500 **OG Page:** 274

In this ***Overlapping Sets*** problem, we are asked to determine the percent of drama club members who are female. There are several ways to figure this out without knowing any specific numbers (e.g., using *Ratios, Percents* or *Fractions*), so we should not worry about finding specific values. However, we will still need either a percent or a ratio of female members of the drama club to total members of the drama club.

(1): INSUFFICIENT: Knowing the percent of female students who are drama club members does not tell us the percent of drama club members who are female. For example, say there are 100 female students and 40%, or 40, of them are in the drama club. If the drama club has 200 members, then the percent would be 40/200 = 1/5 = 20%. But if the club has 400 members, then the percent would be 40/400 = 1/10 = 10%. In both cases, the percent of female students in the club was the same.

(2): INSUFFICIENT. Knowing the percent of male students who are members of the club does not tell us anything about the percent of drama

club members who are female. Keep in mind that this statement is NOT telling us that 25% of the club is male but rather that 25% of male students are in the club. Since we do not know the percent of the club that is male, we cannot deduce the percent that is female.

(1) and (2): INSUFFICIENT. 40% of the female students in the school are in the drama club, and 25% of the male students in the school are in the drama club. However, without knowing how many male and female students are in the school, we have no way of knowing what percent of the drama club is female. Different ratios of male to female students in the school will make different ratios of male to female students in the drama club.

Thus, even using both statements together, we cannot determine the percent of drama club members who are female.

In this problem, we wound up using ***Percent Reasoning,*** but we could have set up a ***Double-Set Matrix*** to solve.

The correct answer is (E): Statements (1) and (2) TOGETHER are not sufficient.

DS 22. Word Translations: Algebraic Translations
Difficulty: 500–600 **OG Page:** 274

This ***Algebraic Translations*** problem asks us for the cost per ounce of a family-size box of cereal. Cost per ounce is total cost divided by the number of ounces. There is nothing to rephrase, so we can go into the statements.

(1): INSUFFICIENT. This statement tells us that the family-size box of cereal contains 10 more ounces of cereal than does a regular-size box, but we do not know how many ounces of cereal are in the latter. We also do not know the cost of a family-size box of cereal.

(2): INSUFFICIENT. This statement tells us the cost of a family-size box of cereal, but we do not know anything about the number of ounces of cereal it contains.

(1) and (2): INSUFFICIENT. Put the information from the two statements into a ***Tracking Chart.***

Cereal Box	Size of Box (oz.)	Cost of Box ($)	Cost per Oz. ($/oz.)
regular size	s		
family size	$s + 10$	$5.40	

With the information provided, we still have no way of knowing the cost per ounce of the cereal in the family-size box of cereal. The overall **Cost Relationship** is still unknown.

The correct answer is (E): Statements (1) and (2) TOGETHER are not sufficient.

DS 23. <u>Word Translations</u>: Minor Question Types
Difficulty: 300–500   **OG Page:** 274

In this **Miscellaneous Cost** problem, we are told that profit increases, *though not proportionally*, with the number of units sold.

This tells us that "more means more"—but we do not know *how much* more. For instance, if 5 units generate $5 in profit, 6 units could generate $5.01, $10, or $1 million—all we know is that selling more than 5 units would generate more than $5 in profit. Put another way, if we graphed units vs. profits, the graph would always go up, but it would not be a straight line through the origin.

To answer the question, "Did the profit exceed $4 million on sales of 380,000 units?", we would need to know that $4 million in profit had already been exceeded by some smaller number of units. Even knowing that 379,999 units generated $3,999,999.00 would not be enough (for instance, maybe that last unit generated only one penny of profit). To answer the question with a *Yes*, we need to know that *less than* 380,000 units generated *at least* $4 million in profit.

(1): INSUFFICIENT. If 200,000 units generated at least $2 million in profit, then all we know is that more than 200,000 units must generate more than $2 million in profit. This is not enough to tell us whether 380,000 units generated more than $4 million in profit.

(2): SUFFICIENT. If 350,000 units generated $5 million in profit, then more than 350,000 units must generate more than $5 million in profit. Even without knowing *how much more*, this is

enough to tell us that 380,000 units would generate more than $4 million in profit.

The correct answer is (B): Statement (2) ALONE is sufficient, but statement (1) alone is not sufficient.

DS 24. <u>Number Properties</u>: Odds & Evens
Difficulty: 500–600   **OG Page:** 274

There is no particular rephrasing of this question, which asks us whether n is even.

(1): SUFFICIENT. We can use **Properties of Odds & Evens** to rephrase this statement. If $n^2 - 1$ is an odd number, then n^2 must be an even number. n^2 is an even number only if integer n is even.

n	n^2	$n^2 - 1$
~~Odd~~	~~Odd~~	~~Even~~
Even	Even	Odd

(2): SUFFICIENT. We can again use **Properties of Odds & Evens** to rephrase this statement. If $3n + 4$ is an even integer, then $3n$ must be even. The only way for (odd) × (n) to be even is if n is even.

n	$3n$	$3n + 4$
~~Odd~~	~~Odd~~	~~Odd~~
Even	Even	Even

The correct answer is (D): EACH statement ALONE is sufficient.

DS 25. <u>Word Translations</u>: Algebraic Translations
Difficulty: 500–600   **OG Page:** 274

This **Algebraic Translations** problem specifies that Carmen works 30 hours per week but it does not specify her hourly pay. We can now **Name a Variable** and call her hourly pay x. Her total weekly pay would be $30x$, according to her **Wage Relationship**.

If Carmen's hourly wage is increased by $1.50, then her new hourly wage is $x + 1.5$, but the number of hours she works will not stay the same. Call her new number of hours y. Her total weekly pay after the wage increase would be $(x + 1.5)y$.

The problem specifies that Carmen wants to earn the *same* weekly pay, so we can set the two total weekly pays equal to each other:

$$30x = (x + 1.5)y.$$

The question asks how many fewer hours she could work to earn the same pay? That would be represented by $30 - y$. If we can find y, then we can find $30 - y$, so we can **Rephrase** the question to "what is the value of y?"

If we know what x is, then we can solve for y. If we can find either the value of x or the value of y, then the information is sufficient.

(1): SUFFICIENT. If her current weekly pay is $225, then $225 = 30x$. We can solve for x. Therefore, we can solve for y.

(2): SUFFICIENT. If $1.50 represents 20% of her current hourly wage, then $1.5 = 0.2x$. We can solve for x. Therefore, we can solve for y.

The correct answer is (D): EACH statement ALONE is sufficient.

DS 26. <u>EIVs:</u> Formulas & Functions
Difficulty: 500–600   **OG Page:** 274

We are asked for the number of units n produced by Company X according to this **New Formula**
$$n = \frac{900}{1 + c2^{-t}}.$$

We are asked for the number of units produced in month 6, so $t = 6$. We can therefore **Rephrase** the question: "What is $\frac{900}{1 + c2^{-6}}$?" Since the value of this entire expression depends on the value of one variable, c, we can rephrase this question as "What is the value of c?"

(1): SUFFICIENT. When $t = 1$, $n = 180$. Substitute these values into the original formula:
$$180 = \frac{900}{1 + c2^{-1}}$$

The only variable in the expression is c. Since c has an exponent of 1 and there are no other variables, this is a **Linear Equation** (although this might not be obvious until we cross-multiply and replace 2^{-1} with 1/2).

A one-variable linear equation can always be solved to determine a unique value for the variable. We should not actually solve this equation. We should simply note that we can obtain a value for c, satisfying our rephrasing.

(2): SUFFICIENT. Similarly, by substituting $t = 2$ and $n = 300$ into the original formula, we can obtain a value for c.

The correct answer is (D): EACH statement ALONE is sufficient.

DS 27. <u>FDPs:</u> Fractions
Difficulty: 300–500   **OG Page:** 275

Let's **Name a Variable** in this **Fractions** problem. If we let x designate the amount of oil in the tank before the removal of the 200 gallons, then the first sentence in the question stem translates to this equation:

$$x - 200 = 3/7 \times Capacity$$

The question asks for the capacity. Let's name another variable and call the capacity C. If we can find the value of x, we can find the value of C from the equation above. We can **Rephrase** the question as "What is C, or what is x?"

Furthermore, this equation is linear (it would represent a line in a coordinate plane). In a **Linear Equation**, the variables have no exponents. They are only multiplied by constants and added or subtracted.

If either statement gives us a distinct linear equation relating x and C, we will have enough information to find C.

(1): SUFFICIENT. This statement translates to the equation $x = 1/2(C)$, which is another linear equation. Together with the stem equation, we now have **Two Different Linear Equations** and **Two Unknowns**. We can stop right now, because we know that we can solve for the variables x and C.

If we feel the need to verify, we can **Substitute** $1/2(C)$ for x in the stem equation. This gives us $1/2(C) - 200 = 3/7(C)$, a linear equation that can be solved for a unique value of C.

(2): SUFFICIENT. This statement translates to the equation $x - 200 = C - 1,600$, another linear equation. We therefore have two independent linear equations, and we can again solve for the variables x and C.

Again, if we feel the need to verify, we can substitute $C - 1,400$ for x in the stem equation. This gives us $(C - 1,400) - 200 = 3/7(C)$, a linear equation that can be solved for a unique value of C.

The correct answer is (D): EACH statement ALONE is sufficient.

DS 28. <u>Word Translations:</u> Statistics
Difficulty: 300–500   **OG Page:** 275

To answer this *Statistics* problem, we can use the *Average Formula* to determine the average annual salary of the employees at Company Q:

$$\text{Avg. Salary} = \frac{\text{Sum of Salaries (all Employees)}}{\text{Total \# of Employees}}$$

We know that there are 1,000 employees in Division R, so the missing information is (a) the number of employees at Company Q who are *not* in Division R and (b) the sum of all employee salaries.

(1): INSUFFICIENT. If the average salary of the employees in Division R is $30,000, then the total salary for Division R is ($30,000)(1,000) = $30 million. However, we do not know anything about the salaries or the number of employees who are *not* in Division R.

(2): INSUFFICIENT. This statement gives us the average salary for the employees at Company Q who are *not* in Division R, but not the number of such employees.

(1) and (2): INSUFFICIENT. Combining the statements, we still have no information about the number of employees who are not in Division R.

Algebraically, we could set up a *Table* to express the *Salary Relationships*, proving that the answer cannot be determined.

Division	Employees	Avg. Salary	Total Salaries
R	1,000	$30,000	$30,000,000
not R	x	$35,000	$35,000x
Total	1,000 + x		$30,000,000 + $35,000x

The average salary of the employees at Company

$$Q = \frac{\$30,000,000 + \$35,000\,x}{1,000 + x}, \text{ which will vary}$$

depending on the unknown value x.

We have *almost* enough information to compute the **Weighted Average** of the salaries. For instance, we would need to know the **Ratio** of employees in each division, in order to compute this average.

The correct answer is (E): Statements (1) and (2) TOGETHER are not sufficient.

DS 29. <u>Geometry:</u> Circles & Cylinders
Difficulty: 500–600   **OG Page:** 275

For this *Cylinders* problem, we should first *Redraw the Picture:*

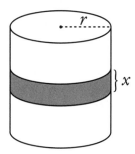

To crack this problem, we must consider how to calculate the surface area of a band that goes around the circumference of a cylinder.

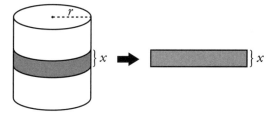

As we can see from the picture, once we unwrap the band from the cylinder, the band is actually a *Rectangle.* So the surface area of the band is actually the area of the rectangle. The width of the rectangle is x, while the length of the rectangle is the circumference of the circle. Pay attention to how the dimensions relate between the two figures.

To find the surface area of the painted stripe, we need either the circumference of the base (our length), or the radius of the base, which will allow us to calculate the circumference. We also need x (our width).

(1): INSUFFICIENT. This statement just gives us the value of x, the height of the cylindrical band.

(2): INSUFFICIENT. This statement provides us with no information about the height of the cylindrical band or the radius of the base. The height of the entire cylindrical tub is irrelevant.

(1) & (2): INSUFFICIENT. With both statements we are still lacking information about the radius of the cylinder, and therefore cannot calculate circumference.

The correct answer is (E): Statements (1) and (2) TOGETHER are not sufficient.

DS 30. <u>EIVs:</u> Quadratic Equations
Difficulty: 500–600   **OG Page:** 275

We are asked for the value of n. Finding one and only one value of n will be sufficient.

(1): INSUFFICIENT. As we have been told that n is an integer, many people will see that the expression $n(n + 1)$ is the product of two consecutive integers. Because this product is equal to 6, it is easy to assume that the integers in question are 2 and 3 (thus $n = 2$). No other positive integers fit.

However, we do not know that n is positive. In fact, this equation is **Quadratic.** We need to solve for the two solutions of n:

$$n(n + 1) = 6$$
$$n^2 + n = 6$$
$$n^2 + n - 6 = 0$$
$$(n + 3)(n - 2) = 0$$
$$n = 2, -3$$

If $n = -3$, then $n + 1 = -2$, and $n(n + 1) = 6$, in fact. Since there are two possible values of n that satisfy $n(n + 1) = 6$, the statement is insufficient.

(2): SUFFICIENT. We can simplify the given **Equation with Exponents** as follows:

$$2^{2n} = 16$$
$$4^n = 16$$
$$4^n = 4^2$$
$$n = 2$$

The correct answer is (B): Statement (2) ALONE is sufficient, but statement (1) alone is not sufficient.

DS 31. <u>FDPs:</u> Digits & Decimals
Difficulty: 500–600   **OG Page:** 275

In this **Decimals** problem, we are told that $d = 0.43t7$, where t is a **Digit**. We are then asked to determine the value of t. There is no need to rephrase, and we can go into the statements.

(1): INSUFFICIENT. When d is **Rounded** to the nearest hundredth, $d = 0.44$. We should **Test Possible Cases** for d. We cannot determine the value of t from this information, because several possible values of d, namely 0.4357, 0.4367, 0.4377, 0.4387, and 0.4397, would all yield 0.44 when rounded to the nearest hundredth.

(2): SUFFICIENT. When d is rounded to the nearest thousandth, $d = 0.436$. The only value of t that will yield 0.436 when d is rounded to the nearest thousandth is 5. If $t = 5$, then $d = 0.4357$. Rounding this decimal to the nearest thousandth yields 0.436, since the digit in the ten-thousandths place (in this case, 7) is greater than or equal to 5. Therefore, we must round up by 1 in the thousandths place.

The correct answer is (B): Statement (2) ALONE is sufficient, but statement (1) alone is not sufficient.

DS 32. <u>Word Translations:</u> Statistics
Difficulty: 500–600   **OG Page:** 275

In this **Statistics** problem, which also involves **Tax Relationships** and **Percents,** we are told that the sum of the prices of 7 items is $365. Furthermore, there is no sales tax on items under $100 in price, whereas a 7% sales tax is applied to all other items.

We are asked for the total sales tax on the purchase. In order to answer this question, we need to determine the total price of all items that were at least $100 in price and multiply that quantity by 7%. Therefore, a good **Rephrasing** is, "What is the total pre-tax cost for all of the items that are priced at $100 or above?"

(1): INSUFFICIENT. This statement gives us the price of the coat as $125. We can see that this item would be subject to a 7% sales tax. However, we don't learn anything more about what other items may or may not be over $100.

(2): INSUFFICIENT. According to this statement, the average price of the remaining 6 items was $40. Using the **Average Law**, we can determine the total price of those 6 items as $240. Knowing the total price of the other items allows us to determine the price of the coat—$125. Still, we do not know how many of those other items, if any, were priced at $100 or above.

(1) and (2): INSUFFICIENT. Both statements give us essentially the same information. No new insight is gained by combining them.

The correct answer is (E): Statements (1) and (2) TOGETHER are not sufficient.

DS 33. <u>FDPs</u>: Percents
Difficulty: 300–500   **OG Page:** 275

The question does not require rephrasing. We are seeking the selling price of the appliance.

(1): INSUFFICIENT. This statement gives only a **Percent.** We know only that the profit = 20% of the selling price. We are not given a dollar figure. Thus, we cannot find the price of the appliance.

(2): INSUFFICIENT. The selling price was $50 more than the wholesale cost. Without knowing the wholesale cost, we still do not know the selling price of the appliance.

(1) and (2): SUFFICIENT. We know from (1) that the profit was 20% of the selling price and from (2) that the profit was $50. Therefore, $50 is 20% of the selling price, which we can now solve for:

$50 = 0.2 × (selling price)

The item sold for $50 divided by 0.2 = $250.

The correct answer is (C): BOTH statements TOGETHER are sufficient, but NEITHER statement ALONE is sufficient.

DS 34. <u>Geometry</u>: Circles & Cylinders
Difficulty: 500–600   **OG Page:** 275

We are asked to find *k*, the number of 15-centimeter high **Cylindrical** cans that can fit into a **Rectangular** box. Because the height of both the box and the cans is 15 cm, we only care about how many circles (from the base of the cans) fit into the

48 cm × 32 cm rectangular base of the box. In this way, we can reduce a **3-D Geometry** question to a **2-D Geometry** question.

If we can find out how many cans can fit along the length and the width of the box, we can find *k*.

We can figure out how many cans fit if we know the diameter of each can. Additionally, if we know the radius or the circumference of a circle, we can find the diameter. This is true because

$$\text{Diameter} = 2 \times \text{Radius} = \frac{\text{Circumference}}{\pi}$$

So we can finally **Rephrase** the question as "What is any key dimension (radius, diameter, circumference, or area) of the circular base of a can?"

(1): SUFFICIENT. We are provided with the radius, which allows us to calculate the diameter, and therefore the number of cans. We know that the diameter is 8 cm, so 6 cans fit along the length and 4 cans fit along the width of the box, totaling 24 cans.

(2): SUFFICIENT. Knowing how many cans fit alongside the length allows us to calculate the diameter of each can and thus the number of cans in the box. If 6 cans fit exactly along the 48 cm length, then each can's diameter is 8 cm. We can now determine that 4 cans fit along the width, for a total of 24 cans.

Note: If the word *exactly* were not in statement (2), then the statement would not have been sufficient. With possible space left over along the length, the diameter could be shorter, and we might be able to add another cylinder along the width.

The correct answer is (D): EACH statement ALONE is sufficient.

DS 35. <u>EIVs</u>: Basic Equations
Difficulty: 300–500   **OG Page:** 275

This **Basic Equations** problem gives us a system of equations and asks for the value of *z*. This is a **Combined Expression** or Combo problem in disguise, since a combination of variables could be sufficient to solve for *z*. For Combo problems, we should figure out what knowledge would be sufficient before we look at the statements. Let's examine the given system of equations:

$$\begin{cases} x - 4 = z \\ y - x = 8 \\ 8 - z = t \end{cases}$$

Equation #1: if we can find x, we can find z.

Equation #2: if we can find y, we can find x. Therefore, if we can find y, we can find z.

Equation #3: if we can find t, we can find z.

In short, if we can find x, y, or t, then we can find z. Our **Rephrased** question is "What is the value of any given variable?"

(1): SUFFICIENT. This statement gives us the value of x. No further work is required.

(2): SUFFICIENT. This statement gives us the value of t. No further work is required.

The correct answer is (D): EACH statement ALONE is sufficient.

DS 36. EIVs: Formulas & Functions
Difficulty: 300–500   **OG Page:** 276

This problem gives us the **Function** $f(n) = a^n$ and asks for the value of $f(1)$. Substituting $n = 1$ into the function, we get $f(1) = a^1$. So the **Rephrased** question is actually "What is a^1?" or simply "What is a?"

(1): INSUFFICIENT. If $f(2) = 100$, then we know that $a^2 = 100$. Remember, **Even Exponents** are dangerous: they hide the sign of the base. The variable a could be 10 or −10. We cannot find a unique value for a.

(2): SUFFICIENT. If $f(3) = -1000$, then $a^3 = -1000$. The only value of a that can satisfy this equation containing an **Odd Exponent** is −10. We have a unique value for a, so we can answer the question.

The correct answer is (B): Statement (2) ALONE is sufficient, but statement (1) alone is not sufficient.

DS 37. FDPs: Percents
Difficulty: 500–600   **OG Page:** 276

This **Percents** problem involves **Algebraic Translation**.

First, we should **Name Variables**, so that we can translate the **Cost Relationship**. Let's make the following assignments:

Selling price = S
Cost = C
Markup = M

The first sentence of the problem can be translated into an equation: $S = C + M$.

We are looking for the markup as a percent of the selling price. If we name another variable and designate the desired percent as x, then we can write an equation: $M = \dfrac{x}{100}S$. This equation can be solved to yield $x = \dfrac{M}{S} \times 100$. If we know the markup and the selling price, we will have enough information to answer the question.

Notice that the question only asks for the percent of the markup, not the actual markup. If that is the case, then the **Ratio** of the markup to the selling price would also be enough information to answer the question.

(1): SUFFICIENT. If the markup is 1/4 of the cost then the cost is 4 times the markup. Thus, we can **Substitute** in the above equation, plugging in $4M$ for C:

$$S = 4M + M$$
$$S = 5M$$

This equation gives the ratio of the markup to the selling price. The markup is 1/5, or 20%, of the selling price.

(2): INSUFFICIENT. This statement tells us that the *sum* of the cost and markup is $250, but the cost and markup could be any two numbers summing to that amount. Thus, the markup could be anywhere from 0% to 100% of the cost. The markup-price ratio is not fixed.

The correct answer is (A): Statement (1) ALONE is sufficient, but statement (2) alone is not sufficient.

DS 38. <u>EIVs</u>: Inequalities
Difficulty: 300–500   **OG Page:** 276

We can set up a *Table* to keep track of the variables and the question.

District	Population	# of reps.	Ratio (pop. to reps.)
1	p_1	r_1	p_1/r_1
2	p_2	r_2	p_2/r_2

This *Inequalities* problem asks "which *Ratio* is greater?" Since the answer is either one or the other (a binary response) we can *Rephrase* this question as the Yes/No question, "Is $\dfrac{p_1}{r_1} > \dfrac{p_2}{r_2}$?"

(also a binary response).

Further manipulation is possible by cross-multiplication: "Is $p_1 r_2 > p_2 r_1$?" We did not have to worry about flipping the sign of the inequality, as all the variables represent numbers of people, which cannot be negative. To answer the question, we need to know something about the values of the products $p_1 r_2$ and $p_2 r_1$, or the values of all four variables individually.

(1): INSUFFICIENT. This gives us a relationship between the populations (p_1 and p_2), but no information about the number of representatives (r_1 and r_2).

(2): INSUFFICIENT. This gives us a relationship between the number of representatives (r_1 and r_2), but no information about the populations (p_1 and p_2).

(1) and (2): SUFFICIENT. We can think about the situation using *Algebraic Reasoning*. If the District 1 population is *greater* than the District 2 population, but the number of representatives for District 1 is *less* than the number of representatives for District 2, then the District 1 ratio (p_1/r_1) is definitely greater than the District 2 ratio (p_2/r_2).

Alternatively, we can use *Direct Algebra* to combine the inequalities for the two statements. Because we know that all the variables are positive, we can line the inequalities up and safely multiply them together. This gives us:

$$\begin{array}{r} p_1 > p_2 \\ \times \; r_2 > r_1 \\ \hline p_1 r_2 > p_2 r_1 \end{array}$$

The new equations matches the rephrasing we did at the beginning of the question.

Notice that we know the variables are all positive because there is a *Hidden Constraint*. All the variables count people, so the variables cannot be negative.

The correct answer is (C): BOTH statements TOGETHER are sufficient, but NEITHER statement ALONE is sufficient.

DS 39. <u>Word Translations</u>: Algebraic Translations
Difficulty: 300–500   **OG Page:** 276

In this *Algebraic Translations* question, we know that there are 80 adults, some of which are college graduates, and some of which are not. Let's *Name Variables:*

n = not college graduates
c = number of college graduates
$n + c = 80$

The question asks us to find the number of college graduates, or c. Using the given information, we can *Rephrase* the question as "What is $80 - n$?" or simply "What is n?"

We should also notice that we have a *Linear Equation* ($n + c = 80$) in the question stem. All we need is one more distinct linear equation in n and c, and we will have sufficiency.

(1): SUFFICIENT. There are 3 times as many non-college graduates as graduates, so $n = 3c$.

We now have *Two Different Linear Equations* relating n and c. Thus, we know that we will be able to find a unique value for c. No further work is required.

If we really want to solve for c using *Direct Algebra,* we can use the equation $n = 3c$ together with the stem equation to solve for c.

$n + c = 80$
$(3c) + c = 80$ *Substitute* $n = 3c$
$4c = 80$
$c = 20$

(2): SUFFICIENT. Since the number of non-college graduates is 40 more than the number of college graduates, $n = c + 40$.

Once again, we have two distinct linear equations relating n and c. We know that we can find a unique value for c. No further work is required.

The correct answer is (D): EACH statement ALONE is sufficient.

DS 40. Word Translations: Minor Question Types
Difficulty: 600–700   **OG Page:** 276

The given table lists the distances between four different cities. By ***Reading the Table*** and ***Rephrasing*** the question, we can determine that we are looking for the value of x, which represents the distance between city R and city T.

(1): INSUFFICIENT. This statement tells us that the distance from S to T, which is known to be 56, is twice the distance from S to R, labeled y. Thus, we can create an equation:

$$56 = 2y$$

This allows us to solve for y. However, knowing y does not allow us to solve for x.

(2): SUFFICIENT. This statement tells us that the distance between T and U, known to be 69, is 1.5 times the distance between R and T, labeled x. Thus, we can create an equation:

$$69 = 1.5x$$

This is a straightforward ***Linear Equation,*** which will result in only one value for x.

The correct answer is (B): Statement (2) ALONE is sufficient, but statement (1) alone is not sufficient.

DS 41. FDPs: Digits & Decimals
Difficulty: 500–600   **OG Page:** 276

In this ***Digits*** problem, we are asked for the value of the two-digit integer x. Since there is need to rephrase the question, we can move into the statements:

(1): INSUFFICIENT. Knowing that the sum of the two digits in x is 3 does not tell us the value of x, since 12, 21, and 30 all satisfy this requirement.

Remember to ***Consider Possible Cases*** skeptically. Do not just find a single case that fits the statement and call it a day.

(2): INSUFFICIENT. There are many two-digit numbers that are divisible by 3: 12, 15, 16, 18, 21, 24....

(1) and (2): INSUFFICIENT. Knowing that the sum of the two digits is 3 already tells us that x is divisible by 3, so combining the two statements does not yield anything useful. Moreover, we can see that 12, 21, and 30 all satisfy both statements. Thus, we cannot determine the value of x.

The correct answer is (E): Statements (1) and (2) TOGETHER are not sufficient.

DS 42. Geometry: Circles & Cylinders
Difficulty: 500–600   **OG Page:** 276

In this ***Circles*** problem, we are trying to find the inside radius of the pipe, r. No rephrase is required, and we can move ahead to the statements.

(1): SUFFICIENT. According to this statement,

$$\frac{t - r}{r} = 0.15 \text{ and } t - r = 0.3 \text{ foot}$$

Combining these two equations through ***Direct Algebra*** allows us to solve for the value of r:

$$\frac{0.3}{r} = 0.15$$

$$r = \frac{0.3 \text{ foot}}{0.15} = 2 \text{ foot}$$

Alternatively, we could recognize that we have ***Two Different Linear Equations*** and ***Two Unknowns,*** which give us enough information to solve.

(2): INSUFFICIENT. This statement tells us that the area of the concrete in the cross section (that is, the space between the internal circle and the external circle) is 1.29π square feet.

We can visualize the cross section as what remains when a circle of radius r is subtracted from a larger circle of radius t. Frequently, the area *between* two figures or in their *overlap* is found by ***Subtracting Areas.***

Using the formula for the ***Area of a Circle,*** we obtain the area of the cross section:

$$A = \pi t^2 - \pi r^2 = \pi(t^2 - r^2) = 1.29\pi$$

so that

$$t^2 - r^2 = 1.29$$

However, without knowing the value of t, we cannot use this information to solve for r.

The correct answer is (A): Statement (1) ALONE is sufficient, but statement (2) alone is not sufficient.

DS 43. FDPs: FDP Connections
Difficulty: 300–500   **OG Page:** 276

What is the tenths ***Digit*** in the ***Decimal*** representation of a certain number? The question does not require rephrasing.

(1): INSUFFICIENT. The number is less than 1/3. Since the decimal representation of 1/3 is $0.\overline{3}$, a number less than 1/3 could have a tenths digit of 3, 2, 1, or 0 (and, if it is a negative number, 9, 8, 7, 6, 5, or 4).

Notice that we must ***Relate Fractions and Decimals*** to think this issue through.

(2): INSUFFICIENT. The number is greater than 1/4. Since the decimal representation of 1/4 is 0.25, a number greater than 1/4 could have a tenths digit of 2, 3, 4, 5, 6, 7, 8, or 9 (and, if the number is greater than 1, 0 or 1).

(1) and (2): INSUFFICIENT. A number between 1/4 and 1/3 is between 0.25 and $0.\overline{3}$. Therefore, its tenths digit could be 2 or 3. Therefore, we cannot answer the question.

The correct answer is (E): Statements (1) and (2) TOGETHER are not sufficient.

DS 44. Word Translations: Ratios
Difficulty: 500–600   **OG Page:** 276

In this problem, we can ***Name Variables*** to represent the ***Work Rates*** of each robot:

x = rate of Robot X
y = rate of Robot Y
z = rate of Robot Z

In this case, $r_x = x/z$, and $r_y = y/z$. We want to find out whether z is the largest. Notice that all variables are positive by the ***Hidden Constraint*** that work rates must be positive.

Rephrasing the question leads to:

Is $z > x$ and $z > y$?

Notice that the word *and* means that both parts need to be true, if we are to answer *Yes.*

(1): INSUFFICIENT. We can replace the ratio with the rates:

$$\frac{x}{z} < \frac{y}{z}$$

We can multiply both sides of the inequality by z (because z cannot be negative) and get $x < y$. However we do not know how z compares to both x and y.

(2): INSUFFICIENT. We can replace the ratio with the rates:

$$\frac{y}{z} < 1$$

When we multiply both sides by z, which again we know to be positive, we get $y < z$. However, this does not provide any information about how z compares to x.

(1) and (2): SUFFICIENT. From (1), we know that $x < y$. From (2), we know that $y < z$. Putting these relationships together, we get:

$$x < y < z$$

Here, we see that $z > x$ and $z > y$, and we can answer our rephrased question.

The correct answer is (C): BOTH statements TOGETHER are sufficient, but NEITHER statement ALONE is sufficient.

DS 45. EIVs: Formulas & Functions
Difficulty: 500–600   **OG Page:** 276

The problem gives a particular ***Sequence*** formula: $a_n = rn$. It further specifies that r is a constant and n is represented by the set of all positive integers $\{1, 2, 3, \ldots\}$. We are asked to determine for how many values of n it is true that $a_n < 100$.

If we know the value of the constant, r, then we can always calculate the number of values of n for which it is true that $a_n < 100$. For example, if r is 20, then there are four values of n for which $a_n < 100$: namely, 20×1, 20×2, 20×3, and 20×4. We can **Rephrase** the question as "What is r?"

(1): SUFFICIENT. If $a_{50} = 500$, then $n = 50$, and we can solve for r using the formula $a_n = rn$:

$500 = r \times 50$. Therefore, $r = 10$.

(2): SUFFICIENT. If $a_{100} + a_{105} = 2{,}050$, we know $r \times 100 + r \times 105 = 2{,}050$, and we can solve for r:

$2{,}050 = r \times 205$. Therefore, $r = 10$.

The correct answer is (D): EACH statement ALONE is sufficient.

DS 46. FDPs: FDP Connections
Difficulty: 300–500   **OG Page:** 277

We are asked to determine the **Digit** t in the **Decimal** $0.t5$. There is no meaningful rephrasing for this question.

(1): INSUFFICIENT. When we want to **Relate Fractions and Decimals,** it is useful to know **Benchmark Values.**

If $r < 1/3$, then $r < 0.\overline{3}$. So r could be 0.05, 0.15, or 0.25, and therefore t could be 0, 1, or 2.

(2): SUFFICIENT. If $r < 1/10$, then $r < 0.1$.

Since $r = 0.t5$, the only possibility for r is 0.05. Therefore, the only possible value for t is 0.

The correct answer is (B): Statement (2) ALONE is sufficient, but statement (1) alone is not sufficient.

DS 47. Geometry: Polygons
Difficulty: 300–500   **OG Page:** 277

In this **Polygons** problem, we are given the distance between floors. We need to know how many steps there are between the first and second floors. We ought to consider **Possible Scenarios:** either the steps have a uniform height, or they don't.

If each step has a uniform height, we can write an equation: (Height of each stair) × (# of stairs) = 9

feet. In this scenario, knowing the height of each stair will be sufficient to solve the problem.

If each step does NOT have a uniform height, we will need more information to determine how many steps there are.

(1): SUFFICIENT. This statement tells us the steps have a uniform height, and tells us the height of each step. The statement is sufficient. The number of stairs may be found by dividing the total height (9 feet) by the height of each stair.

(2): INSUFFICIENT. The width of the stairs is irrelevant to the question at hand.

The correct answer is (A): Statement (1) ALONE is sufficient, but statement (2) alone is not sufficient.

DS 48. FDPs: Percents
Difficulty: 500–600   **OG Page:** 277

First, we can survey this **Percents** question to see what we need to keep track of: two salespeople (X and Y), two months (May and June), and the number of transactions for both employees in both months. We can set up a **Table** to stay organized.

Salesperson	June Transactions	May Transactions
X		
Y		

The question asks for the **Ratio** of the number of sales transactions made by Salesperson X in June to the number made by Salesperson Y in June. In order to answer the question, we will need values for both of the shaded cells above, or we will need expressions that allow us to calculate the ratio.

(1): INSUFFICIENT. Let's **Name a Variable** and assign T to the number of transactions made by Salesperson Y in May. Then the number of transactions made by Salesperson X in June is $1.5T$. We do not have all of the information needed in the shaded cells.

Salesperson	June Transactions	May Transactions
X	$1.5T$	
Y		T

(2): INSUFFICIENT. Using the same variable T, we can see that we still do not have all of the information needed in the shaded cells. Be sure to draw a new table or otherwise prevent statement (1) data from interfering at this point.

Salesperson	June Transactions	May Transactions
X		
Y	1.25T	T

(1) and (2): SUFFICIENT. We have information in all of the shaded cells and the information yields a definite value for the ratio.

Salesperson	June Transactions	May Transactions
X	1.5T	
Y	1.25T	T

The ratio of transactions made by X to transactions made by Y in June is $1.5T/1.25T = 1.5/1.25 = 6/5$.

The correct answer is (C): BOTH statements TOGETHER are sufficient, but NEITHER statement ALONE is sufficient.

DS 49. EIVs: Inequalities
Difficulty: 500–600   **OG Page:** 277

No rephrasing is required. This **Inequalities** question is asking us whether $x < y$.

(1): INSUFFICIENT. If $a < c$, we know that the lower range of possibilities for x is smaller than the lower range for y. Using only this information, we cannot say with certainty that x itself is smaller than y.

We can **Test Numbers** to verify our thinking. For instance, suppose $a = 0$ and $c = 2$. If $x = 2$ and $y = 3$, $x < y$. However, if $x = 4$ and $y = 3$, then $y < x$.

(2): SUFFICIENT. If $b < c$, the upper limit for x is smaller than the lower limit for y. What this means is that the biggest x can be is smaller than the smallest y can be. Therefore, x must be smaller than y.

We could test numbers, but this **Algebraic Reasoning** is both solid and quick.

The correct answer is (B): Statement (2) ALONE is sufficient, but statement (1) alone is not sufficient.

DS 50. Word Translations: Overlapping Sets
Difficulty: 600–700   **OG Page:** 277

For this **Overlapping Sets** problem, we can create a **Double-Set Matrix**. We are looking for the number that goes in the upper-left box—people who are directors of both Company R and Company K.

Director of R?		Director of K?		
		Yes	No	Total
	Yes			
	No			
	Total			

(1): INSUFFICIENT. We can plug in this information as follows:

Director of R?		Director of K?		
		Yes	No	Total
	Yes			
	No		0	
	Total			17

Note that we have placed a 0 in the center box. This is because the 17 represents the total number of directors. Thus, each of the 17 people is a member of at least 1 board. No one is on *neither* board. This "0 in Neither" represents an important insight. Nonetheless, we cannot arrive at a value for the upper-left box.

(2): INSUFFICIENT. We can plug in this information as follows:

Director of R?		Director of K?		
		Yes	No	Total
	Yes			8
	No			
	Total	12		

From the above, we cannot solve for the value of the upper-left box.

(1) and (2): SUFFICIENT. We can now place all of the information into the same matrix:

		Director of K?		
Director of R?		*Yes*	*No*	*Total*
	Yes		5	8
	No	9	0	9
	Total	12	5	17

From here, we can easily fill in every other box. 3 people are directors of both Company R and Company K.

Notice that *without* the "0 in Neither," we would not have sufficiency at this point.

The correct answer is (C): BOTH statements TOGETHER are sufficient, but NEITHER statement ALONE is sufficient.

DS 51. **EIVs:** Inequalities
Difficulty: 500–600   **OG Page:** 277

In this **Inequalities** problem, we are asked whether $x/y > 1$. In order for this to be true, given that both x and y are positive, x must be greater than y. We can thus **Rephrase** the question as "Is $x > y$?"

(1): INSUFFICIENT. Knowing that the product of x and y is greater than 1 does NOT establish whether $x > y$.

(2): SUFFICIENT. If $x - y > 0$, then we can add y to both sides and get $x > y$. This result satisfies our rephrased question.

The correct answer is (B): Statement (2) ALONE is sufficient, but statement (1) alone is not sufficient.

DS 52. **FDPs:** FDP Connections
Difficulty: 500–600   **OG Page:** 277

In this problem, which involves **Connections Between Fractions and Percents**, we are told that a store bought an item for x dollars and sold it for y dollars. We are asked to determine the profit on the sale as a percentage of the initial cost.

Because we are being asked for a value that can be represented algebraically, our first step should be to **Algebraically Translate** the question into an expression. We calculate Percent Profit by dividing the dollar profit by the dollar cost and multiplying the result by 100. By the **Profit Relationship**, Profit = Revenue − Cost = $y - x$. Cost is x, so

$$\text{Percent Profit } = \frac{y - x}{x} \times 100.$$

Before moving on to the statements, we should see whether we can simplify this expression using **Direct Algebra:**

$$\frac{y - x}{x} \times 100 = \left(\frac{y}{x} - \frac{x}{x}\right) \times 100 = \left(\frac{y}{x} - 1\right) \times 100$$

This problem involves a **Combined Expression**, or Combo. To find the Combo y/x, we don't necessarily need the value of x and the value of y. We will be able to answer the **Rephrased** question if we can find the **Ratio** of y to x.

(1): INSUFFICIENT. This statement tells us that the dollar amount of the profit was equal to 20. However, without knowing the cost x, we cannot determine a profit percentage.

(2): SUFFICIENT. From this statement, we learn that the ratio y/x is equal to 5/4. This answers our rephrased question.

If we wish, we can **Substitute** this value into the equation for percent profit to obtain

$$\text{Percent profit} = \left(\frac{5}{4} - 1\right) \times 100 = \frac{1}{4} \times 100 = 25$$

The correct answer is (B): Statement (2) ALONE is sufficient, but statement (1) alone is not sufficient.

DS 53. Word Translations: Statistics
Difficulty: 500–600   **OG Page:** 277

First, simplify the given expression:

$(n - x) + (n - y) + (n - z) + (n - k)$
$4n - x - y - z - k$

Notice that it is possible to factor out a negative:

$4n - (x + y + z + k)$

Our **Rephrased** question is therefore "What is $4n - x - y - z - k$?" or "What is $4n - (x + y + z + k)$?"

This problem involves a **Combined Expression**, or Combo. We do not necessarily need the separate values of $n, x, y, z,$ and k to answer the question.

(1): SUFFICIENT. The **Average** of $x, y, z,$ and k is n. Therefore:

$$\frac{x + y + z + k}{4} = n$$

$$x + y + z + k = 4n$$

Substitute into the question "What is $4n - (x + y + z + k)$?" to yield:

What is $4n - (4n)$?

The answer is 0. Rather amazingly, every variable cancels out. We can answer the question definitively, no matter the values of any of the variables.

(2): INSUFFICIENT. Knowing that $x, y, z,$ and k are **Consecutive Integers** does not tell us anything about their actual values. We also lack information about n.

The correct answer is (A): Statement (1) ALONE is sufficient, but statement (2) alone is not sufficient.

DS 54. Word Translations: Algebraic Translations
Difficulty: 500–600   **OG Page:** 277

Algebraically Translate the **Cost Relationship** in the question stem

To find the charge for a 10-mile ride in terms of f and m, we need to **Algebraically Translate** the **Cost Relationship** in the question stem. Specifically, the charge for a 10-mile ride is $f + 9m$.

We can answer this question if we know both f and m, or if we know the value of the **Combined Expression** $f + 9m$.

(1): INSUFFICIENT: From this statement, we can derive the following equation:

$f + m = 90$

(Since f and m are in cents, our total should also be in cents.)

We cannot arrive at values for either f or m.

Likewise, we cannot determine the value of the Combo $f + 9m$.

(2): INSUFFICIENT: We can rephrase this statement by translating it:

$f + 3m = 120$

We cannot determine the value of f, the value of m, or the value of the combined expression $f + 9m$.

(1) and (2): SUFFICIENT. We can use both equations to find the values of both variables. Right away, we should notice that we have **Two Different Linear Equations** and **Two Unknowns**, so the information is sufficient.

If we really want to find the values of the variables, we can use **Elimination**.

$$\begin{array}{rl} f + 3m &= 120 \\ -(f + m &= 90) \\ \hline 2m &= 30 \\ m &= 15 \\ f &= 75 \end{array}$$

Knowing the values of f and m is sufficient to answer the question.

The correct answer is (C): BOTH statements TOGETHER are sufficient, but NEITHER statement ALONE is sufficient.

DS 55. FDPs: Successive Percents & Percent Change
Difficulty: 500–600   **OG Page:** 277

In order to know the **Percent Change** of Guy's net income, we must know his original net income and the change in his net income, or at least the **Ratio** of these quantities.

Percent change is calculated by the following formula:

$$\frac{\text{Dollar change in net income}}{\text{Starting net income in dollars}}$$

Without these two values, we cannot calculate percent change.

Note that we also have a ***Profit-like Relationship***:

Gross Income − Deductions = Net Income

This relationship behaves mathematically just like the normal profit relationship (Revenue − Cost = Profit).

(1): INSUFFICIENT. Guy's gross income increased by 4% on the specific date in question. This does not allow us to calculate either the change in net income or the starting net income.

(2): INSUFFICIENT. Guy's deductions increased by 15% on the specific date in question. This does not allow us to calculate either the change in net income or the starting net income.

(1) and (2): INSUFFICIENT. Guy's gross income increased by 4% and his deductions increased by 15%. We do not know the starting or ending values for the actual dollar amounts, so we cannot calculate either the change in net income or the starting net income. Thus, both statements together are insufficient.

Note that if both gross income and deductions grew by 4%, then so would his net income. If two percent changes are the same in a profit-like relationship, then the third percent change will equal the other two.

But some of the percent changes are different for the gross income and the deductions, we cannot tell what percent change will happen to the net income. We can prove this by creating two ***Scenarios***:

	Example 1	*Example 2*
starting gross income	$100	$50
starting deduction	$10	$30
starting net income	100 − 10 = 90	50 − 30 = 20
new gross income (+4%)	$104	$52
new deductions (+15%)	$11.50	$34.50
new net income	104 − 11.5 = 92.5	52 − 34.50 = 17.5
percentage change	(92.5 − 90)/90 = 2.5/90 = 2.78%	(20 − 17.5)/20 = 2.5/20 = 12.5%

In the last step, notice that the first example returns 2.5/90 and the second example returns 2.5/20. We do not need to calculate the actual percentages in order to see that these numbers are not equal.

The correct answer is (E): Statements (1) and (2) TOGETHER are not sufficient.

DS 56. <u>Geometry:</u> Triangles & Diagonals
Difficulty: 300–500   **OG Page:** 277

The sum of the ***Angles of a Triangle*** is 180. Therefore, $x + y + z = 180$. Since the problem asks for the value of z, we start by isolating z:

$$z = 180 − (x + y)$$

In order to find the value of z, we need to answer the question "What is the value of $180 − (x + y)$?" More simply, we can ask the ***Rephrased*** question "What is the value of $x + y$?" Here, $x + y$ is a ***Combined Expression,*** or Combo.

(1): SUFFICIENT. We are given the value of $x + y$, directly matching our rephrasing, so we can stop here.

If we know the value of $x + y$, we can solve for the value of z (though it is unnecessary to do so).

$$z = 180 − (x + y)$$
$$z = 180 − (139)$$
$$z = 41$$

(2): INSUFFICIENT. Knowing the value of $y + z$ is neither sufficient to calculate $x + y$ nor sufficient to calculate z itself.

The correct answer is (A): Statement (1) ALONE is sufficient, but statement (2) alone is not sufficient.

DS 57. <u>Word Translations</u>: Algebraic Translations
Difficulty: 500–600   **OG Page:** 277

This *Algebraic Translations* problem involves a disguised *Cost Relationship*. The number of bills, multiplied by the worth or "cost" of each bill, equals the total value (in dollars).

To represent this relationship algebraically, we can *Name Variables*. If we let f stand for the number of five-dollar bills, and t the number of twenty-dollar bills, then the cost relationship translates to $5f + 20t = 125$.

There is also a *Hidden Constraint* in this problem. We know that f and t must be positive integers, since it is impossible for Max to have fractional or negative numbers of bills. This integer constraint will greatly restrict the number of possible combinations of f and t.

For problems involving linear equations with integer constraints, *Testing Values* is often the most efficient method of solution.

(1): SUFFICIENT. Since $5f + 20t$ must equal 125, we may find $20t$ in each case by subtraction: $20t = 125 - 5f$. We are looking for values of f that allow t to be a positive integer.

We know that f is less than 5, so let's test only values less than 5. Make a *Table* to organize the job.

$125 - 5f = 20t$. Therefore, if $125 - 5f$ is not a multiple of 20, then t can't be an integer.

f	$125 - 5f$	$\div 20 = t$
4	105	not an integer
3	110	not an integer
2	115	not an integer
1	120	6
0	125	not an integer

The only possible solution is 1 five-dollar bill and 6 twenty-dollar bills.

(2): SUFFICIENT. Since $5f + 20t$ must equal 125, we may find $5f$ in each case by subtraction: $5f = 125 - 20t$.

We know that t is greater than 5, so only test values that are greater than 5. Make another table to organize the job:

t	$125 - 20t = 5f$	f
6	5	1
7	Negative	negative
8	Negative	negative

All values of t greater than 6 will produce negative values for f. These values are impossible. Again, 1 five-dollar bill and 6 twenty-dollar bills is the only solution.

Notice that, in both statements, an *Inequality* turned out to be sufficient information for precise values of f and t. This is frequently the case in problems with hidden integer constraints.

The correct answer is (D): EACH statement ALONE is sufficient.

DS 58. <u>Word Translations</u>: Ratios
Difficulty: 500–600   **OG Page:** 277

First, survey the question to see what we need to keep track of: two districts (M and P), teachers in both districts, students in both districts, and a *Ratio* of teachers to students in both districts. Set up a *Table* to stay organized.

District	Teachers	Students	Ratio (Teacher to Student)
M			x
P			x

Some information is given. The ratio of teachers to students is the same in both districts, so we can *Name a Variable* and put x in both rows of the ratio column above. This way, we can easily remember that these cells have the same value.

The question asks for the ratio of the number of students in District M to the number of students in District P. We will need values for both of the shaded cells above or expressions that will allow us to calculate the ratio in order to answer the question.

(1): INSUFFICIENT. We can place information in both of the shaded cells. Naming another variable, we can assign s to represent the number of students in District P. However, the information does not yield a definite value for the ratio.

District	Teachers	Students	Ratio (Teacher to Student)
M		$s + 10{,}000$	x
P		s	x

The ratio of students in M to students in P is $\dfrac{s+10{,}000}{s}$, which depends on the unknown value s.

(2): INSUFFICIENT. We can replace the x's in the chart with 1/20, but that does not tell us much. We do not have any information in either of the shaded cells.

District	Teachers	Students	Ratio (Teacher to Student)
M			1/20
P			1/20

(1) and (2): INSUFFICIENT. The value given for the ratio of teachers to students does not resolve the uncertainty about s.

District	Teachers	Students	Ratio (Teacher to Student)
M		$s + 10{,}000$	1/20
P		s	1/20

The ratio of students in M to P is still $\dfrac{s+10{,}000}{s}$, which depends on the unknown value s.

The correct answer is (E): Statements (1) and (2) TOGETHER are not sufficient.

DS 59. **FDPs:** Fractions
Difficulty: 500–600   **OG Page:** 278

This **Overlapping Sets** problem, which also involves **Fractions,** describes a group of 84 calculus students who are either male or female and in either Section 1 or Section 2 of calculus. The question is how many of the students are *female*? Using a **Double-Set Matrix**, we can shade the question:

Gender?	Section?		
	1	2	Total
Male			
Female			
Total			84

(1): INSUFFICIENT. We can *Name a Variable* and assign x as the number of students in Section 1. Thus, $(2/3)x$ are females in Section 1 and $(1/3)x$ are males in Section 1. This does not help us calculate the total number of females.

Gender?	Section?		
	1	2	Total
Male	$(1/3)x$		
Female	$(2/3)x$		
Total	x		84

(2): INSUFFICIENT. We can assign y as the number of students in Section 2. Thus, $(1/2)y$ are males in Section 2 and $(1/2)y$ are females in Section 2. This does not help us calculate the total number of females.

Gender?	Section?		
	1	2	Total
Male		$(1/2)y$	
Female		$(1/2)y$	
Total		y	84

(1) and (2): INSUFFICIENT. With both statements, we can construct an equation for the total number of females. However, the problem is that this equation still has two variables related to the number of students in each section. Without this additional information, we can not get an actual value for the number of female students.

Gender?	Section?		
	1	2	Total
Male	$(1/3)x$	$(1/2)y$	
Female	$(2/3)x$	$(1/2)y$	$(2/3)x + (1/2)y$
Total	x	y	84

To solve this problem, we do not have to use a Double-Set Matrix, but it helps to keep the categories straight.

The correct answer is (E): Statements (1) and (2) TOGETHER are not sufficient.

DS 60. <u>EIVs</u>: Basic Equations
Difficulty: 300–500   **OG Page:** 278

We can begin by manipulating the given **Basic Equation** to isolate *n*:

$$-25 + 19 + n = s$$
$$-6 + n = s$$
$$n = s + 6$$

The question asks us for the value of *n*. We can answer if we know the value of either *n* or *s*. Thus, we can **Rephrase:** "What is the value of *n* or *s*?"

(1): SUFFICIENT. We are given the value of *s*. This satisfies our rephrased question.

(2): SUFFICIENT. Combining this statement with the information from the question stem, we have **Two Different Linear Equations** with **Two Unknowns.** We can stop here, since we have sufficient information to solve for either unknown.

If we really want to know what *n* is, we can solve by **Substitution.**

Begin by putting *s* in terms of *n*:

$$n/s = 4$$
$$n = 4s$$
$$s = \tfrac{1}{4}n$$

Next, plug this value for *s* into the first equation:

$$n = (\tfrac{1}{4}n) + 6$$
$$\tfrac{3}{4}n = 6$$
$$n = 8$$

Of course, the calculations are unnecessary, once we are certain that we can arrive at a definite value for *n*.

The correct answer is (D): EACH statement ALONE is sufficient.

DS 61. <u>FDPs</u>: Percents
Difficulty: 500–600   **OG Page:** 278

In this **Percents** problem, which also involves **Algebraic Translations**, we are asked to determine the number of guests who received double scoops of ice cream. Because we can approach the solution in many different ways, we should go to the statements without a specific rephrase.

(1): INSUFFICIENT. Knowing the percent of guests who received double scoops is not enough, if we do not know the total number of guests.

(2): INSUFFICIENT. Knowing the total number of scoops does not tell us how many guests received double scoops.

(1) and (2): SUFFICIENT. If we know that 60% of the guests received a double scoop, then we know the ratio of single-scoop guests to double-scoop guests. If we know the total number of scoops, we can use the ratio to determine the number of guests who received double scoops.

Naming a Variable, let's label the total number of guests at the picnic *x*. If 60% of the guests received a double scoop, then $0.6x$ people received double scoops. The total number of scoops received by these guests was $2 \times 0.6x$. Similarly, 40% of the guests, or $0.4x$, received a single scoop, so the number of single scoops received by these guests was $1 \times 0.4x$. We know the total number of scoops served, so $0.4x + 2 \times 0.6x = 120$.

This equation will allow us to solve for the total number of guests at the picnic. Once we know the total number of guests, we will be able to determine the number of guests who were served a double scoop.

A **Table** can help us stay organized, if we're having trouble keeping track of all the pieces. Here's what a table could look like for statements (1) and (2) together:

	Guests	Scoops per Guests	Total Scoops
Single Scoop	0.4x	1	0.4x
Double Scoop	0.6x	2	1.2x
Total	x		1.6x

Since we know $1.6x = 120$, we can solve for *x* and calculate every cell, in theory.

The correct answer is (C): BOTH statements TOGETHER are sufficient, but NEITHER statement ALONE is sufficient.

DS 62. Word Translations: Algebraic Translations
Difficulty: 600–700   **OG Page:** 278

In this *Algebraic Translations* problem, we are given a *Cost Relationship.* We are told that the cost of a hotel room is $120 for the first person, plus x dollars for each additional person, and we are asked to find x. If we know the number of people sharing the room and the total cost of the room, we will be able to find x.

(1): SUFFICIENT. The *Average Law* states that $A = \dfrac{S}{N}$, in which A is the average, S is the sum of all terms, and N is the number of terms. Therefore, the average cost per person for four people sharing the room is

$$A_4 = \frac{\$120 + (3x)}{4} = \$45,$$

so that

$$\$120 + (3x) = 4 \times \$45 = \$180.$$

This *Linear Equation* allows us to solve for the value of x. (Although it is not necessary to do the actual calculation, the result is 20.)

(2): SUFFICIENT. Proceeding similarly, we can write the average cost per person for *two* people sharing the room. We can also write the average cost per person for *four* people sharing the room. Lastly, we can use the fact that the former is $25 more than the latter:

$$A_2 = \frac{\$120 + x}{2} = A_4 + \$25$$

$$A_4 = \frac{\$120 + (3x)}{4}$$

$$\frac{\$120 + x}{2} = \frac{\$120 + (3x)}{4} + \$25$$

Again, we have a linear equation that we can solve for x. Multiply both sides by 4 in order to eliminate the fractions:

$$2 \times (\$120 + x) = \$120 + (3x) + (4 \times 25)$$

$$\$240 + (2x) = \$220 + (3x)$$

$$\$20 = x$$

The correct answer is (D): EACH statement ALONE is sufficient.

DS 63. FDPs: Percents
Difficulty: 500–600   **OG Page:** 278

In this *Percents* problem, we are asked "Is the discount price at Store M less than the discount price at Store L?" For both stores, we need either the discount price or the original price AND the amount (or percent) of the discount.

This problem also involves a *Discount Relationship:*

Original Price − Discount = Discount Price

This relationship is mathematically similar to a profit or markup relationship.

(1): INSUFFICIENT. Knowing the *percent* discount at each store does not tell us whether the discount price at Store M is less than the discount price at Store L, because we do not know the original prices of the items. For instance, if Store M's original price is much higher than Store L's, Store M's discount price could be higher even with a larger percent taken off the original price.

(2): INSUFFICIENT. Store L gives $5 off and Store M gives $6 off. Without knowing the original prices for the product at both stores, we cannot answer the question.

(1) & (2): SUFFICIENT. Combining both statements, we know that Store L's discount is 10% and that its discount is $5.

Thus, $5 = 0.1 × Store L's original price. This equation allows us to calculate the original price ($50) and the discount price ($50 − $5 = $45).

Store M's discount is 15%, which is equal to $6. We are given the same type of information for Store M as for Store L, so we will also be able to calculate the discount price at Store M. No further calculation is required.

The correct answer is (C): BOTH statements TOGETHER are sufficient, but NEITHER statement ALONE is sufficient.

DS 64. FDPs: Digits & Decimals
Difficulty: 500–600   **OG Page:** 278

There is no rephrasing needed for this *Decimals* question, which also involves *Inequalities.*

(1): INSUFFICIENT. When *Rounding a Decimal* the nearest tenth, we have to look at the hundredths digit and *Test Possible Cases.*

If *d* is rounded *down* to 0.5 (for example, 0.53), then $d > 0.5$. Here, the answer to the question is *Yes.* If *d* is rounded *up* to 0.5 (for example, 0.47), then $d < 0.5$. Here, the answer to the question is *No.*

As we can create two different scenarios, this statement is insufficient.

Alternately, we can *Algebraically Translate* this statement. According to this statement, the values for *d* are defined as $0.45 \le d < 0.55$. This clearly shows that it is only sometimes true that $d \le 0.5$.

(2): SUFFICIENT. When rounding a number to the nearest units digit, we have to look at the tenths digit. We can translate this statement, saying that the values for *d* are defined as $0.5 \le d < 1.5$. This clearly shows that it is always the case that $d \ge 0.5$.

The correct answer is (B): Statement (2) ALONE is sufficient.

DS 65. Number Properties: Consecutive Integers
Difficulty: 500–600   **OG Page:** 278

If we know the values of *r* and *s*, we can calculate the number of integers between them. These integers will form a *Consecutive Integer* set.

Furthermore, if we know the difference between *r* and *s*—that is, how far apart they are on a number line—then we can also calculate the number of integers between them, even if we do not know what the specific values are. It does not matter whether *s* or *r* is larger.

(1): SUFFICIENT. If $s - r = 10$, then *s* and *r* are 10 units apart on a number line. Therefore, there must be nine integers between them on a number line. For example, if *s* is 3 and *r* is 13, then the nine integers 4, 5, 6, 7, 8, 9, 10, 11, and 12 are between the two. This is true no matter where we place *s* and *r*.

By the way, the problem specifies "between, but not including." This definition may seem unusual, because with consecutive integer sets, we more typically include the endpoints. But for this problem, it does not matter which way we define "between,"

as long as the definition stays consistent through the problem.

(2): SUFFICIENT. If there are 9 integers between, but not including, $r + 1$ and $s + 1$, then $r + 1$ and $s + 1$ are 10 units apart on a number line. As a result, *r* and *s* must also be 10 units apart on a number line.

Again, this is true no matter where we place *s* and *r*. For example, if $r + 1$ is 11, then the 9 integers are 12, 13, 14, 15, 16, 17, 18, 19 and 20. Therefore $s + 1$ is 21. That means that *r* is 10 and *s* is 20. We can determine how many integers are between *r* and *s*.

The correct answer is (D): EACH statement ALONE is sufficient.

DS 66. Number Properties: Divisibility & Primes
Difficulty: 500–600   **OG Page:** 278

This *Divisibility & Primes* problem asks whether *n* is a factor of *t*. This is equivalent to asking whether *t* is equal to *n* times some integer.

We can *Name a Variable,* such as *m*, to stand for this arbitrary integer. We can then *Rephrase* the question as "Is $t = n \times m$?"

Remember that we know that *n* and *t* are positive integers.

(1): INSUFFICIENT. Use *Direct Algebra* to manipulate the given equation, which involves tricky *Exponents.*

$$n = 3^{n-2}$$
$$n = \frac{3^n}{3^2} = \frac{3^n}{9}$$
$$9n = 3^n$$

Without any information about *t*, we cannot determine whether $t = n \times m$.

However, we must check to see whether it is possible that $n = 1$, since 1 is a factor of every positive integer.

Since $9(1) \ne 3^1$, *n* is not equal to 1. We cannot determine whether *n* is a factor of *t*, and so this statement is insufficient.

(2): INSUFFICIENT. $t = 3^n$ just tells us that t is some power of 3. We cannot determine whether n is a factor of t.

Let's *Test Numbers* to verify. If n is a multiple of 3, then n will be a factor of t. If $n = 2$, then $t = 3^2 = 9$ and n is not a factor of t. However, if $n = 3$, then $t = 3^3 = 27$ and n is a factor of t.

(1) and (2): SUFFICIENT. Combining statements (1) and (2), we know that $3^n = 9n$ and we also know that $t = 3^n$. Substituting t for 3^n in the first equation, we get $t = 9n$. This equation directly matches our rephrasing, "Is $t = n \times m$?" In this case, $m = 9$.

The correct answer is (C): BOTH statements TOGETHER are sufficient, but NEITHER statement ALONE is sufficient.

DS 67. Word Translations: Overlapping Sets
Difficulty: 500–600   **OG Page:** 278

This standard *Overlapping Sets* problem presents two binary criteria: student loans vs. no student loans, and scholarship vs. no scholarship. Construct a *Double-Set Matrix* according to these criteria, filling in the information from the prompt and circling the desired quantity.

Note that, since we know the total number of students surveyed (200), we can multiply the given *Percents* by 200 to yield concrete numbers.

As is customary on all double-set matrix problems, we fill in the third entry in any row that contains two existing entries (in italics).

	Student Loans	*No Loans*	*Total*
Sch.			80
No Sch			*120*
Total	60	*140*	200

(1): SUFFICIENT. According to this statement, 50 students received scholarships but no loans. Add this number into the matrix (in bold), and then fill in the third entry in all rows and columns containing two existing entries (in italics):

	Student Loans	*No Loans*	*Total*
Sch.	30	**50**	80
No Sch	30	*90*	120
Total	60	140	200

The desired answer is thus 90 students.

(2): SUFFICIENT. According to this statement, 50 percent *of the 60 students who had received loans* said that they had also received scholarships. Therefore, 30 students had received both loans and scholarships. Add this number into the matrix (in bold), and then fill in the third entry in all rows and columns containing two existing entries (in italics):

	Student Loans	*No Loans*	*Total*
Sch.	**30**	*50*	80
No Sch	*30*	*90*	120
Total	60	140	200

The desired answer is thus 90 students.

The correct answer is (D): EACH statement ALONE is sufficient.

DS 68. Word Translations: Rates & Work
Difficulty: 500–600   **OG Page:** 278

Survey this *Rates & Work* question to see what we need to keep track of: three machines (K, M, and P), as well as Rate, Time, and Work for each and every machine. We should set up an *Rate–Time–Work Chart* to stay organized.

We know that when they work together, the machines can complete the task in 24 minutes. Using the property that $R = W/T$, we can fill in the entire bottom row of the chart.

Machine	*Rate*	*Time*	*Work*
K	a.	?	1 task
M	b.	c.	1 task
P			1 task
All (together)	1/24 task/min.	24 min.	1 task

The question asks for the time it takes Machine K to complete the task, so we place a question mark in the chart to represent that time.

We would be able to solve for K's time if we had some other information, namely any of the following:

- K's rate, because $T = \dfrac{W}{R} = \dfrac{1 \text{ task}}{\text{rate at which K works}}$

- M and P's combined rate, because the three machines in this problem work together, meaning that we can ***Add the Rates*** (i.e., the rate for the three machines working together is equal to the sum of their individual rates). Let's Name Variables as simply as we can, and call K's rate k, M's rate m, and P's rate p. (This differs from the way the OG explanation uses these letters, by the way.) Thus, $k + m + p =$ Total Rate = 1/24.

- The time it takes M and P working together to complete the task, because $R = W/T$ so

$$m + p = \dfrac{1 \text{ task}}{\text{time for M \& P}}.$$

Therefore, we can ***Rephrase*** the original question to "What is k?" or "What is the combined rate of m and p?" OR "How long does it take m and p working together to complete the task?" These questions are represented by "a." "b." and "c." respectively in the chart above.

(1): SUFFICIENT. This statement provides the time it takes M and P together to complete the task, the answer to one of our rephrased questions.

It is not necessary to fill in the entire chart, though we can do so here:

Machine	Rate	Time	Work
K	a.	?	1 task
M	1/36	36	1 task
P			1 task
All (together)	1/24	24	1 task

We know that $k + m + p =$ Total Rate = 1/24. So $k + (1/36) = 1/24$. This allows us to solve for the rate at which K works and thus find the amount of time it takes for K to complete the task.

Notice that $m + p$, a ***Combined Expression*** or Combo, is sufficient to answer the question. The GMAT loves this kind of trick: it gives us a relationship among *three* variables ($k + m + p =$ Total Rate = 1/24) and asks us for the value of one of the variables ($k = ?$). The right Combo of the other variables will do the trick.

Specifically, since $k = 1/24 - (m + p)$, we needed $m + p$, the combined rates of machines M and P.

(2): INSUFFICIENT. This statement gives the time necessary for K and P to complete the task when working together. This time could be used to compute the *combined* rate of K and P ($k + p$). However, we cannot determine the *individual* rate of K.

The correct answer is (A): Statement (1) ALONE is sufficient, but statement (2) alone is not sufficient.

DS 69. Number Properties: Positives & Negatives
Difficulty: 500–600   **OG Page:** 278

By asking whether r is the closest to zero of the four numbers on the ***Number Line***, this ***Positives & Negatives*** question is really asking about the positioning of zero on the number line. In the number line below, the four numbers have been intentionally placed with uneven spacing, since the question says nothing about even spacing. Sometimes, it is good to ***Exaggerate the Picture*** somewhat to ensure that we don't find unjustified features, such as even spacing.

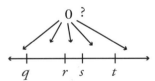

(1): SUFFICIENT. If $q = -s$ then q and s are equally spaced on opposite sides of zero. That is to say, zero is *halfway* between q and s. To prove this, we can ***Test Numbers.*** If $q = 5$, then $s = -5$. If $q = 3$, then $s = -3$, etc. In all cases, 0 is halfway between q and s.

If zero is *halfway* between q and s, r must be closer to zero than either one of them because it is definitely somewhere between q and s. If r is between 0 and s, then it is closer to 0 than s is. But s and q

are equidistant from 0, which means that r is also closer to 0 than q. The logic is the same if r is between q and 0. Finally, t is definitely farther from zero than s since t is to the right of s (and thus a larger positive number). Therefore, r is the closest to zero.

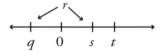

(2): INSUFFICIENT. If $-t < q$, then all we know is that $-t$ is left of q. That means t is farther from zero than q, so zero is to the left of the halfway point between t and q. But this is not enough to tell us whether r is closest to zero.

The correct answer is (A): Statement (1) ALONE is sufficient, but statement (2) alone is not sufficient.

DS 70. Word Translations: Algebraic Translations
Difficulty: 600–700   **OG Page:** 279

In this *Algebraic Translations* problem, we know that n people each donated $500, for a total of $500n$. Each of these n people, in turn, convinced n more people to donate $500. Thus, the number of people donating in the second round will be n times n, or n^2, for a total of $500n^2$ raised in the second round. The total amount raised will therefore be equal to $500n + 500n^2$. This may be seen as a complicated *Cost Relationship.*

We can answer this question if we are given the total amount raised (*Rephrasing* the question), or if we can create an equation to solve for the value of n directly.

(1): SUFFICIENT. We can create and solve the following equation using *Direct Algebra:*

$$500n = \tfrac{1}{16}(500n + 500n^2)$$
$$500n = \tfrac{1}{16}(500)(n + n^2)$$
$$n = \tfrac{1}{16}(n + n^2)$$
$$16n = n + n^2$$
$$15n = n^2$$
$$n^2 - 15n = 0$$
$$n(n - 15) = 0$$
$$n = 0, 15$$

We have two solutions. However, 0 is invalid: there is an implicit constraint that n is positive. (Mary must have found at least *some* people to donate or else there could not have been a second round of fundraising.) Thus, $n = 15$.

(2): SUFFICIENT. If given the total raised, we can create and solve the following equation:

$$\$500n + \$500n^2 = \$120{,}000$$
$$\$500(n + n^2) = \$120{,}000$$
$$(n + n^2) = 240$$
$$n + n^2 = 240$$
$$n^2 + n - 240 = 0$$

We can stop at this point. We have a **Quadratic Equation** that will result in one positive and one negative solution for n. However, given the implicit constraint that n must be positive (Mary could not have encouraged a negative number of people to donate), we will have only one valid solution.

Of course, we can finish the computation as well:

$$(n + 16)(n - 15) = 0$$
$$n = 15, -16$$

Only the positive solution is valid. Thus, $n = 15$.

The correct answer is (D): EACH statement ALONE is sufficient.

DS 71. Word Translations: Rates & Work
Difficulty: 500–600   **OG Page:** 279

In this *Rates* problem, we are asked for the length of the shorter of the two possible routes that Carlotta can take. *Naming Variables,* we can assign s as a variable for the shorter route and l as a variable for the longer route, but there is nothing else for us to rephrase. The slightly *Rephrased* question is simply "What is s?"

(1): INSUFFICIENT. We know that $s + l = 42$, but we cannot use this to solve for s.

(2): INSUFFICIENT. Here, we know that the length of the longer route (l) must be $46/2 = 23$ kilometers. This tells us nothing about the length of the shorter route.

(1) and (2): SUFFICIENT. If we know that $s + l = 42$ and that $l = 23$, then it must be true that $s = 42 - 23 = 19$.

Notice that our initial instinct is to classify this problem with Rates, but it's really a disguised *Algebraic Translations* problem. Essentially, we are asked "What is s?" and we are given $s + l = 42$ and $l = 23$. This distance language is just a disguise. We do not need the *Rate–Time–Distance Formula*.

The correct answer is (C): BOTH statements TOGETHER are sufficient, but NEITHER statement ALONE is sufficient.

DS 72. EIVs: Inequalities
Difficulty: 500–600   **OG Page:** 279

This *Inequalities* question, which asks whether x is greater than y, cannot be rephrased, so we can proceed directly to the statements.

(1): SUFFICIENT. According to this statement, x is 2 more than y. Therefore, regardless of how large or small y may be, x will always be greater than y by 2 units.

We can just intuitively grasp this point, or we can see it by doing a little *Direct Algebra.* Take the statement equation $x = y + 2$ and *Substitute* into the question. After subtracting y from both sides, we can answer the question definitively:

Is $x > y$?
Is $y + 2 > y$?
Is $2 > 0$? *Yes.*

(2): INSUFFICIENT. Multiplying the given equation by 2, in order to eliminate the fraction, results in:

$x = 2y - 2$

This does not allow us to determine which of x and y is greater, as we can show by *Picking Numbers.* For instance, if $y = 0$, then $x = 2(0) - 2 = -2$ and $x < y$.

However, if $y = 3$, then $x = 2(3) - 2 = 4$, so $x > y$.

Alternatively, we can substitute $x = 2y - 2$ into the question and then simplify:

Is $x > y$?
Is $2y - 2 > y$?
Is $y - 2 > 0$?
Is $y > 2$?

Since we do not know whether y is greater than 2, we cannot answer the question definitively.

The correct answer is (A): Statement (1) ALONE is sufficient, but statement (2) alone is not sufficient.

DS 73. Number Properties: Odds & Evens
Difficulty: 300–500   **OG Page:** 279

If m is an integer, is m odd? The question is obviously about *Odds & Evens,* but no rephrasing is needed.

(1): INSUFFICIENT. We are told that $m/2$ is NOT an even integer. This does NOT mean that $m/2$ is an odd integer! Rather, it may be that $m/2$ is not an integer at all.

Let's set up a quick *Table* to *Test Possible Cases.*

m	$m/2$ = not even	m = odd int?
1	1/2	No
2	1	Yes

Since both examples conform to the condition "$m/2$ is NOT an even integer" yet give different answers to the question, the statement is not sufficient.

(2): SUFFICIENT. Apply *Properties of Odds & Evens.* If $m - 3$ is an even integer, then m − Odd = Even. That means that m = Even + Odd, which is *always* Odd.

The correct answer is (B): Statement (2) ALONE is sufficient, but statement (1) alone is not sufficient.

DS 74. Geometry: Triangles & Diagonals
Difficulty: 500–600   **OG Page:** 279

The *Area of a Triangle* can be found with the following formula:

$$\text{Area} = \frac{1}{2}(\text{base})(\text{height})$$

$$\text{Area} = \frac{1}{2}(AC)(BD)$$

Thus, we can *Rephrase* the question as "What is the product $(AC)(BD)$?" We need either the lengths of the two segments or their product.

(1): SUFFICIENT. This statement tells us that $(BD)(AC) = 20$, directly answering the rephrased question.

(2): INSUFFICIENT. Knowing the measure of x without any lengths does not help us find either AC or BD.

The correct answer is (A): Statement (1) ALONE is sufficient, but statement (2) alone is not sufficient.

DS 75. <u>Geometry:</u> Coordinate Plane
Difficulty: 600–700   **OG Page:** 279

This problem does not specify that a, b, and c are constants. However, we need to know that only x and y are variables "in the xy-plane," also known as the xy **Coordinate Plane**. All other letters therefore do represent constants.

Because we are given a **Linear Equation** and because a **Slope** is specified, we can first manipulate the equation into **Slope-Intercept Form,** which is generally $y = mx + b$. Do not confuse this "b," which stands for the y-intercept in the general equation for slope-intercept, with the "b" we are given.

$ax + by + c = 0$ Use **Direct Algebra** to
$by = -ax - c$ isolate y.

$$y = -\frac{a}{b}x - \frac{c}{b}$$

Matching up to the slope-intercept form, we can see that $-a/b$ is equivalent to the slope, m. Therefore, $-a/b = 2/3$. This relationship is the crux of the problem. (Note: we *cannot* determine individual values for a and b without further information.)

We are asked for the value of b. Since we know $-a/b = 2/3$, we can **Rephrase** the question to this: "What is a or b?"

(1): SUFFICIENT. If $a = 4$, we can answer the rephrased question.

If we really want, we can solve for b:

$$-\frac{4}{b} = \frac{2}{3} \rightarrow -12 = 2b \rightarrow -6 = b$$

(2): INSUFFICIENT. If $c = -6$, we can plug that into our linear equation, but we cannot solve further to determine a particular value for a or b:

$$y = -\frac{a}{b}x - \frac{(-6)}{b}$$

The correct answer is (A): Statement (1) ALONE is sufficient, but statement (2) alone is not sufficient.

DS 76. <u>Number Properties:</u> Odds & Evens
Difficulty: 500–600   **OG Page:** 279

In this **Odds & Evens** problem, we are asked about the product mpt. If any one of the integers m, p, or t is even, the product mpt will be even. We can **Rephrase** the question as "Is any one of the integers m, p, or t even?"

(1): INSUFFICIENT. Manipulate the equation using **Direct Algebra**.

$t - p = p - m$ Add m and p to both sides
$t + m = 2p$ Divide by 2
$(t + m)/2 = p$

p is the **Average** of t and m. This does not tell us whether one of the numbers is even.

We can **Test Possible Values** to verify this point. The values of m, p, and t could be 1, 2, and 3, in which case we do have an even integer. Alternatively, the values could also be 1, 3, and 5, in which case we do not have any even integers.

(2): INSUFFICIENT. $t - m = 16$ just tells us that integers t and m are 16 units apart. We have no information on whether the integers are odd or even.

Again, we can use actual numbers to ensure that our understanding is correct. The values of m, p, and t could be 1, 3, and 17, or 1, 2, and 17. We do not know whether an even integer is present.

(1) and (2): INSUFFICIENT. Knowing that t and m are 16 units apart and that p is the average of these 2 integers is still not enough information to determine whether one or more of these integers are even.

We can again test numbers. For instance, the values of m, p, and t could be 1, 9 and 17, or 2, 10, and 18.

The correct answer is (E): Statements (1) and (2) TOGETHER are not sufficient.

DS 77. <u>FDPs</u>: Percents
Difficulty: 500–600   **OG Page:** 279

We can rewrite the opening sentence in this *Percents* problem using *Algebraic Translations.*

The salesman is paid a fixed sum of $300, plus 5% of all sales *over* $1,000. If we *Name Variables* and designate the salesman's total sales for the week as x, then the amount on which the commission is paid is given by $x - 1,000$ (which is the amount of sales *over* 1,000). This is a typical *Cost Relationship.* We therefore have:

$$300 + 0.05(x - 1,000) = ?$$

If we can determine the amount of sales made by the salesman last week, we can answer the question.

We can therefore *Rephrase* the question as "What is x?"

(1): SUFFICIENT. This statement declares that the salesman's total pay, represented by $300 + 0.05(x - 1,000)$, equals 10 percent of the total sales. Since x represents the total sales, we can write an equation:

$$300 + 0.05(x - 1,000) = 0.10x$$

This *Linear Equation* has one unknown. We can definitely solve for a unique value of x.

(2): SUFFICIENT. This statement gives us the value of x directly.

The correct answer is (D): EACH statement ALONE is sufficient.

DS 78. <u>Word Translations</u>: Statistics
Difficulty: 600–700   **OG Page:** 279

In this *Statistics* problem, which also involves *Simple Interest*, a total of $60,000 was invested. Some of this money was invested at x% simple annual interest, and the rest was invested at y% simple annual interest. By the end of the year, $4,080 was earned in interest overall.

As we try to *Rephrase* the question, we should use the *Simple Interest Formula*:

Interest Rate (%) × Original Investment ($) = Interest Paid ($)

We can use this formula to calculate the overall interest rate. (It turns out that this quick *Decimals and Percents* calculation is not absolutely necessary, but it's an good first step toward understanding the real meaning of this problem. The most important thing to know is that this overall interest rate is a fixed, given number.)

Overall Interest Rate = Interest Paid / Original Investment = $4,080 / $60,000 = 0.068 = 6.8%

Conceptually, this 6.8% is a *Weighted Average* of x% and y%. The number 6.8 will be somewhere between x and y. Where exactly it falls will depend on how much money we have invested at each interest rate. For instance, if we invested almost all the $60,000 at x%, then 6.8 has to be much closer to x than to y. The money invested at each rate is the weight of that investment.

Let's now *Name a Variable* and designate P as the amount invested at x% (P stands for "Principal.") Then $60,000 - P$ = the amount invested at y%. (At this point, with three variables, let's not name a fourth.)

We can now write a master equation to represent the Total Interest Paid ($) as a sum of interest paid on each of the two investments:

$$4,080 = \left(\frac{6.8}{100}\right)(60,000) = \left(\frac{x}{100}\right)P + \left(\frac{y}{100}\right)(60,000 - P)$$

We are asked for the value of x. One viable option is to do *Direct Algebra*, rearranging this equation to isolate x. However, that would be a lot of work. At this point, we can stop and say that if we know the values of the other variables P and y, we can plug them into the master equation and find x.

(1): INSUFFICIENT. This statement gives us a specific relationship between x and y. In fact, we should notice that x and y have a *Constant Ratio*, according to this statement. Such relationships can typically take us far on Data Sufficiency.

Rearranging to solve for y, we get $y = 4x/3$, which we can plug into our master equation:

$$4,080 = \left(\frac{x}{100}\right)P + \left(\frac{4x/3}{100}\right)(60,000 - P)$$

Although we can combine the terms somewhat, there's no way to cancel out the P, so we cannot get a number for x with this information alone. This time, a Constant Ratio was not in fact sufficient by itself.

(2): INSUFFICIENT. We can *Algebraically Translate* this information into an equation. A ratio can be written as a fraction:

$$\frac{\text{amount at } x\%}{\text{amount at } y\%} = \frac{P}{60,000 - P} = \frac{3}{2}$$

We should recognize that we can get a value for P, because we have a *Linear Equation with One Unknown*.

If necessary, we can actually solve for P. The earlier we can stop, however, the better. Remember that on Data Sufficiency problems, we do not need to report the specific numbers we find. We just need to know *when* we can find those numbers.

Here is the algebra to solve for P. The first step is to *Cross-Multiply* the equation above.

$$2P = 3(60,000 - P)$$
$$2P = 180,000 - 3P$$
$$5P = 180,000$$
$$P = 36,000$$

Since $60,000 - P = 60,000 - 36,000 = 24,000$, our master equation now looks like this:

$$4,080 = \left(\frac{x}{100}\right)(36,000) + \left(\frac{y}{100}\right)(24,000)$$

However, without knowing y, we cannot solve for x. This statement by itself is not enough.

(1) and (2): SUFFICIENT. Statement (1) gives us y as a constant (4/3) times x, and statement (2) gives us the value of P. Together, they provide enough information to solve for x, and so we can stop here.

If necessary, we can substitute information from both statements into our master equation and solve to confirm. Again, we should stop as soon as we are confident that we see the rest of the path toward a particular value for x.

$$4,080 = \left(\frac{x}{100}\right)(36,000) + \left(\frac{4x/3}{100}\right)(24,000)$$

This equation may seem complex, but it is actually just a linear equation in x. For this reason, we can solve for a unique value of x. It matters now that x and y are related by a Constant Ratio. For instance, if y were instead equal to x^2, we would now have a quadratic equation, which would not necessarily have just one solution.

Here's the algebra to find x:

$$4,080 = 360x + \left(\frac{4x}{100}\right)(8,000)$$
$$4,080 = 360x + 4x(80)$$
$$4,080 = 360x + 320x$$
$$4,080 = 680x$$
$$6 = x$$

The correct answer is (C): BOTH statements TOGETHER are sufficient, but NEITHER statement ALONE is sufficient.

DS 79. FDPs: Percents
Difficulty: 600–700   **OG Page:** 279

Since we are given 4 variables, we should make sure that we are clear on all definitions:

p_1 = price of computer in State A
p_2 = price of computer in State B
t_1 = percent sales tax in State A
t_2 = percent sales tax in State B

The total cost of the computer in State A and State B can be calculated by adding the amount of tax to the base price. Note that the sales tax rates are expressed as *Percents*. Before multiplying by the price, we must convert t_1 and t_2 to *Decimals* by dividing by 100. This is the typical way we translate a given percent: we divide by 100.

We can now *Algebraically Translate* the quantities given in words:

Total cost of computer in State A $= p_1 + p_1\left(\dfrac{t_1}{100}\right)$

Total cost of computer in State B $= p_2 + p_2\left(\dfrac{t_2}{100}\right)$

The question is asking whether the total cost of the computer is greater in State A than in State B. In algebraic terms, we have the following *Inequality:*

$$p_1 + p_1\left(\frac{t_1}{100}\right) > p_2 + p_2\left(\frac{t_2}{100}\right)?$$

We can factor the price of the computers out of each expression:

$$p_1\left(1+\frac{t_1}{100}\right) > p_2\left(1+\frac{t_2}{100}\right)?$$

This is as far as we can *Rephrase*. We will make use of both forms of the question.

(1): INSUFFICIENT. Knowing that $t_1 > t_2$ tells us that the expression $\left(1+\dfrac{t_1}{100}\right)$ on the left side of the second inequality is greater than the expression $\left(1+\dfrac{t_2}{100}\right)$ on the right side of that inequality. However, since we know nothing about the relative sizes of p_1 and p_2, this is insufficient.

(2): INSUFFICIENT. Knowing that $p_1t_1 > p_2t_2$ tells us that the expression $p_1\left(\dfrac{t_1}{100}\right)$ on the left side of the first inequality is greater than the expression $p_2\left(\dfrac{t_1}{100}\right)$ on the right side of that inequality. However, since we know nothing about the relative sizes of p_1 and p_2, this is insufficient.

(1) and (2): INSUFFICIENT. Combining the two statements we still have no information about the relative sizes of p_1 and p_2.

We know that the tax rate in State A (t_1) is higher and that the tax paid in dollars in State A (p_1t_1) is higher as well.

But p_1t_1 might be greater than p_2t_2 for two different reasons:

(a) *Because of* the greater tax rate t_1. That is, p_1 is actually less than p_2, but the higher tax rate pushes the sales tax in dollars higher in State *A*.

OR

(b) *Regardless of* the greater tax rate. That is, p_1 is greater than p_2, so even if the tax rates were the same, we would pay more in tax in State *A*.

If we don't which original price is greater, we cannot calculate which total price, including tax, will be greater.

Testing Numbers is a possible approach. However, since there are four variables, this approach quickly becomes unwieldy, as the Official Guide explanation demonstrates. We still need to *Consider Possible Cases*, but for this problem, we should do so conceptually, as we have done above.

The correct answer is (E): Statements (1) and (2) TOGETHER are not sufficient.

DS 80. EIVs: Inequalities
Difficulty: 600–700   **OG Page:** 279

Because we are told that r and s are both positive, we can *Cross-Multiply* the given *Inequality* without flipping the sign:

Is $r/s > s/r$?

Is $r^2 > s^2$?

Furthermore, because we know that r and s are both positive, we can take the square root of both sides without altering the meaning of the inequality. Thus, our *Rephrased* question is really

Is $r > s$?

(1): SUFFICIENT. Begin by cross-multiplying:

$$\frac{r}{3s} = \frac{1}{4}$$

$$4r = 3s$$

Next, simplify for *r*:

$$r = \frac{3s}{4}$$

Because *r* is a fraction of *s* and both are positive, *r* must be less than *s*.

(2): SUFFICIENT. *s* is 4 greater than *r*. Thus, *s* > *r*.

The correct answer is (D): EACH statement ALONE is sufficient.

DS 81. <u>Word Translations</u>: Statistics
Difficulty: 600–700   **OG Page:** 279

In this **Statistics** problem, we are given the set {*k*, *n*, 12, 6, 17} and asked for the value of *n*. There is no useful way to rephrase this question, so we must proceed directly to the statements.

(1): INSUFFICIENT. Knowing that *n* is greater than *k* does not tell us the value of *n*.

(2): INSUFFICIENT. Knowing that the **Median** is 10 tells us that either *n* or *k* must equal 10. This is true because in a set containing an odd number of terms, as we have here, the median will always be one of the terms of the set. Since none of the given values is 10, either *k* or *n* must be 10. But since we cannot tell whether *n* is the median from this information, this statement is insufficient.

(1) and (2): SUFFICIENT. In a set with an odd number of terms, the median will be the term exactly in the middle. If *k* is less than *n*, we know that the elements of the set, written in numeric order, would look either like this:

{6, *k*, *n*, 12, 17} or like this:

{*k*, 6, *n*, 12, 17}

There is remaining uncertainty about whether *k* is smaller than or greater than 6, but that is of no consequence for the question at hand. *n* is in the middle regardless, so *n* is the median and *n* = 10.

The correct answer is (C): BOTH statements TOGETHER are sufficient, but NEITHER statement ALONE is sufficient.

DS 82. <u>Number Properties</u>: Divisibility & Primes
Difficulty: 600–700   **OG Page:** 280

This **Divisibility & Primes** problem asks us whether *xy* is a multiple of 105, given that *x* is a multiple of 6 and *y* is a multiple of 14.

105 has prime factors 3, 5 and 7 in its **Prime Box**. Therefore, for *xy* to be divisible by 105, it needs to have at least one factor each of 3, 5 and 7 in its prime box.

Because *xy* is the product of *x* and *y*, it must be divisible by the individual factors of *x* and *y*, namely, 2 and 3 for *x*, and 2 and 7 for *y*. This assures us that the prime box of *xy* already contains at least one 3 and one 7 (as well as two 2's, which are not relevant to the question at hand). The remaining question is whether *xy* also contains a 5. To answer this question with a *Yes*, we need to know that a 5 shows up in either *x* or *y*.

Thus, we can **Rephrase** the question as "Is *x* or *y* divisible by 5?"

(1): INSUFFICIENT. The fact that *x* is divisible by 9 does not tell us whether it is also divisible by 5.

(2): SUFFICIENT. This statement tells us that *y* is divisible by 25. Any number that is divisible by 25 is also divisible by 5, since 5 is a factor of 25. Thus, *y* is divisible by 5, and we can answer the rephrased question.

The correct answer is (B): Statement (2) ALONE is sufficient, but statement (1) alone is not sufficient.

DS 83. <u>EIVs</u>: Basic Equations
Difficulty: 600–700   **OG Page:** 280

In this **Basic Equations** problem, we are asked for the value of the **Combined Expression** *b* + *c*, also known as a Combo. No rephrasing is needed.

(1): INSUFFICIENT. It is not possible to manipulate *ab* + *cd* + *ac* + *bd* = 6 to get a numeric value for *b* + *c*.

(2): INSUFFICIENT. This tells us nothing about *b* + *c*.

(1) and (2): SUFFICIENT. We will take a **Direct Algebra** approach.

Since we do have a value for $a + d$, we can manipulate $ab + cd + ac + bd = 6$ to isolate $a + d$. Begin by re-ordering the terms to make factoring easier:

$$ab + cd + ac + bd = 6$$
$$ab + ac + cd + bd = 6$$
$$a(b + c) + d(c + b) = 6$$

Now **Factor** out the common term $(b + c)$:

$$(b + c)(a + d) = 6$$

Plug in statement (2): $a + d = 4$:

$$(b + c)(4) = 6$$

At this point we see that we can solve for $b + c$, which equals 6/4, or 1.5.

Notice that we never find out what b or c is individually. As it turns out, we do not need the values of the separate variables. This is why we do not rephrase a question about a Combo, such as $b + c$, into a question about b and c separately.

The correct answer is (C): both statements TOGETHER are SUFFICIENT.

DS 84. Word Translations: Statistics
Difficulty: 500–600   **OG Page:** 280

According to the **Average Formula,** the average of j and k is:

$$\text{Average} = \frac{\text{Sum of Terms}}{\text{Number of Terms}} = \frac{j + k}{2}$$

If we know the values of j and k, or of the **Combined Expression** $j + k$, we will have enough information to answer the question.

(1): SUFFICIENT. This statement allows us to find the sum of the two variables. We can **Algebraically Translate** the statement and use the average formula:

$$\frac{(j + 2) + (k + 4)}{2} = 11$$

We should be able to tell that we can theoretically solve for the Combo $j + k$.

If necessary, actually do the algebra:

$$j + 2 + k + 4 = 22$$
$$j + k = 16$$

(2): SUFFICIENT. We can translate this statement using the average formula and solve for the sum of $j + k$:

$$\frac{j + k + 14}{3} = 10$$

Again, we should be able to tell that we can theoretically solve for the Combo $j + k$.

If necessary, actually do the algebra:

$$j + k + 14 = 30$$
$$j + k = 16$$

Notice that we never find out what j or k is individually. As it turns out, we do not need the values of the separate variables. This is why we do not rephrase a question about a Combo, such as $j + k$, into a question about j and k separately.

The correct answer is (D): EACH statement ALONE is sufficient.

DS 85. FDPs: FDP Connections
Difficulty: 600–700   **OG Page:** 280

We are given one equation, $P + S = 100$, and we are asked to find P. In order to do so, we must know the value of S or a relationship between P and S such that we can solve for P. Notice that we already have one **Linear Equation**, so if we get another, we will be able to solve for P.

This problem involves both **Fractions** and **Percents** along the way.

(1): SUFFICIENT. Combine the equation given in this statement, $S = (2/3)P$, with the equation given in the question stem.

We now have **Two Different Linear Equations** with **Two Variables,** so it is possible to solve for the value of P. We should stop now to save time.

If we really want to do the algebra for practice, here it is:

$$S + P = 100$$
$$\left(\frac{2}{3}P\right) + P = 100$$
$$\frac{5}{3}P = 100$$
$$P = 60$$

(2): INSUFFICIENT. This statement does not provide any information about the number of tickets Sandy sold, because we don't know the total number of tickets sold. We can't figure out how many tickets Paula sold.

Be careful of the problem's wording. We may incorrectly assume that Paula and Sandy were the *only* people who sold tickets, but we are not told this. Moreover, the numbers in the statements do not support that assumption.

The correct answer is (A): Statement (1) ALONE is sufficient, but statement (2) alone is not sufficient.

DS 86. Word Translations: Minor Question Types
Difficulty: 300–500   **OG Page:** 280

This is a *Grouping* problem that also involves *Inequalities*. Each person has 30 integers to choose from. Thus, if there are fewer than 30 people, everyone can choose a different number. But if there are more than 30 people but only 30 integers to choose from, at least two people will have to write down the same number. Some number (or numbers) will have to be repeated.

If we have fewer than 30 people, we cannot guarantee that everyone will write down a different number. But if we have more than 30 people, we can guarantee that they *will not* all write down different numbers.

Therefore, we can usefully *Rephrase* the question as "Were there more than 30 people?"

(1): SUFFICIENT. We know that there were more than 40 people. Therefore, there were more than 30 people as well. This answers our rephrased question.

In other words, at least one of the numbers *must* have been written down more than once.

(2): INSUFFICIENT. We do not know whether there were more than 30 people. We are told that there were fewer than 70 people. There could have been 50 people or 10 people.

The correct answer is (A): Statement (1) ALONE is sufficient, but statement (2) alone is not sufficient.

DS 87. Word Translations: Rates & Work
Difficulty: 600–700   **OG Page:** 280

This *Rates* problem makes use of the usual *Rate–Time–Work Formula:*

$$\text{Rate} \times \text{Time} = \text{Distance}$$

Since both quantities mentioned in the prompt are *times* (in seconds), we can solve for time in the equation above:

$$\text{Time} = \frac{\text{Distance}}{\text{Rate}}$$

Using this formula for time, we can *Rephrase* the question this way: Is $\dfrac{d_1}{r_1} > \dfrac{d_2}{r_2}$?

Since rates are positive numbers, we can multiply this *Inequality* by the *Common Denominator* of these two fractions, which is $r_1 r_2$. This yields a further rephrasing:

Is $d_1 r_2 > d_2 r_1$?

(1): INSUFFICIENT. We can *Substitute* $d_2 + 30$ for d_1 in either version of the prompt question:

Is $\dfrac{d_2 + 30}{r_1} > \dfrac{d_2}{r_2}$? or Is $(d_2 + 30)r_2 > d_2 r_1$?

We can't determine an answer because we don't know anything about the rates.

(2): INSUFFICIENT. We can substitute $r_2 + 30$ for r_1 in either version of the prompt question:

Is $\dfrac{d_1}{r_2 + 30} > \dfrac{d_2}{r_2}$? or Is $d_1 r_2 > d_2(r_2 + 30)$?

We can't determine an answer because we don't know anything about the distances.

(1) & (2): INSUFFICIENT. Continuing with a *Direct Algebra* approach, we can substitute $r_2 + 30$ for r_1, and $d_2 + 30$ for d_1, in either version of the prompt question:

Is $\dfrac{d_2 + 30}{r_2 + 30} > \dfrac{d_2}{r_2}$? or Is $(d_2 + 30)r_2 > d_2(r_2 + 30)$?

Using the second version, let's distribute and simplify:

$$d_2r_2 + 30r_2 > d_2r_2 + 30d_2 \text{?}$$
$$30r_2 > 30d_2 \text{?}$$
$$r_2 > d_2 \text{?}$$

Since we do not know whether r_2 is larger than d_2, we still cannot resolve the question.

The correct answer is (E): Statements (1) and (2) TOGETHER are not sufficient.

DS 88. FDPs: Percents
Difficulty: 500–600   **OG Page:** 280

In this **Percents** problem, we can set up a **Table** to keep track of the money Arturo spent last year:

Expense	Amount
Real Estate Taxes	?
Home Insurance	
Mortgage Payments	
Total	$12,000

We should be on the lookout for statements that give information about home insurance and mortgage payments or about the two as a combined sum. In other words, if we know the **Combined Expression** $H + M$, then we can answer the question.

(1): INSUFFICIENT. This statement gives us neither the combined mortgage payments and home insurance expenses, nor these expenses individually.

If the sum of real estate taxes and home insurance equals $33\frac{1}{3}\%$ of the mortgage payments, then the sum of real estate taxes and home insurance is 1/3 the total mortgage payments. **Naming a Variable,** we can let x be the amount spent on real estate taxes and M be the amount spent on mortgage payments. The amount spent on real estate taxes and home insurance has to add up to 1/3 the amount spent on mortgage payments, or $M/3$.

Expense	Amount	
Real Estate Taxes	x	} Sum = $M/3$
Home Insurance	$M/3 - x$	
Mortgage Payments	M	
Total	$12,000	

We can extract the following equation:

$$x + \left(\frac{M}{3} - x\right) + M = 12{,}000$$
$$\frac{4}{3}M = 12{,}000$$
$$M = 9{,}000$$

This statement gives us M, the mortgage payments, but the real estate taxes could be any value less than or equal to 1/3 of $9,000, or $3,000.

(2): SUFFICIENT. This statement relates the combined mortgage payment and home insurance expenses to the real estate taxes. Let y be the total amount spent on home insurance and mortgage payments. In other words, $y = H + M$.

Expense	Amount
Real Estate Taxes	0.2y
Home Insurance	y
Mortgage Payments	
Total	$12,000

$$0.2y + y = 12{,}000$$
$$1.2y = 12{,}000$$
$$y = \frac{12{,}000}{1.2}$$
$$y = 10{,}000$$

Therefore, Arturo paid 0.2($10,000) = $2,000 in real estate taxes.

The correct answer is (B): Statement (2) ALONE is sufficient, but statement (1) alone is not sufficient.

DS 89. Word Translations: Overlapping Sets
Difficulty: 600–700   **OG Page:** 280

This question asks about the number of members of two clubs, Club X and Club Y. When we read the statements, we see that we can consider this an **Overlapping Sets** problem, since the question also describes people who are members of both Club X and Club Y.

The stem does not give us much information for the **Double Set Matrix**. All we can really do is **Name Variables**. We can designate the total number of members in Club X as x and the total number of members in Club Y as y. In these terms, the question asks whether $x > y$.

We cannot **Rephrase** any further, but we can observe that **Inequalities** are involved.

		Club X?		
		Yes	*No*	*Total*
Club Y?	*Yes*			y
	No			
	Total	x		

(1): INSUFFICIENT. This statement tells us that 20% of the members of Club X are actually members of both Y and X. We can place a $0.2x$ in the "Yes-Yes" cell at the upper left (Yes to both clubs). This does not help us to decide whether $x > y$.

		Club X?		
		Yes	*No*	*Total*
Club Y?	*Yes*	$0.2x$		y
	No			
	Total	x		

(2): INSUFFICIENT. This statement tells us that 30% of the members of Club Y are actually members of both X and Y. We can place a $0.3y$ in the Yes-Yes cell. This does not help us to decide whether $x > y$.

		Club X?		
		Yes	*No*	*Total*
Club Y?	*Yes*	$0.3y$		y
	No			
	Total	x		

(1) and (2): SUFFICIENT. Both statements gave us an expression for the Yes-Yes cell. This is the key step: we can set these two expressions equal to each other and solve for x in terms of y:

$$0.2x = 0.3y$$
$$2x = 3y$$
$$x = 1.5y$$

Since x is 1.5 times the value of y, x is in fact greater than y. Even though we do not know the value of either x or y, we know that $1.5y\ (= x)$ is greater than y. This is true because y is definitely positive: it represents a number of people. Any positive number multiplied by 1.5 becomes larger.

The correct answer is (C): BOTH statements TOGETHER are sufficient, but NEITHER statement ALONE is sufficient.

DS 90. Number Properties: Divisibility & Primes
Difficulty: 600–700   **OG Page:** 280

The first step in this **Divisibility & Primes** problem is to create a **Prime Box** for 12:

12

$$\boxed{2,\ 2,\ 3}$$

For t and 12 to have a common factor greater than 1, t must share at least one of the primes in 12's prime box. Thus, our **Rephrased** question becomes "Is t a **Multiple** of either 2 or 3?"

Given that we are asked about t, we should simplify the given equation for t at the outset, using **Direct Algebra** to get rid of fractions:

$$\frac{k}{6} + \frac{m}{4} = \frac{t}{12}$$
$$2k + 3m = t$$

(1): SUFFICIENT. Given that k is a multiple of 3, we know that $2k$ will also be a multiple of 3. Moreover, since m is an integer, $3m$ is a multiple of 3. We can now draw conclusions about t.

$$t = 2k + 3m$$
$$t = \text{(a multiple of 3)} + \text{(another multiple of 3)}$$

By the **Properties of Multiples**, we know that the sum, which equals t, is a multiple of 3 as well. Thus, we can answer the rephrased question.

(2): INSUFFICIENT. Knowing that m is a multiple of 3 does not help us, since our expression already multiplied m by 3. Thus, $3m$ will be a multiple of 3 whether or not m itself is a multiple of 3. Furthermore, we know nothing about k:

$$t = 2k + 3m$$
$$t = 2k + \text{(some multiple of 3)}$$

Therefore, we cannot answer the rephrased question.

We can verify our conclusion by **Testing Numbers.** If $m = 3$ and $k = 1$, then $t = 2(1) + 3(3) = 11$, and t does not share any common factors with 12 apart from 1. If, however, $m = 2$ and $k = 4$, then we know that $t = 2(4) + 3(2) = 14$, and t and 12 share 2 as a factor.

The correct answer is (A): Statement (1) ALONE is sufficient, but statement (2) alone is not sufficient.

DS 91. <u>Geometry</u>: Lines & Angles
Difficulty: 600–700   **OG Page:** 280

In this *Lines* problem, we are shown a line segment with four points on it. We are asked whether the distance from C to D is greater than the distance from B to C. We cannot base our determination on the appearance of the diagram. We need to have specific information about the various lengths between the points.

Since the question asks about whether one distance is greater than another, *Inequalities* are involved as well.

(1): INSUFFICIENT. Knowing that the length of the entire line segment AD is 20 does not tell us anything about the various distances between the intervening points.

(2): INSUFFICIENT. Knowing that $AB = CD$ does not tell us whether $CD > BC$. It may be that all three segments (AB, BC, and CD) are equal, or it may be that AB and CD are both less than or both greater than BC.

(1) and (2): INSUFFICIENT. Without knowing the specific distances of the line segments, we cannot determine whether $CD > BC$. *Drawing Possible Cases* will help us visualize extremes. For example, AD and CD could both equal 2 and BC could equal 16.

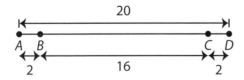

In this case $BC > CD$. Or AD and CD could both equal 9 and BC could equal 2.

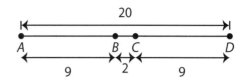

In this case $CD > BC$.

The correct answer is (E): Statements (1) and (2) TOGETHER are not sufficient.

DS 92. <u>FDPs</u>: Percents
Difficulty: 600–700   **OG Page:** 280

In this *Percents* problem, we are told that 30% of the employees at a certain office who are over 40 years old have master's degrees. We are asked for the actual *number* of employees over 40 who have master's degrees. In order to answer this question, we need to determine the number of employees at the office who are over 40.

Since the problem involves *Overlapping Sets*, we can visualize the given data in the form of a *Double Set Matrix*, as shown below, with the desired number shaded. We can *Name a Variable* and use x to indicate the total number of people at the office:

		Over 40?		
		Yes	No	*Total*
College?	*Yes*			0.5x
	No			0.5x
	Total	0.6x	0.4x	x

If we can determine how many people are in the office, we can find out how many people in the office are over 40. Once we know how many people are over 40, we can figure out how many of them have master's degrees.

A good *Rephrasing* of the question is simply "What is x?"

(1): SUFFICIENT. This statement tells us that $0.5x = 100$. From this, we can solve for x and for $0.6x$. Remember that we do not actually need to report that value.

(2): INSUFFICIENT. This statement does not give us any hard numbers. Instead, it only specifies a percent, making it impossible to solve for x.

The correct answer is (A): Statement (1) ALONE is sufficient, but statement (2) alone is not sufficient.

DS 93. Word Translations: Statistics
Difficulty: 500–600   **OG Page:** 280

In this **Statistics** problem, we are told that p, q, r, s, and t are five consecutive even integers in increasing order. Notice that the number line is beside the point. The question asks for the **Average** of the five integers.

In any **Evenly Spaced Set** (such as a list of consecutive integers, consecutive even integers, etc.), the average is simply the middle number (or the average of the two middle numbers if there is an even number of terms). Thus, the average of this list is equal to the value of r. We can **Rephrase** this question as "What is the value of r?"

Since p, q, r, s, and t are evenly spaced and in increasing order, knowing any one of them would allow us to find r. For example, we know that r is 4 greater than p. So if we knew the value of p, we would know the value of r.

Therefore, we can rephrase even further: "What is the value of any of the variables?"

(1): SUFFICIENT. If $q + s = 24$, the average of q and s is 12. Since the list is evenly spaced, and q and s are equidistant from the average, we know that r simply equals 12.

Alternatively, we can use **Substitution**. Note that q equals $r - 2$ (because q is the next lower even number) and s equals $r + 2$ (because s is the next higher even number).

Therefore, $q + s = 24$ can be rewritten as follows:

$$(r - 2) + (r + 2) = 24$$
$$2r = 24$$
$$r = 12$$

(2): SUFFICIENT. If the average of q and r is 11, then q and r sum to 22. Since r is 2 more than q, we know that q and r are simply 10 and 12, respectively. To verify, we can substitute $(r - 2)$ for q and solve:

$$\frac{(r - 2) + r}{2} = 11$$
$$2r - 2 = 22$$
$$2r = 24$$
$$r = 12$$

The correct answer is (D): EACH statement ALONE is sufficient.

DS 94. Geometry: Coordinate Plane
Difficulty: 600–700   **OG Page:** 281

In this **Coordinate Plane** problem, the **Equation for a Line** k is presented in the standard slope-intercept form of $y = mx + b$.

Since we are asked for the slope of the line, we can **Rephrase** the question as "What is m?"

(1): SUFFICIENT. The equation for the second line can be written in slope-intercept form:

$$y = (1 - m)x + (b + 1)$$

By definition, **Parallel** lines have the same slopes. The slope of the second line is $1 - m$. We can set this slope equal to the slope of line k, which is m:

$$m = 1 - m$$
$$2m = 1$$
$$m = 1/2$$

This answers our rephrased question.

(2): INSUFFICIENT. Knowing that two lines intersect does not tell us enough information about their slopes. All we know is that, because they intersect, they are not parallel. Thus, they do not have the same slope. However, we know nothing more about m.

The correct answer is (A): Statement (1) ALONE is sufficient, but statement (2) alone is not sufficient.

DS 95. EIVs: Basic Equations
Difficulty: 600–700   **OG Page:** 281

There is no rephrasing to be done for this **Basic Equations** question, which asks whether the product rst equals 1.

(1): INSUFFICIENT. If $rs = 1$, t could be any

number. We can **Test Numbers** to confirm. If t is also 1, then we have a *Yes* answer. If t is 42, then we have a *No* answer. Thus, the statement is insufficient.

(2): INSUFFICIENT. If $st = 1$, then r could be anything, just as in statement (1).

(1) and (2): INSUFFICIENT. We can do **Direct Algebra** to combine the equations, trying to put rst on one side of the resulting equation.

$$(rs)(st) = (1)(1)$$
$$rs^2t = 1$$
$$rst = 1 / s$$

We cannot isolate rst on one side of the equation and have a number by itself on the other side. Therefore, we cannot find a specific value for rst, and we cannot confirm or deny that $rst = 1$.

Alternatively, we can prove this point with real numbers. If $r = s = t = 1$, then $rs = 1$, $st = 1$, and $rst = 1$. We have a *Yes* answer to our question.

On the other hand, if $r = t = 42$ and $s = 1/42$, then $rs = 1$, $st = 1$, but $rst = 42$. We have a *No* answer. Thus, the statements are insufficient.

The correct answer is (E): Statements (1) and (2) TOGETHER are not sufficient.

DS 96. <u>Geometry</u>: Circles & Cylinders
Difficulty: 300–500   **OG Page:** 281

In a **Circle** graph representing total expenses, the number of degrees in each **Sector** is proportional to the expenses for the corresponding division. For example, if a sector occupies 90 degrees of the circle, then the corresponding division accounts for $90/360 = 1/4$ of the total expenses.

We know that the total expenses for Company H are $5,400,000. Thus, to determine the expenses for Division R, we only need to know the value of x, the number of degrees in the Division R sector.

The **Rephrased** question is therefore "What is x?"

(1): SUFFICIENT. We are given the value of x.

(2): INSUFFICIENT. We can conclude that the sectors corresponding to Divisions S and T take up

twice as much of the circle as Division R, but we do not have enough information to solve for x.

The correct answer is (A): Statement (1) ALONE is sufficient, but statement (2) alone is not sufficient.

DS 97. <u>EIVs</u>: Inequalities
Difficulty: 500–600   **OG Page:** 281

In this **Inequalities** problem, we are asked whether $x < -3$, given that x < 0. No rephrase is necessary.

(1): SUFFICIENT. Like all inequalities involving x^2, this one has a solution involving both positive and negative numbers. If x^2 is greater than some number, then x must be larger in magnitude (or absolute value) than the square root of that number *but can be either positive or negative*. Therefore, if $x^2 > 9$, then $x > 3$ or $x < -3$. Recall that **Even Exponents** hide the sign of the base.

Since we are told up front that x must be negative, it follows that $x < -3$. This statement is sufficient.

(2): INSUFFICIENT. To evaluate this statement, we need to isolate x by getting rid of the exponent. If x were raised to an even power, we could have potential sign issues, because both positives and negatives raised to an even power will be positive. However, because x is raised to the third power, we have no problem. **Odd Exponents** keep the sign of the base. If x^3 is negative, then x must be negative as well. We can isolate x by taking the cube root of both sides of the equations. $\sqrt[3]{x^3} < \sqrt[3]{-9}$, becomes $x < \sqrt[3]{-9}$.

Now we are faced with a different problem—the cube root of -9 is not an integer. In this situation, we can **Estimate** the value of the **Cube Root** by comparing it to cube roots we do know that are both greater than and less than -9. The perfect cube greater than -9 is -8, and $-8 = (-2)^3$. The perfect cube less than -9 is -27, and $-27 = (-3)^3$. Therefore $\sqrt[3]{-27} < \sqrt[3]{-9} < \sqrt[3]{-8}$, meaning that $-3 < \sqrt[3]{-9} < -2$.

$\sqrt[3]{-9}$ is between -2 and -3, and $x < \sqrt[3]{-9}$. That means x could be greater than -3, in which case the answer to the question would be *No*. But there are also possible values of *x* less than −3. In those cases, the answer to the question would be *Yes*.

The correct answer is (A): Statement (1) ALONE is sufficient, but statement (2) alone is not sufficient.

DS 98. Number Properties: Divisibility & Primes
Difficulty: 600–700   **OG Page:** 281

This **Divisibility & Primes** problem deals with **Remainders** after division by 7. When integers are divided by 7, the possible remainders are 0, 1, 2, 3, 4, 5, and 6. We can never have a negative remainder or a remainder of 7 or larger. Notice that there are exactly 7 possible remainders.

(1): INSUFFICIENT. If the range of the seven remainders is 6, the lowest remainder must be 0 and the highest remainder must be 6. However, we do not know anything about the other 5 remainders. **Test Possible Cases** to verify. For example, the sum of the remainders could be

$$0 + 0 + 0 + 0 + 0 + 0 + 6 = 6,$$
$$0 + 6 + 6 + 6 + 6 + 6 + 6 = 30, \text{ or}$$
$$0 + 1 + 2 + 3 + 4 + 5 + 6 = 21.$$

(2): SUFFICIENT. If the seven numbers selected are **Consecutive Integers**, they will each have a different remainder, and the remainders themselves will be consecutive.

For instance, if the 7 numbers chosen were 7, 8, 9, 10, 11, 12, and 13, the remainders would be 0, 1, 2, 3, 4, 5, and 6, respectively. If the numbers chosen were 16, 17, 18, 19, 20, 21 and 22, the remainders would be 2, 3, 4, 5, 6, 0 and 1, respectively. No matter what 7 numbers are chosen, we know that the remainders 0 to 6 will each be represented once. Moreover, the order does not matter for a sum.

Therefore, the sum of the remainders must be $0 + 1 + 2 + 3 + 4 + 5 + 6 = 21$.

The correct answer is (B): Statement (2) ALONE is sufficient, but statement (1) alone is not sufficient.

DS 99. Word Translations: Minor Question Types
Difficulty: 500–600   **OG Page:** 281

r	s	t
u	v	w
x	y	z

This is Sudoku!

The key to this question is carefully following the rules set out in the question about the values of the 9 letters. Each of the 9 letters has a value of 1, 2 or 3, and neither a column nor a row can have more than one instance of a 1, 2 or 3.

This means that each digit must occur exactly once in each column and each row. This also means that there will be a total of three 1's, three 2's and three 3's.

The question asks us for the value of *r*, the letter in the top left cell.

(1): SUFFICIENT. If $v + z = 6$, both *v* and *z* must equal 3, since $3 + 3$ is the only way to achieve 6 if only 1's, 2's and 3's can be used. If *v* and *z* are 3, then we know the other numbers sharing either a row or a column with *v* or *z* cannot be 3. We should record our thinking by crossing out rows and columns in the **Table** we've drawn.

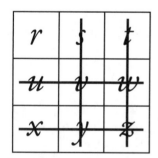

We know there must be a third 3 somewhere in the grid. The only remaining possibility is *r*, so *r* = 3.

(2): SUFFICIENT. We know that $s + t + u + x = 6$. Using only 1's, 2's and 3's, there are only two ways for four integers to sum to 6:

$1 + 1 + 1 + 3 = 6$
$1 + 1 + 2 + 2 = 6$

However, since u and x are in the same column they cannot have the same value, and since s and t are in the same row, they too cannot have the same value. The first scenario is not a possibility (three 1's would require either u and x or s and t to have the same value). Furthermore, s and t must be 1 and 2 (not necessarily in that order), and the same is true of u and x.

Therefore, we know that r, which is in the same row as s and t (and in the same column as u and x) must be 3.

Again, we should **Consider Possible Cases** by putting them on paper in our table.

The correct answer is (D): EACH statement ALONE is sufficient.

DS 100. FDPs: Digits & Decimals
Difficulty: 600–700   **OG Page:** 281

This **Decimals** problem defines a **New Function** for us: $[x]$ is the greatest integer less than or equal to x. For $[x]$ to be 0, x must be greater than or equal to 0 but less than the integer 1.

Thus, our **Rephrased** question becomes this:

Is $0 \le x < 1$?

Notice that our rephrased question involves a **Compound Inequality**.

(1): SUFFICIENT. Here we are given a **Linear Equation** for x. We do not actually need to solve it. We already know that we will be *able* to solve for x, from which we can determine the value of $[x]$. Thus we would be able to answer the question definitively.

If we do decide to solve for x, we get:

$5x + 1 = 3 + 2x$
$5x = 2 + 2x$
$3x = 2$
$x = 2/3$

Because x is between 0 and 1, the greatest integer less than x will be 0.

(2): SUFFICIENT. The range given falls completely within the range in our rephrased question. If we choose to consider the original question, we can see that because x is between 0 and 1, the greatest integer less than x will be 0.

The correct answer is (D): EACH statement ALONE is sufficient.

DS 101. Word Translations: Statistics
Difficulty: 600–700   **OG Page:** 281

We are told in this **Statistics** problem that Material A costs \$3 per kilogram and Material B costs \$5 per kilogram. We are also told that 10 kilograms of Material K is composed of x kilograms of Material A and y kilograms of Material B. We are then asked whether $x > y$.

Since $x + y = 10$, we know that $y = 10 - x$. We can **Rephrase** the question:

Is $x > 10 - x$?
Is $2x > 10$?
Is $x > 5$?

At this point, we may recognize that the **Cost Relationship** will become important, but we do not have enough information about it yet.

(1): INSUFFICIENT. If y is greater than 4, it could equal 5, in which case $x = y$, since $x + y = 10$ from the question stem. Or y could equal 6, in which case x would equal 4 and $y > x$. Or it could even equal 4.1, in which case x would equal 5.9 and $y < x$. Since we cannot tell which of these scenarios we have, we cannot answer the question.

(2): SUFFICIENT. We know from the question stem that $x + y = 10$. Thus, $x = 10 - y$. We also know from this statement that the total cost is less than \$40. **Algebraically Translating** the cost relationship, we can write $3x + 5y < 40$.

Now we can **Substitute** and simplify:

$$3x + 5y < 40$$
$$3(10 - y) + 5y < 40$$
$$30 - 3y + 5y < 40$$
$$-3y + 5y < 10$$
$$2y < 10$$
$$y < 5$$

If $y < 5$, then $x > 5$, and we can answer the question.

We might also recognize **Weighted Averages** in this statement. The average cost per kilogram of mixture K is a weighted average of $3 (the cost per kg of Material A) and $5 (the cost per kg of Material B).

The weights are the literal weights of A and B in mixture K. For instance, the per-kilogram cost of K will be closer to $3 (that is, lower than $4, the midpoint between $3 and $5) if there is more 3-dollar A in K than there is 5-dollar B. In effect, statement (2) tells us exactly this. The per-kilogram cost of K is below $4, so we must be using more of the cheap stuff (x kilograms of A) than of the expensive stuff (y kilograms of B). Thus $x > y$.

The correct answer is (B): Statement (2) ALONE is sufficient, but statement (1) alone is not sufficient.

📌 **DS 102. Word Translations:** Rates & Work
   Difficulty: 600–700   **OG Page:** 281

In this **Rates** problem, we are told that two cars are traveling on the same road at constant rates. Car X is now 1 mile ahead of Car Y. The question is when (in terms of minutes from now) Car X will be 2 miles ahead of Car Y. It may be helpful to **Draw a Picture** to ensure that you can visualize the problem. Exaggerate the differences so you can see what's happening.

We could answer this question with an **Rate-Time-Distance Chart**. However, we are interested in *relative* distances (how far one car is ahead of the other), not absolute distances along the road.

Thus, a better approach is to use **Relative Rates**. Because these cars are moving in the same direction, their rates can be subtracted. It is the *difference* of the rates (speeds) of Cars X and Y that determines how rapidly the distance between them grows.

The general **Rate-Time-Distance Formula** states that distance equals the product of rate and time. In this problem, we are given the change in distance (1 mile) and asked for the time.

Therefore, a good **Rephrasing** is to ask, "What is the difference between the rates (speeds) of Cars X and Y?"

(1): SUFFICIENT. This statement gives us the speeds of Cars X and Y directly, so we can compute the difference of their speeds through subtraction.

(2): SUFFICIENT. This statement tells us that 3 minutes ago, the distance between the two cars was 1/2 mile. Therefore, in those three minutes, the distance grew by $1 - 1/2 = 1/2$ mile.

We can substitute this intermediate result into the rate equation to solve for the rate R, which is really the difference of the speeds of Cars X and Y:

$$R \times 3 \min = \frac{1}{2} \mi$$

Once we obtain a value for R, we can solve for the time (in minutes) that it would take for the distance to grow an additional mile, that is, from 1 mile to 2 miles. Incidentally, this time is 6 minutes, as we would suspect.

The correct answer is (D): EACH statement ALONE is sufficient.

DS 103. Word Translations: Rates & Work
   Difficulty: 500–600   **OG Page:** 281

In this **Rates & Work** problem, we are told that an animated cartoon consists of 17,280 frames. We want to know how many minutes it will take to run the cartoon.

We can determine this time using the **Rate–Time–Work Formula** ($RT = W$) if we know the rate (R) at which the cartoon runs, since we already know the work (W).

The question can be **Rephrased** as "What is the cartoon's running time, OR what is the rate at which the cartoon runs?"

(1): SUFFICIENT. This statement gives us the rate explicitly, although this rate is in frames per second. The question seems to require frames per *minute*, but we could easily convert the units. This statement provides enough information to find the unknown time.

(2): SUFFICIENT. It takes six times as long to run the cartoon as to rewind it, and it takes 14 minutes to complete both acts. Express this 6 to 1 **Ratio** with an **Unknown Multiplier** x:

$$6x + 1x = 14$$
$$7x = 14$$
$$x = 2$$

Since $x = 2$, it takes $6x$, or 12 minutes, to run the cartoon.

The correct answer is (D): EACH statement ALONE is sufficient.

DS 104. <u>Word Translations</u>: Rates & Work
Difficulty: 600–700   **OG Page:** 282

The first thing to consider in this **Rates** problem is whether the speed of the train was constant. Unless the speed was constant, we can only determine **Average Speed** between two points, not the instantaneous speed at a specific point.

(1): INSUFFICIENT. With the total distance and total time, we can compute the average speed for the entire trip, using the **Rate–Time–Distance Formula** ($RT = D$). However, we do not know whether the train was traveling at a *constant* speed through the entire trip.

(2): INSUFFICIENT. This gives us the average speed through the trip, but we still do not know whether the speed was constant.

(1) and (2): INSUFFICIENT. Both statements essentially provide the same information: the average speed. Thus, we get nothing new when we put them together, and we cannot determine whether the speed was constant.

The correct answer is (E): Statements (1) and (2) TOGETHER are not sufficient.

DS 105. <u>Word Translations</u>: Statistics
Difficulty: 600–700   **OG Page:** 282

This **Statistics** problem tells us that the **Mean** price of the three homes is $120,000. We are asked to find the **Median** (middle) price of the three houses.

(1): INSUFFICIENT. Knowing that Tom's house cost $110,000 allows us to determine that Tom's house was not the most expensive. If it were, then the average price could not be $120,000. However, we do not know whether Tom's house was the least expensive house or the "middle" house.

We should **Consider Possible Cases.** If Tom's house is the least expensive, then the middle house would cost more than $110,000, and the median would be some number greater than $110,000. If Tom's house is the middle house, however, then the median would be $110,000.

Here, we have used **Algebraic Reasoning.** Alternatively, to think through the possibilities, we could have **Tested Numbers.**

(2): SUFFICIENT. We know that Jane's house cost $120,000. Again, we consider possible cases by algebraic reasoning. Jane's house cannot be less expensive than both of the others, or else the average would have been higher than $120,000. By the same token, we know that Jane's house cannot be more expensive than both of the others. Otherwise, the overall average would have to be less than $120,000.

There are only two viable scenarios. One is that the three houses are worth different amounts, and Jane's house (worth $120,000) is in the middle. The second scenario is that all three houses are worth $120,000. In either case, the median is $120,000.

The correct answer is (B): Statement (2) ALONE is sufficient, but statement (1) alone is not sufficient.

DS 106. <u>Number Properties</u>: Odds & Evens
Difficulty: 500–600   **OG Page:** 282

In this **Odds & Evens** problem, we are asked whether xy is even. In order for this to be true, just one of the two integers needs to be even. By the

Properties of Odds & Evens, an even integer multiplied by any other integer produces an even product.

Therefore, we can ***Rephrase*** the question as "Is x OR y even?"

(1): SUFFICIENT. If $x = y + 1$, then we are dealing with two ***Consecutive Integers***. In any pair of consecutive integers, one of the integers must be even. The answer to the rephrased question is *Yes.*

(2): SUFFICIENT. If x/y is an even integer, x must be even. An odd number contains only odd prime factors, so if x were odd and divided by y, the quotient would be either an odd integer or a fraction.

Since x is definitely even, the answer to the rephrased question is *Yes.*

Alternatively, we can do ***Direct Algebra*** with Odds & Evens rules:

$x/y = $ Even

$x = (y)($Even$) = $ Another even

The correct answer is (D): EACH statement ALONE is sufficient.

DS 107. Word Translations: Probability
Difficulty: 500–600   **OG Page:** 282

This question asks for the ***Probability*** of selecting a chip that is either white or blue. Since there are only three chips—white, blue, and red—we can use the ***1 − x Principle*** to simplify the question. The only chips that are *not* white or blue are red, so the question can be ***Rephrased*** as "What is the probability that the chip is red?"

(1): INSUFFICIENT. This statement gives us two pieces of information. First, we know the literal content: the probability that the chip is blue (1/5). Second, by the 1 − x Principle, this statement also gives us the probability that the chip is either white *or* red (4/5).

However, we do not have any way of determining the probability that the chip is red. All we know is that this probability is between 0 and 4/5.

(2): SUFFICIENT. This statement provides the answer to our rephrased question above. If the

probability that the chip will be red is 1/3, the probability that the chip will be white or blue is 2/3.

The correct answer is (B): Statement (2) ALONE is sufficient, but statement (1) alone is not sufficient.

DS 108. Number Properties: Consecutive Integers
Difficulty: 600–700   **OG Page:** 282

On the ***Number Line*** shown, x is at the third tick mark to the right of 0, and y is at the seventh tick mark to the right of 0. The tick marks are equally spaced, so let's ***Name a Variable*** and call the constant spacing k.

Thus, by looking at the number line, we can write the following relationships:

$x = 3k$
$y = 7k$
$y - x = 4k$

The question asks "What is y?" We can ***Rephrase*** this question in any of several ways:

"What is k?" (because y is determined by k)

OR "What is x?"

OR "What is $y - x$?" (because these two questions will also give us a value for k).

(1): SUFFICIENT. This provides the value of x, answering one of the rephrased questions.

If $x = 1/2 = 3k$, then $k = 1/6$ and $y = 7/6$.

(2): SUFFICIENT. This statement gives us the value of $y - x$, answering one of the rephrased questions.

If $y - x = 2/3 = 4k$, then $k = 1/6$ and $y = 7/6$.

The tick marks in this problem turn out not to be ***Consecutive Integers***, in fact. However, the tick marks represent an ***Evenly Spaced Set***, of which consecutive integer sets are a special example.

The correct answer is (D): EACH statement ALONE is sufficient.

DS 109. Geometry: Triangles & Diagonals
Difficulty: 700–800   **OG Page:** 282

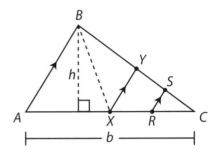

This is a complicated **Triangles** problem. We should first **Draw a Diagram** carefully.

As shown above, $\overline{XY}$ is drawn by connecting the midpoints of $\overline{AC}$ and $\overline{BC}$. Because points X and Y are the midpoints of $\overline{AC}$ and $\overline{BC}$, respectively, we can draw certain conclusions about $\triangle XYC$. First, the base of triangle XYC will be half the base of $\triangle ABC$. Second, because Y is halfway between B and C, we also know that the height of $\triangle XYC$ will be half the height of $\triangle ABC$. Finally, we should notice that $\overline{AB}$ is parallel to $\overline{XY}$, so $\triangle ABC$ and $\triangle XYC$ are **Similar Triangles**.

Now we can compare the areas of $\triangle ABC$ and $\triangle XYC$. The **Triangle Area Formula** multiplies together the base AND the height ($A = \frac{1}{2}bh$). If the base and height of $\triangle XYC$ are each half the base and height of $\triangle ABC$, respectively, than the area of $\triangle XYC$ will be $(1/2)^2$ or $1/4$ that of $\triangle ABC$. This follows a general rule for any two similar figures (not just triangles). If one figure has lengths that are $1/2$ those of a second similar figure, then the first figure will have $1/4$ the area of the second.

Using this same reasoning, $\triangle RSC$ will also be similar to $\triangle XYC$ and have an area that is $1/4$ that of $\triangle XYC$.

$$\text{Area}_{\triangle RSC} = \frac{1}{4}\text{Area}_{\triangle XYC}$$

$$\text{Area}_{\triangle XYC} = \frac{1}{4}\text{Area}_{\triangle ABC}$$

Then $\text{Area}_{\triangle RSC} = \frac{1}{4}\left(\frac{1}{4}\right)\text{Area}_{\triangle ABC} = \frac{1}{16}\text{Area}_{\triangle ABC}$.

We are directly asked for the area of $\triangle RSC$. We can **Rephrase** the question as "What is the area of $\triangle ABC$?"

(1): SUFFICIENT. This statement tells us the area of $\triangle ABX$. While this triangle was not discussed above, this triangle can be related to the larger $\triangle ABC$. Since X is the midpoint of $\overline{AC}$, this triangle has a base that is exactly half that of $\triangle ABC$. (If the base of $\triangle ABC$ is b as pictured above, the base of $\triangle ABX$ will be $\frac{1}{2}b$).

Both $\triangle ABX$ and $\triangle ABC$ have a height of h, as shown in the diagram above. This means that the area of $\triangle ABX$ is $1/2$ that of $\triangle ABC$, so $\text{Area}_{\triangle ABC} = 64$. While it is unnecessary to do so, from this we can calculate the area of

$$\triangle RSC = \frac{1}{16}\text{Area}_{\triangle ABC} = \frac{1}{16}(64) = 4.$$

(2): INSUFFICIENT. Knowing the length of one of the heights (altitudes) of $\triangle ABC$ tells us nothing about the area of $\triangle ABC$. We would need to know the length of the corresponding base to which the height is drawn. In fact, we don't even know which side of the triangle to consider the base for the given height of 8.

The correct answer is (A): Statement (1) ALONE is sufficient, but statement (2) alone is not sufficient.

DS 110. FDPs: Digits & Decimals
Difficulty: 600–700   **OG Page:** 282

In this **Digits** problem, we are asked for the **Units Digit** of a positive integer m.

First, let's **Name Variables** and assign letters to the unknown digits:

$$m = \underline{x}\,\underline{y}\,\underline{z}$$

Here, $\underline{x}$ represents the unit in the hundreds place, $\underline{y}$ represents the unit in the tens place, and $\underline{z}$ represents the unit in the ones place. m is NOT the product of these three integers. Instead, the above equation simply represents m in terms of its digits.

We are told that the product of the three digits equals 96. Thus, $x \times y \times z = 96$. Notice that we have not written the product as xyz, since we might confuse that with the digit representation for *m*.

The unknown digits are factors of 96, but not just any factors. *x, y,* and *z* must each be single digits.

To determine possible values of *x, y,* and *z,* let's now break 96 down into its **Prime Factors**. 96 can be broken down to $(2^5)(3)$. Thus, we know that these factors will be contained within the product *xyz*. We do not know, however, which variables contain which factor(s).

We are asked for the units digit of *m*. In other words, according to our **Rephrased** question, we wish to find the value of *z*.

(1): SUFFICIENT. *m* is odd. We must now **Consider Possible Cases** in an organized, thorough way. The digit *z* could be 1, 3, 5, 7, or 9. However, given that the product of *x, y,* and *z* (96) does not contain 5, 7, or 9 as factors, *z* cannot be any of those three numbers.

We are left with 1 and 3 as possibilities. However, the value of 1 will not work. For *z* to be 1, the other two digits *x* and *y* would have to multiply up to 96. However, the largest product of two single-digit numbers is 9 times 9, or 81. We can also observe that *x* and *y* cannot contain all of the prime factors of 96 without some help from *z*.

Since *z* cannot be 1, we know that *z* must be 3.

(2): INSUFFICIENT. If *x* is 8, then *x* will account for three of the 2's. However, we still have two 2's and a 3 to distribute among *y* and *z*. In other words, *yz* = 12.

Considering possible cases again, we can generate more than one valid value of *z* (2, 3, 4, or 6), so we cannot determine the value of *z*.

The correct answer is (A): Statement (1) ALONE is sufficient, but statement (2) alone is not sufficient.

DS 111. <u>Word Translations</u>: Ratios
Difficulty: 600–700   **OG Page:** 282

In this **Ratios** problem, we are told that the manager distributed *x* pens, *y* pencils, and *z* pads to each staff member. We are asked how many staff members are in the department.

(1): INSUFFICIENT. The **Ratio** of pens to pencils to pads that each employee received does not tell us the number of employees. If we wanted to use an **Unknown Multiplier**, say *w*, we could write

$$x = 2w$$
$$y = 3w$$
$$z = 4w$$

But this doesn't get us very far.

(2): INSUFFICIENT. We do not know how the 18 pens, 27 pencils, and 36 pads were divided among the employees. Let's **Consider Possible Cases.** If there were 3 employees, then each would have received 6 pens, 9 pencils, and 12 pads. But if there were 9 employees, each would have received 2 pens, 3 pencils, and 4 pads.

The possible number of employees is restricted to common factors of 18, 27, and 36, so we know that there could be just 1 employee, 3 employees, or 9 employees. But we cannot narrow the cases down any further.

(1) and (2): INSUFFICIENT. Using the work we have already done for statement (2), we can see that in both scenarios described the ratio of pens to pencils to pads is 2 : 3 : 4.

Therefore, statement (1) does not give us any new information to help us narrow down the cases to just one possibility.

The correct answer is (E): Statements (1) and (2) TOGETHER are not sufficient.

DS 112. <u>Word Translations</u>: Rates & Work
Difficulty: 600–700   **OG Page:** 282

This **Rates & Work** problem involves two machines X and Y that produce identical bottles at different constant rates. We want to know how many hours it would take Machine X to fill a production lot by itself.

The general equation governing such situations is the **Rate-Time-Work Formula**, which states that work equals the product of rate and time. Typically the amount of work is left in vague terms, such as a production lot. In such cases we can just regard the total work as 1, as in "one lot" or "one job." This leaves the rate as the only variable we need to determine the time it would take to complete the work.

We can **Rephrase** the question as "What is the rate at which Machine X fills the production lot?"

(1): INSUFFICIENT. This statement tells us the rate at which Machine X produces bottles. However, without knowing how many bottles constitute one lot, we cannot determine how long it would take Machine X to fill the lot.

(2): SUFFICIENT. From the problem statement, we know that Machine X working alone for 4 hours, followed by Machine Y working alone for 3 hours, filled one production lot. This statement further tells us that Machine X produced *twice* as much as Machine Y.

Therefore, Machine X produced 2/3 of the lot, and Machine Y produced 1/3 of the lot, since 2/3 + 1/3 = 1.

If Machine X produces 2/3 of the lot in 4 hours, we can solve for the rate R of Machine X, using the relationship $RT = W$ as follows:

$$R(4) = 2/3$$
$$R = 2/12$$
$$R = 1/6$$

If we know the rate of Machine X, we can calculate how long it would take for Machine X to fill the lot by itself (6 hours).

Alternatively, we could have picked numbers or set up a chart. However, by not picking numbers, we avoid being distracted by irrelevant information such as the number of bottles in a lot or an actual rate of production in bottles per minute.

The correct answer is (B): Statement (2) ALONE is sufficient, but statement (1) alone is not sufficient.

DS 113. FDPs: Fractions
Difficulty: 600–700   **OG Page:** 282

In this **Fractions** problem, we are given a situation in which a group is split into two binary categories. Each person is an employee or a guest, and furthermore each person is a manager or a non-manager (with the caveat that no guests are managers).

One way to handle this situation is to consider **Overlapping Sets** and set up a **Double-Set Matrix** with a zero in the Manager-Guest box:

		Employee?		
		Yes	No	Total
Manager?	**Yes**		0	
	No	?		
	Total			

Since we do not yet know a total, we have to fill in the givens by **Naming a Variable**. The problem is overrun with fractions, so let t stand for the total.

		Employee?		
		Yes	No	Total
Manager?	**Yes**	1/2 t	0	
	No	1/6 t		
	Total	2/3 t	1/3 t	t

Using the givens that 2/3 of the passengers are employees and 3/4 of those employees are managers, we can determine that 3/4 of 2/3, or 3/4 × 2/3 = 1/2, of the total are employees who are managers.

Also, 2/3 − 1/2 = 1/6, so (1/6)t is the number of employees who are *not* managers.

Since the number of employees who are not managers is equal to (1/6)t, the question can now be **Rephrased** as "What is (1/6) t?" or more simply, "What is t?"

(1): SUFFICIENT. The value of t is 690.

(2): SUFFICIENT. There are 230 guests, or:

$$(1/3)t = 230$$

This **Linear Equation** can be quickly solved for t.

The correct answer is (D): EACH statement ALONE is sufficient.

DS 114. Geometry: Circles & Cylinders
Difficulty: 600–700   **OG Page:** 283

We know that both gardens are **Circular**.

As a first step, we can **Algebraically Translate** the phrase "*length of edging that surrounds circular garden...*" into **Circumference.** Thus, we can simply write:

Circumference of $K = 1/2$(Circumference of G)

We can use r_K and r_G to represent the radii of circles K and G, respectively. The formula for the circumference of a circle is $C = 2\pi r$. We can apply this formula to the equation above and simplify with **Direct Algebra**:

$$2\pi r_K = {}^1\!/_2(2\pi r_G)$$

$$2\pi r_K = \pi r_G$$

$$r_K = {}^1\!/_2 r_G$$

We now have a relationship between the radii of the two circles. In order to find the area of garden K, we need r_K, because $A = \pi r^2$.

Moreover, because we have a relationship between r_K and r_G, knowing r_G will also be enough information to answer this question. Furthermore, knowing the diameter, the area or the circumference of garden G will also be sufficient, because any of those values could be used to solve for r_G.

Essentially, we can **Rephrase** this question as "What is any dimension of either circular garden?" If we know one number, we know them all.

(1): SUFFICIENT. This statement provides us with the area of circle G. With this area, we can find its radius, and thus the radius and area of circle K.

(2): SUFFICIENT. This statement provides the perimeter of circle G. With this perimeter, we can find its radius, and thus the radius and area of circle K.

Although unnecessary, we can find the actual area of circle K. From each of the statements, $r_G = 5$, so $r_K = 2.5$. Then $A_K = \pi(2.5)^2 = 6.25\pi$ square meters.

The correct answer is (D): EACH statement ALONE is sufficient.

◢ **DS 115. EIVs:** Formulas & Functions
Difficulty: 600–700   **OG Page:** 283

The problem introduces **New Functions**, along with illustrative examples. These functions, min and max, have to do with **Inequalities**.

We are told that the variable w represents an integer and asks us to find the value of min$(10, w)$. Let's consider three cases:

If $w < 10$, then the value of min$(10, w) = w$.
If $w > 10$, then the value of min$(10, w) = 10$.
If $w = 10$, then the value of min$(10, w) = 10$ or w (same thing).

So the **Rephrased** question has two parts: "Is w less than or equal to 10? And if so, what is its value?" Notice that we don't care what w is exactly if w is greater than 10.

(1): SUFFICIENT. If $w = $ max$(20, z)$ for some integer z, then w is the greater of 20 or z. If 20 is higher, then $w = 20$. If z is higher, then $w = z$ AND $w > 20$.

Therefore, w is either 20 or greater than 20. We can answer the rephrased question.

Going back to the original question, we can see that the value of min$(10, w)$ must equal the smaller value, 10.

(2): SUFFICIENT. If $w = $ max$(10,w)$, then w is either equal to or larger than 10. As such, the value of min$(10,w)$ must equal 10.

The correct answer is (D): EACH statement ALONE is sufficient.

DS 116. Word Translations: Statistics
Difficulty: 500–600   **OG Page:** 283

If the average number of people registered for the 6 days of the trade show is to be greater than 90, then from the **Average Formula** *(Average × number of terms = Sum)*, we know that the sum of all the registrants must be greater than 90×6, or 540.

We can **Rephrase** the question as "Were there more than 540 registrants in total, over all 6 days?" This question involves **Inequalities**, as do the statements.

(1): SUFFICIENT. For the 4 days with the greatest number of people registered, the average number registered per day was 100. Therefore, the sum over these 4 days was $4 \times 100 = 400$.

Now let's **Apply Constraints** that we are given. The question tells us that the least number of people registered in a single day was 80, so the smallest possible sum for the 6 days is $400 + 80 + 80 = 560$. We can guarantee that there were more than 540 registrants.

(2): INSUFFICIENT. For the three days with the smallest number of registrants per day, there were 85 × 3 = 255 registrants. Since we know that the lowest number of people registered for one day was 80, we know that the next two smallest numbers must have totaled 255 − 80 = 175.

In order to calculate a *minimum* for the sum of all six days, we want the third smallest number to be as low as possible, so that we can minimize the remaining unknown values. The smallest possible value for the third lowest number registered in a single day is 88 people (175/2 = 87.5, but the number of people must be a whole number).

Let's **Test Possible Cases**. List all the days from smallest to largest number registered, fill in the first three days, and **Name Variables** for the remaining days:

80, 87, 88, *x*, *y*, *z*

The least that *x*, *y* and *z* can each be is 88. If that was the case, the total number of registrants would be 80 + 87 + 88 + 88 + 88 + 88 = 519. This represents the smallest total possible based on this statement.

Note that we have no upper limits on *x*, *y* and *z*, so there is no upper limit for the sum. We know that the sum is greater than 519, but nothing else.

Knowing that there were more than 519 registrants does not answer our rephrased question.

The correct answer is (A): Statement (1) ALONE is sufficient, but statement (2) alone is not sufficient.

DS 117. Geometry: Circles & Cylinders
Difficulty: 600–700   **OG Page:** 283

In this **Circles** problem, it will be helpful to **Name Variables** as follows. Let *R* ("big *R*") be the radius of the larger circle, and let *r* ("little *r*") be the radius of the smaller circle. We are asked for the difference in **Areas** of these circles, i.e. $\pi R^2 - \pi r^2$.

Dividing by π, we can **Rephrase** the question as "What is $R^2 - r^2$?" We can loosely rephrase even further: "What are *R* and *r*?"

(1): SUFFICIENT. *AB* is a radius of the smaller circle, so *r* = 3. Furthermore, *AC* is a radius of the

larger circle, so *R* = 3 + 2 = 5. We thus have the values of both *R* and *r* directly.

(2): SUFFICIENT. *CE* is a radius of the larger circle, so *R* = *CD* + *DE* = 1 + 4 = 5. Using the fact that all radii of a circle are equal, we can also establish that *AC* = 5. Since *CD* = 1, we know that the diameter of the small circle, *AD*, equals *AC* + *CD* = 5 + 1 = 6. Therefore, *r* = 3, and again, we have both *R* and *r*.

This statement wound up being harder to figure out than the first statement, but it is also sufficient.

The correct answer is (D): EACH statement ALONE is sufficient.

DS 118. Word Translations: Minor Question Types
Difficulty: 600–700   **OG Page:** 283

To attack this problem, which involves a complicated **Wage Relationship**, we should **Name Variables**:

R = regular hourly rate
W = hours worked on "weekdays" (i.e., not Sunday)
S = hours worked on Sunday

Next, we use **Algebraic Translations** to turn the words into math. If the employee worked 40 hours or fewer on the weekdays, plus some hours on Sunday, then the employee was paid as follows:

(Regular Hourly Wage) × (Weekday Hours) + (2 × Hourly Wage) × (Sunday Hours)

= *RW* + 2*RS*

If the employee worked more than 40 hours on the weekdays, plus some hours on Sunday, then the employee was paid as follows:

(Regular Hourly Wage) × (40 Hours) + (1.5 × Hourly Wage) × (Overtime Hours) + (2 × Hourly Wage) × (Sunday Hours)

40*R* + (1.5*R*)(*W* − 40) + 2*RS*

To figure out how much the employee was paid last week, we need to know the actual values of *R*, *W*, and *S*. If *W* ≤ 40, then we use the first wage relationship. If *W* > 40, then we use the second.

(1): INSUFFICIENT. *R* = $10, but we do not know the value of *W* or *S*.

(2): INSUFFICIENT. The total hours worked last week is $W + S = 54$. The constraint that the employee did not work more than 8 hours per day can be expressed as $S \leq 8$ and $W \leq 48$ (that is, 6 days × 8 hours/day).

Not only is the value of R unknown, but also there are several possibilities for S and W.

We can **Test Numbers** to confirm our understanding. For instance, S could equal 6 and W could equal 48, or S could equal 7 and W could equal 47.

(1) and (2): INSUFFICIENT. The value of R is known, but there are still several possible values for S and W.

Intuitively, the lack of sufficiency should make sense. Since the employee is paid a different amount for Sunday hours than he or she is for "weekday" hours (whether regular or overtime), we need to know the exact value of S (Sunday hours) to determine the total amount paid.

The correct answer is (E): Statements (1) and (2) TOGETHER are not sufficient.

DS 119. Word Translations: Minor Question Types
Difficulty: 500–600   **OG Page:** 283

In this problem, which involves **Algebraic Translations**, we can **Name Variables** as follows:

x = number of tickets sold at full price
$400 - x$ = number of tickets sold at reduced price
p_1 = price of tickets sold at full price
p_2 = price of tickets sold at reduced price

The question asks us for the **Total Revenue** of tickets sold (both at full and reduced price). Using our new variables, we can **Rephrase** the question as "What is the value of $xp_1 + (400 - x)p_2$?" Notice that this expression contains three separate variables.

(1): INSUFFICIENT. Since the number of tickets sold at full price was 1/4 of the total number of tickets sold, the number of tickets sold at full price was $\frac{1}{4}(400) = 100$. Likewise, the number of tickets sold at the reduced price was $400 - 100 = 300$.

This does not provide us with enough information, since we still need the values of p_1 and p_2 to find the total revenue, which can now be written as $100p_1 + 300p_2$.

(2): INSUFFICIENT. Knowing that the full price of the ticket is $25 would not be enough to solve the expression above. We still need the values of p_2 and x to find the total revenue, which can now be written as $x(25) + (400 - x)p_2$.

(1) and (2): INSUFFICIENT. Combining the two statements still fails to provide an answer, since we do not know the reduced ticket price, p_2. The total revenue is $100(25) + 300p_2$, but we still have one variable lurking.

The correct answer is (E): Statements (1) and (2) TOGETHER are not sufficient.

DS 120. FDPs: Successive Percents & Percent Change
Difficulty: 700–800   **OG Page:** 283

In this difficult **Percent Changes** problem, we can manipulate these changes with **Direct Algebra** to simplify the question drastically.

First, let's **Name Variables** and assign r to the rent in 1997. Since the rent in 1998 is x% more, the 1998 rent is $r(1 + \frac{x}{100})$.

Likewise, since the rent in 1999 is y% less, the 1999 rent is $r(1 + \frac{x}{100})(1 - \frac{y}{100})$. Thus, our question becomes:

$$\text{Is } r\left(1 + \frac{x}{100}\right)\left(1 - \frac{y}{100}\right) > r?$$

We shouldn't stop here. Because we know that the rent must have been some positive amount, we can divide by r without flipping the **Inequality** sign:

$$\left(1 + \frac{x}{100}\right)\left(1 - \frac{y}{100}\right) > 1?$$

Next, express each term with a **Common Denominator**. This continued simplification may seem like a lot of work, but it will pay off.

$$\left(\frac{100 + x}{100}\right)\left(\frac{100 - y}{100}\right) > 1?$$
$$\frac{(100 + x)(100 - y)}{10,000} > 1?$$
$$(100 + x)(100 - y) > 10,000?$$
$$10,000 + 100x - 100y - xy > 10,000?$$
$$100x - 100y - xy > 0?$$
$$100(x - y) > xy?$$

This question cannot be **Rephrased** any further, and we can move on to the statements.

(1): INSUFFICIENT. Given that $x > y$, we know that $x - y$ will be positive. Thus, for our rephrased question, we know that $100(x - y)$ will be positive. However, we do not know whether this amount will be greater than xy.

(2): SUFFICIENT. If we have manipulated properly, as shown above, this is now an easy statement to evaluate.

$$\frac{xy}{100} < x - y$$
$$xy < 100(x - y)$$

This inequality perfectly matches our rephrased question, which we can now answer with a definitive *Yes*.

This problem is difficult to solve by picking numbers, especially since the final inequality is not intuitive. In this case, the algebraic approach is faster, easier, and more secure.

The correct answer is (B): Statement (2) ALONE is sufficient, but statement (1) alone is not sufficient.

DS 121. <u>Geometry:</u> Coordinate Plane
Difficulty: 600–700   **OG Page:** 283

This question, though presented as **Coordinate Geometry**, may be easier to deal with if we **Algebraically Translate** the information.

By asking us whether point (r, s) is in region R, the problem is asking whether the pair of numbers r and s satisfies the **Inequality** $2r + 3s \leq 6$.

(1): INSUFFICIENT. Let's **Test Possible Cases**. We can pick points on the given **Line** $3r + 2s = 6$ with one variable equal to 0, since these coordinates are easy to generate. If $r = 2$ and $s = 0$, for example, then $3r + 2s = 6$ and $2r + 3s \leq 6$.

But if $r = 0$ and $s = 3$, then $3r + 2s = 6$, but it is NOT true that $2r + 3s \leq 6$.

Alternatively, we can use the coordinate plane conceptually. Imagine region R in the coordinate plane as a shaded part of the plane with a boundary line $2r + 3s = 6$. The line $3r + 2s = 6$ has a different slope, as we can see without needing to solve for

the slopes. (The slope would be m in the equation $s = mr + b$, similar to $y = mx + b$.)

Since the lines have different slopes, they must intersect. This means that some of the line $3r + 2s = 6$ is in shaded region R, but the rest is not. As a result, if we know a point is on the line $3r + 2s = 6$, we cannot tell whether it is in region R.

(2): INSUFFICIENT. Again, we can test quickly computable cases that are significantly different from each other. If r and s both equal 0, for example, then both values satisfy this statement and also satisfy $2r + 3s \leq 6$. But if $r = 3$ and $s = 2$ (the largest each can be) both values satisfy this statement but do NOT satisfy $2r + 3s \leq 6$.

(1) and (2): INSUFFICIENT. Try points that are on the statement (1) line and that satisfy the statement (2) inequalities. Good candidates are points at the ends of the overlap, where one or the other inequality constraint is at its limit. We always have the best chance of forcing different outcomes if we **Pick Extremes**.

For instance, we know this inequality from statement (2): $r \leq 3$

Let's make r as big as possible, so that $r = 3$ itself. Now solve for s in the equation from statement (1):

$$3r + 2s = 6$$
$$3(3) + 2s = 6$$
$$s = -1.5$$

Does this pair $(3, -1.5)$ satisfy the question inequality $2r + 3s \leq 6$?

$$2(3) + 3(-1.5) \leq 6? \quad Yes$$

Now, let's use the other inequality from statement (2): $s \leq 2$

Let's make s as big as possible, so that $s = 2$ itself. Now solve for r in the equation from statement (1):

$$3r + 2s = 6$$
$$3r + 2(2) = 6$$
$$r = 2/3$$

Does this pair (2/3, 2) satisfy the question inequality $2r + 3s \leq 6$?

$$2(2/3) + 3(2) \leq 6? \qquad No$$

We can satisfy both statements but still be unable to answer the question definitively *Yes* or *No*.

In coordinate-plane language, the line $3r + 2s = 6$ evidently crosses the boundary line of region *R*, as defined by $2r + 3s \leq 6$, somewhere within the segment defined by $r \leq 3$ and $s \leq 2$, so part of the line segment lies within *R*, but part does not.

The correct answer is (E): Statements (1) and (2) TOGETHER are not sufficient.

DS 122. <u>Geometry:</u> Polygons
Difficulty: 600–700   **OG Page:** 283

In this *Polygons* problem, we are asked for the *Volume of a Rectangular Solid.* This volume is equal to the area of its base times its height or, put differently, it is the product of the three different side lengths (length × width × height).

(1): INSUFFICIENT. This statement gives us the areas of two adjacent rectangular faces of the solid. We can regard one of those areas as the base, but we cannot get a unique value for the height.

Two adjacent faces share one edge. We can *Name Variables* and assign *x* to the length of that edge, assigning *y* and *z* to the lengths of the other sides of the box. Thus we know

$$xy = 15$$

and

$$xz = 24$$

However, more than one rectangular solid can be constructed with these measurements. Two possibilities are shown below:

1.

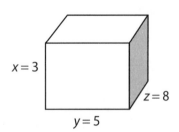

$x = 3$

$z = 8$

$y = 5$

2.

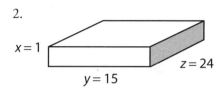

$x = 1$

$y = 15$

$z = 24$

(2): INSUFFICIENT. This statement tells us that the area of two opposite faces of the solid is 40. Even if we regard this face as the base of the solid, we have no way of knowing the height.

(1) and (2): SUFFICIENT. Because 40 is different from the two areas given in Statement (1), we can see that the faces with area equal to 40 are not among those sharing an edge of length *x*. Therefore, 40 must equal the product of the remaining two side lengths:

$$yz = 40$$

In terms of *x*, *y*, and *z*, the volume of the solid is simply *xyz*. We can now do a little *Direct Algebra.*

Multiplying the three known areas together gives us $(xy)(yz)(xz)$, which can be rewritten as $x^2y^2z^2$. Taking the square root of this will allow us to find the volume:

$$V = \sqrt{x^2 y^2 z^2}$$

or

$$V = \sqrt{15 \times 40 \times 24}$$

We do not have to worry about negative possibilities, because all the variables represent positive lengths.

While it is not necessary to actually solve for *V*, the calculations result in a volume of 120.

The correct answer is (C): BOTH statements TOGETHER are sufficient, but NEITHER statement ALONE is sufficient.

DS 123. <u>Word Translations:</u> Algebraic Translations
Difficulty: 700–800   **OG Page:** 283

Joanna bought only $0.15 stamps and $0.29 stamps. How many of each did she buy?

A way to *Rephrase* this Algebraic Translations problem may not be immediately clear. But consider what would happen if Joanna spent exactly $0.44 on stamps. If she spent $0.44 on stamps, then she bought one of each—$0.15 stamps and $0.29 stamps cannot add up to $0.44 in any other way.

There is a **Hidden Constraint** in this question. We cannot have fractional or negative amounts of stamps.

If we **Name Variables,** we can write down the **Cost Relationship**. Let x be the number of $0.15 stamps, and let y be the number of $0.29 stamps. Then the total cost = $0.15x + $0.29y$. We are looking for x.

(1): SUFFICIENT. Joanna bought $4.40 worth of stamps. Note that $4.40 ends in 0. Any multiple of $0.15 must end in 5 or 0. Therefore, whatever multiple of $0.29 stamps Joanna bought must also end in 5 or 0 (so that the value of the $0.15 stamps plus the value of the $0.29 stamps can add to $4.40).

If Joanna must have bought $0.29 stamps in multiples of 5, there are only a few possibilities before the $0.29 stamps alone add up to more than $4.40. Thus, we can simply test which combination(s) are possible:

Number of $0.29 stamps	Actual Value	Amount Left for $0.15 Stamps
5	$1.45	$2.95
10	$2.90	$1.50
15	$4.35	$0.05

Only one of these combinations leaves an "Amount Left for $0.15 Stamps" that is actually divisible by $0.15. Joanna must have purchased 10 $0.29 stamps and 10 $0.15 stamps.

This is a very tricky problem. Consider the cost equation in x and y:

$$0.15x + 0.29y = 4.40$$

Normally, a solitary linear equation with two unknowns x and y cannot be solved for a definite value for either unknown.

However, if x and y are restricted to positive integers, and if the other numbers in the equation are

chosen carefully, there may only be one possible solution for the equation.

(2): INSUFFICIENT. Knowing only that Joanna bought equal numbers of each type of stamp does not tell us how many $0.15 stamps she bought. For instance, she could have bought one of each or one million of each.

The correct answer is (A): Statement (1) ALONE is sufficient, but statement (2) alone is not sufficient.

DS 124. <u>Word Translations</u>: Overlapping Sets
Difficulty: 600–700   **OG Page:** 284

This is an advanced version of the standard **Overlapping Sets** question type, so we want to adapt our overlapping sets strategy.

One approach might be to set up a **Triple-Set Matrix**, which is similar to the **Double-Set Matrix**. The only difference is that there is an extra row and column to take care of the additional choices. The shaded box represents the answer to the question.

		Candidate M			
		Fav.	Unfav.	Not Sure	Total
Candidate N	Fav.	?			30
	Unfav.				35
	Not Sure				35
	Total	40	20	40	100

Since we are only finding voters who had responded "Favorable" to the candidates, we can also simplify this into a **Double-Set Matrix** by combining the "Unfavorable" and "Not Sure" responses:

		Candidate M		
		Fav.	Unfav./Not Sure	Total
Candidate N	Fav.	?		30
	Unfav./Not Sure			70
	Total	40	60	100

(1): SUFFICIENT. Since this statement deals with voters that responded with "Favorable," insert this information into the Double-Set Matrix. We find that 10 voters had responded "Favorable" for both candidates.

		Candidate M		
		Fav.	Unfav./Not Sure	Total
Candidate N	Fav.	10	20	30
	Unfav./Not Sure	30	40	70
	Total	40	60	100

(2): INSUFFICIENT. Since this statement deals with voters that responded with "Unfavorable," we will use our Triple-Set Matrix. This does not provide enough information to answer the question.

		Candidate M			
		Fav.	Unfav.	Not Sure	Total
Candidate N	Fav.	?			30
	Unfav.		10		35
	Not Sure				35
	Total	40	20	40	100

The Triple-Set Matrix is useful conceptually, but when we break it out in its full glory, we will almost never have enough information to fill it out completely. There are just too many boxes.

The correct answer is (A): Statement (1) ALONE is sufficient, but statement (2) alone is not sufficient.

DS 125. EIVs: Basic Equations
Difficulty: 700–800   **OG Page:** 284

In order to work through this question, which involves disguised **Basic Equations,** let's lay out the different options for the **Strange Symbol** °.

If ° is addition, then we have

$$k + l + m = k + l + k + m$$
$$k + l + m = 2k + l + m$$
$$k = 2k$$
$$0 = k$$

k could be 0, but it does not have to be. Therefore, the equation is *not* true for *all* numbers k, l, and m. If ° represents addition, we can answer the question with a definitive *No*.

What if ° is subtraction? The equation becomes

$$k - (l + m) = (k - l) + (k - m)$$
$$k - l - m = 2k - l - m$$
$$k = 2k$$
$$0 = k$$

Again, k could be 0, but it does not have to be. Therefore, the equation is *not* true for *all* numbers k, l, and m. If ° represents subtraction, we can answer the question with a definitive *No*.

Finally, what if ° is multiplication? Then the equation becomes

$$k(l + m) = kl + km$$
$$kl + km = kl + km \qquad \text{Subtract}$$
$$0 = 0$$

What happens when we get $0 = 0$? Well, $0 = 0$ is always true. This means that the original equation is always true as well. It is true for all values of k, l, and m. Therefore, knowing that ° represents multiplication, we can answer the question with a definitive *Yes*.

Thus, we can **Rephrase** the question as "Does ° represent multiplication?" This Yes-No question captures all the logic of the problem.

(1): SUFFICIENT. If $k ° 1 \neq 1 ° k$ for only some values of k, then ° cannot represent multiplication, because $k \times 1 = 1 \times k$ for all values of k. This means that we can answer the question with a definitive *No*.

Incidentally, we can show that ° cannot represent addition either, because $k + 1 = 1 + k$ is also true for all values of k. Therefore, ° must represent subtraction.

(2): SUFFICIENT. This statement indicates that ° must be subtraction. Thus, we can answer the question with a definitive *No*.

The correct answer is (D): EACH statement ALONE is sufficient.

DS 126. Word Translations: Overlapping Sets
Difficulty: 300–500   **OG Page:** 284

This **Overlapping Sets** problem describes cars that either have power windows or do not, and that either have a stereo or do not. The question is how many cars have *neither* power windows *nor* a stereo?

To structure the problem, we can use a **Double-Set Matrix;** the question is shaded below:

		Power Windows?		
		Yes	No	Total
Stereo?	Yes			
	No			
	Total			60

(1): INSUFFICIENT. Knowing that 20 cars had a stereo but not power windows does not help us calculate the number of cars that have neither power windows nor a stereo.

		Power Windows?		
		Yes	No	Total
Stereo?	Yes		20	
	No			
	Total			60

(2): INSUFFICIENT. Knowing that 30 cars had a stereo *and* power windows does not help us calculate the number of cars that have neither power windows nor a stereo.

		Power Windows?		
		Yes	No	Total
Stereo?	Yes	30		
	No			
	Total			60

(1) and (2): INSUFFICIENT. With these combined pieces of information, we know that 50 cars had a stereo, so 10 did not. However, we do not know exactly how many of those cars had power windows.

The number is now bounded between 0 and 10, but we need to know the precise value.

		Power Windows?		
		Yes	No	Total
Stereo?	Yes	30	20	50
	No			10
	Total			60

The correct answer is (E): Statements (1) and (2) TOGETHER are not sufficient.

DS 127. <u>Word Translations:</u> Overlapping Sets
Difficulty: 500–600   **OG Page:** 284

This standard **Overlapping Sets** problem presents two binary criteria: French vs. no French, and Spanish vs. no Spanish. Construct a **Double-Set Matrix** according to these criteria, filling in the information from the prompt and circling the desired quantity. Note that the problem deals only with students who take French or Spanish or both, so that there are 0 students taking *neither* course. This subtle but critical piece of information is easy to miss.

As is customary on all Double-Set Matrix problems, we *immediately* fill in the third entry in any row that contains two existing entries (in italics).

	French	No French	Total
Spanish	?	100	
No Spanish		0	
Total	200	100	300

(1): SUFFICIENT. According to this statement, 60 students do *not* study Spanish. Add this number into the matrix (in bold), and then fill in the third entry in all rows and columns containing two existing entries (in italics):

	French	No French	Total
Spanish	140	100	240
No Spanish	60	0	60
Total	200	100	300

140 students are taking both languages.

(2): SUFFICIENT. According to this statement, 240 students study Spanish. Add this number into the matrix (in bold), and then fill in the third entry in all rows and columns containing two existing entries (in italics):

	French	No French	Total
Spanish	140	100	240
No Spanish	60	0	60
Total	200	100	300

140 students are taking both languages.

The correct answer is (D): EACH statement ALONE is sufficient.

DS 128. <u>Number Properties</u>: Divisibility & Primes
Difficulty: 600–700   **OG Page:** 284

The first step to attacking this initially baffling problem is to understand exactly what we are given and what we are asked for.

Note down the givens. We know $3 < m < 13 < n$.

We know that m and n must be integers, because partial classrooms or partial students are not possible. Thus, $m = 4, 5, 6, 7, 8, 9, 10, 11,$ or 12.

We are asked whether we can assign an equal number of students to each classroom without any leftovers. When will this be possible? What must be true about m and n?

We can and should ***Test Numbers*** to figure out the possibilities. If there are 7 classrooms and we want an equal number of students in each room, there must be exactly 7 students, or 14 students, or 21 students, etc. Thus, we can only put an equal number of students in each classroom if the number of students (n) is a multiple of the number of classrooms (m). Equivalently, we are asking whether n is divisible by m.

Thus, we can ***Rephrase*** the question as "Is n divisible by m?"

By this point, we should realize that the problem is about ***Divisibility & Primes***. In fact, the problem is designed to disguise that fact.

For any fraction to equal an integer, the denominator must be entirely cancelled out by factors in the numerator. Thus, we can rephrase further: "Are all of the ***Prime Factors*** of m included in n?"

(1): INSUFFICIENT. This statement tells us that $3n$ is divisible by m. In other words, $3n$ contains all the factors of m. Thus, either n has all of the factors of m, or n has all of the factors of m *except* 3, because the last factor of 3 in m could be cancelled by the given 3 in the numerator.

Therefore, it is uncertain whether all of the prime factors of m are included in n.

If necessary, we can test numbers again to confirm our understanding.

If $n = 18$ and $m = 6$, then $\dfrac{3n}{m} = \dfrac{3 \times 18}{6} = 9 =$ integer, and $\dfrac{n}{m} = \dfrac{18}{6} =$ integer. We know that n is in fact divisible by m, and the answer to the question would be *Yes*.

If $n = 20$ and $m = 6$, $\dfrac{3n}{m} = \dfrac{3 \times 20}{6} = \dfrac{\cancel{3} \times \cancel{20}^{10}}{\cancel{3} \times \cancel{2}} = 10$, which is an integer, but $\dfrac{n}{m} = \dfrac{20}{6} = \dfrac{10 \times \cancel{2}}{3 \times \cancel{2}} = \dfrac{10}{3}$, which is not an integer. In this case, n is not divisible by m. For these values of n and m, we can see that $3n$ can cancel all the factors of m, but n alone cannot. The answer to the question would be *No*.

(2): SUFFICIENT. This statement tells us that $13n$ is divisible by m. In other words, $13n$ contains all the factors of m. Thus, either n has all of the factors of m, or n has all of the factors of m *except* 13.

However, we know that m is an integer between 3 and 13, so m definitely does not contain 13 as a factor. As a result, 13 does not cancel any of the factors of m. If $13n/m$ is an integer, and 13 did not cancel any of the factors of m, that means that n must have canceled all the prime factors of m. Therefore, all of the prime factors of m are included in n.

The correct answer is (B): Statement (2) ALONE is sufficient, but statement (1) alone is not sufficient.

DS 129. Word Translations: Statistics
Difficulty: 600–700   **OG Page:** 284

This ***Statistics*** question asks for the ***Median*** number of employees assigned per project for the projects at Company Z. The median of a set is the value that falls in the middle of the set, when the set is arranged in increasing order.

(1): INSUFFICIENT. Knowing that 25% of the projects at Company Z have 4 *or more* employees assigned to each project tells us that 75% have less than 4 (i.e., 3 or less). While the median will definitely be less than 4 (i.e., in the 75% region), it could be 1, 2, or 3.

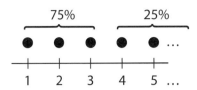

At this point, the problem has introduced both *Percents* and *Inequalities* as relevant issues.

(2): INSUFFICIENT. Knowing that 35% of the projects at Company Z have 2 or fewer employees assigned to each project tells us that 65% have more than 2 (i.e., 3 or more). While the median will definitely be greater than 2, it could be 3, 4, 5, etc.

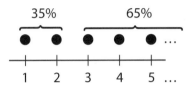

(1) and (2): SUFFICIENT. Combining the two statements gives us enough information to locate the median. If 35% of the projects have 2 or fewer employees and 25% of projects have 4 or more employees, the median value will be in the middle 40% of projects.

The number of employees assigned to any project must be an integer, and there is only one integer value between 2 and 4, namely 3.

Therefore the median number of employees assigned per project for the projects at Company Z must be 3.

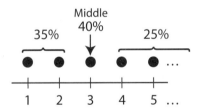

Notice how the *Hidden Constraint* on the number of employees (there must be a whole number of employees) operates to create sufficiency. There are many numbers between 2 and 4, but only one *integer*.

The correct answer is (C): BOTH statements TOGETHER are sufficient, but NEITHER statement ALONE is sufficient.

DS 130. Word Translations: Minor Question Types
Difficulty: 500–600   **OG Page:** 284

This is a yes/no question about a *Scheduling* issue. Was the appointment on a Wednesday?

(1): INSUFFICIENT. 60 hours is exactly 2½ days. Knowing that two and a half days before the appointment it was Monday does not tell us what day the appointment was. The appointment could have been on Wednesday or Thursday and still satisfied this condition.

To verify, we can *Test Extremes*: early Monday morning and late Monday night. If 60 hours prior to the appointment it was 12:01 AM Monday morning, then the appointment was at 12:01 PM Wednesday afternoon. At the other extreme, if 60 hours prior to the appointment was midnight Monday, then the appointment was at noon on Thursday.

We can see that the appointment could have been on a Wednesday or a Thursday.

(2): INSUFFICIENT. This tells us nothing about the day of the week.

(1) and (2): SUFFICIENT. The second statement tells us that the appointment was in the latter half of the day. Therefore, Thursday is no longer an option. We cannot reach from Monday into the latter half of Thursday in only 2.5 days, no matter how late we start on Monday. The appointment must have been on a Wednesday.

The correct answer is (C): BOTH statements TOGETHER are sufficient, but NEITHER statement ALONE is sufficient.

DS 131. Word Translations: Algebraic Translations
Difficulty: 600–700   **OG Page:** 284

In this *Algebraic Translations* problem, we are told that there were 4 more heads than tails. Thus, $h = t + 4$, where h is the number of heads and t is the number of tails.

If we have one more distinct *Linear Equation* with h and t, we can solve for both variables.

(1): SUFFICIENT. This statement tells us that $h + t = 24$. We now have *Two Different Linear Equations* and *Two Unknowns.* Knowing that we could solve for h with these two equations, we can stop at this point.

To illustrate that we could indeed solve for h, we can **Substitute** $t + 4$ for h in this equation and get

$$(t + 4) + t = 24$$
$$2t + 4 = 24$$
$$2t = 20$$
$$t = 10$$

Since $h = t + 4$, we know $h = 14$.

(2): SUFFICIENT. This statement gives us another equation: $3h + t = 52$. Again, we have a second distinct equation and can solve for h.

If we really want, we can substitute $t + 4$ for h and get

$$3(t + 4) + t = 52$$
$$4t + 12 = 52$$
$$4t = 40$$
$$t = 10$$

Since $h = t + 4$, $h = 14$.

The correct answer is (D): EACH statement ALONE is sufficient.

DS 132. <u>Geometry</u>: Lines & Angles
Difficulty: 600–700   **OG Page:** 284

In this problem, we need to determine what information, given the diagram of crisscrossing **Lines & Angles,** will be sufficient to find the sum of x and y. A quick glance at the statements reveals that we are given neither value directly. Thus, we need to figure out if there's any kind of relationship between one pair of variables, x & y, and either of the other two variables, w and z.

The key is the **Quadrilateral** formed by the four lines in the figure. While we do not initially know anything about any *individual* angle, we do know that the four interior angles of the quadrilateral must sum to 360°. We can **Name Variables** and label these four internal angles p, q, r and s.

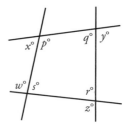

We also know that $x + p = 180$ and $y + q = 180$, because these angles pair up to form straight lines, Therefore, $x + p + y + q = 360$. That means $x + y = 360 - p - q$, which can be restated as $x + y = 360 - (p + q)$. We can **Rephrase** the question as "What is the value of $p + q$?"

(1): INSUFFICIENT. Knowing the value of w allows us to calculate the value of s, because $w + s = 180$. Unfortunately, this does not allow us to find the value of p or q, or the sum of p and q.

(2): INSUFFICIENT. Knowing the value of z allows us to calculate the value of r, because $z + r = 180$. Unfortunately, this does not allow us to find the value of p or q, or the sum of p and q.

(1) and (2): SUFFICIENT. If $w = 95$, then $s = 85$. If $z = 125$, the $r = 55$. $s + r = 140$. That means that $p + q$ must equal 220, because $p + q + r + s = 360$. We can stop here, because we have answered our rephrased question.

If we really want to solve for $x + y$, we can do so easily:

$$x + y = 360 - (p + q) = 360 - 220 = 140$$

The correct answer is (C): BOTH statements TOGETHER are sufficient, but NEITHER statement ALONE is sufficient.

DS 133. <u>Word Translations</u>: Statistics
Difficulty: 600–700   **OG Page:** 284

We want to know if all of the numbers in a certain list of 15 numbers are equal. The question cannot be usefully rephrased, but we should recognize that we are dealing with **Sets** and may need to run **Statistics** on the members of the set.

(1): INSUFFICIENT. The sum of the 15 numbers is 60. Each of the numbers *could* be 4, but there are many other possibilities. For instance:

$$4 + 4 + 4 + 4 + 4 + 4 + 4 + 4 + 4 + 4 + 4$$
$$+ 4 + 4 + 4 + 4 = 60$$

$$4 + 4 + 4 + 4 + 4 + 4 + 4 + 4 + 4 + 4 + 4$$
$$+ 4 + 4 + 7 + 1 = 60$$

(2): SUFFICIENT. The sum of *any* 3 of the numbers is 12. While it is possible to use this statement to prove that each of the numbers is therefore 4, it is reasonable to simply *Test Possible Cases.* Go ahead and try to make a list of numbers of which any 3 sum to 12. It will quickly become apparent that this is impossible unless each number is equal to 4.

Even if we construct a list such that only two numbers are not 4, we see that we cannot guarantee that *any* three numbers in the list sum to 12.

$$4, 4, 4, 4, 4, 4, 4, 4, 4, 4, 4, 4, 4, 5, 3$$

Example 1: $4 + 5 + 3 = 12$

Example 2: $4 + 4 + 5 = 13$

Although we did not wind up computing any statistics, for other problems we should recognize the consequences of having all the numbers in the set be equal. For instance, the standard deviation will be zero.

The correct answer is (B): Statement (2) ALONE is sufficient, but statement (1) alone is not sufficient.

DS 134. <u>Word Translations</u>: Statistics
Difficulty: 600–700   **OG Page:** 284

Conceptually, the **Standard Deviation** is a measure of spread: how *wide* does our data spread from the average? The closer the values are to each other, the smaller the standard deviation. If the values are scattered, then the standard deviation might be large.

Standard deviation is calculated as follows:

(1) For each value, find its difference from the average.

(2) Square these differences.

(3) Find the average of all the squared differences for all the values. This average is called the variance.

(4) Take the square root of this variance.

Because computing standard deviation is tedious, the GMAT will probably not require an actual calculation. To find the standard deviation without doing a computation, however, we need to know how far each number is from the mean.

(1): INSUFFICIENT. Knowing the **Average** does not give us information about how spread out the individual values are. Thus, the statement is insufficient.

(2): SUFFICIENT. Conceptually, if all the nests have the same number of eggs, then the values are not spread out at all. They have zero spread.

Looking at this issue computationally, we can see that if all the nests have the same number of eggs, then the average *is* the number of eggs in each basket. Therefore the difference between each term and the average is 0. The standard deviation must be 0.

The correct answer is (B): Statement (2) ALONE is sufficient, but statement (1) alone is not sufficient.

DS 135. <u>Geometry</u>: Polygons
Difficulty: 600–700   **OG Page:** 285

This **Polygons** problem provides a diagram of a **Trapezoid** with certain information given:

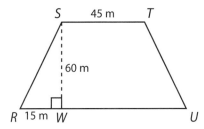

The **Area of the Trapezoid** is represented by the following formula:

$$A = \frac{1}{2}(b_1 + b_2)h$$

In this formula, b_1 and b_2 represent the lengths of the parallel sides and h represents the height of a perpendicular line drawn between the two parallel sides.

The base *ST* and the height *SW* are given. To determine the area of the trapezoid, we need to find the value for b_2, which is *RU* in the diagram.

Thus, we can ***Rephrase*** the question as "What is the length of *RU*?"

(1): SUFFICIENT. This statement directly answers our question. We can stop here, knowing that *RU* = 80.

(2): SUFFICIENT. Given that $TU = 20\sqrt{10}$, we can find *RU*. First, we ***Draw a Line*** parallel to *SW*, starting at point *T* and dropping to line *RU*. Label this line 60 m, since it the same length as *SW*. We label the new point at which this new line crosses *RU*. Let's call it *X*. Finally, we can label line *WX* 45 m, since it is the same length as *ST*.

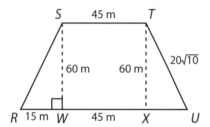

The only missing information to determine the length of line *RU* is the length of line *XU*. This can be calculated using the ***Pythagorean Theorem:***

$$(60)^2 + XU^2 = (20\sqrt{10})^2$$

Since *XU* is a positive length, we know that we can solve this equation for *XU* and therefore compute *RU*. At this point, we should stop.

For algebra practice, we can calculate *XU*:

$$(60)^2 + XU^2 = (20\sqrt{10})^2$$
$$3,600 + XU^2 = 4,000$$
$$XU^2 = 400$$
$$XU = 20$$

The correct answer is (D): EACH statement ALONE is sufficient.

DS 136. **Word Translations:** Statistics
Difficulty: 500–600   **OG Page:** 285

This ***Statistics*** problem asks us about the makeup of a set of six numbers with a predetermined ***Average*** or mean.

The strategy of using ***Residuals*** works well here. Residuals are the differences between a set's data points and its average—in other words, the "overs" and "unders" relative to the mean. For any set, the residuals sum to zero. The positive residuals and negative residuals must cancel out.

For example, in the set {10, 20, 30, 40} the mean is 25 and the residuals are {−15, −5, +5, +15}. Notice that the sum of the residuals is zero.

All this is a fancy way of saying that numbers *over* the mean must be balanced out by numbers *under* the meant, and vice versa.

Since the set in question has a mean of 75 and we are asked how many of the numbers are equal to 75, we can ***Rephrase*** this question as "How many of the six numbers have a residual of zero?"

(1): SUFFICIENT. If none of the six numbers is less than 75, there can be no negative residuals. There are no numbers *under* the mean. Thus, there cannot be any numbers *over* the mean.

With no positive or negative residuals, all of the numbers must be equal to the mean, so all 6 of the numbers are equal to 75.

(2): SUFFICIENT. Similarly, if none of the six numbers is greater than 75, there are no numbers *over* the mean. Thus, there cannot be any numbers *under* the mean.

All six of the numbers must again be equal to 75.

The correct answer is (D): EACH statement ALONE is sufficient.

DS 137. **Word Translations:** Algebraic Translations
Difficulty: 300–500   **OG Page:** 285

In this ***Algebraic Translations*** problem, we have a typical ***Cost Relationship*** involving prices and quantities of two baked goods.

We can ***Name Variables,*** letting *d* be the price of a doughnut and *b* be the price of a bagel. The ***Rephrased*** question is asking for a ***Combined Expression,*** or a Combo:

What is $5d + 3b$?

As in other Combo problems, finding the values of the individual variables (in this case b and d) is unnecessary.

(1): SUFFICIENT. This statement specifies the value of $10d + 6b$, which is exactly twice the desired combo. Therefore, dividing the given price in half will yield the price for the desired Combo: $5d + 3b = (12.90/2) = 6.45$.

(2): INSUFFICIENT. This statement tells us that $d = b - 0.15$. However, we have no information about the actual prices of either bagels or doughnuts and are thus unable to come up with a total cost. The statement gives us the value of $b - d$, but we cannot get the desired Combo.

The trick in this problem is that we might not recognize that what we are given in statement (1) is exactly twice the desired Combo. We might think that we need both equations to solve for the values of b and d separately. This is incorrect. Statement (1) gives us all we need.

Be aware of the ratios of coefficients. If the ratios are the same, one Combo might be just a scaled up version of the other. For instance, the desired Combo in this problem has coefficients 5 and 3, and the Combo in statement (1) has 10 and 6. These coefficients are in the same ratio.

The correct answer is (A): Statement (1) ALONE is sufficient, but statement (2) alone is not sufficient.

DS 138. <u>Word Translations</u>: Minor Question Types
Difficulty: 700–800   **OG Page:** 285

This problem has many moving parts, including *Algebraic Translations* and *Percents*. To get started, let's *Name Variables* and list all the relevant quantities:

F = Full ticket price

x = percent of full price paid for discount tickets

$\dfrac{x}{100} F$ = discount price

d = number of discounted tickets sold

$400 - d$ = number of full-price tickets sold, since 400 tickets in all were sold.

Now we can set up the following equation for the *Cost Relationship*:

$$\text{Revenue} = \left(\frac{x}{100} F \right) d + F(400 - d)$$

Notice that this equation expresses revenue in terms of three variables. Moreover, the relationship is complicated.

To determine the total revenue for the theater, we most likely will need the values of x, F, and d individually.

(1): INSUFFICIENT. $x = 50$, but we do not know the values of F and d. We cannot compute the total revenue.

(2): INSUFFICIENT. $F = \$20$, but we do not know the values of x and d. Again, we cannot compute the total revenue.

(1) and (2): INSUFFICIENT. We still know the values of both x and F, but we do not know the value of d.

The lack of sufficiency should make sense intuitively. For one thing, we have an equation with three unknowns, but we are only given two of the needed values in the statements.

Putting those values in, we can see that the full price tickets sold for $20 and discounted tickets for 50% of that, or $10. Even with both statements, we don't know how many tickets were sold at a discount. If no tickets sold at a discount, the revenue would be $400(\$20) = \$8,000$. If all the tickets sold at a discount, the revenue would be $400(\$10) = \$4,000$.

The correct answer is (E): Statements (1) and (2) TOGETHER are not sufficient.

DS 139. <u>FDPs</u>: FDP Connections
Difficulty: 600–700   **OG Page:** 285

This problem involves *Connections between Fractions and Decimals*. Specifically, we have to deal with a very specific kind of decimal: a *Terminating Decimal*.

A terminating decimal is one that ends, such as 0.1 or 0.77. These decimals have a finite number of nonzero digits after the decimal. Integers count as terminating decimals, too.

All fractions with integers on top and bottom can be expressed *either* as terminating decimals *or* as infinitely repeating decimals—e.g., $0.\overline{6}$. (By the way, a decimal that continues infinitely *without* a repeating pattern, on the other hand, is irrational and *cannot* be expressed as a fraction. $\sqrt{2}$ or π are two examples of non-terminating, non-repeating decimals.)

Note that in determining whether a fraction will be equivalent to a terminating or non-terminating decimal, the most important element is the divisor. Certain divisors, such as 2, will always create a terminating decimal when divided into an integer (e.g. 3/2 = 1.5, and 4/2 = 2), and others, such as 3, will only do so in certain situations. For instance, $2/3 = 0.66666666...$ (non-terminating), but 6/3 = 2 (terminating).

The crucial test is whether the denominator has only 2's and/or 5's as Prime Factors, after we cancel common factors with the numerator. Denominators containing *only* 2's and 5's will always produce terminating decimals when divided into integers.

(1): INSUFFICIENT. This only tells us that the numerator r is an integer between 90 and 100. We are given no information about the denominator. Thus, we don't know whether the denominator only contains 2's and 5's as prime factors, and we cannot answer the question.

We can *Test Numbers* to see what happens with different combinations of numbers. For instance, 93/6 will be a terminating decimal (15.5), but 92/3 will not ($30.\overline{6}$).

(2): SUFFICIENT. This tells us that the denominator is 4. Any integer divided by 4 will produce a finite terminating decimal. We can confirm this by trying out a few numbers:

$1/4 = 0.25$
$2/4 = 0.5$
$3/5 = 0.75$
$4/4 = 1$
$5/4 = 1.25$
$6/4 = 1.5$ and so on.

We can also see that 4 only has 2 as a prime factor. 4 fits our criteria for creating terminating decimals.

The correct answer is (B): Statement (2) ALONE is sufficient, but statement (1) alone is not sufficient.

DS 140. **Geometry:** Triangles & Diagonals
Difficulty: 500–600   **OG Page:** 285

For **Geometry** questions in Data Sufficiency, we should assume that the given drawings are NOT to scale. In this **Triangles** problem, it seems as though point D lies at a point equidistant from A, B, and C. However, this is not guaranteed.

We are asked for the value of $x + y$, a **Combined Expression** or Combo.

(1): INSUFFICIENT. We are given the value of x. But can we find the value for y? We know that y must be larger than x, and thus greater than 70. However, we do not know where point D is within the triangle. Thus, we cannot know the value of y. Therefore, we do not know the value of $x + y$.

(2): INSUFFICIENT. Because the triangles are each **Isosceles,** we might assume that $AB = BC$ and $AD = DC$. However, we know nothing about the length of AC, nor do we know the height of B or D above segment AC. It might be helpful for us to **Draw Pictures** displaying two possible variations of the triangle, to show what we know *and* what we do not know:

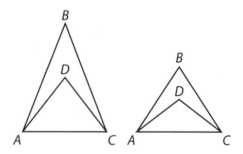

Each of the above triangles fits the current parameters. However, we can clearly see that the angles have changed. Moreover, both angles are larger in the second triangle. Thus, we know for certain that their sum has grown as well.

In fact, we do not technically know which sides of each triangle are meant to be equal. The explanation in the Official Guide assumed that the "sides of each mountain" are meant to be equal, but this assumption is unwarranted. It could certainly be the case that $AB = AC$ rather than $AB = BC$. Remember, the pictures are not necessarily drawn to scale. We already know that this statement is insufficient, but we should be careful about making unjustified assumptions.

(1) and (2): INSUFFICIENT. We still do not know the value of y (because we have not learned the position of point D). Again, we can show this by creating two separate drawings, each of which meets all of the current parameters (even going ahead and assuming $AB = BC$):

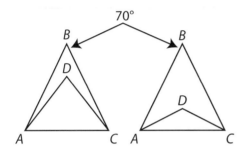

The correct answer is (E): Statements (1) and (2) TOGETHER are not sufficient.

DS 141. <u>Word Translations:</u> Statistics
Difficulty: 600–700   **OG Page:** 285

This **Statistics** problem tells us that the members of Committee X will join the members of Committee Y to form Committee Z. We are asked whether X has more members than Y.

There is no additional rephrasing to be done, but we can predict that we will be dealing with **Sets** and **Statistics** of those sets.

(1): INSUFFICIENT. Knowing only the **Average** ages of each committee does not tell us anything about the number of members on each committee.

(2): INSUFFICIENT. Knowing only the average age of Committee Z does not tell us anything about the number of members on each committee.

(1) and (2): SUFFICIENT. We can think of this as a **Weighted Averages** question. If X and Y have the same number of members, the average age of the joint Committee Z would simply be the average of the average ages of X and Y.

Since the average age of X is 25.7 and the average age of Y is 29.3, the average age of Z would be $(25.7 + 29.3)/2 = 55/2 = 27.5$.

But the actual average age of Z (26.6) is lower than 27.5. The overall average is skewed more towards the average age of X. As a result, we know that Z must have more members from X than from Y.

The correct answer is (C): BOTH statements TOGETHER are sufficient, but NEITHER statement ALONE is sufficient.

DS 142. <u>FDPs:</u> Percents
Difficulty: 500–600   **OG Page:** 285

This **Percents** problem, which involves a **Salary Relationship,** asks us for the dollar amount that Jean earned as commission from her sales in the first half of 1988.

In order to know this dollar amount, we need to know her sales and her rate of commission during that time period, or we need enough information to recreate this data.

(1): INSUFFICIENT. This statement tells us that Jean earned a commission of 5% from her total sales in 1988, but without knowing how much she sold in dollar terms, we cannot determine the actual amount of her commission.

Furthermore, we do not know how much of her yearly commission she earned in the first half of the year.

(2): INSUFFICIENT. From this statement, we learn that Jean's average monthly sales in the second half of 1988 were $10,000 more than her average monthly sales in the first half of the year.

However, we do not know how much she sold in either half of the year, or for the whole year. We also do not know how much commission Jean earned on her sales.

(1) and (2): INSUFFICIENT. Even with both pieces of information, we do not know how much Jean sold in the first half of the year in dollar terms.

As a further subtlety, we do not know that Jean's commission was a *uniform* 5% of sales throughout the year. We only know that what she earned in commission was an amount equal to 5% of her *total* sales for the year.

We can *Algebraically Translate* the information we have and place it in a *Table*. This way, we can see how big the gaps are. We can *Name a Variable* and let *x* be the average monthly sales in the first half of the year.

	Sales ($)	Commission Rate (%)	Commission ($)
First half of 1988	$6x$	?	
Second half of 1988	$6x + 60{,}000$	?	
All of 1988	$12x + 60{,}000$	5%	$5\%(12x + 60{,}000)$

The correct answer is (E): Statements (1) and (2) TOGETHER are not sufficient.

DS 143. FDPs: FDP Connections
Difficulty: 600–700   **OG Page:** 285

This problem, which involves *Connections Between Percents & Fractions* and *Percent Change,* benefits from upfront analysis before we consider the statements.

The price per share of Stock X increased by 10%—that is, it went from *x* to 1.1*x*. Meanwhile, the price of Stock Y decreased by 10%—that is, it went from *y* to 0.9*y*. The question asks, "0.9*y* is what percent of *x*?"

We can *Name Variables* and assign *p* as the percent we are seeking. The question may now be *Algebraically Translated* to an equation:

$$0.9y = \frac{p}{100}x$$

Isolate *p*:

$$90y = px$$
$$p = \frac{90y}{x}$$

Thus, the question may be *Rephrased* as, "What is 90*y*/*x*?" or simply, "What is *y*/*x*?"

Because the question asks us for a percentage and not the actual values, a *Ratio* of *y* to *x* will be sufficient to answer this question.

(1): SUFFICIENT. The increased price of X was equal to the original price of Y. This provides a ratio and is sufficient. Algebraically, we have:

$$1.1x = y$$
$$\frac{y}{x} = 1.1$$

(2): SUFFICIENT. The increase in X was 10/11 the decrease in Y. This also provides a ratio and is sufficient.

If we write out the algebraic steps, we get:

$$0.1x = \frac{10}{11}(0.1y)$$
$$x = \frac{10}{11}y$$
$$\frac{11}{10} = \frac{y}{x}$$

The correct answer is (D): EACH statement ALONE is sufficient.

DS 144. Geometry: Triangles & Diagonals
Difficulty: 600–700   **OG Page:** 286

Both *Right Triangles* and *Squares* are involved in this problem. To know the area of *A*, we need to find the length of a side of square *A*.

We can *Name Variables* to represent the sides of the three squares:

a = length of a side of square *A*
b = length of a side of square *B*
c = length of a side of square *C*

We can use the formula for the *Area of a Triangle* and set up an equation for the area of triangle *D*, which we know is 4.

Area = ½(base)(height)
4 = ½*bc*
bc = 8

Because triangle *D* is a right triangle, we also can use the *Pythagorean Theorem* to relate its sides:

$$b^2 + c^2 = a^2$$

Because $bc = 8$, if we know either b or c, we can find the other. We can then find out a^2 by using the Pythagorean Theorem equation.

Thus, we can **Rephrase** the question as "What is the value of either b or c?"

(1): SUFFICIENT. We can use the formula for the **Area of a Square** and to translate this statement:

$$b^2 = 9$$
$$b = 3$$

This directly answers the rephrased question.

Although it's unnecessary, we can compute the value of a for practice. We can use the value of b to solve for c because $bc = 8$.

$$(3)c = 8$$
$$c = 8/3$$

Now we can plug b and c into the Pythagorean Theorem to solve for a.

$$(3)^2 + \left(\frac{8}{3}\right)^2 = a^2$$

$$9 + \frac{64}{9} = a^2$$

$$\frac{145}{9} = a^2$$

$$\frac{\sqrt{145}}{3} = a$$

(2): SUFFICIENT. We can use the formula for the area of a square and translate this statement:

$$c^2 = \frac{64}{9}$$

$$c = \frac{8}{3}$$

This directly answers the rephrased question.

Although it's unnecessary, we could solve for a using the same method we used for statement (1).

The correct answer is (D): EACH statement ALONE is sufficient.

DS 145. <u>Word Translations</u>: Algebraic Translations
Difficulty: 600–700   **OG Page:** 286

In this **Algebraic Translations** problem, we know that $S = 2B$. In order to solve for S, we need the value of B, or another **Linear Equation** involving just S and B.

(1): SUFFICIENT. We can create a linear equation from this statement. Since we will then have **Two Different Linear Equations** with **Two Unknowns**, we can stop right here. Under exam conditions, we should certainly move on right now.

For algebra practice, we can continue solving. We know that four years ago, Sara was $S - 4$, whereas Bill was $B - 4$. Put this data in an **Age Chart**:

	4 years ago	now
Sara	$S - 4$	S
Bill	$B - 4$	B

At that time, Sara's age was three times Bill's age. Write a relationship:

$$S - 4 = 3(B - 4).$$

Substitute the original equation ($S = 2B$) into this equation

$$(2B) - 4 = 3(B - 4)$$
$$2B - 4 = 3B - 12$$
$$8 = B$$

Now that we have the value for B, we can solve for S.

$$S = 2B$$
$$S = 2(8)$$
$$S = 16$$

(2): SUFFICIENT. Again, this relationship will produce a distinct linear equation relating Sara's age and Bill's age. With two different linear equations at our disposal, we know right now that we have sufficiency.

Again for practice, let's lay out the algebra. Eight years from now, Sara will be $S + 8$ and Bill will be $B + 8$.

	now	*8 years from now*
Sara	S	S + 8
Bill	B	B + 8

At that time, Sara's age will be 1.5 times Bill's age.

$$S + 8 = 1.5(B + 8)$$

Combine this with the original equation: $S = 2B$:

$$(2B) + 8 = 1.5(B + 8)$$
$$2B + 8 = 1.5B + 12$$
$$0.5B = 4$$
$$B = 8$$

Just as we did in Statement (1), we can use the value of B to solve for S.

The correct answer is (D): EACH statement ALONE is sufficient.

DS 146. <u>Word Translations</u>: Statistics
Difficulty: 500–600   **OG Page:** 286

In this **Statistics** problem, we are asked whether the average number of words per paragraph for 25 paragraphs is less than 120.

Using the **Average Formula**, Sum = Average × Number of Terms, we must actually determine whether the sum of the number of words in all 25 paragraphs is less than 120 × 25 = 3,000. We already know that the report originally consisted of 2,600 words. For the sum to be less than 3,000, the two new paragraphs must consist of less than 400 words in total.

The **Rephrased** question is therefore "Do the two new paragraphs in the preface contain less than 400 words in total?"

As is common for Yes-No questions on Data Sufficiency, this question involves **Inequalities.**

(1): INSUFFICIENT. If each paragraph of the preface has more than 100 words, then the total number of words for the two new paragraphs is greater than 200. Knowing that the total number of words was greater than 200 does not tell us whether the total was less than 400.

(2): SUFFICIENT. If each paragraph of the preface has fewer than 150 words, the total number of

words in these two new paragraphs is less than 300. Thus, we know that the new paragraphs have less than 400 words in total.

The correct answer is (B): Statement (2) ALONE is sufficient, but statement (1) alone is not sufficient.

DS 147. <u>Word Translations</u>: Statistics
Difficulty: 500–600   **OG Page:** 286

This *Statistics* problem also involves *Algebraic Translations*. We must interpret a complicated scenario.

From the information presented in the prompt, we can determine that *any* book on the lower shelf will have more pages than *any* book on the upper shelf. This must be so because the *shortest* book on the lower shelf has more pages than the *longest* book on the upper shelf.

We are asked for the **Median** number of pages among the books on the shelves. We must keep careful track of the relative numbers of books on each shelf.

(1): INSUFFICIENT. This statement provides no information about the number of books on the lower shelf and is thus insufficient.

If there are *more* books on the lower shelf than on the upper shelf, then the median number of pages will be that of some book on the lower shelf, or halfway between two such books (and will thus be 475 pages or more).

If there are *fewer* books on the lower shelf than on the upper shelf, then the median number of pages will be that of some book on the upper shelf, or halfway between two such books (and will thus be less than or equal to 400 pages).

Finally, if the two shelves are holding an equal numbers of books, then the median number of pages will be halfway between 400 and 475 (the two middle numbers).

(2): INSUFFICIENT. This statement provides no information about the number of books on the upper shelf, and is thus insufficient for the same reasons statement (1) is.

(1) and (2): SUFFICIENT. If there are a total of 49 books, then the median number of pages is that of the 25th book in either increasing or decreasing order (halfway between 1st and 49th). Since the upper shelf contains all of the 25 shortest books, the longest book on that shelf determines the median: 400 pages.

The correct answer is (C): BOTH statements TOGETHER are sufficient, but NEITHER statement ALONE is sufficient.

DS 148. <u>Geometry:</u> Polygons
Difficulty: 600–700   **OG Page:** 286

In this ***Polygons*** problem, each leg of the jogging path has a positive length, as is normal for lengths. This imposes the ***Hidden Constraint*** that $x > 0$.

The total distance around the path is $x + x + 3x + (x + 60)$ or $6x + 60$. Thus, we can ***Rephrase*** the question as "What is the value of x?"

(1): INSUFFICIENT. One of the sides of the path is 120 meters, but which side is it? There are three possibilities:

$x = 120$ or $3x = 120$ or $x + 60 = 120$

These three cases lead to three different possible values for x: 120, 40, or 60.

(2): SUFFICIENT. The two shortest sides of the path are each x meters long. One of the other sides of the path is twice as long as each of the shortest sides. In other words, one of the other sides has length $2x$.

This constraint cannot refer to the side that is $3x$ meters long, because $3x \neq 2x$ for all $x > 0$.

Therefore, this constraint must refer to the side that is $x + 60$ meters long.

$$x + 60 = 2x$$
$$60 = x$$

The correct answer is (B): Statement (2) ALONE is sufficient, but statement (1) alone is not sufficient.

DS 149. <u>Geometry:</u> Coordinate Plane
Difficulty: 700–800   **OG Page:** 286

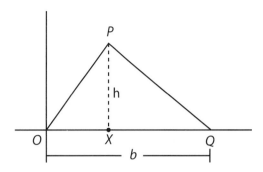

The question is asking whether the area of $\triangle OPQ$ is greater than 48, given that $OP < PQ$. We will need to consider the ***Area of a Triangle*** and ***Inequalities*** as well.

We should ***Redraw the Picture***, adding labels and ***Naming Variables*** as necessary. We can label $\overline{OQ}$ as b, the base of the triangle. We can also drop a height from P to a point X and label this distance h, the height of the triangle.

We should also ***Exaggerate Constraints***. For instance, we are told that $OP < PQ$. In the diagram given, PQ is barely longer than OP, if at all. In our picture, we should make sure that PQ is *substantially* longer than OP. This way, our eyes will be working for us as we make sense of the diagram.

We can ***Rephrase*** the question as "Is $\frac{1}{2}bh > 48$?" or "Is $bh > 96$?"

(1): SUFFICIENT. Knowing the coordinates of point P tells us the value of $h = 8$, the y-coordinate of P. It also tells that $OX = 6$, the x-coordinate of P. This, however, is only *part* of the base b.

To understand why this statement is sufficient, first consider what would happen if $OP = PQ$. If $OP = PQ$, then $\triangle OPQ$ will be isosceles, and the height drawn to base OQ will be the perpendicular bisector of that base. Thus, we have $OX = XQ = 6$ (as shown below).

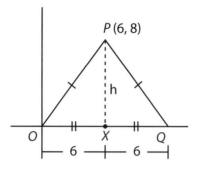

Since $OP < PQ$, however, PQ must extend further out, making $XQ > OX$ (shown below).

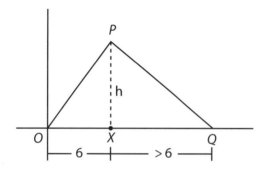

Therefore XQ must be greater than 6 and OQ must be greater than 12.

$$\text{Area}_{\triangle OPQ} = \frac{1}{2}bh$$

$$= \frac{1}{2}(\text{greater than } 12)(8)$$

$$= \text{greater than } 48$$

(2): INSUFFICIENT. Knowing the coordinates of point Q tells us nothing about the height of $\triangle OPQ$.

The correct answer is (A): Statement (1) ALONE is sufficient, but statement (2) alone is not sufficient.

DS 150. EIVs: Basic Equations
Difficulty: 500–600   **OG Page:** 286

To attack this **Basic Equations** problem, we should first do **Direct Algebra**.

Simplify this **Complicated Fraction**, starting with the denominator:

$$S = \frac{\dfrac{2}{n}}{\dfrac{1}{x} + \dfrac{2}{3x}} = \frac{\dfrac{2}{n}}{\dfrac{3}{3x} + \dfrac{2}{3x}}$$

$$= \frac{\dfrac{2}{n}}{\dfrac{3+2}{3x}} = \frac{\dfrac{2}{n}}{\dfrac{5}{3x}} = \left(\frac{2}{n}\right)\left(\frac{3x}{5}\right) = \frac{6x}{5n}$$

Alternatively, we can simplify by using the universal **Common Denominator**. This is the **Least Common Multiple** of each of the individual denominators within the fraction. Since the individual denominators are n, x, and $3x$, we know that $3xn$ is the universal common denominator:

$$S = \frac{\dfrac{2}{n}}{\dfrac{1}{x} + \dfrac{2}{3x}} = \frac{\left(\dfrac{2}{n}\right)(3xn)}{\left(\dfrac{1}{x} + \dfrac{2}{3x}\right)(3xn)} = \frac{6x}{3n+2n} = \frac{6x}{5n}$$

Either way, we are asked for the value of S. Thus, we can **Rephrase** this question as "What is the value of $\dfrac{6x}{5n}$?"

The key piece of information here is the **Ratio** x/n. If we have the value for x/n, we can multiply it by 6/5 to solve for S.

Thus, we can rephrase further: "What is the value of x/n?"

(1): SUFFICIENT. This gives us a value for the ratio x/n. Namely, $x/n = 2$, so we can answer the rephrased question.

(2): INSUFFICIENT. This gives us a value for n, but we do not know the value for x.

A trap in this problem is that we might think we need both statements. After all, with both statements, we get values of both n and x. If we have both these values, we can solve for the value of any Combo of the two variables, including S.

However, it turns out that we only need the ratio of x to n, in order to find S.

The correct answer is (A): Statement (1) ALONE is sufficient, but statement (2) alone is not sufficient.

DS 151. FDPs: Digits & Decimals
Difficulty: 600–700 **OG Page:** 286

In this **Digits & Decimals** problem, we are told that $k = 5.1 \times 10^n$, with n as a positive integer. We are then asked for the value of k.

We can see that we will need to make use of **Powers of Ten**. Since the value of n dictates the value of k, we can **Rephrase** the question as "What is n?"

(1): SUFFICIENT. If it is true that $6,000 < k < 500,000$ and that $k = 5.1 \times 10^n$, then it must be true that $k = 51,000$.

Since n is a positive integer, the only possible values of k are 51, 510, 5,100, 51,000, 510,000, etc. The only one of these values in the given range is 51,000.

(2): SUFFICIENT. If we know that $k^2 = 2.601 \times 10^9$, then we theoretically know the value of k, since 2.601×10^9 is a specific numeric value.

We do not need to compute the value of k. We simply need to recognize that we *could* find it.

We do not need to worry about the negative root of k^2, since we know that k must be positive. No matter the value of n, if $k = 5.1 \times 10^n$, then k is greater than zero.

The correct answer is (D): EACH statement ALONE is sufficient.

DS 152. Word Translations: Algebraic Translations
Difficulty: 700–800 **OG Page:** 287

In this **Algebraic Translations** problem, we are asked whether Carmen has fewer tapes than Rafael. We are given a relationship between the number of tapes that each person has.

We can **Name Variables** and assign C to the number of tapes that Carmen has. We can also assign R to the number of tapes that Rafael has.

The question stem states that $C + 12 = 2R$. We can solve this equation for C to yield $C = 2R - 12$. The question asks whether Carmen has fewer tapes than Rafael, which we can **Rephrase** as:

Is $C < R$?

If we replace C with $2R - 12$, we get:

Is $2R - 12 < R$?
Is $R < 12$?

Alternatively, we could simplify the expression in terms of C. If $C = 2R - 12$, then $R = \frac{C+12}{2}$. The inequality becomes:

Is $C < \frac{C+12}{2}$?
Is $2C < C + 12$?
Is $C < 12$?

We have two rephrasings for this question, either of which would be sufficient: "Is $R < 12$ OR is $C < 12$?"

Either way, the question involves **Inequalities**.

(1): INSUFFICIENT. This statement tells us that $R > 5$. R could be either greater than or less than 12.

(2): SUFFICIENT. This statement tells us that C is less than 12. According to the work we did above, this is a direct answer to the second rephrasing of the original question.

The correct answer is (B): Statement (2) ALONE is sufficient, but statement (1) alone is not sufficient.

DS 153. EIVs: Inequalities
Difficulty: 500–600 **OG Page:** 287

This **Inequalities** problem involves **Exponents** and **Absolute Values**.

Let's consider the possibilities for the given inequality when x is positive and when it is negative.

$|x|$ is always positive, regardless of whether x itself is positive. 2^x is also always positive, since we cannot take a positive base, raise it to some exponent, and get a negative number.

Therefore, the only quantity in $x|x| < 2^x$ that could be negative is x. Thus, if x is negative, then the answer to the question is definitely *Yes*, since a negative will always be less than a positive.

If x is zero, the answer to the question will be *Yes*, since 0 is less than 2^0, which is 1.

If x is positive, however, we will need more information, such as its exact value, in order to evaluate the statement.

Therefore, we can **Rephrase** the question in two parts: "Is x negative or zero? If *Yes*, we are done. If *No*, there is one more question: is $x|x| < 2^x$?"

(1): SUFFICIENT. x is negative. This answers the first part of the rephrased question. From the reasoning above, the answer to the question is *Yes*.

(2): SUFFICIENT. x is negative. This also answers the first part of the rephrased question. From the reasoning above, the answer to the question is *Yes*.

The correct answer is (D): EACH statement ALONE is sufficient.

DS 154. EIVs: Equations with Exponents
Difficulty: 600–700　　**OG Page:** 287

This problem involves not only **Equations with Exponents** but also **Inequalities**.

We can **Rephrase** the question, translating from words to symbols:

Is $b - a \geq 2(3^n - 2^n)$?

Go further by distributing the 2:

Is $b - a \geq 2(3^n) - 2(2^n)$?

(1): SUFFICIENT. We can manipulate the information in this statement to get $b - a$ on one side of an equation. To do so, we **Subtract Equations**: that is, subtract the equation for a from the equation for b.

The tricky step is that we have to rewrite 3^{n+1} as $(3^n)(3^1)$, which equals $(3)(3^n)$. This applies a very subtle **Exponents Rule**.

Do the same thing for 2^{n+1} to get $(2)(2^n)$.

$$b - a = 3^{n+1} - 2^{n+1} = (3)(3^n) - (2)(2^n)$$

Now we plug this equation into the rephrased question:

Is $b - a \geq 2(3^n) - 2(2^n)$?

Is $(3)(3^n) - (2)(2^n) \geq 2(3^n) - 2(2^n)$?

Is $(3)(3^n) \geq 2(3^n)$?

Is $3 \geq 2$?

The answer to this question will always be *Yes*. Thus, this statement is sufficient.

(2): INSUFFICIENT. This statement does not tell us anything about a or b.

The correct answer is (A): Statement (1) ALONE is sufficient, but statement (2) alone is not sufficient.

DS 155. Word Translations: Ratios
Difficulty: 700–800　　**OG Page:** 287

In this **Ratios** problem, we are asked to find the price of the mixer in 1970, given the inflation index. If we **Name Variables** and label the 1970 price x, then the price of the mixer in 1989 will be $3.56x$. The question is "What is x?"

If we can find the price in 1970 or the price in 1989, then we can answer the question. We will also have enough information if we are given a relationship between the two prices that we can use to solve for x.

(1): SUFFICIENT. The difference between the two prices is \$102.40. In other words, we know that the 1989 price − the 1970 price = 102.4.

We can now calculate the price in 1970. The 1989 price ($3.56x$) minus the 1970 price (x) equals $3.56x - x = 2.56x$. Therefore, $2.56x = 102.40$. We can stop here, because this is a **Linear Equation** in just one variable.

Remember, we don't have to actually solve for x. Once we know we can find the value of x, we know the statement is sufficient, and we can move on.

(2): SUFFICIENT. Knowing the price of the mixer in 1989 allows us to calculate the price of the mixer in 1970, using the following relationship.

$$3.56x = 142.4$$

If we do compute x in either case, we get $x = \$40$. However, we should not take the time to do so under exam-like conditions.

The correct answer is (D): EACH statement ALONE is sufficient.

DS 156. <u>EIVs</u>: Equations with Exponents
Difficulty: 600–700   **OG Page:** 287

No rephrasing is required: "Is $5^k < 1,000$?"

In theory, we can rephrase to a more specific question about k itself. But we may as well leave the question in terms of 5^k and see where the statements lead.

This problem involves both *Equations with Exponents* and *Inequalities*.

(1): INSUFFICIENT. Manipulate the inequality using *Direct Algebra*:

$5^{k+1} > 3,000$ Write 5^{k+1} as $5^k \times 5^1 = 5^k \times 5$

$5^k \times 5 > 3,000$ Divide both sides by 5

$5^k > 600$

We know that $5^k > 600$, but this information does not tell us whether 5^k is less than 1,000.

(2): SUFFICIENT. Manipulate the equation:

$5^{k-1} = 5^k - 500$ Move powers of 5 to one side

$5^{k-1} - 5^k = -500$ Write 5^{k-1} as $5^k \times 5^{-1} = \dfrac{5^k}{5}$
(very tricky!)

$\dfrac{5^k}{5} - 5^k = -500$ Factor out 5^k on the left side

$5^k (1/5 - 1) = -500$

$5^k (-4/5) = -500$ Subtract 1 from 1/5

$5^k = 625$ Multiply both sides by $-5/4$

We can and should stop, once we know that we can arrive at a definite value for 5^k. After all, with a definite value for 5^k, we can answer any Yes-No question about 5^k.

The correct answer is (B): Statement (2) ALONE is sufficient, but statement (1) alone is not sufficient.

DS 157. <u>Geometry</u>: Triangles & Diagonals
Difficulty: 700–800   **OG Page:** 287

In this *Triangles* problem, we can *Name Variables* and assign x and y to the lengths of the two legs of the triangle.

We are told that we have a *Right Triangle*. Using the *Pythagorean Theorem*, which applies to all right triangles, we can determine from the prompt that $x^2 + y^2 = 100$.

The prompt question asks for the sum $x + y$. This is a *Combined Expression*, or Combo. No rephrase is necessary.

(1): SUFFICIENT. Since the triangle is a right triangle, the legs x and y are also the base and height of the triangle.

Therefore, the area of the triangle is $1/2 xy$. We have $1/2 xy = 25$. Therefore, $xy = 50$.

To finish the calculations, we can rearrange this new equation: $y = 50/x$.

Next, substitute for y in the equation from the question:

$x^2 + (50/x)^2 = 100$, or $x^2 + 2,500/x^2 = 100$

Multiply by the denominator, x^2, on both sides to produce $x^4 + 2,500 = 100x^2$, which can be rearranged into a *Quadratic Equation:*

$x^4 - 100x^2 + 2,500 = 0$

This equation factors to

$(x^2 - 50)(x^2 - 50) = 0$ or $(x^2 - 50)^2 = 0$

x^2 must equal 50. Thus x has the unique value $\sqrt{50}$.

Note that we don't need to consider negative solutions, because x represents a positive length. Moreover, we can plug this value back into $y = 50/x$ to determine a unique value for y (which will also be $\sqrt{50}$, as it turns out).

Since we have unique values of both x and y, the sum $x + y$ is uniquely determined.

Alternatively, we might recognize that we nearly have a *Special Product* with $x^2 + y^2 = 100$. The form on the left is not quite the same as $(x + y)^2$, which expands as follows:

$(x + y)^2 = x^2 + 2xy + y^2$

All we are missing is the xy cross-term. This statement supplies it. Since $xy = 50$, we also know that $2xy = 100$. Hence, we have the right side of the equation:

$$(x + y)^2 = x^2 + 2xy + y^2$$
$$= (x^2 + y^2) + 2xy$$
$$= 100 \quad + 100$$
$$= 200$$

Taking the square root, we find that $x + y$ is $\sqrt{200}$.

(2): SUFFICIENT. If the right triangle has two legs of equal length, then it must be a **45–45–90** triangle. The sides of such triangles are in the fixed ratio $1 : 1 : \sqrt{2}$, so the length of the legs may be found from that of the hypotenuse. Therefore, the length of each leg can be determined, and the sum of the two legs can likewise be determined.

The correct answer is (D): EACH statement ALONE is sufficient.

DS 158. <u>EIVs:</u> Quadratic Equations
Difficulty: 700–800   **OG Page:** 287

In this **Quadratic Equations** problem, which also involves **Algebraic Translations**, we have the following relationship:

60 = (# of members)(contribution per person)

We can **Name Variables**:

m = number of club members
c = dollars each member contributes

Thus, we can rewrite the equation as $60 = mc$.

The original question asks "What is m?" We can **Rephrase** this question as "What is $60/c$?" or simply "What is c?" Having the value of c will allow us to determine the value of m.

(1): SUFFICIENT. If $c = 4$, then we can answer the rephrased question. $m = 60/4 = 15$.

(2): SUFFICIENT. The gift certificate costs $60 no matter how many members actually contribute. If 5 of the members do not contribute, then the rest of the members ($m - 5$ members) do contribute. The contributing members have to pay $2 more than they otherwise would if everyone contributed. That is, they each pay $c + 2$.

Thus, we can set up a second equation for the (hypothetical purchase of the gift certificate:

$$60 = (m - 5)(c + 2)$$

Using **Direct Algebra**, we can solve for m by combining the two equations. First, solve the equation from the question stem for c:

$$60 = mc$$
$$c = \frac{60}{m}$$

Substitute into the equation from (2):

$$60 = (m - 5)(c + 2)$$
$$60 = (m - 5)\left(\frac{60}{m} + 2\right)$$
$$\left[60 = (m - 5)\left(\frac{60}{m} + 2\right)\right] \times m$$
$$60m = (m - 5)(60 + 2m)$$
$$60m = 60m + 2m^2 - 300 - 10m$$
$$0 = 2m^2 - 300 - 10m$$
$$0 = m^2 - 5m - 150$$
$$0 = (m - 15)(m + 10)$$
$$m = 15 \; or \; -10$$

Since the number of club members most be positive, the only valid solution is $m = 15$.

Beware of assuming that a quadratic will always produce two solutions and thus fail to provide a sufficient answer for a value question. On difficult GMAT questions, one of the solutions may be either invalid or redundant, leaving only one (therefore sufficient) answer. The safest policy is to factor and solve any quadratic before answering the original question.

The correct answer is (D): EACH statement ALONE is sufficient.

DS 159. <u>Number Properties:</u> Positives & Negatives
Difficulty: 500–600   **OG Page:** 287

While this question may look like an **Inequality** question on the surface, it is really testing **Positives & Negatives**. The question stem tells us that x is negative and asks us whether y is positive.

(1): SUFFICIENT. If $x/y < 0$, then by **Rules of Positives & Negatives**, we know that x and y must have opposite signs (x positive and y negative, or vice versa). Since we already know that x must be negative from the question stem, y must be positive.

(2): INSUFFICIENT. We are told that $y - x > 0$. If we add x to both sides of the inequality we get $y > x$. While we know that x is negative, all we know is that y is greater than some negative number. y could be either negative or positive.

The correct answer is (A): Statement (1) ALONE is sufficient, but statement (2) alone is not sufficient.

DS 160. <u>Geometry</u>: Circles & Cylinders
Difficulty: 500–600   **OG Page:** 287

We know from the given drawing that triangle OXZ is a **Right Triangle**. We also know (from the question stem) that O is the center of the **Circle**. Thus, we know that the arc XYZ represents one quarter of the total **Circumference**, because $90/360 = 1/4$.

We are asked for this total circumference. We can calculate the circumference if we know the radius of the circle, which is equal to the length of each of the legs of the right triangle. Thus, we can **Rephrase** the question as "What is the radius of the circle?"

(1): SUFFICIENT. We are told that the **Perimeter** of the triangle OXZ is $20 + 10\sqrt{2}$. Because OX and OZ are each radii of the circle, $OX = OZ$. This means that triangle OXZ is **Isosceles**.

Furthermore, because triangle OXZ is also a right triangle, it must be a **45–45–90** triangle. Such triangles have a special property: their sides must be in the ratio of $1 : 1 : \sqrt{2}$.

We do not know the value of the radius, so let's **Name a Variable** and call it r. We know that $OX = OZ = r$, and that $XZ = \sqrt{2}\,r$. Thus, the perimeter of triangle OXZ must be $r + r + \sqrt{2}\,r$. Statement (1) gives us a value for that overall perimeter, from which we can create an equation:

$$r + r + \sqrt{2}\,r = 20 + 10\sqrt{2}$$
$$2r + \sqrt{2}\,r = 20 + 10\sqrt{2}$$
$$r(2 + \sqrt{2}) = 10\,(2 + \sqrt{2})$$
$$r = 10$$

Now that we know the value of r, we can easily determine the value of the overall circumference:

$$C = 2\pi r$$
$$C = 2\pi(10)$$
$$C = 20\pi$$

Of course, this final process is unnecessary. Once we know that we can compute r, we know that the statement is sufficient.

(2): SUFFICIENT. We are told that arc XYZ is 5π. We know that this arc is one fourth the overall circumference. Thus, the overall circumference is 20π.

The correct answer is (D): EACH statement ALONE is sufficient.

DS 161. <u>Word Translations</u>: Statistics
Difficulty: 600–700   **OG Page:** 287

In this **Statistics** problem, we are told that Carl deposited $120 into his account on the 15th of every month for several consecutive months, starting in January, and then withdrew $50 on the 15th of every month for the remainder of the year. We are also told that his balance at the end of May was $2,600.

We are asked for the range of monthly closing balances for the year. In order to know this range, we need to know for how many months Carl deposited $120 and for how many months he withdrew $50 or, in other words, the month in which he switched from deposits to withdrawals.

To work through this problem, we need a clear understanding of this Carl's strange story (how his deposits and withdrawals work in sequence). As we proceed, we will have to **Consider Possible Cases** logically. We will also have to think about **Inequalities**, since these are the constraints imposed by the statements.

(1): INSUFFICIENT. We know that Carl could not have withdrawn $50 in April, because his closing balance for April would need to have been at least $50 greater than it was in May. From this statement, we know that this was not the case.

So Carl did not begin withdrawing from the account until at least June 15. (We know he did not withdraw in May, since he would have needed

$2,650 in his account in April to afford such a withdrawal and still have a balance of $2,600.)

Thus, Carl must have deposited $120 into his account every month through at least May. If he had $2,600 in the account in May, the fifth month, he must have made 5 deposits of $120 apiece, for a total of $600 in deposits. So he began the year with $2,000 in the account.

But we do not know when he began withdrawing, so we cannot say what the range of balances was for the whole year.

(2): INSUFFICIENT. Again, we must consider possible cases. If Carl had deposited into his account in June, his balance would have been $2,800. Since his balance for June was less than that, he must have withdrawn on June 15. But we cannot tell whether June was the first month in which Carl withdrew or the second, third, etc.

(1) and (2): SUFFICIENT. We know from statement (1) that Carl did not begin withdrawing until at least June. We know from statement (2) that he definitely did withdraw in June.

If June was the first possible month in which Carl could have withdrawn and he actually did withdraw in June, then we know in how many months Carl deposited and in how many months he withdrew.

We can thus figure out the range of balances for the entire year.

The correct answer is (C): BOTH statements TOGETHER are sufficient, but NEITHER statement ALONE is sufficient.

DS 162. EIVs: Inequalities
Difficulty: 600–700   **OG Page:** 287

In this problem, which involves both *Inequalities* and *Roots*, we are told that n and k are positive integers. We are asked whether $\sqrt{n+k}$ is greater than $2\sqrt{n}$. Because n and k must be positive, we can square both sides of the inequality without introducing any complications. We arrive at an equivalent question:

Is $\sqrt{n+k} > 2\sqrt{n}$?

Is $n + k > (2\sqrt{n})^2 = 4n$?

Simplifying further, we can **Rephrase** the question as "Is $k > 3n$?"

(1): SUFFICIENT. This gives a direct answer to the rephrased question.

(2): INSUFFICIENT. This statement tells us that $n + k > 3n$, or that $k > 2n$. However, we cannot determine whether k is greater than $3n$, even with the restriction that k and n are positive integers.

We can **Test Numbers** to confirm. For example, if we choose $n = 1$ and $k = 3$, then k is not greater than $3n$. However, for the same n, if $k = 4$, then k is greater than $3n$.

The correct answer is (A): Statement (1) ALONE is sufficient, but statement (2) alone is not sufficient.

DS 163. Word Translations: Ratios
Difficulty: 600–700   **OG Page:** 287

In this **Ratios** problem, we are asked to find a value for p if $i = 70$. We are told that p is directly proportional to e, which is directly proportional to i. From this we can deduce that p is directly proportional to i.

To answer the question, we need to know both the relationship between p and e and between e and i (that is, a relationship between p and i using e as the "middleman"). Alternately, because we know that p is directly proportional to i, the relationship between p and i would also be sufficient.

Any set of two values of p and i in proportion will tell us the constant by which they are proportional. Alternatively, any set of two values for p and e in proportion and e and i in proportion will also tell us the constant that relates p and i.

(1): INSUFFICIENT. This tells us the relationship between e and i, but we lack the relationship between p and e or p and i.

(2): SUFFICIENT. This tells us the relationship between p and i directly. It is not necessary to know anything about e to answer the question.

Although we may certainly stop here, a numeric solution can be found for practice. We **Name a Variable** and call the proportionality constant m:

$p = mi$
$2 = m (50)$
$m = 1/25$

Thus, the proportionality constant is 1/25. If we know that $i = 70$:

$$p = \frac{1}{25}(70)$$
$$p = \frac{70}{25}$$
$$p = \frac{14}{5}$$

The correct answer is (B): Statement (2) ALONE is sufficient, but statement (1) alone is not sufficient.

DS 164. <u>Geometry:</u> Coordinate Plane
Difficulty: 600–700   **OG Page:** 288

This **Coordinate Plane** question requires us to use the **Distance Formula** to ascertain whether two points are equidistant from the origin, which is point (0,0). The distance between any two points (x_1, y_1) and (x_2, y_2) is

$$d = \sqrt{(x_2 - x_1)^2 + (y_2 - y_1)^2}$$

This formula is based directly on the **Pythagorean Theorem**.

We can write expressions for the distance between point (r, s) and the origin and between (u, v) and the origin.

$$d_1 = \sqrt{(r-0)^2 + (s-0)^2} = \sqrt{r^2 + s^2}$$
$$d_2 = \sqrt{(u-0)^2 + (v-0)^2} = \sqrt{u^2 + v^2}$$

We can thus **Rephrase** the question:

Is $d_1 = d_2$?

Is $\sqrt{r^2 + s^2} = \sqrt{u^2 + v^2}$?   Square both sides

Is $r^2 + s^2 = u^2 + v^2$?

(1): INSUFFICIENT. Knowing $r + s$ does not provide information about u or v. We cannot answer the rephrased question with this statement.

(2): INSUFFICIENT. We can plug in these expressions for u and v into our rephrased question. Simplify using **Direct Algebra**:

Is $r^2 + s^2 = u^2 + v^2$?
Is $r^2 + s^2 = (1 - r)^2 + (1 - s)^2$?
Is $r^2 + s^2 = 1 - 2r + r^2 + 1 - 2s + s^2$?
Is $0 = 2 - 2r - 2s$?
Is $2r + 2s = 2$?
Is $r + s = 1$?

We do not have information about r or s to know if this is true or not.

(1) and (2): SUFFICIENT. Our final rephrased question from Statement (2) is:

Is $r + s = 1$?

Statement (1) tells us that

$r + s = 1$

The answer to this rephrased question is *Yes*. We have sufficiency.

Alternatively, we can combine the statements algebraically.

From statement (1), we know that

$s = 1 - r$ and $r = 1 - s$.

From statement (2), we know that

$u = 1 - r$ and $v = 1 - s$.

If we combine these statements, we know that

$s = u$ and $v = r$.

This means that (r, s) and (u, v) have the same coordinates, but in reverse order. As a result, the points must be equidistant from the origin.

The correct answer is (C): BOTH statements TOGETHER are sufficient, but NEITHER statement ALONE is sufficient.

DS 165. <u>EIVs:</u> Equations with Exponents
Difficulty: 700–800   **OG Page:** 288

We cannot easily rephrase this question, which involves **Equations with Exponents**.

We must simply find out whether a definite *Yes* or *No* answer can be reached.

(1): SUFFICIENT. The equation contains a *Square Root* sign. Our first move should be to square both sides:

$$3^x + 3^{-x} = \sqrt{b+2}$$
$$(3^x + 3^{-x})^2 = b + 2$$

We can recognize that the left side of the equation is a *Special Product Quadratic*. Distribute and simplify. Note that we will have to make liberal use of *Exponent Rules*:

$$(3^x)(3^x) + 2(3^x)(3^{-x}) + (3^{-x})(3^{-x}) = b + 2$$
$$3^{2x} + 2(3^0) + 3^{-2x} = b + 2$$
$$3^{2x} + 2 + 3^{-2x} = b + 2$$
$$3^{2x} + 3^{-2x} = b$$

At this stage, the terms on the left have a base of 3, but the terms in the question stem have a base of 9. We need to use exponent rules again to make the final leap.

$$3^{2x} + 3^{-2x} = (3^2)^x + (3^2)^{-x}$$
$$(3^2)^x + (3^2)^{-x} = b$$
$$9^x + 9^{-x} = b$$

This equation directly answers the question.

(2): INSUFFICIENT. This statement provides no information about the value of b. Therefore, we cannot determine whether the equation is true.

The correct answer is (A): Statement (1) ALONE is sufficient, but statement (2) alone is not sufficient.

DS 166. Number Properties: Exponents & Roots
Difficulty: 600–700   **OG Page:** 288

In this *Exponents* problem, manipulate the *Inequality* in the question as much as possible before evaluating the statements.

Notice that both sides of the inequality can be expressed as *Powers of Ten*:

$$(1/10)^n < 0.01 ?$$
$$(10^{-1})^n < 10^{-2} ?$$

$$10^{-n} < 10^{-2} ?$$

When both sides of an inequality share the same positive base (not equal to 1), we can drop the bases and compare the exponents:

Is $-n < -2$?
Is $n > 2$?   This is our *Rephrased* question.

(1): SUFFICIENT. This statement matches our rephrasing directly.

(2): SUFFICIENT. Manipulate the inequality:

$$(1/10)^{n-1} < 0.1$$
$$(10^{-1})^{n-1} < 10^{-1}$$
$$10^{-n+1} < 10^{-1}$$
$$-n + 1 < -1$$
$$-n < -2$$
$$n > 2$$

The correct answer is (D): EACH statement ALONE is sufficient.

DS 167. FDP: Digits & Decimals
Difficulty: 500–600   **OG Page:** 288

No rephrase is necessary for this *Digits* question.

(1): SUFFICIENT. If n is multiplied by 10 to produce $10n$, each digit moves "up" by one place. The ones (units) digit of n becomes the tens digit of $10n$, the tens digit of n becomes the hundreds digit of $10n$, and so on.

We can *Test Numbers* to verify these relationships. For instance, let $n = 352$, so that $10n = 3,520$. Note that the "2," which is the units digit of n, becomes the tens digit of $10n$. The "5," which is the tens digit of n, becomes the hundreds digit of $10n$. Finally, the "3," which is the hundreds digit of n, becomes the thousands digit of $10n$.

This statement gives us the hundreds digit of $10n$, which is exactly the same as the tens digit of n. Therefore, the tens digit of n is 6.

(2): INSUFFICIENT. The addition of 1 may or may not change the original tens digit of n.

We should *Consider Possible Cases.* For instance, if $n + 1$ is 70, then n is 69. The tens digit of the original n would be 6.

On the other hand, if $n + 1$ is 71, then n is 70. The tens digit of the original n is 7.

Therefore, the tens digit of n could be either 6 or 7. This is not specific enough information.

The correct answer is (A): Statement (1) ALONE is sufficient, but statement (2) alone is not sufficient.

DS 168. <u>EIVs</u>: Basic Equations
Difficulty: 700–800   **OG Page:** 288

This **Basic Equations** problem contains a **Complicated Fraction**. In this case, we can split the numerator. The common term of $t - x$ in both the numerator and denominator allows us to do strategic **Direct Algebra**:

$$\frac{2t + t - x}{t - x} = \frac{(2t) + (t - x)}{(t - x)}$$

$$= \frac{2t}{(t - x)} + \frac{(t - x)}{(t - x)}$$

$$= \frac{2t}{(t - x)} + 1$$

The problem hinted at this manipulation by writing the numerator as $2t + t - x$, rather than as the more normal form $3t - x$.

The only value that is still unknown is $\frac{2t}{(t - x)}$.

With that value, we will be able to determine the value of $\frac{2t + t - x}{t - x}$. Thus, the **Rephrased** question is "What is the value of $\frac{2t}{(t - x)}$?"

(1): SUFFICIENT. This answers the rephrased question directly. If $\frac{2t}{(t - x)} = 3$, then $\frac{2t + t - x}{t - x} = 3 + 1 = 4$.

(2): INSUFFICIENT. We cannot manipulate $t - x = 5$ to determine the value of $\frac{2t}{(t - x)}$.

The correct answer is (A): Statement (1) ALONE is sufficient, but statement (2) alone is not sufficient.

DS 169. <u>Number Properties</u>: Exponents & Roots
Difficulty: 700–800   **OG Page:** 288

This deceptively simple question is asking whether n is an integer. As we shall see, this problem involves both **Exponents** and **Roots**.

(1): INSUFFICIENT. It is crucial to read this statement *without* assuming that n is an integer, since that is actually the question at hand. This only tells us that n, when multiplied by itself, results in an integer.

We must **Consider Possible Cases**. It is possible that n is an integer: $2 \times 2 = 4$. But it is equally possible that n is not an integer. For instance, n could be $\sqrt{2}$, since $\sqrt{2} \times \sqrt{2} = 2$. One thing that makes this problem difficult is that we are so accustomed to having n represent integers, that we fail to consider alternatives.

(2): SUFFICIENT. $\sqrt{n} \times \sqrt{n} = n$. We know that $\sqrt{n}$ is an integer, so we know that (integer) × (integer) = n. Any integer times another integer will always yield an integer.

The correct answer is (B): Statement (2) ALONE is sufficient, but statement (1) alone is not sufficient.

DS 170. <u>Number Properties</u>: Consecutive Integers
Difficulty: 700–800   **OG Page:** 288

The problem asks us about the **Divisibility** of the expression $n^3 - n$. Divisibility is difficult to determine for sums and differences. We can deal much more easily with a product. Thus, we ought to **Factor** the given expression:

$$n^3 - n$$
$$n(n^2 - 1)$$
$$n(n + 1)(n - 1)$$

We now have the difference expressed as the product of three terms. At this point, we can reorder the terms to show that they are, in fact, **Consecutive Integers**:

$$(n - 1)(n)(n + 1)$$

Thus, we are really asked whether the product of three consecutive integers is divisible by 4.

For divisibility by 4, we must have at least two 2's as factors. We should **Consider Possible Cases**. We will have at least two 2's whenever n is odd, because the terms to either side will be even (and thus each term will contribute at least one 2 to the factors of the overall product).

What if n itself is even? In exactly half of those cases, n will be a multiple of 4, making the product divisible by 4. Thus, we can **Rephrase** the question as "Is n either odd or a multiple of 4?"

(Note: We are told that n must be a positive integer. Thus, the lowest possible value of $n - 1$ is zero. Even in this case, the product will be divisible by 4, since 0 is divisible by 4.)

(1): SUFFICIENT. If k is an integer, then $2k$ must be an even integer. $2k + 1$ will therefore be odd. Thus, n is odd, and we can answer the question *Yes*.

(2): INSUFFICIENT. Here we are told about the divisibility of a sum. Let's express this sum as a product instead, by factoring out the common term:

$$n^2 + n = n(n + 1)$$

We now have the product of two consecutive integers. For this product to be divisible by 6, it must have at least one 2 and one 3 as factors.

However, this does not mean that the numbers are *themselves* 2 and 3. For instance, they could be 5 and 6, or they could be 6 and 7. Thus, we do not know whether n is odd. Nor do we know whether n is a multiple of 4.

The correct answer is (A): Statement (1) ALONE is sufficient, but statement (2) alone is not sufficient.

DS 171. Number Properties: Divisibility & Primes
Difficulty: 600–700   **OG Page:** 288

The question is asking us for the value of the **Tens Digit** of positive integer x. The topic of **Divisibility** will come into play in the statements.

(1): SUFFICIENT. Often, the simplest way to deal with **Remainder** questions is to **Test Numbers**. We know that when x is divided by 100, the remainder is 30. This means that every

possible x will be 30 more than a multiple of 100. Recast language such as "*when x is divided by 100, the remainder is 30*" in terms of multiples ("*x is 30 more than a multiple of 100*"), since multiples make more intuitive sense to most people.

Let's set up a **Table** to find the pattern.

Possible values for x	The tens digit of x?
$100(0) + 30 = 30$	3
$100(1) + 30 = 130$	3
$100(2) + 30 = 230$	3

The tens digit of all such possible x values is 3.

We can actually start with $(100)(0)$ as the first multiple of 100, since zero is technically a multiple of all numbers.

(2): INSUFFICIENT. We can again generate a list of possible x values. Each x must be 30 more than a multiple of 110.

Possible values for x	The tens digit of x?
$110(0) + 30 = 30$	3
$110(1) + 30 = 140$	4
$110(2) + 30 = 250$	5

The results show three different values for the tens digit of x, although two are enough to prove the point.

The correct answer is (A): Statement (1) ALONE is sufficient, but statement (2) alone is not sufficient.

DS 172. Number Properties: Odds and Evens
Difficulty: 600–700   **OG Page:** 288

In this **Odds & Evens** problem, we are asked about the **Combined Expression** $x - y$.

For the Combo $x - y$ to be odd, one of these terms must be odd and the other even.

Thus, we can **Rephrase** the question somewhat clumsily as "Are x and y opposites in terms of Odds & Evens?"

(1): INSUFFICIENT. Create an **Odd/Even Table**:

z	z^2	x
Odd	Odd	Odd
Even	Even	Even

x could be either odd or even. Moreover, we know nothing about y.

(2): INSUFFICIENT. Create an *Odd/Even Table*:

z	$z-1$	y
Even	Odd	Odd
Odd	Even	Even

y could be either odd or even. Moreover, we know nothing about x.

(1) and (2): SUFFICIENT. Combine the tables:

z	$z-1$	y	x
Even	Odd	Odd	Even
Odd	Even	Even	Odd

We can see that whenever x is even, y will be odd, and vice versa. Thus, x and y are opposites in terms of Odds & Evens, and $x - y$ must be odd.

Alternatively, we could do *Direct Algebra*:

$y = (z - 1)^2$
$y = z^2 - 2z + 1$

Next, subtract the y equation from the x equation:

$$\begin{array}{l} x = z^2 \\ - \; [\, y = z^2 - 2z + 1 \,] \\ \hline x - y = z^2 - (z^2 - 2z + 1) \\ x - y = z^2 - z^2 + 2z - 1 \\ x - y = 2z - 1 \end{array}$$

$2z$ must be even. Thus, $2z - 1$ is odd, and $x - y$ is odd as well.

The correct answer is (C): BOTH statements TOGETHER are sufficient, but NEITHER statement ALONE is sufficient.

DS 173. Geometry: Triangles & Diagonals
Difficulty: 700–800   **OG Page:** 288

A preliminary note about this problem: the problem is clearly intended to be difficult, yet the answer to the actual question, "What is the length of *PR*?" is very easy to get to using both statements: $4 + 1 = 5$. This should be an excellent clue that answer choice (C) might be too simple. Incidentally, this clue also completely rules out (E), since we actually can answer the question with the two statements together. The question is whether we can answer the question with even less.

Now we should study the figure. A *Triangle Inscribed in a Semicircle* is necessarily a right triangle, so mark the angle at Q as 90 degrees.

Note that each of the smaller triangles (the one with one side of a and the one with one side of b) has a right angle, and that they "share" the right angle at Q. This means that all three triangles (the two smaller and the larger one that encompasses them both) are *Similar*. Similar triangles have the same angles and, thus, their legs are in proportion.

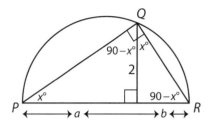

To see this point, let's *Name a Variable* and label an unknown angle as x. It follows that the other unmarked angle in that triangle must be $90 - x$, since the angles in any triangle must add to 180.

Moreover, the two angles that add up to the 90 degree angle at Q must also be x and $90 - x$, since together they must sum to 90. Since the triangles each have angles of 90, x, and $90 - x$, the triangles are similar.

Redraw the two smaller similar triangles so that they are facing the same direction:

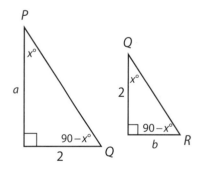

As the sides of similar triangles are in proportion:

$a/2 = 2/b$
$ab = 4$

Thus, if we know a, we know b. If we know b, we know a.

We can ***Rephrase*** the question as "What is *a* OR what is *b*?"

(1): SUFFICIENT. $a = 4$. From $ab = 4$, $b = 1$.

(2): SUFFICIENT. $b = 1$. From $ab = 4$, $b = 4$.

These relationships can be derived from repeated application of the ***Pythagorean Theorem*** within the three triangles, but the process is more cumbersome.

The correct answer is (D): EACH statement ALONE is sufficient.

DS 174. <u>Word Translations</u>: Algebraic Translations
Difficulty: 500–600   **OG Page:** 288

Questions such as this one require us to know either the dimensions of the vessel or how a particular volume relates to some portion of the overall capacity.

We must be ready to do ***Algebraic Translations***, but there is no upfront rephrasing needed.

(1): INSUFFICIENT. This statement tells us nothing about the total capacity of Marcia's bucket. All we know is that it can hold, at minimum, 9 liters.

(2): SUFFICIENT. There is enough information to set up a ***Linear Equation*** with the given ***Fractions***. We can then solve for the capacity of the bucket.

According to this statement, adding 3 liters to a half-full bucket will increase the volume by 1/3. Thus, we know that 3 liters is equal to 1/3 of a half-full bucket. We can ***Name a Variable*** and assign *c* to the capacity of the bucket.

$$3 = (1/3)(1/2)c$$

$$3 = (1/6)c$$

$$18 = c$$

Marcia's bucket has a capacity of 18 liters.

The correct answer is (B): Statement (2) ALONE is sufficient, but statement (1) alone is not sufficient.

g

Part V
of
THE OFFICIAL GUIDE COMPANION

HORACIO'S HOT LIST

Horacio's Hot List

Welcome to the Hot List! If you've run into trouble on any of these problems—or with the explanations printed in the OG—relax. You're in good company. Thousands of other students have knocked their heads against these beauties, too.

Themes

Each of the 33 Hot List problems is unique, but some problems share features. After all, students routinely find certain topics more difficult than others.

Below, we've listed common themes on the Hot List. Since there's a good chance you are using our Strategy Guides as well, we've also included references to the relevant portions of our books.

1) Word Problems with Variables In Choices

Hot List Problem	Beginning of Question	Page in OG	Page in This Book
D 24 (Diagnostic)	Aaron will jog home…	23	29
PS 149	During a trip, Francine traveled…	173	111
PS 163	This year Henry will save…	175	117
PS 204	John and Mary were each paid…	181	138

In word problems such as these, it can be difficult to translate the given information into algebra. Of course, ***don't forget about the Direct Algebra approach***, which is certainly worth learning in each of these cases.

However, you should also ***develop robust alternative methods***, such as ***Picking Numbers and Calculating a Target Value***. These methods may work better for you under exam pressure.

Methods for VICs problems (Variables in Choices) are outlined in Chapter 7 of the Equations, Inequalities, and VICs Strategy Guide. Word problems in general are covered in the Word Translations Strategy Guide—Chapter 1 on Algebraic Translations is a great place to start.

2) Rate & Work Problems

Three of the following four problems are repeated from the first category.

Hot List Problem	Beginning of Question	Page in OG	Page in This Book
D 24 (Diagnostic)	Aaron will jog home…	23	29
PS 149	During a trip, Francine traveled…	173	111
PS 204	John and Mary were each paid…	181	138
DS 87	Is the number of seconds…	280	194
DS 102	While on a straight road…	281	202

Rate & Work problems on the Hot List go far beyond simple applications of $RT = D$ or $RT = W$. Each of these problems has two parts: two legs of a trip, two moving objects, or two employees. ***Clearly distinguish between the two parts*** with a table, a picture, or both. Also be sure to ***articulate the relationship between the two parts***. The distance may be the same for both legs of a trip, or the distances may add up to a certain total. The wage may be the same for both employees. Or there may be a more complicated relationship, but it will always be stated in the problem.

Rate & Work problems that have two parts *and* have variables in the answer choices are particularly difficult. If you are picking numbers, "nice" numbers that simplify the calculation are not always obvious. If you don't spot a perfectly nice number ahead of time, just **pick a reasonable number** and get started. Along the way, you may come across an ugly fraction, but keep going.

Strategies for Rate & Work problems are outlined in Chapter 2 (General) and Chapter 11 (Advanced) of our Word Translations Strategy Guide.

3) Problems with Exponential Expressions to Factor

Hot List Problem	Beginning of Question	Page in OG	Page in This Book
DS 154	If *n* is a positive integer…	287	230
DS 156	Is 5^k less than…	287	231

Students generally know how to **Combine Exponents** when multiplying two expressions with the same base, especially when the exponents are numbers, not variables: $2^3 \times 2^4 = 2^{3+4} = 2^7$. However, students are less comfortable combining exponents when variables are involved, or when the exponent is a "hidden 1," as in the following example: $2(2^y) = 2 \times 2^y = 2^1 \times 2^y = 2^{1+y} = 2^{y+1}$. And it seems to be really difficult for folks to go backwards and **Factor** the exponential expression: $2^{y+1} = 2^y \times 2^1 = 2 \times 2^y = 2(2^y)$.

Practice factoring exponential expressions, especially of this type (2^{y+1}), until you can do so smoothly and quickly.

Strategies for Exponents are outlined in Chapter 5 (General) and Chapter 12 (Advanced) of our Number Properties Strategy Guide.

4) Problems involving Remainders

Hot List Problem	Beginning of Question	Page in OG	Page in This Book
D 13 (Diagnostic)	If *s* and *t* are positive integers…	22	25
DS 171	What is the tens digit…	288	238

The topic of **Remainders** is straightforward when you're dealing with actual numbers—for instance, 17 divided by 5 is 3, with a remainder of 2. But when you're dealing with variables, remainders are another matter. You should actually **study this topic**, learning how to set up variable expressions involving remainders and how to draw conclusions about variables when you know the remainder. You should also **study the connections among related subtopics**: integer remainders (17 divided by 5 leaves remainder 2), decimal remainders (e.g., 17 divided by 5 is 3.4), and digits (17 divided by 10 leaves remainder 7, which is also the units digit of 17).

Strategies for Remainders are outlined in the Divisibility & Primes chapters of our Number Properties Strategy Guide. Chapter 1 contains a quick introduction to the topic, while Chapter 10 covers Advanced Remainders.

5) Problems involving Combinatorics

Hot List Problem	Beginning of Question	Page in OG	Page in This Book
D 11 (Diagnostic)	Of the three-digit integers…	22	24
PS 191	Pat will walk from Intersection X…	179	131

Combinatorics (counting possibilities, such as possible arrangements or groups) strikes fear into the hearts of many students. You're not alone if this is your least favorite math topic.

Outside of straightforward textbook examples, you might not know how to apply combinatorics methods. In other words, you know a few formulas with factorials, but you wind up counting by hand. In fact, on harder combinatorics problems, it's a great strategy to **start by listing cases**. The trick is to figure out how to **save at least some time and effort by rephrasing part or all of the problem**. Sometimes, you can't save all that much time. There simply might not be a great shortcut, and you're stuck counting. Fortunately, that situation is relatively rare.

Strategies for Combinatorics problems are outlined in Chapter 4 (General) and Chapter 12 (Advanced) of our Word Translations Strategy Guide.

The Hot List, with Comments

Below, we discuss typical issues that students face and highlight key takeaways. We'll also evaluate the quality of the answer explanations given in the OG. As previously mentioned, some of these explanations are fine; others should be avoided. In fact, certain problems are on this list in part because the relevant OG explanation is confusing.

Warning: *spoilers ahead!* Don't look at our commentary until you've given the problem a try.

Hot List Problem: D 11 (Diagnostic Test)
Beginning of Question: Of the three-digit integers…
Page in OG: 22
Page in This Book: 24

Comments:
Students frequently ask for a shortcut on this problem. Unfortunately, there's no one-step recipe. However, when faced with a counting problem, you should always ask yourself: should I directly count the outcomes that I *want*, or should I count the outcomes that I *don't* want and subtract from the total number of outcomes? You may be able to solve this problem more quickly with the latter approach.

The OG explanation counts the desired outcomes directly; this approach certainly works and is worth studying.

Hot List Problem: D 13 (Diagnostic Test)
Beginning of Question: If *s* and *t* are positive integers…
Page in OG: 22
Page in This Book: 25

Comments:
This is an infamous problem. Focus on the connection between integer remainders (8 divided by 5 leaves remainder 3) and the decimal part of a quotient (8 divided by 5 equals 1.6).

The OG explanation is cryptic. We would not do it that way ourselves.

Hot List Problem: D 15 (Diagnostic Test)
Beginning of Question: The product of all the...
Page in OG: 22
Page in This Book: 26

Comments:

Focus on the phrase "closest to" and the large spread in the answer choices. You only need to estimate the product. Find ways to round off your computations. You'll save lots of time.

The OG says that you should go ahead and multiply all the numbers up and get 9,699,690. That's downright insane. Do not do this.

Hot List Problem: D 16 (Diagnostic Test)
Beginning of Question: If $\sqrt{3-2x}$ ...
Page in OG: 22
Page in This Book: 26

Comments:

Many people find roots daunting—especially since squaring both sides of the given equation does *not* immediately eliminate all the roots. Also, you may feel a chill when you realize that you can't easily isolate x in this equation. But notice that three of the answer choices have x in them. Since you are asked for $4x^2$, isolate *that* expression on one side of the equation and see what you get on the other side.

The process given in the OG is fine; we would perform the same algebra. It just requires some perseverance.

Hot List Problem: D 24 (Diagnostic Test)
Beginning of Question: Aaron will jog home...
Page in OG: 23
Page in This Book: 29

Comments:

This tough Rates & Work problem has variables in the answer choices, making it extra-difficult. Notice that the problem gives you three variables (x, y, and t), but the quantity you're asked for (the distance) doesn't have a letter. Go ahead and make one up. Or pick a number for that distance. But don't ignore it.

The OG explanation is hard to follow because it doesn't create a letter or pick a number for the distance.

Hot List Problem: PS 11
Beginning of Question: Which of the following...
Page in OG: 153
Page in This Book: 50

Comments:

Roots inside roots are simply frightening. On top of that, how do you take a square root or a third root of a decimal? Try converting the decimal to a power of ten. This should make the calculations easier. You might also learn what roots do to the number of decimal places: for instance, square roots cut the number of decimal places in half. The process shown in the OG is fine. It's worth studying.

Hot List Problem: PS 32

Beginning of Question: $\sqrt{(16)(20)}$...

Page in OG: 156

Page in This Book: 59

Comments:

Notice the plus sign under the square root. That complicates matters. You have to either pull out a common factor (say, 16) or add up the two terms.

The OG explanation doesn't explain why or how you get a 16 out of the second term. To save time, you pull out the largest square you can (16), and you borrow a 2 from the 32 to turn the 8 into a 16.

Hot List Problem: PS 50

Beginning of Question: If y is an integer...

Page in OG: 159

Page in This Book: 66

Comments:

This problem has a lot of great traps. Read it carefully. You need to find the least possible value of $|23 - 5y|$ itself. To do that, you need to test a bunch of y's. But notice that you are NOT asked for the value of y that produces the least possible value. Always double-check what the problem is asking you for. Or you might think, because of the absolute value sign, that you are restricted to positive values *inside* the absolute value. That's not true. Inside an absolute value expression, you can usually put either positive or negative values. The absolute value *turns* those values positive, but they don't have to be positive to begin with.

The OG explanation is needlessly confusing. Feel free to ignore it.

Hot List Problem: PS 82

Beginning of Question: If n is an integer...

Page in OG: 163

Page in This Book: 79

Comments:

This is a forbidding problem. Here's the key idea: when you multiply a group of numbers together, you only get a multiple of 3 if at least one of the numbers in the group is a multiple of 3. For instance, $4 \times 5 \times 7$ is not a multiple of 3, but $4 \times 5 \times 6$ is. So, how can we guarantee that one of the numbers will be a multiple of 3? In this problem, a number line is an effective visual tool.

The first method shown in the OG (picking numbers) isn't bad, but the second explanation is very tough to follow.

Hot List Problem: PS 87

Beginning of Question: A necklace is made...

Page in OG: 164

Page in This Book: 81

Comments:

This question asks what the value of N *could* be. A question asked in this way usually involves a hidden pattern, so look for the pattern. Since there are 5 different colors of beads, the pattern repeats every fifth bead.

The OG explanation is too short. Moreover, it uses a lowercase n to mean something different from the uppercase

N in the problem, despite the availability of every other letter in the alphabet. Given this sort of pointless mix-up, we suspect that the folks who wrote the problem did not write the explanation.

Hot List Problem: PS 89
Beginning of Stem: If *s* is the product...
Page in OG: 164
Page in This Book: 82

Comments:
This problem has variables in the choices, but you cannot plug numbers, since *s* and *t* are defined as particular values (which happen to be very big). Since there is no way to compute those values, look for a lot of numbers to cancel out. What is the *only* difference between *s* and *t*? Use your answer to set up a relationship. This set-up is the crux of the problem.

The OG explanation is technically fine, but it skips right past the hard part as if it were easy.

Hot List Problem: PS 98
Beginning of Question: On a scale that measures...
Page in OG: 166
Page in This Book: 86

Comments:
The wording of this question is quite confusing. You must keep straight the difference between the *reading* and the *intensity*. When you *add* to the reading, you *multiply* the intensity by a factor. Specifically, when you add 1 to the reading, you multiply the intensity by 10. The Richter scale of earthquake intensity works this way, incidentally.

The explanation in the OG is almost criminally brief.

Hot List Problem: PS 130
Beginning of Question: Which of the following inequalities...
Page in OG: 170
Page in This Book: 101

Comments:
Inequalities give people the willies. Regardless of your approach, you should notice the *endpoints* in any question that involves ranges. Here, the endpoints are useful because they represent the extreme values. If you plug either extreme into the correct inequality, you should get the maximum possible absolute value: in this case, 4.

The process described in the OG is correct, of course. However, since the reasons for various moves are unclear, you can easily feel as if the OG is pulling a rabbit out of a hat.

Hot List Problem: PS 148
Beginning of Question: If *x, y,* and *k* are positive numbers...
Page in OG: 176
Page in This Book: 109

Comments:
More than one Manhattan GMAT instructor messed this problem up on the first go-through, so don't feel bad. The GMAT simply loves weighted averages, which are easy to disguise. You should learn the standard formula for weighted averages, as well as relevant applications and disguises. Once you recognize this problem as a weighted-average problem, you're almost done.

The OG explanation is particularly poor. Please spend no time trying to recreate its bewildering, unmotivated steps.

Hot List Problem: PS 149
Beginning of Question: During a trip, Francine traveled...
Page in OG: 173
Page in This Book: 111

Comments:
Avoid taking the simple average of rates. You might think that if you pick $x = 50$, then the average rate will be halfway between 40 and 60 miles per hour, or 50 miles per hour. Wrong—you will have spent a longer *time* going 40 miles per hour, so your average speed would wind up being closer to 40 than to 60.

The answer choices here were designed to foil a simple picking-numbers approach. It's easy to see that if you pick $x = 100$, the average speed for the whole trip is 40 miles per hour. Well, guess what? *Every* answer choice gives you 40 if you plug in 100 for x. That's how these choices were evidently designed. Moreover, if you plug in $x = 0$, two choices still give you the value you expect (60).

The OG explanation of the algebraic solution is fine, but you'll need time to work through it. This problem is flat-out tough.

Hot List Problem: PS 157
Beginning of Question: For any positive integer n...
Page in OG: 174
Page in This Book: 115

Comments:
This question is unusually evil, because you do not need the given formula. In fact, you shouldn't even touch it, because there is a much easier path to the answer. (Fortunately, it seems that GMAT problems pull this sort of trick very rarely. They almost never give you pointless information.) To add up the members of an evenly spaced set, you just need to know this equation: Sum = (Average) × (Number of members).

The OG explanation is extraordinarily complicated and annoying. For instance, it contains unexplained notation (Σ), which is not used anywhere else in the OG or on the GMAT itself. If you haven't yet read the OG explanation, completely avoid doing so.

Hot List Problem: PS 163
Beginning of Question: This year Henry will save...
Page in OG: 175
Page in This Book: 117

Comments:
Several Manhattan GMAT instructors commented on this difficult word problem when it appeared. What makes the problem especially gruesome is that only some of the variables you need to think about are defined for you. Whether you write algebraic equations or pick numbers, you must consider several quantities, such as income, money spent, and money saved, for which you don't have pre-made letters.

The OG explanation outlines the algebraic path correctly and decently. No matter which explanation you go through, you'll need to put in serious work on your own to master it. Do not expect simply to read either our explanation or the OG's and be finished.

Hot List Problem: PS 191
Beginning of Question: Pat will walk from Intersection X…
Page in OG: 179
Page in This Book: 131

Comments:
The key to this problem is the wording "how many routes." If you are asked for how many ways you can do something, you're facing a combinatorics (counting) problem. Look for ways to use combinatorics methods instead of counting the routes manually, which takes time and is prone to error. The real trick here is to code every move as a letter (U or R), in order to transform the problem into an anagram puzzle. That's a big conceptual leap.

The OG explanation is adequate, but it fails to acknowledge how big a deal it is to transform the problem from counting routes on a map to counting anagrams of the letters U and R. Moreover, the explanation does you the favor of showing you all the possible anagrams, but it implies that you must simply list them out to count them. Instead, you can use the anagram formula or the combinations formula.

Hot List Problem: PS 192
Beginning of Question: The ratio, by volume, of soap…
Page in OG: 179
Page in This Book: 131

Comments:
Three-part "multiple" ratios (such as 2 : 50 : 100) can be tricky, since they contain more than one normal two-part ratio (e.g., 2 : 50). You start by adjusting one number (doubling the amount of soap), but that throws off the ratio of soap to water, and then you're not sure what to do. The safest method is to break the multiple ratio down to normal two-part ratios, make your adjustments, and then recombine. Remember also that ratios are fundamentally fractions. A ratio of 2 : 50 is really 2/50. To double this ratio, multiply 2/50 by 2. You get 4/50.

The OG explanation relies a great deal on subscripts and is rather hard to follow.

Hot List Problem: PS 202
Beginning of Question: If $m > 0$…
Page in OG: 181
Page in This Book: 137

Comments:
Translating "y is what percent of x" into an equation is hard for many folks, but you can learn the process. The word "IS" becomes the equals sign (=), "percent" becomes "/100," and "of" becomes "times." The most important step is to name a new variable to stand for the "what." Then you can solve for that variable. Alternatively, you can pick numbers, as long as you're organized and quick with calculation.

The OG explanation is fine until the last step (multiplying by 100 to convert a fraction into an equivalent percent). This is mystifying as written. What the OG means is that a fraction such as ½, or its equivalent decimal 0.50, can also be written as 50%. To get the number 50 that you write in front of the % sign, you multiply the 1/2 or the 0.50 by 100. Likewise, 1/4 or 0.25 is 25%, where 25 = 1/4 × 100. But doing this multiplication to a variable expression, while technically correct, seems to come totally out of the blue.

Hot List Problem: PS 204
Beginning of Question: John and Mary were each paid...
Page in OG: 181
Page in This Book: 138

Comments:

It's trickier than it looks to find simple values of *x* and *y* fitting the condition (making the hourly wage the same for each person). Think of this problem as a variation on a work problem. The work done is the dollars earned. The hourly wage, in dollars per hour, is the rate. Dollars earned divided by hours worked is the wage rate.

The OG solution is worth studying, as it's relatively good.

Hot List Problem: DS 45
Beginning of Question: If *r* is a constant...
Page in OG: 276
Page in This Book: 173

Comments:

Sequences can be daunting. For one thing, people rarely learned sequences that well in the first place, back in school. Moreover, anything with subscripts is automatically scary. Make sure that you clearly distinguish *n* (the position of the term in the sequence) from a_n (the actual value of that term). For instance, take the sequence 2, 4, 8, 16. When $n = 1$, $a_n = 2$. When $n = 2$, $a_n = 4$. The value of the second ($n = 2$) term is 4.

The OG explanation doesn't rephrase the question, which can be made much more straightforward. The sequence part of this problem is a disguise for a much simpler question and much simpler facts.

Hot List Problem: DS 69
Beginning of Question: Of the four numbers...
Page in OG: 278
Page in This Book: 185

Comments:

No actual values are given on this number line. That's terrifying. All you know is the relative order of the variables, and you have to deal with various scenarios. Replacing variables with numbers is an excellent strategy for abstract problems such as this one. For instance, when looking at Statement 1, assign values to *q* and *s*.

To its credit, the OG explanation uses diagrams and takes up a full column, but the content is overly dense in places, relying on extended mathematical inequalities that can be expressed more simply in words and pictures.

Hot List Problem: DS 73
Beginning of Question: If *m* is an integer...
Page in OG: 279
Page in This Book: 187

Comments:

The phrasing in Statement 1 is cunning. You are told that *m*/2 is <u>not</u> an even integer. That does not mean that *m*/2 is an odd integer. It might not be an integer at all! Here's an analogy: if you are told that a number is <u>not</u> negative, you can't say that it's definitely positive. After all, it might be zero. Your brain can also get scrambled if you mix up what's given and what you're asked for. There are very similar terms (even/odd and integer) all over the place, and the "not" will short-circuit your wiring if you don't write anything down. Keep good track of your cases on paper.

The OG solution gives you examples but doesn't really walk you through them. If m is the odd integer 3, then it's true that $m/2$ (= 3/2) is <u>not</u> an even integer (since it's not an integer at all). But if m is the even integer 10, then it's also true that $m/2$ (= 10/2 = 5) is <u>not</u> an even integer. Both $m = 3$ and $m = 10$ fit the condition, but they answer the question differently.

Hot List Problem: DS 87
Beginning of Question: Is the number of seconds…
Page in OG: 280
Page in This Book: 194

Comments:
We don't often rewrite the $RT = D$ equation to solve for time (number of seconds). The rewritten form $T = D/R$ ("Time equals Distance over Rate") is simply not as intuitive as either $R = D/T$ ("Rate equals Distance over Time") or $RT = D$ ("Rate times Time equals Distance"). You just have to trust the algebra. This problem also involves sub-scripted variables and inequalities, both of which are nasty.

The OG explanation plucks various sets of 4 numbers at a time out of thin air to justify its claims about each statement. How would you ever know to pick those numbers? On problems with this many variables, it's generally a better move to do Direct Algebra.

Hot List Problem: DS 89
Beginning of Question: Is the number of members…
Page in OG: 280
Page in This Book: 195

Comments:
The setup here is typical of Overlapping Sets problems. However, you have to make a key logical inference: $0.2x$ EQUALS $0.3y$. Despite the differences in language, the two statements are actually talking about the *same* sub-group: the people who are in both clubs.

The explanation in the OG is tremendously confusing. Please don't try to figure it out; it's all pain and no gain. We would never do this problem the way the OG proposes.

Hot List Problem: DS 90
Beginning of Question: If k, m, and t are positive integers…
Page in OG: 280
Page in This Book: 196

Comments:
It's not immediately obvious how to prove that a number and a variable share common factors. Even after you rephrase the given equation to $2k + 3m = t$, you may not know how to use the information in the statements. In the end, you have to think about what happens when you add multiples. Some multiple of 3 plus another multiple of 3 will always give you a multiple of 3.

The OG explanation is not all bad, but it takes a harder road needlessly. For instance, the given equation is simplified to $2k + 3m = t$, but then the statements randomly return to the original, more complicated form.

Hot List Problem: DS 102
Beginning of Question: While on a straight road…
Page in OG: 281
Page in This Book: 202

Comments:
Setting up $RT = D$ relationships for each car can make this problem very difficult. All we really care about is the rate at which the distance between the cars is changing. Thus, a relative rates approach is simpler and faster.

The OG explanation is too brief; it simply doesn't do this problem justice.

Hot List Problem: DS 115
Beginning of Question: For any integers x and y…
Page in OG: 283
Page in This Book: 208

Comments:
This problem introduces new terminology and functions. Moreover, you often have to think out a couple of cases. Statement 1 is the crux. It is easy to see that if $w = 20$, then min$(10, w) = 10$. But what if $w = z$? It's easy to assume that we know nothing about z, but that's not true. If $w = z$, then z has to be greater than or equal to 20. This tells us that w itself has to be greater than or equal to 20.

The OG explanation skirts too quickly over the mental challenge of thinking out the two cases and their consequences.

Hot List Problem: DS 128
Beginning of Question: A school administrator will assign…
Page in OG: 284
Page in This Book: 216

Comments:
This question hides the real topic very well. Asking whether students can be assigned to rooms so that each room has the same number of students is a sneaky way of asking about divisibility. Plug in numbers temporarily for n and m to make sense of the question.

In the solution, the OG assumes that you figure out right away that the question is asking about divisibility. That may be the hardest part of the problem! In addition, the content of the explanation itself is rather dense, with 4 or 5 propositions in a single sentence. That's tough to follow.

For additional practice with a similar problem, check out page 97 of our Number Properties Strategy Guide (4th edition).

Hot List Problem: DS 154
Beginning of Question: If n is a positive integer…
Page in OG: 287
Page in This Book: 230

Comments:
As mentioned above, this problem requires you to manipulate an exponential expression in a way most folks dislike. You might recognize that $2 \times 2^n = 2^{n+1}$, but it's easy to miss that the logic works in reverse, too.

The OG explanation is generally okay, although the discussion of statement 1 could be clarified. What's hard about this problem is the process of manipulating exponents. Redo this problem until you can do it in your sleep.

Hot List Problem: DS 156
Beginning of Question: Is 5^k less...
Page in OG: 287
Page in This Book: 231

Comments:
This problem is very similar to DS 154. In both cases, you have to break apart an exponent such as $n + 1$ or $k + 1$.

Again, the OG explanation is pretty good. It's the problem itself that's evil. As with DS 154, practice the exponent manipulations until you have them down cold.

Hot List Problem: DS 171
Beginning of Question: What is the tens digit...
Page in OG: 288
Page in This Book: 238

Comments:
As mentioned above, remainders (when you're dealing with variables) are frightening. Rephrase the statements from "remainder" language to "multiple" language, which is much easier to understand. Instead of "x divided by 110 has a remainder of 30," think "x is 30 more than a multiple of 110." Then come up with possible values for x in each case.

In the explanation, the OG uses "R" notation for remainders. This notation, while useful in some contexts, is overkill in this one. The explanation is a little too short overall.

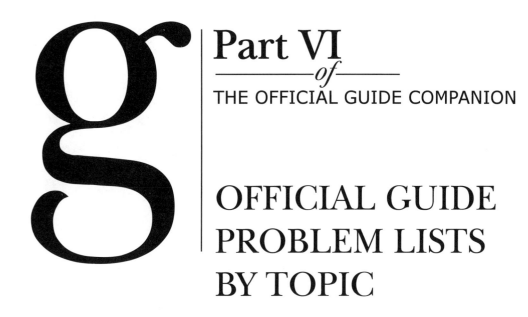

Part VI

of

THE OFFICIAL GUIDE COMPANION

OFFICIAL GUIDE
PROBLEM LISTS
BY TOPIC

Official Guide Problem Lists by Topic

PROBLEM SOLVING GENERAL SET— NUMBER PROPERTIES

Divisibility & Primes
12th Edition: 3, 7, 23, 36, 72, 82, 87, 106, 107, 110, 142, 159, 198, 217, D13, D15, D18, D23
Odds & Evens
12th Edition: 40, 185
Positives & Negatives
12th Edition: 22, 29, 50
Consecutive Integers
12th Edition: 85, 116, 157, 201, 219, 224, D2
Exponents & Roots
12th Edition: 11, 32, 46, 51, 54, 73, 117, 137, 164, 216, 230, D17

PROBLEM SOLVING GENERAL SET— FRACTIONS, DECIMALS, & PERCENTS

Fractions
12th Edition: 24, 37, 43, 45, 74, 95, 138, 175, 176, 181, 186, 225, D8
Digits and Decimals
12th Edition: 15, 28, 79, 108, 114, 129, 133, 143, 182, 190, 203, 211, 226, D1, D11
Percents
12th Edition: 8, 13, 19, 47, 61, 78, 123, 128, 131, 139, 156, 166, 193, 223, D21
Successive Percents and Percent Change
12th Edition: 17, 60, 64, 92, 94, 109, 111, 115, 151, 220, D12
FDPs
12th Edition: 10, 56, 187

DATA SUFFICIENCY GENERAL SET— NUMBER PROPERTIES

Divisibility & Primes
12th Edition: 16, 66, 82, 90, 98, 128, 171, D26, D42
Odds & Evens
12th Edition: 6, 12, 17, 24, 73, 76, 106, 172
Positives & Negatives
12th Edition: 69, 159, D41
Consecutive Integers
12th Edition: 65, 108, 170
Exponents & Roots
12th Edition: 166, 169, D44

DATA SUFFICIENCY GENERAL SET— FRACTIONS, DECIMALS, & PERCENTS

Fractions
12th Edition: 9, 27, 59, 113
Digits and Decimals
12th Edition: 31, 41, 64, 100, 110, 151, 167, D25
Percents
12th Edition: 2, 7, 33, 37, 48, 61, 63, 77, 79, 88, 92, 142, D40
Successive Percents and Percent Change
12th Edition: 55, 120
FDPs
12th Edition: 43, 46, 52, 85, 139, 143

PROBLEM SOLVING GENERAL SET— EQUATIONS, INEQUALITIES, & VICs

Basic Equations
12th Edition: 2, 38, 44, 58, 70, 100, 168, 196, 218

Equations with Exponents
12th Edition: 104, 150, 172

Quadratic Equations
12th Edition: 41, 97, 144, 155, 215, 222, D16

Formulas & Functions
12th Edition: 42, 68, 98, 136, 146, 171, 188, 228, D3

Inequalities
12th Edition: 49, 71, 119, 125, 130, 161, 173

VICs
12th Edition: 6, 31, 34, 84, 89, 112, 120, 122, 127, 158, 163, 165, 202, 204, 208, 212, 213, 227, D24

PROBLEM SOLVING GENERAL SET— WORD TRANSLATIONS

Algebraic Translations
12th Edition: 26, 59, 65, 77, 83, 90, 91, 140, 153, 195

Rates and Work
12th Edition: 21, 80, 81, 86, 101, 126, 149, 154, 183, 206

Ratios
12th Edition: 20, 52, 55, 63, 66, 76, 96, 103, 118, 162, 169, 179, 192

Combinatorics & Probability
12th Edition: 12, 67, 105, 121, 135, 174, 191, 214, D7

Statistics
12th Edition: 5, 14, 27, 57, 69, 93, 99, 132, 148, 180, 184, 199, 207, D9

Overlapping Sets
12th Edition: 124, 167, 170, 178, 200, 221, D4, D6, D14

Miscellaneous (Graphs, Computation, and Non-Standard Problems)
12th Edition: 1, 30, 35, 75, 141

DATA SUFFICIENCY GENERAL SET— EQUATIONS, INEQUALITIES, & VICs

Basic Equations
12th Edition: 1, 15, 35, 60, 83, 95, 125, 150, 168, D35, D37

Equations with Exponents
12th Edition: 154, 156, 165

Quadratic Equations
12th Edition: 30, 158

Formulas & Functions
12th Edition: 19, 26, 36, 45, 115

Inequalities
12th Edition: 11, 38, 49, 51, 72, 80, 97, 153, 162, D30, D33, D38

DATA SUFFICIENCY GENERAL SET— WORD TRANSLATIONS

Algebraic Translations
12th Edition: 8, 13, 22, 25, 39, 54, 57, 62, 70, 123, 131, 137, 145, 152, 174, D27

Rates and Work
12th Edition: 10, 14, 68, 71, 87, 102, 103, 104, 112

Ratios
12th Edition: 44, 58, 111, 155, 163

Combinatorics & Probability
12th Edition: 3, 107, 122

Statistics
12th Edition: 28, 32, 53, 78, 81, 84, 93, 101, 105, 116, 129, 133, 134, 136, 141, 146, 147, 161, D31, D32, D43, D46

Overlapping Sets
12th Edition: 4, 21, 50, 67, 89, 124, 126, 127, D29, D34, D47

Miscellaneous (Graphs, Computation, and Non-Standard Problems)
12th Edition: 5, 23, 40, 86, 99, 118, 119, 130, 138, D45

PROBLEM SOLVING GENERAL SET— GEOMETRY

Polygons
12th Edition: 4, 16, 18, 102, 113, 134

Triangles and Diagonals
12th Edition: 48, 145, 147, 152, 177, 205, D19

Circles and Cylinders
12th Edition: 33, 160, 189, 197, D5, D20, D22

Lines and Angles
12th Edition: 53, 62, 209, D10

Coordinate Plane
12th Edition: 9, 25, 39, 88, 194, 210, 229

DATA SUFFICIENCY GENERAL SET— GEOMETRY

Polygons
12th Edition: 18, 47, 122, 135, 148, D48

Triangles and Diagonals
12th Edition: 20, 56, 74, 109, 140, 144, 157, 173, D28

Circles and Cylinders
12th Edition: 29, 34, 42, 96, 114, 117, 160, D36

Lines and Angles
12th Edition: 91, 132

Coordinate Plane
12th Edition: 75, 94, 121, 149, 164, D39

mbaMission

Every candidate has a unique story to tell.

We have the creative experience to help you tell yours.

We are **mbaMission**, published authors with elite MBA experience who will work with you one-on-one to craft complete applications that will force the admissions committees to take notice. Benefit from straightforward guidance and personal mentorship as you define your unique attributes and reveal them to the admissions committees via a story only you can tell.

We will guide you through our "Complete Start to Finish Process":

- ☑ Candidate assessment, application strategy and program selection
- ☑ Brainstorming and selection of essay topics
- ☑ Outlining and essay structuring
- ☑ Unlimited essay editing
- ☑ Letter of recommendation advice
- ☑ Resume construction and review
- ☑ Interview preparation, mock interviews and feedback
- ☑ Post-acceptance and scholarship counseling

Monday Morning Essay Tip: Overrepresenting Your Overrepresentation

Many in the MBA application pool—particularly male investment bankers—worry that they are overrepresented. While you cannot change your work history, you can change the way you introduce yourself to admissions committees. Consider the following examples:

Example 1: "As an investment banking analyst at Bank of America, I am responsible for creating Excel models…."
Example 2: "At 5:30 pm, I could rest easy. The deadline for all other offers had passed. At that point, I knew…."

In the first example, the candidate starts off by mistakenly introducing the reader to the very over-representation that he/she should be trying to avoid emphasizing. In the second example, the banker immerses the reader in an unraveling mystery. This keeps the reader intrigued and focused on the applicant's story and actions rather than making the specific job title and responsibilities the center of the text. While each applicant's personal situation is different, every candidate can approach his/her story so as to mitigate the effects of overrepresentation.

To schedule a free consultation and read more than fifty Monday Morning Essay Tips, please visit our website:
www.mbamission.com

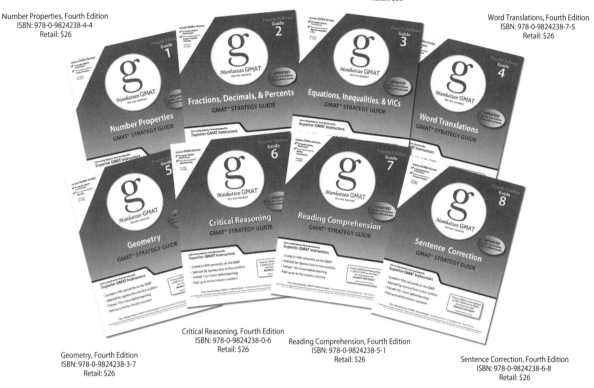